3rd Linguistic Annotation Workshop 2009

(LAW-III)

Held at ACL-IJCNLP 2009

Singapore
6-7 August 2009

ISBN: 978-1-61738-451-6

Printed from e-media with permission by:

Curran Associates, Inc.
57 Morehouse Lane
Red Hook, NY 12571
www.proceedings.com

Some format issues inherent in the e-media version may also appear in this print version.

Printed by Curran Associates, Inc. (2010)

Association for Computational Linguistics
209 N. Eighth Street
Stroudsburg, Pennsylvania 18360

Phone: 1-570-476-8006
Fax: 1-570-476-0860

acl@aclweb.org

Introduction

The Linguistic Annotation Workshop (The LAW) provides a forum to facilitate the exchange and propagation of research results concerned with the annotation, manipulation, and exploitation of corpora; work towards the harmonization and interoperability from the perspective of the increasingly large number of tools and frameworks for annotated language resources; and work towards a consensus on all issues crucial to the advancement of the field of corpus annotation. Although this year's LAW is officially the third edition, LAW itself is the convergence of several previous workshops—including NLPXML, FLAC, LINC, and Frontiers in Corpus Annotation—dating back to the first NLPXML in 2001. This series of workshops attests to the rapid developments in the creation and use of annotated data in both language technology and empirical approaches to linguistic studies over the past 10 years.

The response to this year's Call for Papers was enthusiastic: 43 submissions were received. After careful review, the program committee accepted 10 long papers, 11 short papers, and 15 posters. Selection of the papers was not an easy task, as the papers cover the full range of linguistic facts and their corresponding annotation frameworks, from wordnets to treebanks, emotion to belief, and speech to discourse. The papers also deal with a range of annotation levels, from the macro perspective on infrastructure for international collaboration and interoperability, to the micro perspective on tools to deal with inter-annotator inconsistencies. It is this richness of the topics that attest to the growing maturity of field, which will be represented in a special issue of the journal *Language Resources and Evaluation* devoted to selected papers from the workshop.

We would like to thank SIGANN for its continuing endorsement of the LAW workshops, as well as the support and comments from the ACL-IJCNLP 2009 workshop committee chairs: Jimmy Lin and Yuji Matsumoto. Most of all, we would like to thank all our program committee members and reviewers for their dedication and helpful review comments. Without them, LAW III could not be implemented successfully.

Chu-Ren Huang and Manfred Stede, Program Committee Co-chairs
Nancy Ide and Adam Meyers, Organizers

Workshop Committees

Organizers:

Nancy Ide, Vassar College
Adam Meyers, New York University

Organizing Committee:

Manfred Stede (Program Co-chair), Universität Potsdam
Chu-Ren Huang (Program Co-chair), Hong Kong Polytechnic University / Academia Sinica
Antonio Pareja-Lora, SIC, UCM / OEG, UPM
Sameer Pradhan, BBN Technologies
Nianwen Xue, Brandeis University

Program Committee:

Collin Baker	*ICSI/UC Berkeley*
Timothy Baldwin	*University of Melbourne*
Francis Bond	*NICT*
Nicoletta Calzolari	*ILC/CNR*
Steve Cassidy	*Macquarie University*
Christopher Cieri	*Linguistic Data Consortium/University of Pennsylvania*
Tomaz Erjavec	*Josef Stefan Institute*
Katrin Erk	*University of Texas at Austin*
Alex Chengyu Fang	*City University of Hong Kong*
Christiane Fellbaum	*Princeton University*
Charles Fillmore	*ICSI/UC Berkeley*
Nancy Ide	*Vassar College*
Richard Johansson	*Lund University*
Aravind Joshi	*University of Pennsylvania*
Adam Meyers	*New York University*
Eleni Miltsakaki	*University of Pennsylvania*
Joakim Nivre	*Växjö University and Uppsala University*
Eric Nyberg	*Carnegie-Mellon University*
Antonio Pareja-Lora	*SIC, UCM / OEG, UPM*
Martha Palmer	*University of Colorado*
Sameer Pradhan	*BBN Technologies*
James Pustejovsky	*Brandeis University*
Mihai Surdeanu	*Yahoo! Research, Barcelona*
Theresa Wilson	*University of Edinburgh*
Andreas Witt	*IDS Mannheim*
Nianwen Xue	*Brandeis University*

Table of Contents

A Cognitive-based Annotation System for Emotion Computing
Ying Chen, Sophia Y. M. Lee and Chu-Ren Huang 1

Complex Linguistic Annotation No Easy Way Out! A Case from Bangla and Hindi POS Labeling Tasks
Sandipan Dandapat, Priyanka Biswas, Monojit Choudhury and Kalika Bali 10

Assessing the benefits of partial automatic pre-labeling for frame-semantic annotation
Ines Rehbein, Josef Ruppenhofer and Caroline Sporleder 19

Bridging the Gaps: Interoperability for GrAF, GATE, and UIMA
Nancy Ide and Keith Suderman 27

By all these lovely tokens... Merging Conflicting Tokenizations
Christian Chiarcos, Julia Ritz and Manfred Stede 35

Annotating Subordinators in the Turkish Discourse Bank
Deniz Zeyrek, Ümit Deniz Turan, Cem Bozsahin, Ruket Çakıcı, Ayışığı B. Sevdik-Çallı, Işın Demirşahin, Berfin Aktaş, İhsan Yalçınkaya and Hale Ögel 44

Annotation of Events and Temporal Expressions in French Texts
André Bittar 48

Designing a Language Game for Collecting Coreference Annotation
Barbora Hladká, Jiří Mírovský and Pavel Schlesinger 52

Explorations in Automatic Image Annotation using Textual Features
Chee Wee Leong and Rada Mihalcea 56

Human Evaluation of Article and Noun Number Usage: Influences of Context and Construction Variability
John Lee, Joel Tetreault and Martin Chodorow 60

Stand-off TEI Annotation: the Case of the National Corpus of Polish
Piotr Banski and Adam Przepiórkowski 64

Committed Belief Annotation and Tagging
Mona Diab, Lori Levin, Teruko Mitamura, Owen Rambow, Vinodkumar Prabhakaram and Weiwei Guo 68

Annotation of Sentence Structure; Capturing the Relationship among Clauses in Czech Sentences
Markéta Lopatková, Natalia Klyueva and Petr Homola 74

Schema and Variation: Digitizing Printed Dictionaries
Christian Schneiker, Dietmar Seipel and Werner Wegstein 82

Syntactic annotation of spoken utterances: A case study on the Czech Academic Corpus
Barbora Hladká and Zdenka Uresova 90

High-Performance High-Volume Layered Corpora Annotation
Tiago Luís and David Martins de Matos 99

The Coding Scheme for Annotating Extended Nominal Coreference and Bridging Anaphora in the Prague Dependency Treebank
Anna Nedoluzhko, Jiří Mírovský and Petr Pajas 108

Timed Annotations — Enhancing MUC7 Metadata by the Time It Takes to Annotate Named Entities
Katrin Tomanek and Udo Hahn 112

Transducing Logical Relations from Automatic and Manual GLARF
Adam Meyers, Michiko Kosaka, Heng Ji, Nianwen Xue, Mary Harper, Ang Sun, Wei Xu and Shasha Liao 116

Using Parallel Propbanks to enhance Word-alignments
Jinho Choi, Martha Palmer and Nianwen Xue 121

WordNet and FrameNet as Complementary Resources for Annotation
Collin F. Baker and Christiane Fellbaum 125

Annotating language errors in texts: investigating argumentation and decision schemas
Camille Albert, Laurie Buscail, Marie Garnier, Arnaud Rykner and Patrick Saint-Dizier 130

Developing Novel Multimodal and Linguistic Annotation Software
Alexey Podlasov, Kay O'Halloran, Sabine Tan, Bradley Smith and Arun Nagarajan 134

Unsupervised Detection of Annotation Inconsistencies Using Apriori Algorithm
Václav Novák and Magda Razímová 138

Towards a Methodology for Named Entities Annotation
Karën Fort, Maud Ehrmann and Adeline Nazarenko 142

Online Search Interface for the Sejong Korean-Japanese Bilingual Corpus and Auto-interpolation of Phrase Alignment
Sanghoun Song and Francis Bond 146

Annotating Semantic Relations Combining Facts and Opinions
Koji Murakami, Shouko Masuda, Suguru Matsuyoshi, Eric Nichols, Kentaro Inui and Yuji Matsumoto 150

Ingesting the Auslan Corpus into the DADA Annotation Store
Steve Cassidy and Trevor Johnston 154

The Hindi Discourse Relation Bank
Umangi Oza, Rashmi Prasad, Sudheer Kolachina, Dipti Misra Sharma and Aravind Joshi 158

Simple Parser for Indian Languages in a Dependency Framework
Akshar Bharati, Mridul Gupta, Vineet Yadav, Karthik Gali and Dipti Misra Sharma 162

Annotating Discourse Anaphora
Stefanie Dipper and Heike Zinsmeister 166

Annotating Wall Street Journal Texts Using a Hand-Crafted Deep Linguistic Grammar
Valia Kordoni and Yi Zhang 170

A general scheme for broad-coverage multimodal annotation
Philippe Blache 174

The SILT and FlaReNet International Collaboration for Interoperability
Nancy Ide, James Pustejovsky, Nicoletta Calzolari and Claudia Soria 178

Building a Large Syntactically-Annotated Corpus of Vietnamese
Phuong Thai Nguyen, Xuan Luong Vu, Thi Minh Huyen Nguyen, Van Hiep Nguyen
and Hong Phuong Le 182

A Multi-Representational and Multi-Layered Treebank for Hindi/Urdu
Rajesh Bhatt, Bhuvana Narasimhan, Martha Palmer, Owen Rambow, Dipti MIsra Sharma
and Fei Xia 186

Conference Program

Thursday, August 6, 2009

8:50–9:00 Opening Remarks

9:00–9:30 *A Cognitive-based Annotation System for Emotion Computing*
Ying Chen, Sophia Y. M. Lee and Chu-Ren Huang

9:30–10:00 *Complex Linguistic Annotation—No Easy Way Out! A Case from Bangla and Hindi POS Labeling Tasks*
Sandipan Dandapat, Priyanka Biswas, Monojit Choudhury and Kalika Bali

10:00–10:30 Break

10:30–11:00 *Assessing the benefits of partial automatic pre-labeling for frame-semantic annotation*
Ines Rehbein, Josef Ruppenhofer and Caroline Sporleder

11:00–11:30 *Bridging the Gaps: Interoperability for GrAF, GATE, and UIMA*
Nancy Ide and Keith Suderman

11:30–12:00 *By all these lovely tokens... Merging Conflicting Tokenizations*
Christian Chiarcos, Julia Ritz and Manfred Stede

12:00–13:30 Lunch Break

13:30–13:50 *Annotating Subordinators in the Turkish Discourse Bank*
Deniz Zeyrek, Ümit Deniz Turan, Cem Bozsahin, Ruket Çakıcı, Ayışığı B. Sevdik-Çallı, Işın Demirşahin, Berfin Aktaş, İhsan Yalçınkaya and Hale Ögel

13:50–14:10 *Annotation of Events and Temporal Expressions in French Texts*
André Bittar

14:10–14:30 *Designing a Language Game for Collecting Coreference Annotation*
Barbora Hladká, Jiří Mírovský and Pavel Schlesinger

14:30–14:50 *Explorations in Automatic Image Annotation using Textual Features*
Chee Wee Leong and Rada Mihalcea

14:50–15:10 *Human Evaluation of Article and Noun Number Usage: Influences of Context and Construction Variability*
John Lee, Joel Tetreault and Martin Chodorow

Thursday, August 6, 2009 (continued)

15:10–15:30 *Stand-off TEI Annotation: the Case of the National Corpus of Polish*
Piotr Banski and Adam Przepiórkowski

15:30–16:00 Break

16:00–17:30 POSTER SESSION

17:30–18:00 SIGANN Annual Meeting

Friday, August 7, 2009

9:00–9:30 *Committed Belief Annotation and Tagging*
Mona Diab, Lori Levin, Teruko Mitamura, Owen Rambow, Vinodkumar Prabhakaram and Weiwei Guo

9:30–10:00 *Annotation of Sentence Structure: Capturing the Relationship among Clauses in Czech Sentences*
Markéta Lopatková, Natalia Klyueva and Petr Homola

10:00–10:30 Break

10:30–11:00 *Schema and Variation: Digitizing Printed Dictionaries*
Christian Schneiker, Dietmar Seipel and Werner Wegstein

11:00–11:30 *Syntactic Annotation of Spoken Utterances: A Case Study on the Czech Academic Corpus*
Barbora Hladká and Zdenka Uresova

11:30–12:00 *High-Performance High-Volume Layered Corpora Annotation*
Tiago Luís and David Martins de Matos

12:00–13:30 Lunch Break

13:30–13:50 *The Coding Scheme for Annotating Extended Nominal Coreference and Bridging Anaphora in the Prague Dependency Treebank*
Anna Nedoluzhko, Jiří Mírovský and Petr Pajas

13:50–14:10 *Timed Annotations — Enhancing MUC7 Metadata by the Time It Takes to Annotate Named Entities*
Katrin Tomanek and Udo Hahn

Friday, August 7, 2009 (continued)

14:10–14:30 *Transducing Logical Relations from Automatic and Manual GLARF*
Adam Meyers, Michiko Kosaka, Heng Ji, Nianwen Xue, Mary Harper, Ang Sun, Wei Xu and Shasha Liao

14:30–14:50 *Using Parallel Propbanks to enhance Word-alignments*
Jinho Choi, Martha Palmer and Nianwen Xue

14:50–15:10 *WordNet and FrameNet as Complementary Resources for Annotation*
Collin F. Baker and Christiane Fellbaum

15:10–15:30 SIGANN Working Group Reports

15:30–16:00 Break

16:00–17:50 PANEL: The Standards Debate: Pro and Con

17:50–18:00 Closing

A Cognitive-based Annotation System for Emotion Computing

Ying Chen, Sophia Y. M. Lee and Chu-Ren Huang
Department of Chinese & Bilingual Studies
The Hong Kong Polytechnic University
{chenying3176,sophiaym,churen.huang}@gmail.com

Abstract

Emotion computing is very important for expressive information extraction. In this paper, we provide a robust and versatile emotion annotation scheme based on cognitive emotion theories, which not only can annotate both explicit and implicit emotion expressions, but also can encode different levels of emotion information for the given emotion content. In addition, motivated by a cognitive framework, an automatic emotion annotation system is developed, and large and comparatively high-quality emotion corpora are created for emotion computing, one in Chinese and the other in English. Such an annotation system can be easily adapted for different kinds of emotion applications and be extended to other languages.

1 Introduction

Affective information is important for human language technology, and sentiment analysis, a coarse-grained affective computing (Shanahan et al., 2006), which is attitude assessment, has become the most salient trend. The polarity-driven approach in sentiment analysis is, however, often criticized as too general to satisfy some applications, such as advertisement design and robot design, and one way to capture more fine-grained affective information is to detect emotion expressions. Unlike sentiment, emotions are cognitive-based, which consistently occur across domains because of its human psychological activities. We believe that emotion computing, which is a fine-grained and cognitive-based framework of affective computing, will provide a more robust and versatile model for human language technology.

Since the concept of emotion is very complicated and subjective, comparing to some annotations such as POS annotation and Chinese word segmentation annotation, emotion annotation is highly labor intensive as it requires careful human judgment. Both explicit and implicit emotions must be recognized and tagged during emotion annotation, therefore, emotion annotation is not a simple assignment exercise as in POS annotation. Technically, emotion annotation can be divided into two subtasks: emotion detection (i.e. differentiate emotional content from neutral content), which is a very important task for affective information extraction, and emotion classification (i.e. assign emotion tags to emotional content.)

Emotion computing often requires a large and high-quality annotated data, however, there is a lack of this kind of corpus. This is not only because of the enormous human involvement, but also because of the unavailability of emotion annotation scheme, which is robust and versatile for both emotion annotation and emotion computing. Tokuhisa et al. (2008) is the only work that explores the issue of emotion detection while most of the previous studies concentrate on the emotion classification given a known emotion context (Mihalcea and Liu, 2006; Kozareva et al., 2007.) Even for emotion classification, some issues remain unresolved, such as the complicated relationships among different emotion types, emotion type selection, and so on. Thus, it is still far from solving the emotion problem if emotion annotation is just considered as emotion-tag assignment.

In this paper, we first explore the relationships among different emotion types with the support of a proposed emotion taxonomy, which combines some psychological theories and linguistic semantics. Based on the emotion taxonomy, a robust and versatile emotion annotation scheme is designed and used in both Chinese and English

Proceedings of the Third Linguistic Annotation Workshop, ACL-IJCNLP 2009, pages 1–9,
Suntec, Singapore, 6-7 August 2009.

emotion corpora. Our emotion annotation scheme is very flexible, which is only a layer added to a sentence, although it can easily be extended to a higher level of a text. Our annotation scheme not only can provide the emotion type information, but also can encode the information regarding the relationship between emotions. With this versatile annotated emotion information, different NLP users can extract different emotion information from a given annotated corpus according to their applications.

With such an emotion annotation scheme, a large and comparatively high-quality annotated emotion corpus is built for emotion computing through an unsupervised approach. Tokuhisa et al. (2008) pointed out that besides emotion corpus, neutral corpus (i.e. sentences containing no emotion) is also very important for emotion computing. Therefore, a high-quality neutral corpus is also automatically collected using contextual information. These two corpora are combined to form a complete emotion-driven corpus for emotion computing. Although the unsupervised method cannot provide a perfectly-annotated corpus, it can easily adapt for different emotion computing.

The remainder of this paper is organized as follows. In Section 2, we give an overview of the previous work on emotion annotation and some related psychological and linguistic theories. In Section 3, we describe our emotion taxonomy and emotion annotation scheme. Section 4 discusses how the unsupervised corpus is created. Section 5 presents the pilot experiments for emotion computing with our corpus, which suggests that the unsupervised approach of our corpus creation is effective. Finally, a conclusion is made in Section 5.

2 Related work

There is no clear consensus among many psychological and linguistic theories on the concept of emotions. Here, we limit our work by the classic definition of "emotions" (Cannon, 1927): Emotion is the felt awareness of bodily reactions to something perceived or thought.

Emotion is a complicated concept, and there are complicated relationships among different emotions. For example, the relationship between "discouraged" and "sad" is different with the one between "remorse" and "sad." Hobbs & Gordon (2008) and Mathieu (2005) explore emotions mainly from a lexical semantics perspective, and Schröder et al. (2006) designed an annotation scheme, EARL, mainly for speech processing. Because of the disagreements in emotion theories, EARL did not explore the relationships among emotion types. In this paper, we focus on emotions in written data, which is very different from that of in spoken data in terms of expressions. Here, we first adopt psychological theories (Plutchik, 1980; Turner, 2000) to create an emotion taxonomy, and then design an emotion annotation scheme based on the taxonomy.

Since most of the previous emotion corpora are either too small (Xu et al., 2008) or comparatively ineffective in terms of accuracy (Tokuhisa et al., 2008), they cannot satisfy the requirements of emotion computing. In this paper, based on Natural Semantic Metalanguage (NSM), a cognitive approach to human emotions (which will be discussed in the later section), we create an automatic emotion annotation system. While this annotation system needs only a little training data and does not require human supervision, the corpus still maintains a comparatively high quality. Another significant advantage of our automatic annotation system is that it can easily adapt to different emotion applications by simply supplying different training data.

Most of the existing emotion theories study emotions from the biological and psychological perspectives, hence they cannot easily apply to NLP. Fortunately, NSM, one of the prominent cognitive models exploring human emotions, offers a comprehensive and practical approach to emotions (Wierbicka 1996.) NSM describes complex and abstract concepts, such as emotions, in terms of simpler and concrete ones. In such a way, emotions are decomposed as complex events involving a cause and a mental state, which can be further described with a set of universal, irreducible cores called semantic primitives. This approach identifies the exact differences and connections between emotion concepts in terms of the causes, which provide an immediate cue for emotion detection and classification. We believe that the NSM model offers a plausible framework to be implemented for automatic emotion computing.

3 Emotion annotation scheme

3.1 The emotion taxonomy

Although there are many emotion theories developed in different fields, such as biology, psychology, and linguistics, most of them agree that emotion can be divided into primary emotions and complex emotions (i.e. the combinations of primary emotions.) There is still controversy over the selection of primary emotions, nonetheless, "happiness", "sadness", "anger", and "fear" are considered as primary emotions by most of emotion theories.

Plutchik's emotion taxonomy (Plutchik 1980), one of the classic emotion taxonomies, also follows the division of primary emotions and complex emotions, and Turner's taxonomy (Turner 2000), which is based on Plutchik's work, allows more flexible combinations of primary emotions. In this paper, we adopt Turner's taxonomy, with the two main points emphasized:

1) For each primary emotion, it is divided into three levels according to its intensity: high, moderate, and low. Besides "happiness," "sadness," "anger" and "fear," Turner also suggests that "disgust" and "surprise" can be primary emotions (Turner 1996; Turner 2007). In Chinese, the character "惊" ("surprise") has a strong ability to form many emotion words, such as 惊喜 (surprise and happiness), and 惊吓 (surprise and fear), which is consistent with the explanation of "surprise" emotion by Plutchik (1991): "when the stimulus has been evaluated, the surprise may quickly change to any other emotion." Therefore, in our annotation scheme, we consider "happiness," "sadness," "anger," "fear," and "surprise" as primary emotions.

2) Complex emotion can be divided into first-order complex emotions (consisting of two primary emotions), second-order complex emotions (consisting of three primary emotions), and so on, according to the number of primary emotions that involves in the complex emotion. For example, "pride" (happiness + fear) is a first-order complex emotion, which contains a greater amount of "happiness" with a lesser amount of "fear."

Tables 1 and 2 show some keywords in Turner's taxonomy, and the symbol "//" is to separate different emotion types. Table 1 lists the five most common English keywords and their corresponding primary emotions, and Table 2 lists the English keywords and their corresponding complex emotions. In Table 2, several emotion keywords, which express similar emotion meaning, are grouped into an emotion type. For example, the emotion keywords "awe, reverence, veneration" are grouped into emotion type "awe." For a complex emotion, the order of primary emotions indicates the importance of those primary emotions for that complex emotion. For examples, "envy" is "fear + anger," which contains a greater amount of "fear" with a lesser amount of "anger" whereas "awe" is "fear + happiness," which contains a greater amount of "fear" with a lesser amount of "happiness."

For English emotion keywords, as Turner's taxonomy missed some common emotion keywords, we add the emotion keywords from Plutchik's taxonomy. Besides, unlike Chinese, English words have morphological variations, for example, the emotion keyword "pride" can occur in text with the various formats: "pride," "prides," "prided," "proud," "proudly." As shown in Tables 1 and 2, there are 188 English lemmas in our taxonomy. In total, there are 720 emotion keywords if morphology is taken into account.

Since Turner's emotion taxonomy is cognitive-based, it is versatile for different languages although there is no one-to-one mapping. We also explore Chinese emotion taxonomy in our previous work (Chen at el., 2009). We first select emotion keywords from the cognitive-based feeling words listed in Xu and Tao (2003), and then map those emotion keywords to Turner's taxonomy with adaptation for some cases. Lastly, some polysemous emotion keywords are removed to reduce ambiguity, and 226 Chinese emotion keywords remain.

Moreover, Turner's taxonomy is a comparatively flexible structure, and more extensions can be done for different applications. For example, for a complex emotion, not only its primary emotions are listed, but also the intensity of the primary emotions can be given. For instance, three emotion types, which belong to "anger + fear," are extended as follows:

Jealousy: Anger (Moderate) + Fear (Moderate)
Suspicion: Anger (Low) + Fear (Low)
Abhorrence: Anger (High) + Fear (Low)

Finally, we should admit that the emotion taxonomy is still an on-going research topic and needs further exploration, such as the position of a given emotion keyword in the emotion taxonomy, whether and how to group similar emotion keywords, and how to decompose a complex emotion into primary emotions.

3.2 The emotion annotation scheme

Given Turner's taxonomy, we design our annotation scheme to encode this kind of emotion information. Our emotion annotation scheme is XML scheme, and conforms with the Text Encoding Initiative (TEI) scheme with some modifications. The emotion scheme is a layer just

Primary Emotions	Keywords
Happiness	High: ecstatic, eager, joy, enthusiastic, happy//Moderate: cheerful, satisfy, pleased, enjoy, interest//Low: sanguine, serene, content, grateful
Fear	High: horror, terror//Moderate: misgivings, self-conscious, scare, panic, anxious//Low: bewilder, reluct, shy, puzzles, confuse
Anger	High: dislike, disgust, outrage, furious, hate//Moderate: contentious, offend, frustrate, hostile, angry//Low: contemptuous, agitate, irritate, annoy, impatient
Sadness	High: deject, despondent, sorrow, anguish, despair//Moderate: gloomy, dismay, sad, unhappy, disappoint//Low: dispirit, downcast, discourage
Surprise	High: astonish//Moderate: startled, amaze, surprise

Table1: Primary emotions and some corresponding keywords

Combinations	Keywords
Happiness + Fear	Wonder: wonder, wondering, hopeful//Pride: pride, boastful
Happiness + Anger	Vengeance: vengeance, vengeful//Calm: appeased, calmed, calm, soothed//Bemused: bemused
Happiness + Sadness	Yearning: nostalgia, yearning
Fear + Happiness	Awe: awe, reverence, veneration
Fear + Anger	Antagonism: antagonism, revulsed//Envy: envy
Fear + Sadness	Worried: dread, wariness, pensive, helpless, apprehension, worried
Anger +Happiness	Unfriendly: snubbing, mollified, rudeness, placated, apathetic, unsympathetic, unfriendly, unaffectionate//Sarcastic: sarcastic
Anger + Fear	Jealousy: jealous//Suspicion: suspicion, distrustful//Abhorrence: abhorrence
Anger + Sadness	Depressed: bitter, depression//Intolerant: intolerant
Sadness +Happiness	Acceptance: acceptance, tolerant//Solace: moroseness, solace, melancholy
Sadness+ Fear	Hopeless: forlorn, lonely, hopeless, miserable//Remorseful: remorseful, ashamed, humiliated
Sadness+ Anger	Discontent: aggrieved, discontent, dissatisfied, unfulfilled//Boredom: boredom//Grief: grief, sullenness
Surprise + Happiness	Delight: delight
Surprise + Sadness	Embarrassed: embarrassed

Table 2: First-order complex emotions and some corresponding keywords

beyond a sentence, and encodes emotion information for a sentence. This annotation scheme can be compatible for any TEI-based annotated corpora as long as sentences are clearly marked.

The emotion-related elements (tags) in our annotation scheme are described as follows. For easy demonstration, our elements are defined with the format of British National Corpus (BNC) annotation scheme[1], and our examples are also based on BNC annotated text. Figure 1 gives the definition of each element, and Figure 2 shows several examples using our annotation scheme. Note that <s> element is a tag for a sentence-like division of a text, and its attribute "n" gives the sentence index. In Figure 2, Sentence 1, which expresses emotions by emotion keywords, contains two types of emotions: "surprise" (primary emotion) and "jealousy" (complex emotion); Sentence 2 is a neutral sentence.

<emotion> element

It is used only when the sentence expresses emotions. It contains a list of <emotionType> elements and a <s> element. As a sentence may express several emotions, an <emotion> element can contain several <emotionType> elements, and each <emotionType> element describes an emotion occurring in that sentence separately.

<neutral> element

It is used only when the sentence does not contain any emotion expression. It contains only a <s> element.

<emotionType> element

It describes a type of emotion in that sentence. It contains an ordered sequence of <primaryEmotion> elements. Attribute "name" provides the name of the emotion type, such as "surprise", "jealousy," and so on, and it is optional. If the emotion type is a primary emotion, the <emotionType> element will have only one <primaryEmotion> element, which encodes the information of this primary emotion. If the emotion is a complex emotion, the <emotionType> element will have several <primaryEmotion> elements (each of them describes the primary emotion involved in that complex emotion.) Attribute "keyword" is an optional attribution if annotators want to provide the indicator of a text for that emotion.

[1] http://www.natcorp.ox.ac.uk/XMLedition/URG/

```
<emotion>
  <emotionType name = "surprise"  keyword ="surprised">
      <primaryEmotion  order =  "1"  name =  "surprise"  intensity = "moderate"></primaryEmotion>
  </emotionType>
  <emotionType name = "jealousy"  keyword = "jealousy">
      <primaryEmotion  order =  "1"  name = "anger" intensity =  "moderate"></primaryEmotion>
      <primaryEmotion  order =  "2"  name =  "fear"  intensity =  "moderate"></primaryEmotion>
  </emotionType>
  <s n = "1"> Hari was surprised at the rush of pure jealousy that swept over her at the mention of Emily Grenfell .</s>
</emotion>
<neutral>
  <s n = "2"> By law no attempts may be made to hasten death or prolong the life of the sufferer . </s>
</neutral>
<emotion>
  <emotionType>
      <primaryEmotion name =  "sadness"></primaryEmotion>
  </emotionType>
  <s n = "3">He looked hurt when she did n't join him , his emotions transparent as a child 's . </s>
</emotion>
```

Figure 2: The example of sentence annotation

```
element emotion
{
 (emotionType)+,
 <s>
}
element emotionType
{
 attribute name (optional),
 attribute keyword (optional),
 (primaryEmotion)+
}
element primaryEmotion
{
 attribute order (optional),
 attribute name (necessary),
 attribute intensity (optional)
}
element neutral
{
 <s>
}
```

Figure 1: The definition of emotion-related elements

<primaryEmtion> element

It describes the property of a primary emotion involved in the emotion type. There are three attributes: "order," "name," and "intensity." "Order" gives the weight of this primary emotion in the emotion type, and the weight value decreases with the ascending "order" value. "Name" and "intensity" provide the name and intensity of a primary emotion. To encode the information in our emotion taxonomy, the value of "order" is {1,2,3,4,5}, the value of "name" is {"happiness," "sadness," "anger," "fear", "surprise" }, and the value of "intensity" is {"high", "moderate", "low".}

The <primaryEmotion> element seems to be redundant because its encoded information can be obtained from the given emotion taxonomy if the name of the emotion type is available, but the presence of this element can make our annotation scheme more robust. Sometimes emotion is so complicated (especially for those emotion expressions without any explicit emotion keyword) that an annotator may not be able to find an exact emotion type to match this emotion, or to list all involved primary emotions. For those subtle cases, emotion annotation can be simplified to list the involved primary emotions as many as possible through <primaryEmotion> elements. For example, in Sentence 3 in Figure 2, although there is no emotion keyword occurring, the word "hurt" indicates the presence of an emotion, which at least involves "sadness." However, because it is hard to explicitly list other primary emotions, therefore, we give only the annotation of "sadness."

Our annotation scheme has the versatility to provide emotion data for different applications. For example, if textual information input annotated with our scheme is provided for the Japanese robot Saya (Hashimoto et al, 2006) to control her facial emotion expression, a simple mapping from our 24 emotion types can be done automatically to Saya's six emotion types, i.e. surprise, fear, disgust, anger, happiness, and sadness. As four of her emotion types are also unique primary emotions, using information encoded in <emotionType> element and <primaryEmotion> element will ensure unique many-to-one mapping and the correct robotic expressions. A trickier case involves her "anger" and "disgust' emotions. The emotion type "anger" in our taxonomy includes emotion words "anger" and "disgust". However, with the "keyword" information provided in <emotionType> element, a small subset of "anger" emotion in our taxonomy can be mapped to "disgust" in Saya's system. For example, we could map keywords "dislike, disgust, hate" to "disgust", and all the remaining ones, such as “outrage, furious,” to “anger.”

4 Emotion-driven corpus creation

Similar to most corpora, our corpus creation is designed to satisfy the requirements of real emotion computing. Emotions can be expressed with or without emotion vocabulary in the text. It seems to be intuitive that emotion computing for a context with emotion keywords can be satisfactory when the collection of emotion vocabulary is comprehensive, such as “joyful” indicates the presence of “happiness” emotion. However, this intuitive approach cannot work well because of the ambiguity of some emotion keywords and the emotion context shift as the sentiment shift (Polanyi and Zaenen, 2004). Moreover, the detection of emotions in a context without emotion keywords is very challenging. To deal with these problems, we build the emotion corpus, which is motivated by the NSM theory.

According to the NSM theory, an emotion is provoked by a stimulus. This indicates one possible way to detect emotions in text, i.e. the detection of emotional stimulus, which is often provided in the text. In other words, emotion corpus is a collection of emotion stimuli. Since emotion is subjective, the stimulus-based approach works only when its context is provided. For example, the stimulus – “build a gym for this community” – may cause different emotions, such as “surprise”, “happy” and so on, depending on its context. We also notice that the text containing an emotion keyword may contain emotional stimulus and its context. Thus, a natural corpus creation approach comes out.

In our system, a pattern-based approach is used to collect the emotion corpus, which is similar to the one used in Tokuhisa et al. (2008), but we do not limit to event-driven emotions (Kozareva et al., 2008), and adjust our rules to improve the quality of emotion annotation. There are five steps in our emotion sentence annotation as given below, and Steps (2) and (3) are to improve the annotation quality.

1) Extract emotion sentences: sentences containing emotion keywords are extracted by keyword matching.
2) Delete ambiguous structures: some ambiguous sentences, which contain structures such as negation and modal, are filtered out.
3) Delete ambiguous emotion keywords: if an emotion keyword is very ambiguous, all sentences containing this ambiguous emotion keyword are filtered out.
4) Give emotion tags: each remaining sentence is marked with its emotion tag according to the emotion type which the focus emotion word belongs to (refer to Tables 1 and 2.)
5) Ignore the focus emotion keywords: for emotion computing, the emotion word is removed from each sentence.

Polanyi and Zaenen (2004) addressed the issue of polarity-based sentiment context shift, and the similar phenomenon also exists in emotion expressions. In our corpus creation, two kinds of contextual structures are handled with: the negation structure and the modal structure. In both English and Chinese, a negated emotion expression can be interpreted as one of the three possible meanings (as shown in Figure 3): opposite to the target emotion (S1), deny the existence of the target emotion (S2), or confirm the existence of the target emotion (S3). The modal structure often indicates that the emotion expression is based on the counter-factual assumption, hence the emotion does not exist at all (S4 and S5 in Figure 3). Although Chinese and English have different interpretations about the modal structure, for emotion analysis, those sentences often do not express an emotion. Therefore, to ensure the quality of the emotion corpus, all sentences containing a negation structure or a modal structure, which are detected by some rules plus a list of keywords (negation polarity words for the negation structure, and modal words for the modal structure), are removed.

S1 (Neg_Happiness): I am not happy about that.
S2 (Netural): Though the palazzo is our family home, my father had never been very happy there.
S3 (Pos_Happiness): I 've never been so happy.
S4 (Netural): I can die happy if you will look after them when I have gone.
S5 (Netural): Then you could move over there and we'd all be happy.

Figure 3: Structures for emotion shift

To overcome the high ambiguity of some emotion keywords, after Step (2), for each emotion keyword, five sentences are randomly selected and annotated by two annotators. If the accuracy of five sentences is lower than 40%, this emotion keyword is removed from our emotion taxonomy. Finally, 191 Chinese keywords and 645 English keywords are remained.

Tokuhisa et al. found that a big challenge for emotion computing, especially for emotion detection, is to collect neutral sentences. Since neutral sentences are unmarked and hard to detect, we develop a naïve yet effective algorithm to create a neutral corpus. A sentence is considered as neutral only when the sentence itself and its context (i.e. the previous sentence and the following sentence) do not contain any of the given emotion keywords.

We run our emotion sentence extraction and neutral sentence extraction on three corpora: the Sinica Corpus (Chinese), the Chinese Gigaword Corpus, and the British National Corpus (BNC, English), and create three emotion corpora and three neutral corpora separately. The Sinica Corpus is a balanced Chinese corpus, which includes documents in 15 kinds of genres; The Chinese Gigaword Corpus is a huge collection of news reports; The BNC is also a balanced corpus, which collects documents from different domains.

To estimate the accuracy of our emotion sentence extraction, we randomly select about 1000 sentences from the three emotion corpora, and have two annotators to check it. Table 3 lists the accuracy of those emotions sentences (emotion corpus.) To test how good this straightforward neutral sentence extraction strategy is, about 1000 sentences are randomly selected from each of the three neutral corpora and are checked by two annotators. Table 3 lists the accuracy of those neutral sentences (neutral corpus.)

	Emotion corpus	Neutral corpus
Gigaword	82.17	98.61
Sinica	77.56	98.39
BNC	69.36	99.50

Table 3: The accuracy of the emotion-driven corpora

From Table 3, the high accuracy of neutral corpus proves that our approach is effective in extracting neutral sentences from the document-based corpus which contains contextual information. Although the accuracy of emotion corpus is lower, it is still much higher than the one reported by Kozareva et al. (2008), i.e. 49.4. The accuracy is significantly increased by deleting ambiguous emotion keywords in Step (3). For the 2,474 randomly selected Chinese sentences, the overall accuracy of the remaining 1,751 sentence is increased by about 14% after Step (3). For the 803 randomly selected English sentences, the accuracy of the remaining 473 sentence is increased about 21% after Step (3). Whether or how the ambiguous emotion keywords in Step 3 are removed is a tradeoff between the coverage and the accuracy of the emotion corpus.

From Table 3, we also find that the accuracy of English emotion corpus is much lower than Chinese emotion corpus, which indicates English emotion sentences expressed by emotion keywords are more ambiguous than that of Chinese. Moreover, during our emotion corpus building, 20.2% of Sinica sentences and 22.4% of Gigaword sentences are removed in Step (2) and (3), on the contrary, 41.2% of BNC sentences are deleted. Although it is more difficult to develop the rules in Step (2) and (3) for Chinese than for English, it also confirms the higher ambiguity of emotion expressions in English due to the ambiguity of emotion keyword. Finally, because of the comparatively-high percentage of the sentences removed in Step (2) and (3), more exploration about those sentences is needed, such as the emotion distribution, the expression patterns and so on, and how to re-incorporate them into the emotion corpus without hurting the whole quality is also our future work.

We also explore emotions through the sentences (no-emotion-keyword sentences) that do not contain any given emotion keyword, because our approach extracts only partial neutral sentences and partial emotion sentences in reality. For each corpus, about 1000 no-emotion-keyword sentences are randomly selected and checked by two annotators. It is surprising that only about 1% of those sentences express emotions. This indicates that it is important for real emotion computing, which mainly works on formal written text, to deal with the emotion expressions which contain emotion keywords and however are ambiguous, such as the sentences deleted in Steps (2) and (3). More exploration is needed for the emotion and neutral sentence distribution on other kinds of written text, such as blogs, and on spoken text.

The unsupervised corpus creation approach can easily be adapted for different languages and different emotion applications, provided that the keyword collection and patterns in Step (2) and (3) need some changes. Moreover, another big advantage of our approach is that it can avoid the controversy during emotion annotation. Emotion is subjective, and therefore disagreement for emotion types often arises if the emotion is not expressed through an explicit emotion keyword.

Overall, the annotated corpus created by the unsupervised approach has a comparatively high quality, and is suitable for the emotion computing. As the size of the neutral corpus is much bigger than its corresponding emotion corpus, to avoid model bias, we randomly select some neutral sentences from the neutral corpus, combining with its corresponding emotion sentences to form a complete emotion-driven corpus.

5 Emotion computing system

In this paper, we present some pilot work to prove that our emotion-driven corpus is useful for emotion computing. With the inclusion of neutral sentences, emotion detection and classification is simplified into a general classification problem, and a supervised machine learning method can be directly applied if enough annotated data are obtained. Here, we choose the MaxEnt learning in Mallet as a classifier.

Both the Sinica Corpus and the Chinese Gigaword Corpus are segmented, and POS-tagged. This allows us to implement the bag-of-words approach in the focus sentences in both Chinese and English. However, emotions are mostly human attitudes or expectations arising from situations, where situations are often expressed in more than a single word. Such kind of situations tends to be more easily extracted by word bigrams (2-gram word) than by word unigram (1-gram word.) To take this into account, besides 1-gram words, we also extract word bi-grams from the focus sentences.

There are too many emotion types in our corpus, which can cause data sparse; therefore, we choose the most frequent emotions to do exploration. Besides the five primary emotions, for Chinese, we select another nine complex emotions, and for English, we select another four complex emotions. Other emotion types are renamed as "Other Emotions."

Since Chinese emotion-driven corpus is much larger than the English one, to fairly compare the performance, we reduce the size of Chinese corpus in our experiments. Then, for each corpus, we reserve 80% as the training data, 10% as the development data, and 10% as the test data (there are two sets of test data as follows.) In the evaluation, for each emotion sentence, if our system detects one of its emotion tags, we consider this sentence is correctly tagged.

Test data set 1 (TDS 1): contains about 10% of the sentences from the complete emotion-driven corpus, and emotion tags are automatically given during the corpus creation.

Test data set 2 (TDS 2): contains the sentences used in Table 3, which is checked by two annotators. If more than one emotion tags co-exist in a sentence, all of them are chosen to label the sentence. If there exists an emotion that does not belong to any of the emotion types, it is labeled as "Other Emotions."

Table 4 shows the performance (accuracy) of our system for Test data set 1 and 2 for both Chinese and English. We notice that our corpus creation approach is effective for emotion computing. As we expect, the 2-gram words can partially catch the emotion stimulus, and improves the performances. However, the overall performance is still very low, which indicates that emotion computing is a difficult task. From the error analysis, it is surprised that for Chinese, the mislabeling of emotion sentences as neutral sentences ("emotion" vs. "neutral") is a common error, and whereas, for English, two kinds of errors: "emotion" vs. "neutral" and "focus emotions" vs. "Other emotions" (the mislabeling of a sentence with a focus emotion as "Other emotions,") occupy at least 50%. The error distribution confirms the importance of emotion detection during emotion computing. The high frequency of the error of "focus emotions" vs. "Other Emotions" in English may be because there are fewer focus emotion types for English.

	1-gram words	{1,2}-gram words
Chinese TDS 1	53.92	58.75
English TDS 1	44.02	48.20
Chinese TDS 2	37.18	39.95
English TDS 2	33.24	36.31

Table 4: The performances of our system for the test data

6 Conclusion

Emotion, no matter its annotation or computing, is still a new and difficult topic. In this paper, we apply emotion theories to design a cognitive-based emotion annotation scheme, which are robust and versatile so that it can encode different levels of emotion information for different emotion computing. Moreover, motivated from NSM, we develop an unsupervised approach to create a large and comparatively high-quality corpus for emotion computing, which is proven in our pilot experiments to be useful. Moreover, this approach makes emotion computing for different applications possible through a little modification.

Certainly, there are some issues remaining unsolved. For corpus construction, we will explore emotion distribution in other kinds of corpora, such as blog and dialog, and make analysis of ambiguous emotion sentences, such as negation structure and modal structure. For emotion computing, we did only pilot experiments and more work needs to be done, such as feature extraction.

References

W. B. Cannon. 1927. The James-Lange theory of emotions: A Critical Examination and an Alternative Theory. *American Journal of Psychology, 39*, 106-124.

Y. Chen, S. Y. M. Lee and C. R. Huang, 2009. Construction of Chinese Emotion Corpus with an Unsupervised Approach. In CNCCL-2009, 2009. (in Chinese)

T. Hashimoto, S. Hiramatsu, T. Tsuji and H. Kobayashi. 2006. Development of the Face Robot SAYA for Rich Facial Expressions. SICE-ICASE International Joint Conference, Busan,Korea.

J. Hobbs and A. Gordon. 2008. The Deep Lexical Semantics of Emotions. Workshop on Sentiment Analysis: Emotion, Metaphor, Ontology and Terminology (EMOT-08), 6th International conference on Language Resources and Evaluation (LREC-08), Marrakech, Morocco, May 27, 2008.

P. Livia, A. Zaenen. 2004. Contextual Valence Shifters. In Shanahan, J. G., Y. Qu, and J. Wiebe (Eds.), *Computing Attitude and Affect in Text: Theory and Applications*, pp. 1-10.

Z. Kozareva, Borja Navarro, Sonia Vazquez, and Andres Nibtoyo. 2007. UA-ZBSA: A Headline Emotion Classification through Web Information. In *Proceedings of the 4th International Workshop on Semantic Evaluations*.

Y. Y. Mathieu. 2005. Annotations of Emotions and Feelings in Texts. In Conference on Affective Computing and intelligent Interaction (ACII2005), Beijing, Springer Lecture Notes in Computer Science, pp. 350-357.

R. Mihalcefa, and Hugo Liu. 2006. A Corpus-based Approach to Finding Happiness. In *Proceedings of AAAI*.

R. Plutchik. 1991. *The Emotions*. University Press of America, Inc.

R. Plutchik. 1980. Emotions: A psychoevolutionary synthesis. New York:Harper & Row.

M. Schröder, H. Pirker and M. Lamolle. 2006. First suggestions for an emotion annotation and representation language. In L. Deviller et al. (Ed.), Proceedings of LREC'06 Workshop on Corpora for Research on Emotion and Affect (pp. 88-92). Genoa, Italy.

J. G. Shanahan, Y. Qu and J. Wiebe. 2006. Computing attitude and affect in text: theory and applications, Springer.

R. Tokuhisa, K. Inui, and Y. Matsumoto (Eds.) 2008. Emotion Classification Using Massive Examples Extracted from the Web. COLING.

J. H. Turner. 2007. Human Emotions: A sociological theory. New York : Routledge, 2007.

J. H. Turner. 2000. On the origins of human emotions: A sociological inquiry into the evolution of human affect. Stanford, CA: Stanford University Press.

J. H. Turner. 1996. The Evolution of Emotions in Humans: A Darwinian–Durkheimian Analysis. Journal for the theory of social behaviour26:1-34

L. Xu, H. Lin, J. ZHAO.2008. Construction and Analysis of Emotional Corpus. *JOURNAL OF CHINESE INFORMA TION PROCESSIN*.

X. Y. Xu, and J. H. Tao. 2003. The study of affective categorization in Chinese. The 1st Chinese Conference on Affective Computing and Intelligent Interaction. Beijing, China.

A. Wierzbicka, 1996. *Semantics: Primes and Universals*. Oxford: Oxford University Press.

Complex Linguistic Annotation – No Easy Way Out! A Case from Bangla and Hindi POS Labeling Tasks

Sandipan Dandapat[1] Dublin City University Ireland

Priyanka Biswas[1] LDCIL CIIL-Mysore, India

Monojit Choudhury **Kalika Bali** Microsoft Research Labs India Bangalore, India

E-mail: sdandapat@computing.dcu.ie, biswas.priyanka@gmail.com, monojitc@microsoft.com, kalikab@microsoft.com

Abstract

Alternative paths to linguistic annotation, such as those utilizing games or exploiting the web users, are becoming popular in recent times owing to their very high benefit-to-cost ratios. In this paper, however, we report a case study on POS annotation for Bangla and Hindi, where we observe that reliable linguistic annotation requires not only expert annotators, but also a great deal of supervision. For our hierarchical POS annotation scheme, we find that close supervision and training is necessary at every level of the hierarchy, or equivalently, complexity of the tagset. Nevertheless, an *intelligent annotation tool* can significantly accelerate the annotation process and increase the inter-annotator agreement for both expert and non-expert annotators. These findings lead us to believe that reliable annotation requiring deep linguistic knowledge (e.g., POS, chunking, Treebank, semantic role labeling) requires expertise and supervision. The focus, therefore, should be on design and development of appropriate annotation tools equipped with machine learning based predictive modules that can significantly boost the productivity of the annotators.

1 Introduction

Access to reliable annotated data is the first hurdle encountered in most NLP tasks be it at the level of Parts-of-Speech (POS) tagging or a more complex discourse level annotation. The performance of the machine learning approaches which have become de rigueur for most NLP tasks are dependent on accurately annotated large datasets. Creation of such databases is, hence, a highly resource intensive task both in terms of time and expertise.

While the cost of an annotation task can be characterized by the number of man-hours and the level of expertise required, the productivity or the benefit can be measured in terms of the reliability and usability of the end-product, i.e., the annotated dataset. It is thus no surprise that considerable effort has gone into developing techniques and tools that can effectively boost the benefit-to-cost ratio of the annotation process. These include, but are not limited to:

(a) exploiting the reach of the web to reduce the effort required for annotation (see, e.g., Snow et al. (2008) and references therein)
(b) smartly designed User Interfaces for aiding the annotators (see, e.g., Eryigit (2007); Koutsis et al. (2007); Reidsma et al. (2004))
(c) using supervised learning to bootstrap a small annotated dataset to automatically label a larger corpus and getting it corrected by human annotators (see, e.g., Tomanek et al. (2007); Wu et al. (2007))
(d) Active Learning (Ringger et al. 2007) where only those data-points which are directly relevant for training are presented for manual annotation.

Methods exploiting the web-users for linguistic annotation are particularly popular these days, presumably because of the success of the ESP-Game (von Ahn and Dabbish, 2004) and its successors in image annotation. A more recent study by (Snow et al., 2008) shows that annotated data obtained from non-expert anonymous web-users is as good as those obtained from experts. However, unlike the game model, here the task is distributed among non-experts through an Internet portal such as Amazon Mechanical Turk, and the users are paid for their annotations.

This might lead to an impression that the expert knowledge is dispensable for NLP annotation tasks. However, while these approaches may work for more simple tasks like those described in (Snow et al., 2008), most NLP related annotation tasks such as POS tagging, chunking, semantic role labeling, Treebank annotation and

[1] This work has been done during the authors' internship at Microsoft Research Lab India.

Proceedings of the Third Linguistic Annotation Workshop, ACL-IJCNLP 2009, pages 10–18, Suntec, Singapore, 6-7 August 2009.

discourse level tagging, require expertise in the relevant linguistic area. In this work, we present a case study of POS annotation in Bangla and Hindi using a hierarchical tagset, where we observe that reliable linguistic annotation requires not only expert annotators, but also a great deal of supervision. A generic user interface for facilitating the task of hierarchical word level linguistic annotation was designed and experiments conducted to measure the *inter-annotator agreement* (IA) and annotation time. It is observed that the tool can significantly accelerate the annotation process and increase the IA. The productivity of the annotation process is further enhanced through bootstrapping, whereby a little amount of manually annotated data is used to train an automatic POS tagger. The annotators are then asked to edit the data already tagged by the automatic tagger using an appropriate user interface.

However, the most significant observation to emerge from these experiments is that irrespective of the complexity of the annotation task (see Sec. 2 for definition), language, design of the user interface and the accuracy of the automatic POS tagger used during bootstrapping, the productivity and reliability of the expert annotators working under close supervision of the dataset designer is higher than that of non-experts or those working without expert-supervision. This leads us to believe that among the four aforementioned approaches for improving the benefit-to-cost ratio of the annotation tasks, solution (a) does not seem to be the right choice for involved linguistic annotations; rather, approaches (b), (c) and (d) show more promise.

The paper is organized as follows: Section 2 provides a brief introduction to IL-POST – a hierarchical POS Tag framework for Indian Languages which is used for defining the specific annotation tasks used for the experiments. The design and features of the data annotation tool are described in Section 3. Section 4 presents the experiments conducted for POS labeling task of Bangla and Hindi while the results of these experiments are discussed in Section 5. The conclusions are presented in Section 6.

2 IL-POST

IL-POST is a POS-tagset framework for Indian Languages, which has been designed to cover the morphosyntactic details of Indian Languages (Baskaran et al. 2008). It supports a three-level

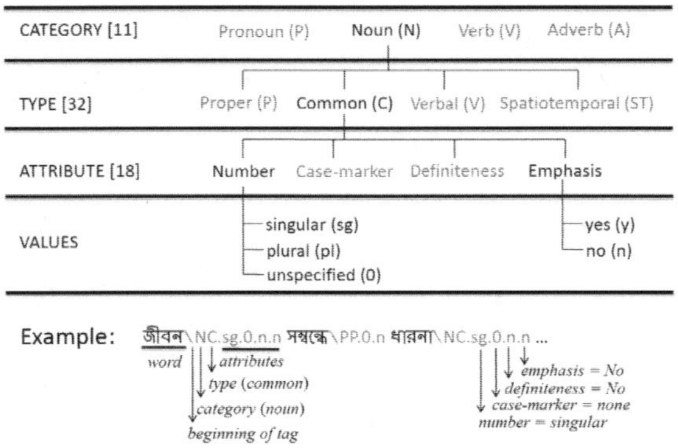

Figure 1: A schematic of IL-POST framework

hierarchy of Categories, Types and Attributes that provides a systematic method to annotate language specific categories without disregarding the shared traits of the Indian languages. This allows the framework to offer flexibility, cross-linguistic compatibility and reusability across several languages and applications. An important consequence of its hierarchical structure and decomposable tags is that it allows users to specify the morpho-syntactic information applicable at the desired granularity according to the specific language and task. The complete framework supports 11 categories at the top level with 32 types at the second level to represent the main POS categories and their sub-types. Further, 18 morphological attributes or features are associated with the types. The framework can thus, be used to derive a flat tagset of only 11 categories or a complex three level tagset of several thousand tags depending on the language and/or application. Figure 1 shows a schematic of the IL-POST framework. The current framework has been used to derive maximally specified tagsets for Bangla and Hindi (see Baskaran et al. (2008) for the descriptions of the tagsets), which have been used to design the experiments presented in this paper.

3 Annotation Tool

Though a number of POS annotation tools are available none are readily suitable for hierarchical tagging. The tools from other domains (like discourse annotation, for example) that use hierarchical tagsets require considerable customization for the task described here. Thus, in order to facilitate the task of word-level linguistic annotation for complex tagsets we developed a generic annotation tool. The annotation tool can be customized to work for any tagset that has up to

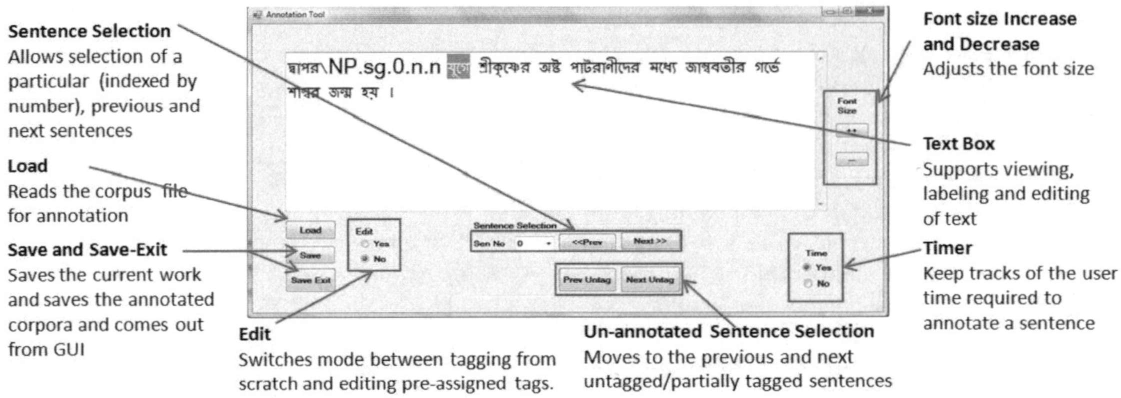

Figure 2: The basic Interface Window and Controls. See the text for details.

three levels of hierarchy and for any word level linguistic annotation task, such as *Named Entity* annotation and *Chunk boundary* labeling. In this section we describe the design of the user interface and other features of the annotation tool.

3.1 Interface Design Principles

The annotation scheme followed for linguistic data creation is heavily dependent on the end-application the data will cater to. Moreover, annotations are often performed by trained linguists who, in the Indian context, are either novice or intermittent users of computer. These observations led us to adopt the following principles: (1) customizability of the interface to any word level annotation task; (2) mouse driven selection of tags for faster and less erroneous annotation; and (3) display of all possible choices at every stage of the task to reduce memorization overload.

3.2 Basic Interface

Figure 2 depicts the basic interface of the annotation tool

3.2.1 Automatic Handling

Apart from the surface controls, the interface also supports automatic selection facility that highlights the next unlabeled word that needs to be annotated. After loading the task (i.e., a sentence) it automatically highlights the first unlabeled word. Once a tag is assigned to the highlighted word, the next unlabeled word is automatically selected. However, the automatic selection module can be stopped by selecting a particular word through a mouse click.

3.2.2 Handling Hierarchical Annotation

The first two levels of the IL-POST hierarchy are displayed (on a right mouse click) as a two level context menu. This is illustrated in Fig. 3(a). On selection of the category and type by left clicks, a window is dynamically generated for the assignment of the attribute values, i.e., the third level of the hierarchy. A drop down box is associated with each attribute for selecting the appropriate values. This is shown in Fig. 3(b). The default values for each of the attributes are set based on the frequency of occurrence of the values in a general corpus. This further reduces the time of tag assignment. When the user clicks "OK" on the attribute assignment window, the system automatically generates the tag as per the user's selection and displays it in the *Text-box* just after the selected word.

3.3 Edit Mode Annotation

While performing the annotation task, human annotators need to label every word of a sentence. Instead of annotating every word from scratch, we incorporate machine intelligence to automatically label every word in a sentence. Suppose that we have an automatic POS tag prediction module that does a fairly accurate job. In that case, the task of annotation would mean editing the pre-assigned tags to the words. We hypothesize that such an editing based annotation task that incorporates some intelligence in the form of a tagger will be much faster than purely manual annotation, provided that the pre-assigned tags are "sufficiently accurate". Thus, human annotators only need to edit a particular word whenever machine assigns an incorrect tag making the process faster. We also make certain changes to the basic interface for facilitating easy editing. In particular, when the corpus is loaded using the interface, the predicted tags are shown for each word and the first *category-type* is highlighted automatically. The user can navigate

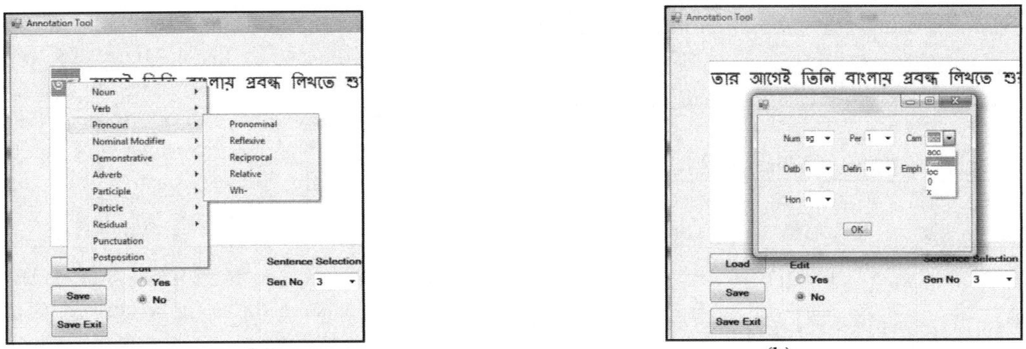

(a) (b)

Figure 3: Annotation at a) Category-Type level, b) Attribute level

to the next or pervious editable positions (*Category-Type* or *Attributes*) by using the *Shift* and the *Ctrl* keys respectively. The user may edit a particular pre-assigned tag by making a right mouse click and choosing from the usual context menus or attribute editing window. The user also has the provision to choose an editable location by left mouse-click.

3.3.1 Automatic POS Tagger

We developed a statistical POS tagger based on *Cyclic Dependency Network* (Toutanova et al., 2003) as an initial annotator for the Edit mode annotation. The tagger was trained for Bangla and Hindi on the data that was created during the first phase of annotation (i.e. annotation from scratch). We developed taggers for both *Category+Type* level (CT) and *Category+Type+ Attribute* level (CTA). We also developed two versions of the same tagger with *high* and *low* accuracies for each level of the annotation by controlling the amount of training data. As we shall see in Sec. 4 and 5, the different versions of the tagger at various levels of the hierarchy and accuracy will help us to understand the relation between the *Edit mode* annotation, and the complexity of the tagset and the accuracy of the tagger used for initial annotation. The taggers were trained on 1457 sentences (approximately 20,000 words) for Bangla and 2366 sentences (approximately 45,000 words) for Hindi. The taggers were tested on 256 sentences (~ 3,500 words) for Bangla and 591 sentences for Hindi, which are disjoint from the training corpus. The evaluation of a hierarchical tagset is non-trivial because the error in the machine tagged data with respect to the gold standard should take into account the level of the hierarchy where the mismatch between the two takes place. Clearly, mismatch at the category or type level should incur a higher penalty than one at the level of the attributes. If for a word, there is a mismatch between the type assigned by the machine and that present in the gold standard, then it is assumed to be a full error (equivalent to 1 unit). On the other hand, if the type assigned is correct, then the error is 0.5 times the fraction of attributes that do not agree with the gold standard.

Table 1 reports the accuracies of the various taggers. Note that the attributes in IL-POST correspond to morphological features. Unlike Bangla, we do not have access to a morphological analyzer for Hindi to predict the attributes during the POS tagging at the CTA level. Therefore, the tagging accuracy in the CTA level for Hindi is lower than that of Bangla even though the amount of training data used in Hindi is much higher than that in Bangla.

4 Experiments

The objective of the current work is to study the *cognitive load* associated with the task of linguistic annotation, more specifically, POS annotation. Cognitive load relates to the higher level of processing required by the working memory of an annotator when more learning is to be done in a shorter time. Hence, a higher cognitive load implies more time required for annotation and higher error rates. The time required for annotation can be readily measured by keeping track of the time taken by the annotators while tagging a sentence. The timer facility provided with the annotation tool helps us keep track of the annotation time. Measuring the error rate is slightly trickier as we do not have any ground truth (gold standard) against which we can measure the accuracy of the manual annotators. Therefore, we measure the IA, which should be high if the error rate is low. Details of the evaluation metrics are discussed in the next section.

Language	CT		CTA	
	High	*Low*	*High*	*Low*
Bangla	81.43	66.73	76.98	64.52
Hindi	87.66	67.85	69.53	57.90

Table 1: Tagging accuracy in % for Bangla and Hindi

The cognitive load of the annotation task is dependent on the complexity of the tagset, (un)availability of an appropriate annotation tool and bootstrapping facility. Therefore, in order to quantify the effect of these factors on the annotation task, annotation experiments are conducted under eight different settings. Four experiments are done for annotation at the Category+Type (CT) level. These are:

- **CT-AT**: without using annotation tool, i.e., using any standard text editor[2].
- **CT+AT**: with the help of the basic annotation tool.
- **CT+ATL**: with the help of the annotation tool in the edit mode, where the POS tagger used has low accuracy.
- **CT+ATH**: in the edit mode where the POS tagger used has a high accuracy.

Similarly, four experiments are conducted at the Category+Type+Attribute (CTA) level, which are named following the same convention: CTA-AT, CTA+AT, CTA+ATL, CTA+ATH.

4.1 Subjects

The reliability of annotation is dependent on the expertise of the annotators. In order to analyze the effect of annotator expertise, we chose subjects with various levels of expertise and provided them different amount of training and supervision during the annotation experiments.

The experiments for Bangla have been conducted with 4 users (henceforth referred to as B1, B2, B3 and B4), all of whom are trained linguists having at least a post-graduate degree in linguistics. Two of them, namely B1 and B2, were provided rigorous training in-house before the annotation task. During the training phase the tagset and the annotation guidelines were explained to them in detail. This was followed by 3-4 rounds of trial annotation tasks, during which the annotators were asked to annotate a set of 10-15 sentences and they were given feedback regarding the correctness of their annotations as judged by other human experts. For B1 and B2, the experiments were conducted in-house and under close supervision of the designers of the tagset and the tool, as well as a senior research linguist.

The other two annotators, B3 and B4, were provided with the data, the required annotation tools and the experimental setup, annotation guidelines and the tool usage guidelines, and the task were described in another document. Thus, the annotators were self-trained as far as the tool usage and the annotation scheme were concerned. They were asked to return the annotated data (and the time logs that are automatically generated during the annotation) at the end of all the experiments. This situation is similar to that of linguistic annotation using the Internet users, where the annotators are self-trained and work under no supervision. However, unlike ordinary Internet users, our subjects are trained linguists.

Experiments in Hindi were conducted with two users (henceforth referred to as H1 and H2), both of whom are trained linguists. As in the case of B1 and B2, the experiments were conducted under close supervision of a senior linguist, but H1 and H2 were self-trained in the use of the tool.

The tasks were randomized to minimize the effect of familiarity with the task as well as the tool.

4.2 Data

The annotators were asked to annotate approximately 2000 words for CT+AT and CTA+AT experiments and around 1000 words for CT-AT and CTA-AT experiments. The *edit mode* experiments (CT+ATL, CT+ATH, CTA+ATL and CTA+ATH) have been conducted on approximately 1000 words. The amount of data was decided based primarily on the time constraints for the experiments. For all the experiments in a particular language, 25-35% of the data was common between every pair of annotators. These common sets have been used to measure the IA. However, there was no single complete set common to all the annotators. In order to measure the influence of the pre-assigned labels on the judgment of the annotators, some amount of data was kept common between CTA+AT and CTA+ATL/H experiments for every annotator.

[2] The experiments without the tool were also conducted using the basic interface, where the annotator has to type in the tag strings; the function of the tool here is limited to loading the corpus and the timer.

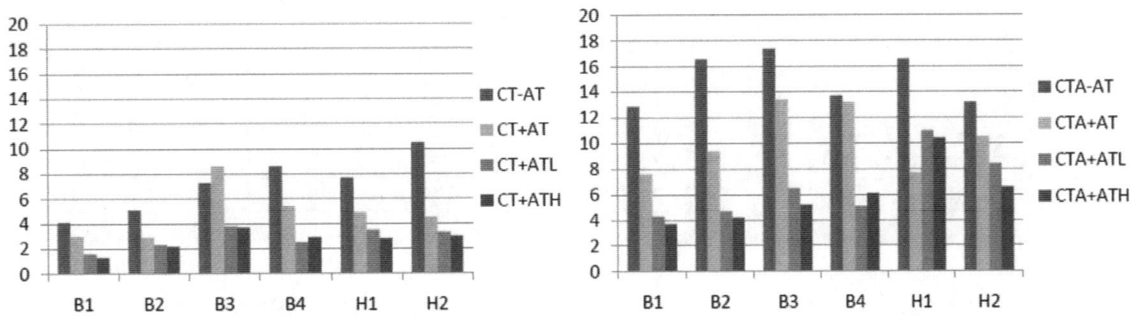

(a) (b)

Figure 4: Mean annotation time (in sec per word) for different users at (a) CT and (b) CTA levels

Level	Mean Time (in Sec)			
	-AT	+AT	+ATL	+ATH
CT	6.3	5.0 (20.7)	2.6 (59.4)	2.5 (59.8)
CTA	15.2	10.9 (28.1)	5.2 (66.0)	4.8 (68.3)

Table 2: Mean annotation time for Bangla experiments (%reduction in time with respect to –AT is given within parentheses).

Level	IA (in %)			
	-AT	+AT	+ATL	+ATH
CT	68.9	79.2 (15.0)	77.2 (12.2)	89.9 (30.6)
CTA	51.4	72.5 (41.0)	79.3 (54.2)	83.4 (62.1)

Table 3: Average IA for Bangla experiments (%increase in IA with respect to –AT is given within parentheses).

5 Analysis of Results

In this section we report the observations from our annotation experiments and analyze those to identify trends and their underlying reasons.

5.1 Mean Annotation Time

We measure the mean annotation time by computing the average time required to annotate a word for a sentence and then average it over all sentences for a given experiment by a specific annotator. Fig. 4 shows the mean annotation time (in seconds per word) for the different experiments by the different annotators. It is evident that complex annotation task (i.e., CTA level) takes much more time compared to a simple one (i.e., CT level). We also note that the tool effectively reduces the annotation time for most of the subjects. There is some variation in time (for example, B3) where the subject took longer to get accustomed to the annotation tool. As expected, the annotation process is accelerated by bootstrapping. In fact, the higher the accuracy of the automatic tagger, the faster is the annotation. Table 2 presents the mean time averaged over the six subjects for the 8 experiments in Bangla along with the %reduction in the time with respect to the case when no tool is present (i.e., "-AT"). We observe that (a) the tool is more effective for complex annotation, (b) on average, annotation at the CTA level take twice the time of their CT level counterparts, and (c) bootstrapping can significantly accelerate the annotation process. We also note that experts working under close supervision (B1 and B2) are in general faster than self-trained annotators (B3 and B4).

5.2 Inter-annotator Agreement

Inter-annotator agreement (IA) is a very good indicator of the reliability of an annotated data. A high IA denotes that at least two annotators agree on the annotation and therefore, the probability that the annotation is erroneous is very small. There are various ways to quantify the IA ranging from a very simple percentage agreement to more complex measures such as the *kappa statistics* (Cohen, 1960; Geertzen and Bunt, 2006). For a hierarchical tagset the measurement of IA is non-trivial because the extent of disagreement should take into account the level of the hierarchy where the mismatch between two annotators takes place. Here we use percentage agreement which takes into consideration the level of hierarchy where the disagreement between the two annotators takes place. For example, the difference in IA at the category level between say, a Noun and a Nominal Modifier, versus the difference at the number attribute level between singular and plural. The extent of agreement for each of the tags is computed in the same way as we have evaluated our POS tagger (Sec.3.2.1). We have also measured the Cohen's Kappa (Cohen, 1960) for the **CT** level experiments. Its behavior is similar to that of percentage agreement.

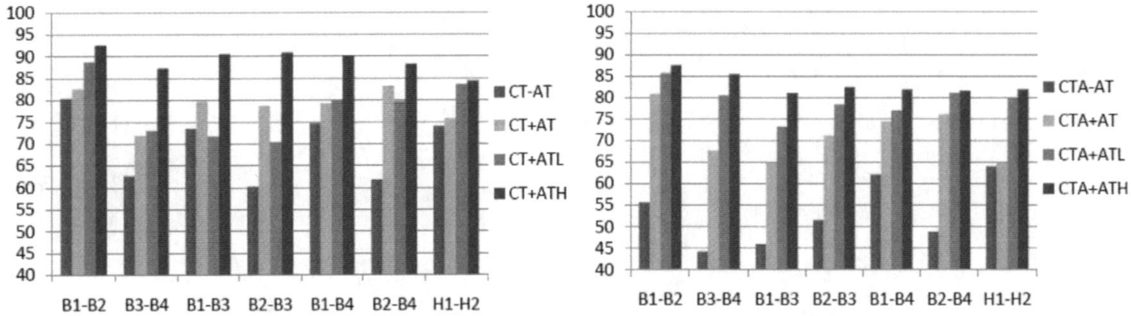

(a) (b)

Figure 5: Pair-wise IA (in %) at (a) CT and (b) CTA levels

Fig. 5 shows the pair-wise percentage IA for the eight experiments and Table 3 summarizes the %increase in IA due to the use of tool/bootstrapping with respect to the "-AT" experiments at CT and CTA levels. We observe the following basic trends: (a) IA is consistently lower for a complex annotation (CTA) task than a simpler one (CT), (b) use of annotation tool helps in improvement of the IA, more so for the CTA level experiments, (c) bootstrapping helps in further improvement in IA, especially when the POS tagger used has high accuracy, and (d) IA between the trained subjects (B1 and B2) is always higher than the other pairs.

IA is dependent on several factors such as the ambiguity in the tagset, inherently ambiguous cases, underspecified or ambiguously specified annotation guidelines, and errors due to carelessness of the annotator. However, manual inspection reveals that the factor which results in very low IA in "-AT" case that the tool helps improve significantly is the typographical errors made by the annotators while using a standard text editor for annotation (e.g., NC mistyped as MC). This is more prominent in the CTA level experiments, where typing the string of attributes in the wrong order or missing out on some attributes, which are very common when annotation tool is not used, lead to a very low IA. Thus, memorization has a huge overload during the annotation process, especially for complex annotation schemes, which the annotation tool can effectively handle. In fact, more than 50% errors in CTA level are due to the above phenomenon. The analysis of other factors that lower the IA is discussed in Sec. 5.4.

We would like to emphasize the fact that although the absolute time difference between the trained and un-trained users reduces when the tool and/or bootstrapping is used, the IA does not decrease significantly in case of the untrained users for the complex annotation task.

Level	Tagger	Subjects			
		B1	B2	B3	B4
CT	*Low*	89.6	89.8	74.2	81.8
	High	90.8	90.1	64.8	77.8
CTA	*Low*	85.4	85.1	68.2	76.1
	High	86.4	85.4	59.1	73.4

Table 4: Percentage agreement between the edit and the normal mode annotations (for Bangla).

5.3 Machine Influence

We have seen that the IA increases in the edit mode experiments. This apparent positive result might be an unacceptable artifact of machine influence, which is to say that the annotators, whenever in confusion, might blindly agree with the pre-assigned labels. In order to understand the influence of the pre-assigned labels on the annotators, we calculate the percentage agreement for a subject between the data annotated from scratch using the tool (+AT) and that in the edit mode (+ATL and +ATH). The results are summarized in Table 4.

The low agreement between the data annotated under the two modes for the untrained annotators (B3 and B4) shows that there is a strong influence of pre-assigned labels for these users. Untrained annotators have lower agreement while using a high accuracy initial POS tagger compared to the case when a low accuracy POS tagger is used. This is because the high accuracy tagger assigns an erroneous label mainly for the highly ambiguous cases where a larger context is required to disambiguate. These cases are also difficult for human annotators to verify and untrained annotators tend to miss these cases during edit mode experiments. The trained annotators show a consistent performance. Nevertheless, there is still some influence of the pre-assigned labels.

5.4 Error Patterns

In order to understand the reasons of disagreement between the annotators, we analyze the confusion matrix for different pairs of users for the various experimental scenarios. We observe that the causes of disagreement are primarily of three kinds: (1) unspecified and/or ambiguous guidelines, (2) ignorance about the guidelines, and (3) inherent ambiguities present in the sentences. We have found that a large number of the errors are due to type (1). For example, in attribute level annotation, for every attribute two special values are '0' (denotes '*not applicable for the particular lexical item*') and 'x' (denotes '*undecided or doubtful to the annotator*'). However, we find that both trained and untrained annotators have their own distinct patterns of assigning '0' or 'x'. Later we made this point clearer with examples and enumerated possible cases of '0' and 'x' tags. This was very helpful in improving the IA.

A major portion of the errors made by the untrained users are due to type (2). For example, it was clearly mentioned in the annotation guidelines that if a borrowed/foreign word is written in the native script, then it has to be tagged according to its normal morpho-syntactic function in the sentence. However, if a word is typed in foreign script, then it has to be tagged as a foreign word. However, none of the untrained annotators adhered to these rules strictly.

Finally, there are instances which are inherently ambiguous. For example, in noun-noun compounds, a common confusion is whether the first noun is to be tagged as a nouns or an adjective. These kinds of confusions are evenly distributed over all the users and at every level of annotation.

One important fact that we arrive at through the analysis of the confusion matrices is that the trained annotators working under close supervision have few and consistent error patterns over all the experiments, whereas the untrained annotators exhibit no consistent and clearly definable error patterns. This is not surprising because the training helps the annotators to understand the task and the annotation scheme clearly; on the other hand, constant supervision helps clarifying doubts arising during annotation.

6 Conclusion

In this paper we reported our observations for POS annotation experiments for Bangla and Hindi using the IL-POST annotation scheme under various scenarios. Experiments in Tamil and Sanskrit are planned in the future.

We argue that the observations from the various experiments make a case for the need of training and supervision for the annotators as well as the use of appropriate annotation interfaces and techniques such as bootstrapping. The results are indicative in nature and need to be validated with larger number of annotators. We summarize our salient contributions/conclusions:

- The generic tool described here for complex and hierarchical word level annotation is effective in accelerating the annotation task as well as improving the IA. Thus, the tool helps reducing the cognitive load associated with annotation.
- Bootstrapping, whereby POS tags are pre-assigned by an automatic tagger and human annotators are required to edit the incorrect labels, further accelerates the task, at the risk of slight influence of the pre-assigned labels.
- Although with the help of the tool and techniques such as bootstrapping we are able to bring down the time required by untrained annotators to the level of their trained counterparts, the IA, and hence the reliability of the annotated data for the former is always poorer. Hence, training and supervision is very important for reliable linguistic annotation.

We would like to emphasize the last point because recently it is being argued that Internet and other game based techniques can be effectively used for gathering annotated data for NLP. While this may be suitable for certain types of annotations, such as word sense, lexical similarity or affect (see Snow et al. (2008) for details), we argue that many mainstream linguistic annotation tasks such as POS, chunk, semantic roles and Treebank annotations call for expertise, training and close supervision. We believe that there is no easy way out to this kind of complex linguistic annotations, though smartly designed annotation interfaces and methods such as bootstrapping and active learning can significantly improve the productivity and reliability, and therefore, should be explored and exploited in future.

Acknowledgements

We would like to thank the annotators Dripta Piplai, Anumitra Ghosh Dastidar, Narayan Choudhary and Maansi Sharma. We would also like to thank Prof. Girish Nath Jha for his help in conducting the experiments.

References

S. Baskaran, K. Bali, M. Choudhury, T. Bhattacharya, P. Bhattacharyya, G. N. Jha, S. Rajendran, K. Saravanan, L. Sobha and K.V. Subbarao. 2008. A Common Parts-of-Speech Tagset Framework for Indian Languages. In *Proc. of LREC 2008.*

J. Cohen. 1960. A coefficient of agreement for nominal scales. Educational and Psychological Measurement, **20** (1):37-46

J. Geertzen, and H. Bunt. 2006. Measuring annotator agreement in a complex hierarchical dialogue act annotation scheme. In *Proc. of the Workshop on Discourse and Dialogue*, ACL 2006, pp. 126-133.

G. Eryigit. 2007. ITU Treebank annotation tool. In *Proc. of Linguistic Annotation Workshop*, ACL 2007, pp. 117-120.

I. Koutsis, G. Markopoulos, and G. Mikros. 2007. Episimiotis: A Multilingual Tool for Hierarchical Annotation of Texts. In *Corpus Linguistics*, 2007.

D. Reidsma, N. Jovanovi, and D. Hofs. 2004. Designing annotation tools based on the properties of annotation problems. *Report, Centre for Telematics and Information Technology*, 2004.

E. Ringger, P. McClanahan, R. Haertel, G. Busby, M. Carmen, J. Carroll, K. Seppi, and D. Lonsdale. 2007. Active Learning for Part-of-Speech Tagging: Accelerating Corpus Annotation. In *Proc. of Linguistic Annotation Workshop*, ACL 2007, pp. 101-108.

R. Snow, B. O'Connor, D. Jurafsky and A. Y. Ng. 2008. Cheap and Fast — But is it Good? Evaluating Non-Expert Annotations for Natural Language Tasks. In *Proc of EMNLP-08*

K. Tomanek, J. Wermter, and U. Hahn. 2007. Efficient annotation with the Jena ANotation Environment (JANE). In *Proc. of Linguistic Annotation Workshop*, ACL 2007, pp. 9-16.

L. von Ahn and L. Dabbish. 2004. Labeling Images with a Computer Game. In *ACM Conference on Human Factors in Computing Systems, CHI 2004.*

Y. Wu, P. Jin, T. Guo and S. Yu. 2007. Building Chinese sense annotated corpus with the help of software tools. In *Proc. of Linguistic Annotation Workshop*, ACL 2007, pp. 125-131.

Assessing the benefits of partial automatic pre-labeling for frame-semantic annotation

Ines Rehbein and **Josef Ruppenhofer** and **Caroline Sporleder**
Computational Linguistics
Saarland University
{rehbein,josefr,csporled}@coli.uni-sb.de

Abstract

In this paper, we present the results of an experiment in which we assess the usefulness of partial semi-automatic annotation for frame labeling. While we found no conclusive evidence that it can speed up human annotation, automatic pre-annotation does increase its overall quality.

1 Introduction

Linguistically annotated resources play a crucial role in natural language processing. Many recent advances in areas such as part-of-speech tagging, parsing, co-reference resolution, and semantic role labeling have only been possible because of the creation of manually annotated corpora, which then serve as training data for machine-learning based NLP tools. However, human annotation of linguistic categories is time-consuming and expensive. While this is already a problem for major languages like English, it is an even bigger problem for less-used languages.

This data acquisition bottleneck is a well-known problem and there have been numerous efforts to address it on the algorithmic side. Examples include the development of weakly supervised learning methods such as co-training and active learning. However, addressing only the algorithmic side is not always possible and not always desirable in all scenarios. First, some machine learning solutions are not as generally applicable or widely re-usable as one might think. It has been shown, for example, that co-training does not work well for problems which cannot easily be factorized into two independent views (Mueller et al., 2002; Ng and Cardie, 2003). Some active learning studies suggest both that the utility of the selected examples strongly depends on the model used for classification and that the example pool selected for one model can turn out to be sub-optimal when another model is trained on it at a later stage (Baldridge and Osborne, 2004). Furthermore, there are a number of scenarios for which there is simply no alternative to high-quality, manually annotated data; for example, if the annotated corpus is used for empirical research in linguistics (Meurers and Müller, 2007; Meurers, 2005).

In this paper, we look at this problem from the data creation side. Specifically we explore whether a semi-automatic annotation set-up in which a human expert corrects the output of an automatic system can help to speed up the annotation process without sacrificing annotation quality.

For our study, we explore the task of frame-semantic argument structure annotation (Baker et al., 1998). We chose this particular task because it is a rather complex – and therefore time-consuming – undertaking, and it involves making a number of different but interdependent annotation decisions for each instance to be labeled (e.g. frame assignment and labeling of frame elements, see Section 3.1). Semi-automatic support would thus be of real benefit.

More specifically, we explore the usefulness of automatic pre-annotation for the first step in the annotation process, namely frame assignment (word sense disambiguation). Since the available inventory of frame elements is dependent on the chosen frame, this step is crucial for the whole annotation process. Furthermore, semi-automatic annotation is more feasible for the frame labeling sub-task. Most automatic semantic role labeling systems (ASRL), including ours, tend to perform much better on frame assignment than on frame role labeling and correcting an erroneously chosen

Proceedings of the Third Linguistic Annotation Workshop, ACL-IJCNLP 2009, pages 19–26,
Suntec, Singapore, 6-7 August 2009.

frame typically also requires fewer physical operations from the annotator than correcting a number of wrongly assigned frame elements.

We aim to answer three research questions in our study: First, we explore whether pre-annotation of frame labels can indeed speed up the annotation process. This question is important because frame assignment, in terms of physical operations of the annotator, is a relatively minor effort compared to frame role assignment and because checking a pre-annotated frame still involves all the usual mental operations that annotation from scratch does. Our second major question is whether annotation quality would remain acceptably high. Here the concern is that annotators might tend to simply go along with the pre-annotation, which would lead to an overall lower annotation quality than they could produce by annotating from scratch.[1] Depending on the purpose for which the annotations are to be used, trading off accuracy for speed may or may not be acceptable. Our third research question concerns the required quality of pre-annotation for it to have any positive effect. If the quality is too low, the annotation process might actually be slowed down because annotations by the automatic system would have to be deleted before the new correct one could be made. In fact, annotators might ignore the pre-annotations completely. To determine the effect of the pre-annotation quality, we not only compared a null condition of providing no prior annotation to one where we did, but we in fact compared the null condition to two different quality levels of pre-annotation, one that reflects the performance of a state-of-the-art ASRL system and an enhanced one that we artificially produced from the gold standard.

2 Related Work

While semi-automatic annotation is frequently employed to create labeled data more quickly (see, e.g., Brants and Plaehn (2000)), there are comparatively few studies which systematically look at the benefits or limitations of this approach. One of the earliest studies that investigated the advantages of manually correcting automatic annotations for linguistic data was carried out by Marcus et al. (1993) in the context of the construction of the Penn Treebank. Marcus et al. (1993) employed a post-correction set-up for both part-of-speech and syntactic structure annotation. For pos-tagging they compared the semi-automatic approach to a fully manual annotation. They found that the semi-automatic method resulted both in a significant reduction of annotation time, effectively doubling the word annotation rate, and in increased inter-annotator agreement and accuracy.

Chiou et al. (2001) explored the effect of automatic pre-annotation for treebank construction. For the automatic step, they experimented with two different parsers and found that both reduce overall annotation time significantly while preserving accuracy. Later experiments by Xue et al. (2002) confirmed these findings.

Ganchev et al. (2007) looked at semi-automatic gene identification in the biomedical domain. They, too, experimented with correcting the output of an automatic annotation system. However, rather than employing an off-the-shelf named entity tagger, they trained a tagger maximized for recall. The human annotators were then instructed to filter the annotation, rejecting falsely labeled expressions. Ganchev et al. (2007) report a noticeable increase in speed compared to a fully manual set-up.

The approach that is closest to ours is that of Chou et al. (2006) who investigate the effect of automatic pre-annotation for Propbank-style semantic argument structure labeling. However that study only looks into the properties of the semi-automatic set-up; the authors did not carry out a control study with a fully manual approach. Nevertheless Chou et al. (2006) provide an upper bound of the savings obtained by the semi-automatic process in terms of annotator operations. They report a reduction in annotation effort of up to 46%.

3 Experimental setup

3.1 Frame-Semantic Annotation

The annotation scheme we use is that of FrameNet (FN), a lexicographic project that produces a database of frame-semantic descriptions of English vocabulary. Frames are representations of prototypical events or states and their participants in the sense of Fillmore (1982). In the FN database, both frames and their participant roles are arranged in various hierarchical relations (most prominently, the is-a relation).

FrameNet links these descriptions of frames with the words and multi-words (lexical units, LUs) that evoke these conceptual structures. It also docu-

[1] This problem is also known in the context of resources that are collaboratively constructed via the web (Kruschwitz et al., 2009)

ments all the ways in which the semantic roles (frame elements, FEs) can be realized as syntactic arguments of each frame-evoking word by labeling corpus attestations. As a small example, consider the Collaboration frame, evoked in English by lexical units such as *collaborate*.v, *conspire*.v, *collaborator*.n and others. The core set of frame-specific roles that apply include Partner_1, Partner_2, Partners and Undertaking. A labeled example sentence is

(1) [The two researchers ^{Partners}] COLLABORATED [on many papers ^{Undertaking}].

FrameNet uses two modes of annotation: full-text, where the goal is to exhaustively annotate the running text of a document with all the different frames and roles that occur, and lexicographic, where only instances of particular target words used in particular frames are labeled.

3.2 Pilot Study

Prior to the present study we carried out a pilot experiment comparing manual and semi-automatic annotation of different segments of running text. In this experiment we saw no significant effect from pre-annotation. Instead we found that the annotation speed and accuracy depended largely on the order in which the texts were annotated and on the difficulty of the segments. The influence of order is due to the fact that FrameNet has more than 825 frames and each frame has around two to five core frame elements plus a number of non-core elements. Therefore even experienced annotators can benefit from the re-occuring of frames during the ongoing annotation process.

Drawing on our experiences with the first experiment, we chose a different experimental set-up for the present study. To reduce the training effect, we opted for annotation in lexicographic mode, restricting the number of lemmas (and thereby frames) to annotate, and we started the experiment with a training phase (see Section 3.5). Annotating in lexicographic mode also gave us better control over the difficulty of the different batches of data. Since these now consist of unrelated sentences, we can control the distribution of lemmas across the segments (see Section 3.4).

Furthermore, since the annotators in our pilot study had often ignored the error-prone pre-annotation, in particular for frame elements, we decided not to pre-annotate frame elements and to experiment with an enhanced level of pre-annotation to explore the effect of pre-annotation quality.

3.3 Annotation Set-Up

The annotators included the authors and three computational linguistics undergraduates who have been performing frame-semantic annotation for at least one year. While we use FrameNet data, our annotation set-up is different. The annotation consists of decorating automatically derived syntactic constituency trees with semantic role labels using the Salto tool (Burchardt et al., 2006) (see Figure 1). By contrast, in FrameNet annotation a chunk parser is used to provide phrase type and grammatical relations for the arguments of the target words. Further, FrameNet annotators need to correct mistakes of the automatic grammatical analysis, unlike in our experiment. The first annotation step, frame assignment, involves choosing the correct frame for the target lemma from a pull down menu; the second step, role assignment, requires the annotators to draw the available frame element links to the appropriate syntactic constituent(s).

The annotators performed their annotation on computers where access to the FrameNet website, where gold annotations could have been found, was blocked. They did, however, have access to local copies of the frame descriptions needed for the lexical units in our experiment. As the overall time needed for the annotation was too long to do in one sitting, the annotators did it over several days. They were instructed to record the time (in minutes) that they took for the annotation of each annotation session.

Our ASRL system for state-of-the-art pre-annotation was Shalmaneser (Erk and Pado, 2006). The enhanced pre-annotation was created by manually inserting errors into the gold standard.

3.4 Data

We annotated 360 sentences exemplifying all the senses that were defined for six different lemmas in FrameNet release 1.3. The lemmas were the verbs *rush, look, follow, throw, feel* and *scream*. These verbs were chosen for three reasons. First, they have enough annotated instances in the FN release that we could use some instances for testing and still be left with a set of instances sufficiently large to train our ASRL system. Second,we knew from prior work with our automatic role labeler that it had a reasonably good performance on these lemmas. Third, these LUs exhibit a range of difficulty in terms of the number of senses they have in FN (see Table 1) and the subtlety of the sense distinc-

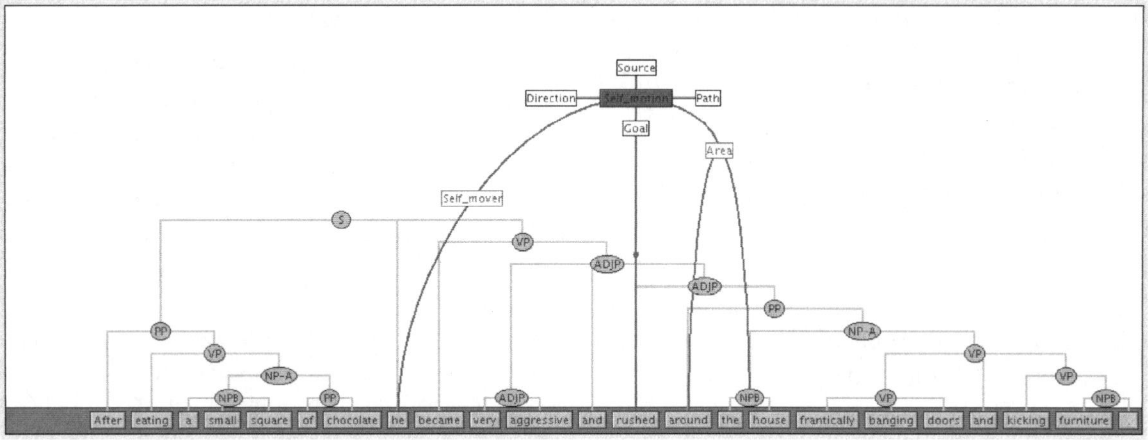

Figure 1: The Salto Annotation Tool

	Instances	Senses
feel	134	6
follow	113	3
look	185	4
rush	168	2
scream	148	2
throw	155	2

Table 1: Lemmas used

tions – e.g. the FrameNet senses of *look* are harder to distinguish than those of *rush*. We randomly grouped our sentences into three batches of equal size and for each batch we produced three versions corresponding to our three levels of annotation.

3.5 Study design

In line with the research questions that we want to address and the annotators that we have available, we choose an experimental design that is amenable to an analysis of variance. Specifically, we randomly assign our 6 annotators (1-6) to three groups of two (Groups I-III). Each annotator experiences all three annotation conditions, namely no pre-annotation (N), state-of-the-art pre-annotation (S), and enhanced pre-annotation (E). This is the within-subjects factor in our design, all other factors are between subjects. Namely, each group was randomly matched to one of three different orders in which the conditions can be experienced (see Table 2). The orderings are designed to control for the effects that increasing experience may have on speed and quality. While all annotators end up labeling all the same data, the groups also differ as to which batch of data is presented in which condition. This is intended as a check on any inherent differences in annotation difficulty that might exist between the data sets. Finally, to rule out difficulties with unfamiliar frames and frame elements needed for the lexical units used in this study, we provided some training to the annotators. In the week prior to the experiment, they were given 240 sentences exemplifying all 6 verbs in all their senses to annotate and then met to discuss any questions they might have about frame or FE distinctions etc. These 240 sentences were also used to train the ASRL system.

	1st	2nd	3rd	Annotators
Group I	E	S	N	5, 6
Group II	S	N	E	2, 4
Group III	N	E	S	1, 3

Table 2: Annotation condition by order and group

4 Results

In addition to time, we measured precision, recall and f-score for frame assignment and semantic role assignment for each annotator. We then performed an analysis of variance (ANOVA) on the outcomes of our experiment. Our basic results are presented in Table 3. As can be seen and as we expected, our annotators differed in their performance both with regard to annotation quality and speed. Below we discuss our results with respect to the research questions named above.

4.1 Can pre-annotation of frame assignment speed up the annotation process?

Not surprisingly, there are considerable differences in speed between the six annotators (Table 3),

Precision		Recall		F	t	p
		Annotator 1				
94/103	91.3	94/109	86.2	88.68	75	N
99/107	92.5	99/112	88.4	90.40	61	E
105/111	94.6	105/109	96.3	95.44	65	S
		Annotator 2				
93/105	88.6	93/112	83.0	85.71	135	S
86/98	87.8	86/112	76.8	81.93	103	N
98/106	92.5	98/113	86.7	89.51	69	E
		Annotator 3				
95/107	88.8	95/112	84.8	86.75	168	N
103/110	93.6	103/112	92.0	92.79	94	E
99/113	87.6	99/113	87.6	87.60	117	S
		Annotator 4				
106/111	95.5	106/112	94.6	95.05	80	S
99/108	91.7	99/113	87.6	89.60	59	N
105/112	93.8	105/113	92.9	93.35	52	E
		Annotator 5				
104/110	94.5	(104/112)	92.9	93.69	170	E
91/103	88.3	(91/113)	80.5	84.22	105	S
96/100	96.0	(96/113)	85.0	90.17	105	N
		Annotator 6				
102/106	96.2	102/112	91.1	93.58	124	E
94/105	89.5	94/112	83.9	86.61	125	S
93/100	93.0	93/113	82.3	87.32	135	N

Table 3: Results for frame assignment: precision, recall, f-score (F), time (t) (frame and role assignment), pre-annotation (p): **N**on, **E**nhanced, **S**halmaneser

which are statistically significant with $p \leq 0.05$. Focussing on the order in which the text segments were given to the annotators, we observe a significant difference ($p \leq 0.05$) in annotation time needed for each of the segments. With one exception, all annotators took the most time on the text segment given to them first, which hints at an ongoing training effect.

The different conditions of pre-annotation (none, state-of-the-art, enhanced) did not have a significant effect on annotation time. However, all annotators except one were in fact faster under the enhanced condition than under the unannotated condition. The one annotator who was not faster annotated the segment with the enhanced pre-annotation before the other two segments; hence there might have been an interaction between time savings from pre-annotation and time savings due to a training effect. This interaction between training effect and degree of pre-annotation might be one reason why we do not find a significant effect between annotation time and pre-annotation condition. Another reason might be that the pre-annotation only reduces the physical effort needed to *annotate* the correct frame which is relatively minor compared to the cognitive effort of *determining* (or verifying) the right frame, which is required for all degrees of pre-annotation.

4.2 Is annotation quality influenced by automatic pre-annotation?

To answer the second question, we looked at the relation between pre-annotation condition and f-score. Even though the results in f-score for the different annotators vary in extent (Table 4), there is no significant difference between annotation quality for the six annotators.

Anot1	Anot2	Anot3	Anot4	Anot5	Anot6
91.5	85.7	89.0	92.7	89.4	89.2

Table 4: Average f-score for the 6 annotators

Next we performed a two-way ANOVA (Within-Subjects design), and crossed the dependent variable (f-score) with the two independent variables (order of text segments, condition of pre-annotation). Here we found a significant effect ($p \leq 0.05$) for the impact of pre-annotation on annotation quality. All annotators achieved higher f-scores for frame assignment on the enhanced pre-annotated text segments than on the ones with no pre-annotation. With one exception, all annotators also improved on the already high baseline for the enhanced pre-annotation (Table 5).

Seg.	Precision		Recall		f-score
		Shalmaneser			
A	(70/112)	62.5	(70/96)	72.9	67.30
B	(75/113)	66.4	(75/101)	74.3	70.13
C	(66/113)	58.4	(66/98)	67.3	62.53
		Enhanced Pre-Annotation			
A	(104/112)	92.9	(104/111)	93.7	93.30
B	(103/112)	92.0	(103/112)	92.0	92.00
C	(99/113)	87.6	(99/113)	87.6	87.60

Table 5: Baselines for automatic pre-annotation (Shalmaneser) and enhanced pre-annotation

The next issue concerns the question of whether annotators make different types of errors when provided with the different styles of pre-annotation. We would like to know if erroneous frame assignment, as done by a state-of-the-art ASRL will tempt annotators to accept errors they would not make in the first place. To investigate this issue, we compared f-scores for each of the frames for all three pre-annotation conditions with f-scores for frame assignment achieved by Shalmaneser. The boxplot in Figure 2 shows the distribution of f-scores for each frame for the different pre-annotation styles and for Shalmaneser. We can see that the same

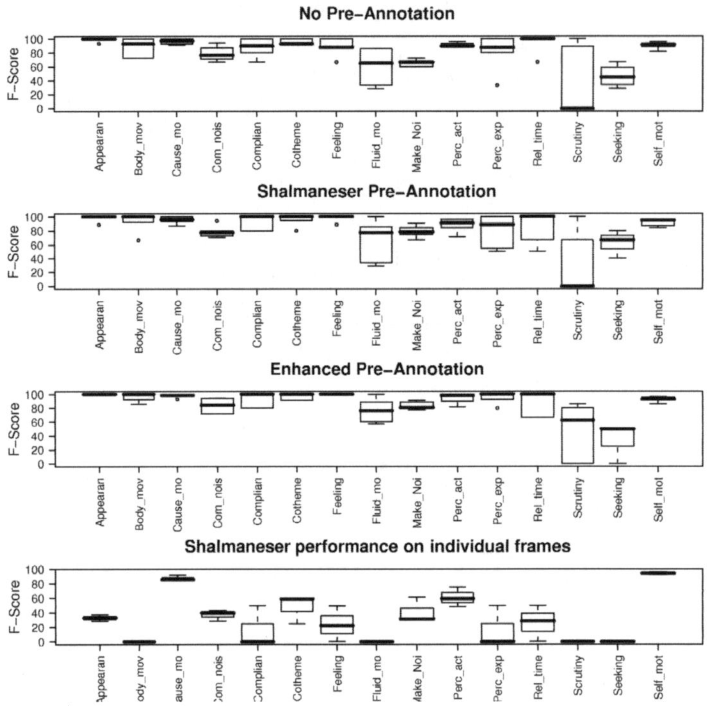

Figure 2: F-Scores per frame for human annotators on different levels of pre-annotation and for Shalmaneser

error types are made by human annotators throughout all three annotation trials, and that these errors are different from the ones made by the ASRL.

Indicated by f-score, the most difficult frames in our data set are Scrutiny, Fluidic_motion, Seeking, Make_noise and Communication_noise. This shows that automatic pre-annotation, even if noisy and of low quality, does not corrupt human annotators on a grand scale. Furthermore, if the pre-annotation is good it can even improve the overall annotation quality. This is in line with previous studies for other annotation tasks (Marcus et al., 1993).

4.3 How good does pre-annotation need to be to have a positive effect?

Comparing annotation quality on the automatically pre-annotated texts using Shalmaneser, four out of six annotators achieved a higher f-score than on the non-annotated sentences. The effect, however, is not statistically significant. This means that pre-annotation produced by a state-of-the-art ASRL system is not yet good enough a) to significantly speed up the annotation process, and b) to improve the quality of the annotation itself. On the positive side, we also found no evidence that the error-prone pre-annotation decreases annotation quality.

Most interestingly, the two annotators who showed a decrease in f-score on the text segments pre-annotated by Shalmaneser (compared to the text segments with no pre-annotation provided) had been assigned to the same group (Group I). Both had first annotated the enhanced, high-quality pre-annotation, in the second trial the sentences pre-annotated by Shalmaneser, and finally the texts with no pre-annotation. It might be possible that they benefitted from the ongoing training, resulting in a higher f-score for the third text segment (no pre-annotation). For this reason, we excluded their annotation results from the data set and performed another ANOVA, considering the remaining four annotators only.

Figure 3 illustrates a noticeable trend for the interaction between pre-annotation and annotation quality: all four annotators show a decrease in annotation quality on the text segments without pre-annotation, while both types of pre-annotation (Shalmaneser, Enhanced) increase f-scores for human annotation. There are, however, differences between the impact of the two pre-annotation types on human annotation quality: two annotators show better results on the enhanced, high-quality pre-

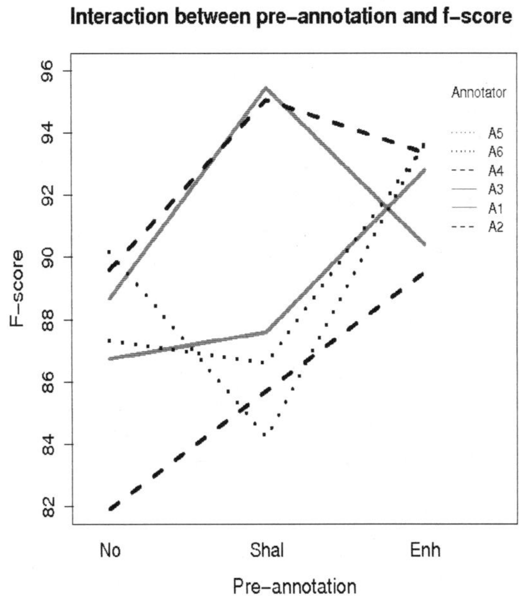

Figure 3: Interaction between pre-annotation and f-score

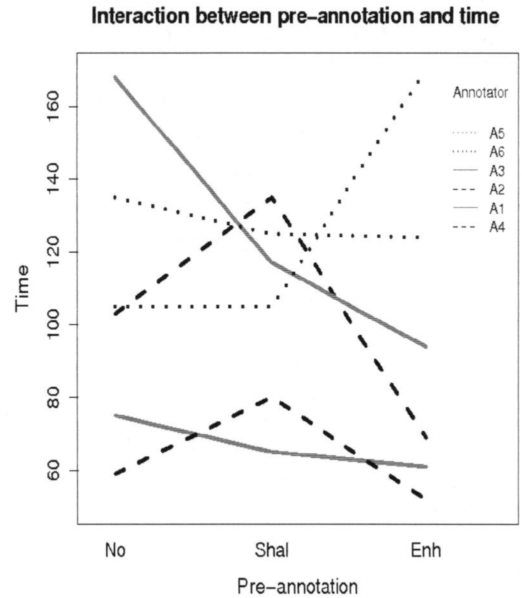

Figure 4: Interaction between pre-annotation and time

annotation, the other two perform better on the texts pre-annotated by the state-of-the-art ASRL. The interaction between pre-annotation and f-score computed for the four annotators is weakly significant with $p \leq 0.1$.

Next we investigated the influence of pre-annotation style on annotation time for the four annotators. Again we can see an interesting pattern: The two annotators (A1, A3) who annotated in the order N-E-S, both take most time for the texts without pre-annotation, getting faster on the text pre-processed by Shalmaneser, while the least amount of time was needed for the enhanced pre-annotated texts (Figure 4). The two annotators (A2, A4) who processed the texts in the order S-N-E, showed a continuous reduction in annotation time, probably caused by the interaction of training and data quality. These observations, however, should be taken with a grain of salt, as they outline trends, but due to the low number of annotators, could not be substantiated by statistical tests.

4.4 Semantic Role Assignment

As described in Section 3.5, we provided pre-annotation for frame assignment only, therefore we did not expect any significant effects of the different conditions of pre-annotation on the task of semantic role labeling. To allow for a meaningful comparison, the evaluation of semantic role assignment was done on the subset of frames annotated correctly by all annotators.

As with frame assignment, there are considerable differences in annotation quality between the annotators. In contrast to frame assignment, here the differences are statistically significant ($p \leq 0.05$). Table 6 shows the average f-score for each annotator on the semantic role assignment task.

Anot1	**Anot2**	**Anot3**	**Anot4**	**Anot5**	**Anot6**
85.2	80.1	87.7	89.2	82.5	84.3

Table 6: Average f-scores for the 6 annotators

As expected, neither the condition of pre-annotation nor the order of text segments had any significant effect on the quality of semantic role assignment.[2]

5 Conclusion and future work

In the paper we presented experiments to assess the benefits of partial automatic pre-annotation on a frame assignment (word sense disambiguation) task. We compared the impact of a) pre-annotations

[2] The annotation of frame and role assignment was done as a combined task, therefore we do not report separate results for annotation time for semantic role assignment.

provided by a state-of-the-art ASRL, and b) enhanced, high-quality pre-annotation on the annotation process. We showed that pre-annotation has a positive effect on the quality of human annotation: the enhanced pre-annotation clearly increased f-scores for all annotators, and even the noisy, error-prone pre-annotations provided by the ASRL system did not lower the quality of human annotation.

We suspect that there is a strong interaction between the order in which the text segments are given to the annotators and the three annotation conditions, resulting in lower f-scores for the group of annotators who processed the ASRL pre-annotations in the first trial, where they could not yet profit from the same amount of training as the other two groups.

The same problem occurs with annotation time. We have not been able to show that automatic pre-annotation speeds up the annotation process. However, we suspect that here, too, the interaction between training effect and annotation condition made it difficult to reach a significant improvement. One way to avoid the problem would be a further split of the test data, so that the different types of pre-annotation could be presented to the annotators at different stages of the annotation process. This would allow us to control for the strong bias through incremental training, which we cannot avoid if one group of annotators is assigned data of a given pre-annotation type in the first trial, while another group encounters the same type of data in the last trial. Due to the limited number of annotators we had at our disposal as well as the amount of time needed for the experiments we could not sort out the interaction between order and annotation conditions. We will take this issue up in future work, which also needs to address the question of how good the automatic pre-annotation should be to support human annotation. F-scores for the enhanced pre-annotation provided in our experiments were quite high, but it is possible that a similar effect could be reached with automatic pre-annotations of somewhat lower quality.

The outcome of our experiments provides strong motivation to improve ASRL systems, as automatic pre-annotation of acceptable quality does increase the quality of human annotation.

References

C. F. Baker, C. J. Fillmore, J. B. Lowe. 1998. The berkeley framenet project. In *Proceedings of the 17th international conference on Computational linguistics*, 86–90, Morristown, NJ, USA. Association for Computational Linguistics.

J. Baldridge, M. Osborne. 2004. Active learning and the total cost of annotation. In *Proceedings of EMNLP*.

T. Brants, O. Plaehn. 2000. Interactive corpus annotation. In *Proceedings of LREC-2000*.

A. Burchardt, K. Erk, A. Frank, A. Kowalski, S. Padó. 2006. SALTO – a versatile multi-level annotation tool. In *Proceedings of LREC*.

F.-D. Chiou, D. Chiang, M. Palmer. 2001. Facilitating treebank annotation using a statistical parser. In *Proceedings of HLT-2001*.

W.-C. Chou, R. T.-H. Tsai, Y.-S. Su, W. Ku, T.-Y. Sung, W.-L. Hsu. 2006. A semi-automatic method for annotation a biomedical proposition bank. In *Proceedings of FLAC-2006*.

K. Erk, S. Pado. 2006. Shalmaneser - a flexible toolbox for semantic role assignment. In *Proceedings of LREC*, Genoa, Italy.

C. J. F. C. J. Fillmore, 1982. *Linguistics in the Morning Calm*, chapter Frame Semantics, 111–137. Hanshin Publishing, Seoul, 1982.

K. Ganchev, F. Pereira, M. Mandel, S. Carroll, P. White. 2007. Semi-automated named entity annotation. In *Proceedings of the Linguistic Annotation Workshop*, 53–56, Prague, Czech Republic. Association for Computational Linguistics.

U. Kruschwitz, J. Chamberlain, M. Poesio. 2009. (linguistic) science through web collaboration in the ANAWIKI project. In *Proceedings of WebSci'09*.

M. P. Marcus, B. Santorini, M. A. Marcinkiewicz. 1993. Building a large annotated corpus of English: The Penn Treebank. *Computational Linguistics*, 19(2):313–330.

W. D. Meurers, S. Müller. 2007. Corpora and syntax (article 44). In A. Lüdeling, M. Kytö, eds., *Corpus linguistics*. Mouton de Gruyter, Berlin.

W. D. Meurers. 2005. On the use of electronic corpora for theoretical linguistics. case studies from the syntax of german. *Lingua*, 115(11):1619–1639. `http://purl.org/net/dm/papers/meurers-03.html`.

C. Mueller, S. Rapp, M. Strube. 2002. Applying co-training to reference resolution. In *Proceedings of 40th Annual Meeting of the Association for Computational Linguistics*, 352–359, Philadelphia, Pennsylvania, USA. Association for Computational Linguistics.

V. Ng, C. Cardie. 2003. Bootstrapping coreference classifiers with multiple machine learning algorithms. In *Proceedings of the 2003 Conference on Empirical Methods in Natural Language Processing (EMNLP-2003)*.

N. Xue, F.-D. Chiou, M. Palmer. 2002. Building a large-scale annotated chinese corpus. In *Proceedings of Coling-2002*.

Bridging the Gaps:
Interoperability for GrAF, GATE, and UIMA

Nancy Ide
Department of Computer Science
Vassar College
Poughkeepsie, New York USA
ide@cs.vassar.edu

Keith Suderman
Department of Computer Science
Vassar College
Poughkeepsie, New York USA
suderman@anc.org

Abstract

This paper explores interoperability for data represented using the Graph Annotation Framework (GrAF) (Ide and Suderman, 2007) and the data formats utilized by two general-purpose annotation systems: the General Architecture for Text Engineering (GATE) (Cunningham, 2002) and the Unstructured Information Management Architecture (UIMA). GrAF is intended to serve as a "pivot" to enable interoperability among different formats, and both GATE and UIMA are at least implicitly designed with an eye toward interoperability with other formats and tools. We describe the steps required to perform a round-trip rendering from GrAF to GATE and GrAF to UIMA CAS and back again, and outline the commonalities as well as the differences and gaps that came to light in the process.

1 Introduction

The creation of language data and linguistic annotations remains a fundamental activity in the field of language technology, in order to develop increasingly sophisticated understanding and generation capabilities for the world's languages. Substantial effort has been devoted to the creation of resources for major languages, and new projects are developing similar resources for less widely-used languages; the cost and effort of resource creation, as well as the possibilities for linking multilingual and multi-modal language data, demands that resources and tools are reusable as well as compatible in terms of their representation. Various representation standards and annotation tools have emerged over the past decade and have contributed to some convergence in practice, but at the same time, there has been growing recognition that *interoperability* among formats and tools, rather than universal use of a single representation format, is more suited to the needs of the community and language technology research in general.

This paper explores interoperability for data represented using the Graph Annotation Framework (GrAF) (Ide and Suderman, 2007) and the data formats utilized by two general-purpose annotation systems: the General Architecture for Text Engineering (GATE) (Cunningham, 2002) and the Unstructured Information Management Architecture (UIMA)[1]. UIMA and GATE are similar in design and purpose: both represent documents as text plus annotations and allow users to define pipelines of processes that manipulate the document. However, there are some differences in implementation and representation format that prohibit direct exchange of data and annotations between the two.

The Graph Annotation Framework (GrAF) (Ide and Suderman, 2007) is intended to serve as a "pivot" to enable interoperability among different formats for data and linguistics annotations and the systems that create and exploit them. In this paper, we describe the steps required to perform a round-trip rendering from GrAF to GATE and GrAF to UIMA CAS and back again, and outline the commonalities as well as the differences and gaps that came to light in the process. In doing so, we hope to shed some light on the design and implementation choices that either contribute to or impede progress toward interoperability, which can feed future development.

2 Background

A handful of formats for linguistic data and annotations have been proposed as standards over the past ten years, including Annotation Graphs (AG) (Bird and Liberman, 2001), and,

[1] http://www.oasis-open.org/committees/uima/

Proceedings of the Third Linguistic Annotation Workshop, ACL-IJCNLP 2009, pages 27–34,
Suntec, Singapore, 6-7 August 2009.

most recently, the Graph Annotation Framework (GrAF) (Ide and Suderman, 2007). UIMA's Common Analysis System (CAS) also provides a "common" way to represent annotations so that they can be shared and reused among UIMA annotator components.

Annotation Graphs were introduced primarily as a means to handle time-stamped speech data, in large part to overcome the problem of overlapping annotations that violate the strict tree structure of XML-based schemes. However, AGs are limited by the inability to represent hierarchical relations among annotations (as, for instance, in a syntax tree). AGs are used in GATE to represent standoff annotations.

GrAF has been developed by the International Standards Organization (ISO)'s TC37 SC4, as a part of the Linguistic Annotation Framework (International Standards Organization, 2008). GrAF provides an XML serialization of an abstract data model for annotations that is intended to serve as a "pivot" for transducing among user-defined and tool input annotation formats. GrAF is intended to function in much the same way as an *interlingua* in machine translation: a common, abstract conceptual representation into and out of which user- and tool-specific formats are transduced, so that a transduction of any specific format into and out of GrAF accomplishes the transduction between it and any number of other GrAF-conformant formats. GrAF is currently an ISO Candidate Draft.

The UIMA framework is a data management system that supports pipelined applications over unstructured data. UIMA was originally developed by IBM and is currently under further development by an OASIS technical committee[2]. Apache UIMA[3] is an Apache-licensed open source implementation of the UIMA specification being developed as an Apache incubator project. UIMA's Common Analysis System (CAS) is used to describe typed objects (annotations) associated with a given text or other media, upon which processing modules ("annotators") operate.

2.1 Annotation models

Each of the formats described above is based on some model of annotations and their relation to the data they describe. The AG model consists of sets of arcs defined over nodes corresponding to timestamps in primary data, each of which is labeled with an arbitrary linguistic description that applies to that region. Multiple annotations over the data produce multiple arcs; there is no provision for arcs associating annotations.

GrAF defines the *regions* to be annotated in primary data as the area bounded by two or more *anchors*. The definition of anchor and the number of anchors needed to define a region depends on the medium being annotated. The only assumption that GrAF makes is that anchors have a natural ordering. For textual data GrAF uses character offsets for anchors, and two anchors bound each region. Regions serve as the leaf nodes of a directed acyclic graph. Annotations in the form of feature structures are associated with nodes in the graph, including nodes associated with both regions and other annotations, via edges in the graph. GrAF can represent common annotation types such as hierarchical syntax trees by allowing, for example, a sentence annotation to have edges to constituent annotations such as NP, VP, etc. As opposed to AGs, annotations typically label nodes rather than edges in GrAF, although labeled edges are allowed, and the information comprising the annotations is represented using feature structures rather than simple labels.

The underlying model of UIMA CAS is similar to GrAF's, due to its hierarchical type system and the use of feature structures to represent annotation information. In fact, the GrAF model, consisting of a directed acyclic graph whose nodes are labeled with feature structures, provides the relevant abstraction underlying UIMA CAS. In principle, then, annotations represented in GrAF and UIMA CAS are trivially mappable to one another. The same is not true for AGs: in GrAF, annotations can be directly linked to other annotations, but in the AG model annotations are effectively independent layers linked to the primary data. As a result, while it is possible to "flatten" a GrAF representation so that it can be represented as an AG, it is not possible to take the round trip back into GrAF without losing information about relations among annotations. An AG can, of course, always be represented in GrAF, since independent graphs layered over data (possibly with shared anchors in the data) are valid GrAF structures.

[2]http://www.oasis-open.org/committees/uima/

[3]http://incubator.apache.org/uima/index.html

3 GrAF → UIMA → GrAF

Conversion of a GrAF data structure into UIMA involves generating (1) a UIMA data structure (a *CAS*), (2) a UIMA *type system*, and a specification of *type priorities*.

The CAS consists of a *subject of analysis* (sofa), which is the data (in our examples here, a text) itself, together with its annotations. The CAS XML representation of the annotations is very similar to the GrAF XML representation: each annotation is identified by its start and end location in the data expressed in terms of virtual nodes between each character in the data, where the position before the first character is node 0. The conversion of GrAF anchors to UIMA indexes is therefore trivial.

3.1 UIMA Type Systems

A UIMA type system specifies the type of data that can be manipulated by annotator components. A type system defines two kinds of objects; types and features. The *type* defines the kinds of data that can be manipulated in a CAS, arranged in an inheritance hierarchy. A *feature* defines a field, or slot, within a type. Each CAS type specifies a single supertype and a list of features that may be associated with that type. A type inherits all of the features from its supertype, so the features that can be associated with a type is the union of all features defined by all supertypes in the inheritance tree. A feature is a name/value pair where the value can be one of UIMA's built in primitive types (boolean, char, int, etc.) or a reference to another UIMA object. UIMA also allows feature values to be arrays of either primitive types or arrays of references to other objects.

UIMA defines a top level type *uima.cas.TOP* which contains no features and serves as the root of the UIMA type system inheritance tree. The root type *uima.cas.TOP* is the supertype of *uima.cas.AnnotationBase*, which is the supertype of *uima.tcas.Annotation*, which in turn is the supertype for *org.xces.graf.uima.Annotation*. All UIMA annotations generated by GrAF use *org.xces.graf.uima.Annotation* as their supertype. Note that the UIMA type hierarchy is strictly an *is-a* hierarchy; for example, there may be an annotation type *pos* with subtypes *penn_pos*, *claws_pos*, etc., indicating that each of these annotations are a kind of part of speech annotation. The hierarchy does not reflect other kinds of relations such as the relation between a "lemma" annotation and a "pos" annotation (i.e., a lemma and a pos are typically companion parts of a morpho-syntactic description, but neither one *is* a morpho-syntactic description), or constituency relations in syntactic annotation schemes.

The GrAF Java API provides a Java class that generates a valid UIMA type system given one or more GrAF objects. The type system is generated by iterating over all the nodes in the graph and creating a new type for each kind of annotation encountered (e.g., token, sentence, POS, etc.). Feature descriptions are generated for each type at the same time.

One drawback of deriving a type system automatically is that some of the power of UIMA type systems is lost in the conversion. For example, in the process of conversion, all feature values are assumed to be strings, even though UIMA allows specification of the type of a feature value. Since in GrAF, feature values have been serialized from the contents of an XML attribute, all feature values are represented internally as strings; to convert a feature value to any other representation would require that GrAF have some external knowledge of the annotation format being deserialized. Therefore, any type checking capability for feature value types in UIMA is lost after automatic generation of the type system. Similarly, it is not possible to determine a supertype for an annotation if it is more specific than *org.xces.graf.uima.Annotation* from the information in the GrAF representation alone, so in effect, it is not possible to derive any meaningful type hierarchy without additional knowledge. For example, it is not possible to include the information in the type system description that *penn_pos* and *claws_pos* are subtypes of *pos* since this information is not represented in the graph. Even in cases where this kind of information is represented in the graph, it is not retrievable; for example, FrameNet annotation includes a *grammaticalFunction* annotation whose children are elements such as `subject`, `object`, etc. However, there is no way to determine what the parent-child relation is between nodes without *a priori* knowledge of the annotation scheme.

Without a source of external knowledge, GrAF does not attempt to make any assumptions about the annotations and features in the graph. However, all of these problems are avoided by providing an XML Schema or other source of information about the GrAF annotations that can be used when generating the type system. The XML schema can specify the type hierarchy, data types and restricted ranges for feature values, etc. (see, for example, the XCES (Ide *et al.*, 2000) schema is used for the data and annotations in the American National Corpus (ANC)[4].)

3.2 UIMA Views and Indexes

A UIMA CAS object may contain more than one view of the artifact being annotated; for example, a CAS may contain an audio stream as one view and the transcribed text as another. Each view contains a copy of the artifact, referred to as the *subject of analysis* (*sofa*), and a set of indexes that UIMA annotators (processing modules) use to access data in the CAS. Each index is associated with one CAS type and indexes that type by its features–that is, the features are the keys for the index.

The indexes are the only way for UIMA annotators to access annotations in the CAS. It is necessary to generate these indexes, which are not provided automatically within UIMA. The GrAF Java API provides a module that generates the indexes at the same time the it generates the type system description. Since we do not know, and make no assumptions about, which annotations might be required by other annotators, all annotations are indexed by all of their features.

3.3 Type Priorities

Type priorities in UIMA are used to determine nesting relations when iterating over collections of annotations. That is, if two annotations have the same start and end offsets, then the order in which they will be presented by an iterator is determined by their type priority; the annotation with the highest priority will be presented first. Type priorities are specified by an ordered listing of annotation types, where order determines priority. In GrAF, annotation nesting is implicit in the graph itself.

To generate an explicit type priority specification for UIMA we must first obtain a list of all annotation types that appear in the graph and then sort the list based on the order they are encountered during a a depth first traversal of the graph. During the depth first traversal a *N x N precedence matrix* is constructed where *N* is the number of annotation types in the graph. If *precedes*[A,B] == *true* then A was encountered as an ancestor of B in the depth first traversal. If *precedes*[A,B] == *precedes*[B,A] == *true* then it is assumed that the annotation types have the same priority. Once the list of annotation types has been collected and the precedence matrix constructed, the matrix can be used to to sort the annotation types:

```
int compare(Annotation A,
            Annotation B,
            PrecedenceMatrix m)
{
   boolean AB = m.precedes(A,B);
   boolean BA = m.precedes(B,A);
   if (AB && BA)
   {
      return 0; // equal
   }
   else if (AB)
   {
      return -1; // A first.
   }
   else if (BA)
   {
      return 1; // B first.
   }
   // Neither AB or BA means A and
   // B are not in connected
   // components.
   return 0;
}
```

Not all nodes in the graph may be reachable in a depth first traversal, particularly if multiple annotations formats have been merged together. Therefore, after the initial traversal has been completed each node is checked to determine if it has been visited. If not, then another traversal is started from that node. This is repeated until all nodes/annotations in the graph have been visited at least once.

We have found that UIMA type priorities impose some limitations because they cannot represent context sensitive annotation orderings. For example, given

<!ELEMENT E1 (A,B)>
<!ELEMENT E2 (B,A)>

The order of `A` and `B` differs depending on whether the parent annotation is `E1` or `E2`. This type of relationship cannot be expressed by a simple ordering of annotations.

3.4 Naming Conflicts

The annotation type names used when generating the UIMA type system are derived automatically based on the annotation names used in the graph. Annotations in GrAF may also be grouped into named annotation sets and the gen-

[4]http://www.anc.org

```
<as type="POS">
   <a label="token">
       <fsr:fs type="PENN">
          <fsr:f name="msd" fVal="NN"/>
       </fsr:fs>
       <fsr:fs type="CLAWS5">
          <fsr:f name="msd" fVal="NN"/>
       </fsr:fs>
   </a>
</as>
```

Figure 1: GrAF representation of alternative POS annotations

erated UIMA type name consists of a concatenation of the nested annotation set names with the annotation label appended. For example, multiple part of speech annotations may be represented in different annotation sets, as shown in Figure 1.[5]

For the above example, two types will be generated: `POS_token_PENN` and `POS_token_CLAWS5`. However, GrAF places no restrictions on the names used for annotation set names, annotation labels, or feature structure types. Therefore, it is possible that the derived type name is not a valid UIMA identifier, which are required to follow Java naming conventions. For example, `Part-Of-Speech` is a valid name for an annotation label in GrAF, but because of the hyphen it is not a valid Java identifier and therefore not valid in UIMA.

To avoid the naming problem, a derived name is converted into a valid UIMA identifier before creating the UIMA type description. To permit round trip engineering, that is, ensuring a GrAF $\rightarrow$ UIMA $\rightarrow$ GrAF transformation results in the same GrAF representation as the original, a `NameMap` file is produced that maps a generated name to the compatible UIMA name. NameMaps can be used in a UIMA $\rightarrow$ GrAF conversion to ensure the GrAF annotations and annotation sets created are given the same names as they had in the original GrAF representation.

3.5 Preserving the Graph Structure

While UIMA does not have any graph-specific functionality, the value of a UIMA feature can be an array of annotations, or more specifically, an array of references to other annotations. In this way, annotations can effectively "point" to other annotations in UIMA. We exploit this capability to preserve the structure of the original graph in the UIMA representation, by adding two features to each annotation: `graf_children` and `graf_ancestors`. This information can be used to recreate the GrAF representation, should that ever be desired. It can also be used by UIMA annotators that have been designed to use and/or manipulate this information.

Although rarely used, GrAF permits edges in the graph to be annotated in the same way that nodes are. For UIMA conversion, if a graph contains labeled edges it must be converted into an equivalent graph without labeled edges. A graph with labeled edges can be converted into an equivalent graph without labeled edges, where a node replaces the original edge. To preserve the original graph structure, an attribute indicating that the node is represented as a a labeled edge in GrAF is included.

4 GrAF $\rightarrow$ GATE $\rightarrow$ GrAF

The conversion to/from GATE is much simpler than conversion to UIMA, since GATE is typeless and does not require the overhead of generating a type system or type priorities list. While GATE does support annotation schemas, they are optional, and annotations and features can be created at will. GATE is also much more lenient on annotation and feature names; names automatically generated by GrAF are typically valid in GATE.

Representing the graph structure in GATE is not as straightforward as it is in UIMA. We have developed a plugin to GATE that loads GrAF standoff annotations into GATE, and a parallel plugin that generates GrAF from GATE's internal format. As noted above, GATE uses annotation graphs to represent annotations, However, because annotation graphs do not provide for annotations of annotations, to transduce from GrAF to the GATE internal format it is necessary to "flatten" the graph so that nodes with edges to other nodes are modified to contain edges directly into the primary data. GATE assigns a unique id value to every annotation, so it is possible to link annotations by creating a special feature and referencing the parent/child annotations by their GATE id values.

The greatest difficulty in a GrAF $\rightarrow$ GATE conversion arises from the fact that in GATE, every

[5] The use of the `fVal` attribute in this example is subject to change according to revisions of ISO/DIS 24610-1 *Language Resource Management - Feature Structures - Part 1: Feature Structure Representation* (International Standards Organization, 2005), to which the representation of feature structures in GrAF adheres.

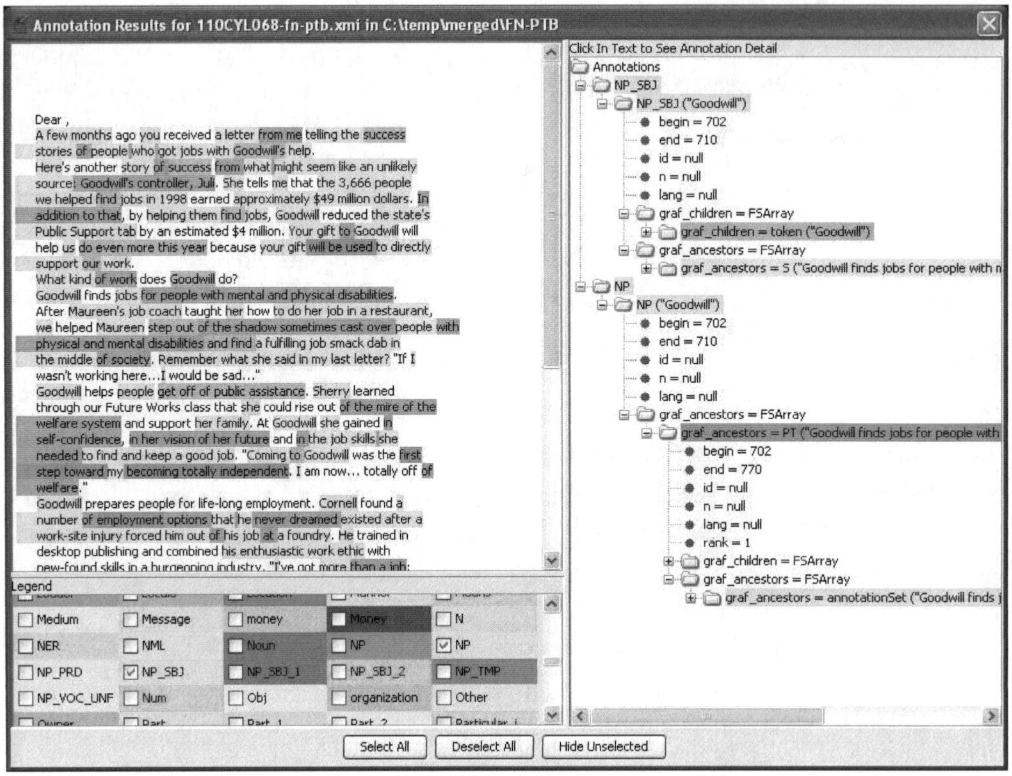

Figure 2: UIMA rendering of GrAF annotations

annotation is expected to have a start and end offset. In GrAF, a node may have multiple edges to other nodes that cover disjoint regions of text. For example, the FrameNet[6] annotation for a given verb typically includes edges to the associated role fillers (e.g., agent, theme, instrument, etc.), which are rarely contiguous in the text itself. Our current solution to this problem is to give a start and end offset that covers the smallest region of the text covering the regions associated with all descendants of the annotation, and recording the information concerning the original graph structure in attributes to enable reconversion into the original GrAF representation.

5 Exploiting Interoperability

GrAF is intended to serve as the *lingua franca* for data and annotations used in processing systems such as GATE and UIMA. As such, it provides a way for users to take advantage of each framework's strengths, e.g., UIMAs capabilities for deploying analysis engines as services that can be run remotely, and GATE's wide array of processing resources and capabilities for defining regular expressions over annotations (JAPE). It should be noted that GATE provides wrappers to allow a UIMA analysis engine to be used within GATE, and to allow a GATE processing pipeline to be used within UIMA. To share data and annotations between the two systems, it is necessary to construct a *mapping descriptor* to define how to map annotations between the UIMA CAS and the GATE Document, which operate similarly to the converters from and to GrAF from data and annotations described above. However, one advantage of using a GrAF representation as a pivot between the two systems is that when an annotation schema is used with GrAF data, the conversion from GATE to UIMA is more robust, reflecting the true type description and type priority hierarchies.

Using GrAF as a pivot has more general advantages, for example, by allowing annotations to be imported from and exported to a wide variety of formats, and also enabling merging annotations from disparate sources into a single annotation graph. Figure 2 shows a rendering of a Penn Treebank annotation (bracketed format) and a FrameNet annotation (XML) that have been transduced to GrAF, merged, and the transduced

[6]http://framenet.icsi.berkeley.edu/

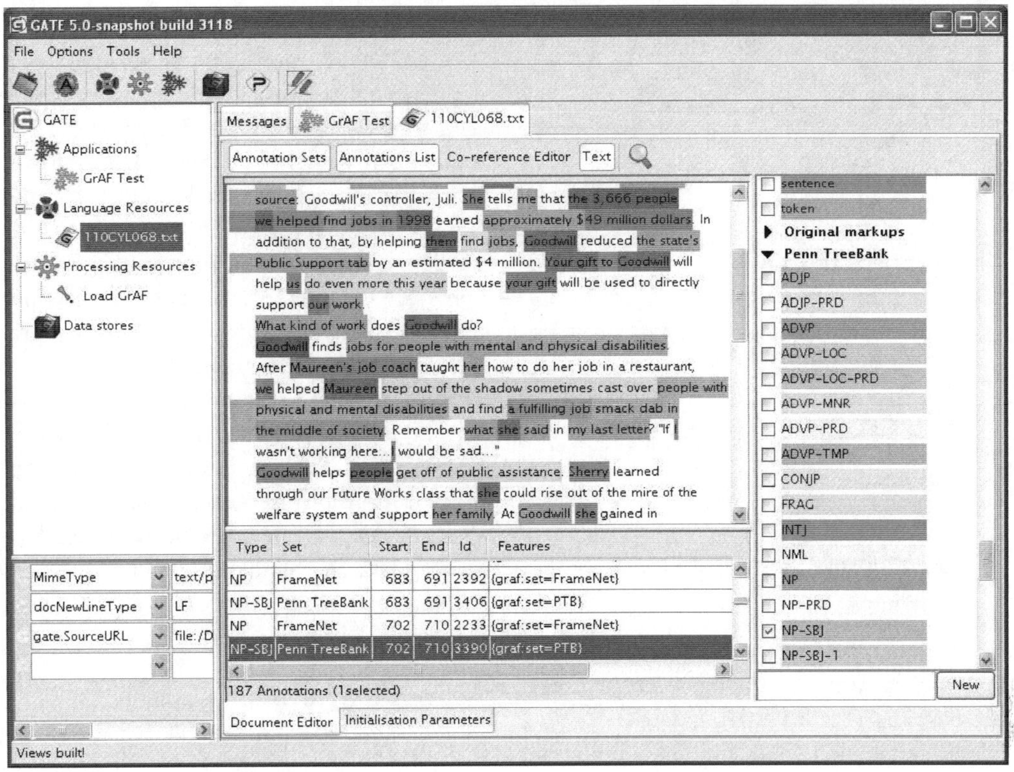

Figure 3: GATE rendering of GrAF annotations

for use in UIMA. The same data is shown rendered in GATE in Figure 3. The two "views" of the data consisting of overlaid annotations for each annotation type are visible in each rendering. There are multiple possibilities for exploiting and exploring merged annotations representing a range of annotation types within these two frameworks. For example, a UIMA analysis engine could be developed to identify regions annotated by both schemes, or all FrameNet elements that are annotated as `agent` and also annotated with Penn Treebank `NP-OBJ`, etc. In GATE, JAPE rules could locate patterns in annotations obtained from different sources, or named entity recognition rules could be enhanced with annotation information from data annotated in other formats. It would also be possible to compare multiple annotations of the same type, such as different tokenizations, different POS taggings , etc.

As a final note, we point out that in addition to conversion to UIMA and GATE, annotations from different sources (singly or merged in any combination) can also be converted to several other formats by using the GrAF Java API. The API allows the user to select from among existing annotations and specify an output format for their merged representation. Currently, in addition to GrAF, the following output formats are supported: XML documents with inline annotations; formats compatible with Monoconc Pro[7] and Wordsmith Tools[8]; NLTK[9]; CONLL (B-I-E) format; and UIMA CAS.[10] So, for example, it is possible to load a collection of standoff annotation files and convert to XML, and then present them to XML-aware applications as XML files with inline annotations. As a result, we are beginning to see possibilities for true interoperability among not only major frameworks like UIMA and GATE, but also applications with more limited functionalities as well as in-house formats. This, in turn, opens up the potential to mix and match among tools for various kinds of processing as appropriate to a given task. In general, the transduction of "legacy schemes" such as Penn Treebank into GrAF greatly facilitates their use in major systems such as UIMA and GATE, as well as

[7]http://www.athel.com/mono.html

[8]http://www.lexically.net/wordsmith/

[9]http://www.nltk.org/

[10]Note that to render GrAF into GATE, a plugin within the GATE environment is used to perform the conversion.

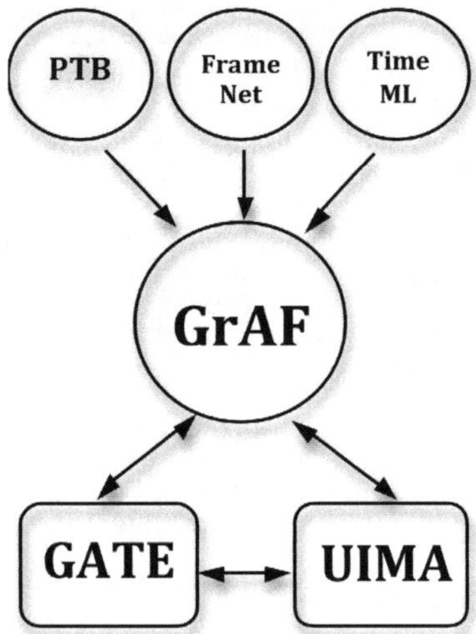

Figure 4: Conversion capabilities

other applications and systems. Figure 4 shows the conversion capabilities among a few annotations schemes, GrAF, and UIMA and GATE.

All of our conversion tools and GATE plugins are freely available for download with no restrictions at http://www.anc.org. The UIMA project has received support to develop a UIMA → GrAF conversion module, which should be available in the near future.

6 Conclusion

Consideration of the transduction from a generic, relatively abstract representation scheme such as GrAF into the formats required for widely adopted frameworks for creating and analyzing linguistically annotated data has several ramifications for interoperability. First, it brings to light the kinds of implementation choices that either contribute to or impede progress toward interoperability, which can feed future development. Second, our work on converting GrAF to the formats supported by UIMA and GATE shows that while minor differences exist, the underlying data models used by the two frameworks are essentially the same, as well as being very similar to the data model underlying GrAF. This is good news for interoperability, since it means that there is at least implicit convergence on the data model best suited for data and annotations; the differences lie primarily in the ways in which the model is serialized internally and as output by different tools. It also means that transduction among the various formats is possible without loss of information.

We have shown that a UIMA → GrAF or GATE → GrAF conversion is fairly straightforward; the expressive power of GrAF can easily represent the data models used by UIMA and GATE. On the other hand, GrAF → UIMA or GrAF → GATE transformations are less straightforward. Both frameworks can represent graphs, but neither provides a standard representation that other components are guaranteed to understand. Given that powerful analysis algorithms for data in graphs are well-established, there may be considerable advantage to using the graph as a general-purpose format for use within various modules and analytic engines. In any case, the generality and flexibility of the GrAF representation has already been shown to be an effective means to exchange linguistic data and annotations that exist in different formats, as well as a model for development of annotation schemes in the future.

Acknowledgments

This work was supported by an IBM UIMA Innovation Award and National Science Foundation grant INT-0753069.

References

Steven Bird and Mark Liberman. 2001. A Formal Framework for Linguistic Annotation. *Speech Communication*, 33:1-2, 23-60.

Nancy Ide and Keith Suderman. 2007. GrAF: A Graph-based Format for Linguistic Annotations. *Proceedings of the First Linguistic Annotation Workshop*, Prague, Czech Republic, June 28-29, 1-8.

International Standards Organization. 2008. Language Resource Management - Linguistic Annotation Framework. ISO Document WD 24611.

International Standards Organization. 2005. Language Resource Management - Feature Structures - Part 1: Feature Structure Representation. ISO Document ISO/DIS 24610-1.

Nancy Ide, Patrice Bonhomme, and Laurent Romary. 2000. XCES: An XML-based Standard for Linguistic Corpora. *Proceedings of the Second Language Resources and Evaluation Conference* (LREC), Athens, Greece, 825-30.

Hamish Cunningham. 2002. GATE, a General Architecture for Text Engineering. Computers and the Humanities, 36:223-254

By all these lovely tokens...*
Merging Conflicting Tokenizations

Christian Chiarcos, Julia Ritz and Manfred Stede
Sonderforschungsbereich 632 "Information Structure"
University of Potsdam
Karl-Liebknecht-Str. 24-25, 14476 Golm, Germany
{chiarcos|julia|stede}@ling.uni-potsdam.de

Abstract

Given the contemporary trend to modular NLP architectures and multiple annotation frameworks, the existence of concurrent tokenizations of the same text represents a pervasive problem in everyday's NLP practice and poses a non-trivial theoretical problem to the integration of linguistic annotations and their interpretability in general. This paper describes a solution for integrating different tokenizations using a standoff XML format, and discusses the consequences for the handling of queries on annotated corpora.

1 Motivation

1.1 Tokens: Functions and goals

For most NLP tasks and linguistic annotations, especially those concerned with syntax (part-of-speech tagging, chunking, parsing) and the interpretation of syntactic structures (esp., the extraction of semantic information), tokens represent the **minimal unit of analysis**: words (lexemes, semantic units, partly morphemes) on the one hand and certain punctuation symbols on the other hand. From a corpus-linguistic perspective, tokens also represent the **minimal unit of investigation**, the minimal character sequence that can be addressed in a corpus query (e.g. using search tools like TIGERSearch (König and Lezius, 2000) or CWB (Christ, 1994)). Tokens also constitute the basis for 'word' **distance** measurements. In many annotation tools and their corresponding formats, the order of tokens provides a **timeline** for the sequential order of *structural* elements (MMAX (Müller and Strube, 2006), GENAU (Rehm et al., 2009), GrAF (Ide and Suderman, 2007), TIGER XML (König and Lezius, 2000)). In several multi-layer formats, tokens also define the **absolute position** of annotation elements, and only by reference to a common token layer, annotations from different layers can be related with each other (NITE (Carletta et al., 2003), GENAU).

Thus, by their function, tokens have the following characteristics: (i) tokens are totally ordered, (ii) tokens cover the full (annotated portion of the) primary data, (iii) tokens are the smallest unit of annotation, and (iv) there is only one single privileged token layer. The last aspect is especially relevant for the study of richly annotated data, as an integration and serialization of annotations produced by different tools can be established only by reference to the token layer. From a corpus-linguistic perspective, i.e., when focusing on querying of annotated corpora, tokens need to be well-defined and all information annotated to a particular text is to be preserved without any corruption. We argue that for this purpose, characteristic (iii) is to be abandoned, and we will describe the data format and an algorithm for merging different tokenizations and their respective annotations.

Our goal is a fully automated merging of annotations that refer to different tokenizations (henceforth T_1 and T_2) of the same text. We regard the following criteria as crucial for this task:

Information preservation. All annotations applied to the original tokenizations should be preserved.

Theoretically well-defined notion of token. It should be possible to give a plausible list of positive criteria that define character sequences as tokens. Knowledge about the token definition is essential for formulating queries for words, e.g. in a corpus search interface.

Integrative representation. All annotations that are consistent with the merged tokenization should refer to the merged tokenization. This is necessary in order to query across multiple annotations orig-

*Taken from the poem *September* by Helen Hunt Jackson.

Proceedings of the Third Linguistic Annotation Workshop, ACL-IJCNLP 2009, pages 35–43,
Suntec, Singapore, 6-7 August 2009.

inating from different annotation layers or tools.
Unsupervised merging. The integration of conflicting tokenizations should not require manual interference.

1.2 Tokenization

Tokenization is the process of mapping sequences of characters to sequences of words (cf. Guo 1997). However, different research questions or applications induce different conceptions of the term 'word'. For a *shallow morphosyntactic analysis* (part of speech tagging), a 'simple' tokenization using whitespaces and punctation symbols as delimiters seems acceptable for the examples in (1). A *full syntactic analysis* (parsing), however, could profit from the aggregation of complex nominals into one token each.

(1) a. department store
b. Herzog-von der Heide[1]
c. Red Cross/Red Crescent movement

Similarly, examples (2a) and (2b) can be argued to be treated as one token for *(morpho)syntactic analyses*, respectively. Despite intervening whitespaces and punctuation symbols, they are complex instances of the 'classical' part-of-speech *adjective*. For certain *semantic analyses* such as in information extraction, however, it may be useful to split these compounds in order to access the inherent complements (*E 605, No. 22*).

(2) a. E 605-intoxicated
b. No. 22-rated

Finally, (3) illustrates a *morphology-based* tokenization strategy: the principle of splitting at morpheme boundaries (Marcus et al., 1993, PTB) (token boundaries represented by square brackets). Morphological tokenization may help distributional (co-occurrence-based) semantics and/or parsing; however, the resulting tokens might be argued as being less intuitive to users of a corpus search tool.

(3) a. [Mitchell]['s], [they]['ve], [do][n't]
b. [wo][n't], [ca][n't], [ai][n't]

These examples show that different applications (tagging, parsing, information extraction) and the focus on different levels of description (morphology, syntax, semantics) require specialized tokenization strategies. When working with multiple tools for standard NLP tasks, thus, it is the norm rather than the exception that they disagree in their tokenization, as shown in ex. (4).

(4) doesn't
a. [does][n't] (Marcus et al., 1993, PTB)
b. [doesn]['][t] (Brants, 2000, TnT)

When creating a corpus that is annotated at multiple levels and/or using several tools, different tokenizations are not always avoidable, as some tools (automatic NLP tools, but also tools for manual annotation) have integrated tokenizers. Another challenge is the representation of token boundaries. Commonly, token boundaries are represented by a line break ('\n') or the whitespace 'character' (' ') – in which case token-internal whitespaces are replaced, usually by an underscore ('_') –, thereby corrupting the original data. This practice makes reconciling/merging the data a difficult enterprise.

Given this background, we suggest an XML-based annotation of token boundaries, such that token boundaries are marked without affecting the original primary data. In a straightforward XML model, tokens are represented by XML elements enclosing primary text slices (c.f. the BNC encoding scheme (Burnard, 2007)). However, treating tokens as spans of text by means of the XML hierarchy is impossible for tokenization conflicts as in (4.a) and (4.b).

2 Conflicting tokenizations: Straightforward strategies

By 'straightforward strategies', we mean approaches that aim to preserve the definition of tokens as atomic, minimal, unambiguous units of annotation when unifying different tokenizations (henceforth T_1 and T_2) of the same text. By 'unsupervised straightforward strategies', we mean tokenization strategies that operate on the primary data only, without consulting external resources such as dictionaries or human expertise.

Unsupervised straightforward strategies to the task include:

1. no merging In a conservative approach, we could create independent annotation projects for every tokenization produced, and thus represent all tokenizations independently. This, however, rules out any integration or combined evaluation of annotations to T_1 and annotations to T_2.

[1] Double surname consisting of *Herzog* and *von der Heide*.

2. normalization Adopt one of the source tokenizations, say T_1, as the 'standard' tokenization. Preserve *only* the information annotated to T_2 that is consistent with T_1. Where tokenization T_2 deviates from T_1, all annotations to T_2 are lost.[2]

3. maximal tokens For every token boundary in T_1 that is also found in T_2, establish a token boundary in the merged tokenization (cf. Guo's 1997 'critical tokenization'). However, with tokens assumed to be the minimal elements of annotation, we lose linguistic analyses of fine-grained tokens. With respect to (4.a) and (4.b), the maximal token would be the whole phrase *doesn't*. Again, this results in a loss of information, as all annotations applied to *does*, *doesn*, *n't*, *'* and *t* refer to units that are smaller than the resulting token.

4. maximal common substrings For every token boundary in T_1 *or* T_2, establish a token boundary, thereby producing **minimal tokens**: one token for every maximal substring shared between T_1 and T_2 (cf. Guo's 1997 'shortest tokenization'). By defining the original tokens ('supertokens') as annotations spanning over tokens, all annotations are preserved. However, the concept of 'token' loses its theoretical motivation; there is no guarantee that maximal common substrings are meaningful elements in any sense: The maximum common substring tokenization of 4.a and 4.b is *[does][n][']][t]*, but *[n]* is not a well-defined token. It is neither defined with respect to morphology (like PTB tokens) nor is it motivated from orthography (like TnT tokens), but it is just the remainder of their intersection.

As shown in Table 1, none of the strategies sketched above fulfills all criteria identified in Section 1.1: Avoiding a merging process counteracts data integration; token normalization and maximal tokens violate information preservation, and maximal common substrings violate the requirement to specify a theoretically well-defined notion of token.

As an alternative, we propose a formalism for the lossless integration and representation of conflicting tokenizations by abandoning the assumption that tokens are an atomic, primitive concept that represents the minimal unit of annotation. Rather, we introduce annotation elements smaller than the actual token – so-called *terminals* or *terms* for short – that are defined according to the maximum common substrings strategy described above.

[2]Alternatively, transformation rules to map annotations from T_2 to T_1 would have to be developed. This does, however, not guarantee information preservation, and, additionally, it requires manual work, as such transformations are annotation-specific. Thus, it is not an option for the fully automated merging of tokenizations.

Table 1: Deficits of 'straightforward' merging approaches

	no merge	normalize	max. tokens	max. common substrings
information preservation	+	−	−	+
well-defined tokens	+	+	(−)	−
integrative	−	+	+	+
unsupervised	(+)	+	+	+

Then, tokens are defined as nodes that span over a certain range of terms similar to phrase nodes that dominate other nodes in syntax annotations. The representation of conflicting tokenizations, then, requires a format that is capable to express conflicting hierarchies. For this purpose, we describe an extension of the PAULA format, a generic format for text-oriented linguistic annotations based on standoff XML.

3 Conflicting tokenizations in the PAULA format

3.1 Annotation structures in PAULA 1.0

The PAULA format (Dipper, 2005; Dipper and Götze, 2005) is a generic XML format, used as a pivot format in NLP pipelines (Stede et al., 2006) and in the web-based corpus interface ANNIS (Chiarcos et al., 2008). It uses standoff XML representations, and is conceptually closely related to the formats NITE XML (Carletta et al., 2003) and GraF (Ide and Suderman, 2007).

PAULA was specifically designed to support the lossless representation of different types of text-oriented annotations (layer-based/timeline annotations, hierarchical annotations, pointing relations), optimized for the annotation of multiple layers, including conflicting hierarchies and simple addition/deletion routines for annotation layers. Therefore, primary data is stored in a separate

Table 2: PAULA 1.0 data types

nodes (structural units of annotation) **token** character spans in the primary data that form the basis for higher-level annotation **markable** (spans of) token(s) that can be annotated with linguistic information. Markables represent flat, layer-based annotations defined with respect to the sequence of tokens as a general timeline. **struct** hierarchical structures (DAGs or trees) are formed by establishing a dominance relation between a struct (e.g., a phrase) node as parent, and tokens, markables, or other struct nodes as children.	**edges** (relational units of annotation, connecting tokens, markables, structs) **dominance relation** directed edge between a struct and its children **pointing relations** directed edge between nodes in general (tokens, markables, structs) **labels** (annotations: node or edge labels) **features** represent annotations attached to a particular (structural or relational) unit of annotation

file. Multiple annotations are also stored in separate files to avoid interference between concurrent annotations. Annotations refer to the primary data or to other annotations by means of XLinks and XPointers.

As types of linguistic annotation, we distinguish nodes (token, markable, struct), edges (dominance and pointing relations) and labels (annotations), as summarized in Table 2. Each type of annotation is stored in a separate file, so that competing or ambiguous annotations can be represented in an encapsulated way.

PAULA 1.0 is already sufficiently expressive for capturing the data-heterogeneity sketched above, including the representation of overlapping segments, intersecting hierarchies, and alternative annotations (e.g., for ambiguous annotations), but only for annotations *above* the token level. Further, PAULA 1.0 relies on the existence of a unique layer of non-overlapping, atomic tokens as minimal units of annotation: For all nodes, their position and sequential order is defined with respect to the absolute position of tokens that they cover; and for the special case of markables, these are defined solely in terms of their token range.

Finally, PAULA 1.0 tokens are *totally ordered*, they *cover* the (annotated) primary data *completely*, and they are *non-overlapping*. Only on this basis, the extension and (token-)distance of annotated elements can be addressed; and only by means of unambiguous reference, information from different layers of annotation can be combined and evaluated.

3.2 Introducing terminal nodes

In our extension of the PAULA format, we introduce the new concept of *term* nodes: atomic terminals that directly point to spans of primary data. *Terms* are subject to the same constraints as tokens in PAULA 1.0 (total order, full coverage, non-overlapping). So, terms can be used in place of PAULA 1.0 *tokens* to define the extension and position of super-token level and sub-token level annotation elements.

Markables are then defined with respect to (spans of) terminal nodes rather than tokens, such that alternative tokenizations can be expressed as markables in different layers that differ in their extensions.

Although terms adopt several functions formerly associated with tokens, a privileged token layer is still required: In many query languages, including ANNIS-QL (Chiarcos et al., 2008), tokens define the application domain of regular expressions on the primary data. More importantly, tokens constitute the basis for conventional ("word") distance measurements and ("word") coverage queries. Consequently, the constraints on tokens (total order, full coverage and absence of overlap) remain.

The resulting specifications for structural units of annotation are summarized in Table 3. Distinguishing terminal elements and re-defining the token layer as a privileged layer of markables allows us to disentangle the technical concept of 'atomic element' and 'token' as the conventionally assumed minimal unit of linguistic analysis.

3.3 A merging algorithm

In order to integrate annotations on tokens, it is not enough to represent two tokenizations side by side with reference to the same layer of terminal nodes. Instead, a privileged token layer is to be established and it has to be ensured that annotations can be queried *with reference to the token layer*.

Table 3: PAULA extensions: revised node types

terms	specify character spans in the primary data that form the basis for higher-level annotation
markable	defined as above, with terms taking the place of tokens
structs	defined as above, with terms taking the place of tokens
tokens	sub-class of structs that are non-overlapping, arranged in a total order, and cover the full primary data

Then, all annotations whose segmentation is consistent with the privileged token layer are directly linked with tokens.

Alg. 3.1 describes our merging algorithm, and its application to the four main cases of conflicting tokenization is illustrated in Figure 1.[3] The following section describes its main characteristics and the consequences for querying.

4 Discussion

Alg. 3.1 produces a PAULA project with one single tokenization. So, it is possible to define queries spanning across annotations with originally different tokenization:

Extension and **precedence** queries are tokenization-independent: Markables refer to the $term$ layer, not the tok layer, structs also (indirectly) dominate $term$ nodes.

Dominance queries for struct nodes and tokens yield results whenever the struct node dominates only nodes with tok-compatible source tokenization: Structs dominate tok nodes wherever the original tokenization was consistent with the privileged tokenization tok (case A and C in Fig. 1).

Distance queries are defined with respect to the tok layer, and are applicable to all elements that are are defined with reference to the tok layer (in figure 1: tok_{1a}, tok_{2a}, tok_{1b}, tok_{2b} in case A; tok_{ab} in case B; tok_{a}, tok_{b}, tok_{ab} in case C; tok_{ab}, tok_{c} in case D). They are not applicable to elements that do not refer to the tok layer (B: tok_{a}, tok_{b}; D: tok_{a}, tok_{bc}).

[3]Notation: $prim$ – primary data / $tok, term$ – annotation layers / $t \in L$ – t is a node on a layer L / $a..b$ – continuous span from tok/term a to tok/term b / a, b – list of tok/term/markable nodes a, b / $t = [a]$ – t is a node (struct, markable, tok) that points to a node, span or list a

The algorithm is unsupervised, and the token concept of the output tokenization is well-defined and consistent (if one of the input tokenizations is adopted as target tokenization). Also, as shown below, it is integrative (enabling queries across different tokenizations) and information-preserving (reversible).

4.1 Time complexity

After a PAULA project has been created, the time complexity of the algorithm is quadratic with respect to the number of characters in the primary data n. This is due to the total order of tokens: Step 2 and 3.a are applied once to all original tokens from left to right. Step 5 can be reformulated such that for every *terminal node*, the relationship between the directly dominating tok_1 and tok_2 is checked. Then, Step 5 is also in $O(n)$. In terms of the number of markables m, the time complexity in Step 3.b is in $O(n\ m)$: for every markable, the corresponding $term$ element is to be found, taking at most n repositioning operations on the $term$ layer. Assuming that markables within one layer are non-overlapping[4] and that the number of layers is bound by some constant c[5], then $m \leq n\ c$, so that 3.b is in $O(n^2\ c)$.

For realistic scenarios, the algorithm is thus quadratic.

4.2 Reversibility

The merging algorithm is reversible – and, thus, lossless – as shown by the splitting algorithm in Alg. 3.2. For reasons of space, the correctness of this algorithm cannot be demonstrated here, but broadly speaking, it just removes every node that corresponds to an original token of the 'other' tokenization, plus every node that points to it, so that only annotations remain that are directly applied to the target tokenization.

4.3 Querying merged tokenizations

We focus in this paper on the merging of analyses with different tokenizations for the purpose of users *querying a corpus across multiple annota-*

[4]Although PAULA supports overlapping markables within one single layer, even with identical extension, this is a reasonable assumption: In practice, overlapping markables within one single layer are rare. More often, there is even a longer sequence of primary data between one markable of a particular layer and the next. In our experience, such 'gaps' occur much more often than overlapping markables.

[5]Again, this is a practical simplication. Theoretically, the number of layers is infinite.

Alg. 3.1 Merging different tokenizations

0. assume that we have two annotations $analysis_1$ and $analysis_2$ for the same primary data, but with different tokenizations

1. create PAULA 1.0 annotation projects for $analysis_1$ and $analysis_2$ with primary data files $prim_1$ and $prim_2$ and token layers tok_1 and tok_2 respectively.

2. harmonize primary data
   if $prim_1$ equals $prim_2$, then
   (i) rename $prim_1$ to $prim$
   (ii) set all references in $analysis_2$ from $prim_2$ to $prim$
   (iii) create a new annotation project $analysis$ by copying $prim$ and all annotation layers from $analysis_1$ and $analysis_2$

   otherwise terminate with error msg

3. harmonize terminal nodes
   create a new annotation layer $term$, then
   (a) for all overlapping tokens $t_1 \in tok_1$ and $t_2 \in tok_2$: identify the maximal common substrings of t_1 and t_2
   for every substring s, create a new element $term_s$ pointing to the corresponding character span in the primary data
   for every substring s, redefine t_1 and t_2 as markables referring to $term_s$

   (b) redefine markable spans as spans of terminal nodes
   for every token $t = [term_{s_1}..term_{s_2}] \in tok_1 \cup tok_2$ and every markable $m = [w..xty..z]$: set $m = [w..xterm_{s_1}..term_{s_2}y..z]$

4. select token layer
   rename tok_1 to tok, or rename tok_2 to tok, (cf. the normalization strategy in Sect. 2) or
   rename $term$ to tok (cf. the minimal tokens strategy in Sect. 2)

5. token integration
   for every original token $ot = [a..b] \in (tok_1 \cup tok_2) \setminus tok$:
   if there is a token $t \in tok$ such that $t = [a..b]$, then define ot as a struct with $ot = [t]$, else
   if there are tokens $t_1, .., t_n \in tok$ such that $t_1..t_n$ form a continuous sequence of tokens and $t_1 = [a..x]$ and $t_n = [y..b]$, then define ot as a struct such that $ot = [t_1, .., t_n]$,
   otherwise: change nothing

Figure 1: Merging divergent tokenizations

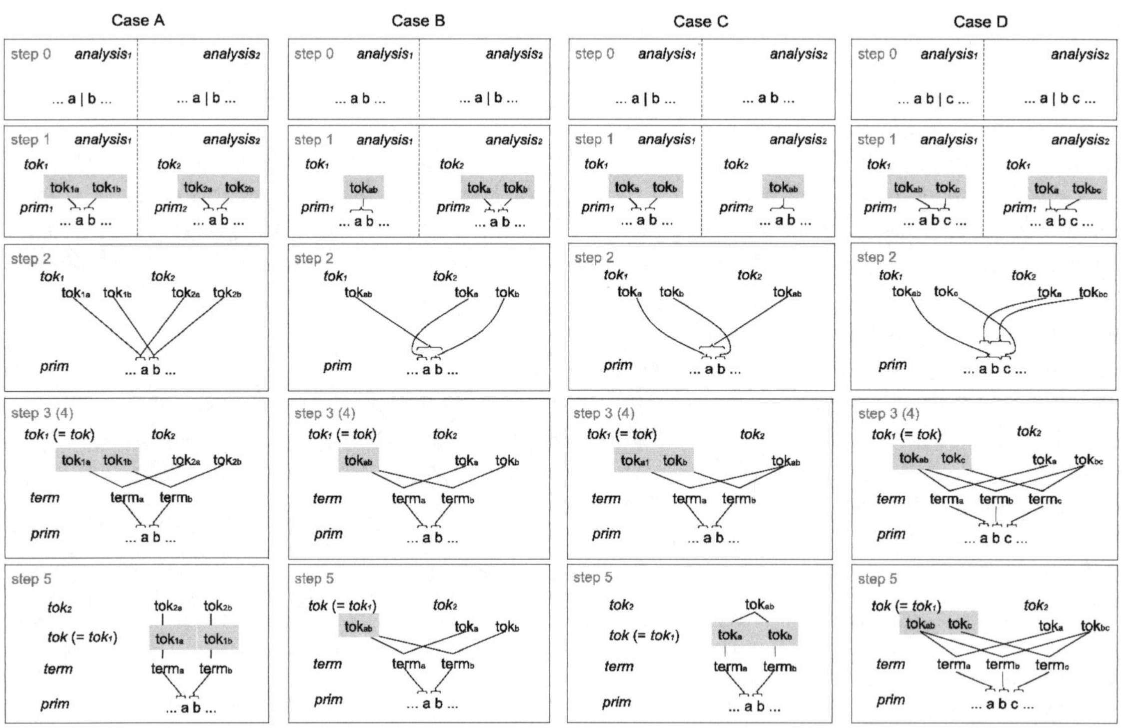

Alg. 3.2 Splitting a PAULA annotation project with two different tokenizations

0. given a PAULA annotation project $analysis$ with token layer tok, terminal layer $term$, and two layers l_1 and l_2 (that may be identical to $term$ or tok) that convey the information of the original token layers tok_1 and tok_2
1. create $analysis_1$ and $analysis_2$ as copies of $analysis$
2. if l_1 represents a totally ordered, non-overlapping list of nodes that cover the primary data completely, then modify $analysis_1$:
   a. for every node in l_1: substitute references to tok_1 by references to $term_1$
   b. remove l_2 from $analysis_1$
   c. if $l_1 \neq tok_1$, remove tok_1 from $analysis_1$
   d. for every annotation element (node/relation) e in $analysis_1$ that directly or indirectly points to another node in $analysis_1$ that is no longer present, remove e from $analysis_1$
   e. remove every annotation layer from $analysis_1$ that does not contain an annotation element
   f. for every markable in l_1: remove references to $term_1$, define the extension of l_1 nodes directly in terms of spans of text in $prim_1$
   g. if $l_1 \neq term_1$, remove $term_1$
3. perform step 2. for l_2 and $analysis_2$

tion layers. Although the merging algorithm produces annotation projects that allow for queries integrating annotations from analyses with different tokenization, the structure of the annotations is altered, such that the behaviour of merged and unmerged PAULA projects may be different. Obviously, token-level queries must refer to the privileged tokenization T_1. Operators querying for the relative **precedence or extension** of markables are not affected: in the merged annotation project, markables are defined with reference to the layer $term$: originally co-extensional elements E_1 and E_2 (i.e. elements covering the same tokens in the source tokenization) will also cover the same *terminals* in the merged project. **Distance operators** (e.g. querying for two tokens with distance 2, i.e. with two tokens in between), however, will operate on the new privileged tokenization, such that results from queries on $analysis$ may differ from those on $analysis_2$. **Dominance operators** are also affected, as nodes that directly dominated a token in $analysis_1$ or $analysis_2$ now indirectly dominate it in $analysis$, with a supertoken as an intermediate node.

Alg. 3.3 Iterative merging: modifications of Alg. 3.1, step.3

if $analysis_1$ has a layer of terminal nodes $term_1$, then let $T_1 = term_1$, otherwise $T_1 = tok_1$
if $analysis_2$ has a layer of terminal nodes $term_2$, then let $T_2 = term_2$, otherwise $T_2 = tok_2$
create a new annotation layer $term$, then

1. for all overlapping terminals/tokens $t_1 \in T_1$ and $t_2 \in T_2$: identify the maximal common substrings of t_1 and t_2
   for every substring s, create a new element $term_s$ pointing to the corresponding character span in the primary data
   for every substring s, redefine t_1 and t_2 as markables referring to $term_s$
2. redefine markable spans as spans of terminal nodes
   for every node $t = [term_{s_1}..term_{s_2}] \in T_1 \cup T_2$ and every markable $m = [w..xty..z]$: set $m = [w..xterm_{s_1}..term_{s_2}y..z]$
3. for all original terminals $t \in T_1 \cup T_2$: if t is not directly pointed at, remove t from $analysis$

Accordingly, queries applicable to PAULA projects *before* the merging are not directly applicable to merged PAULA projects. Users are to be instructed to keep this in mind and to be aware of the specifications for the merged tokenization and its derivation.[6]

5 Extensions

5.1 Merging more than two tokenizations

In the current formulation, Alg. 3.1 is applied to two PAULA 1.0 projects and generates extended PAULA annotation projects with a $term$ layer. The algorithm, however, may be applied iteratively, if step 3 is slightly revised, such that extended PAULA annotation projects can also be merged, see Alg. 3.3.

5.2 Annotation integration

The merging algorithm creates a struct node for every original token. Although this guarantees reversibility, one may consider to remove such redundant structs. Alg. 3.4 proposes an optional postprocessing step for the merging algorithm. This step is optional because these operations are

[6]The information, however, is preserved in the format and may be addressed by means of queries that, for example, operate on the extension of terminals.

Alg. 3.4 Annotation integration: Optional post-processing for merging algorithm

6.a. remove single-token supertoken
for every original token $ot = [t] \in tok_1 \cup tok_2$ with $t \in tok$: replace all references in $analysis$ to ot by references to t, remove ot

6.b. merging original token layers tok_1 and tok_2 (if $tok_1 \neq tok$ and $tok_2 \neq tok$)
define new 'super token' layer $stok$.
for every $ot \in tok_1 \cup tok_2$:

if $ot = [t]$ for some $t \in tok$, then see 6.a

if $ot = [t_1, .., t_n]$ for some $t_1, .., t_n \in tok$, and there is $ot_2 = [t_1, .., t_n] \in tok_1 \cup tok_2 \cup stok$, then replace all references in $analysis$ to ot_2 by references to ot, move ot to layer $stok$, remove ot_2 from $analysis$

move all remaining $ot \in tok_1 \cup tok_2$ to $stok$, remove layers tok_1 and tok_2

6.c. unify higher-level annotations
for every markable $mark_1 = [term_1..term_n]$ and $term_1, .., term_n \in term$:

if there is a markable $mark_2$ in $analysis$ such that $mark_2 = [term_1..term_n]$, then replace all references in $analysis$ to $mark_2$ by references to $mark_1$, remove $mark_2$

for every struct $struct_1 = [c_1, .., c_n]$ that covers exactly the same children as another struct $struct_2 = [c_1, .., c_n]$, replace all references to $struct_2$ by references to $struct_1$, remove $struct_2$

destructive: We lose the information about the origin ($analysis_1$ vs. $analysis_2$) of $stok$ elements and their annotations.

6 Summary and Related Reasearch

In this paper, we describe a novel approach for the integration of conflicting tokenizations, based on the differentiation between a privileged layer of tokens and a layer of atomic terminals in a standoff XML format: Tokens are defined as structured units that dominate one or more terminal nodes.

Terminals are atomic units only *within* the respective annotation project (there is no unit addressed that is smaller than a terminal). By iterative applications of the merging algorithm, however, complex terms may be split up in smaller units, so that they are not atomic in an absolute sense.

Alternatively, terms could be identified a priori with the minimal addressable unit available, i.e., characters (as in the formalization of tokens as *charspan*s and *charseq*s in the ACE information extraction annotations, Henderson 2000). It is not clear, however, how a character-based term definition would deal with sub-character and zero extension terms: A character-based definition of terms that represent traces is possible only by corrupting the primary data.[7] Consequently, a character-based term definition is insufficient unless we restrict ourselves to a particular class of languages, texts and phenomena.

The role of terminals can thus be compared to timestamps: With reference to a numerical timeline, it is always possible to define a new event between two existing timestamps. Formats specifically designed for time-aligned annotations, e.g., EXMARaLDA (Schmidt, 2004), however, typically lack a privileged token layer and a formal concept of tokens. Instead, tokens, as well as longer or shorter sequences, are represented as markables, defined by their extension on the timeline.

Similarly, GrAF (Ide and Suderman, 2007), although being historically related to PAULA, does not have a formal concept of a privileged token layer in the sense of PAULA.[8] We do, however, assume that terminal nodes in GrAF can be compared to PAULA 1.0 tokens.

For conflicting tokenizations, Ide and Suderman (2007) suggest that 'dummy' elements are defined covering all necessary tokenizations for controversially tokenized stretches of primary data. Such dummy elements combine the possible tokenizations for strategies 1 (no merging) and 3 (maximal tokens), so that the information preservation deficit of strategy 3 is compensated by strategy 1, and the integrativity deficit of strategy 1 is compensated by strategy 3 (cf. Table 1). However, tokens, if defined in this way, are overlapping and thus only partially ordered, so that distance operators are no longer applicable.[9]

[7] Similarly, phonological units that are not expressed in the primary data can be subject to annotations, e.g., short *e* and *o* in various Arabic-based orthographies, e.g., the Ajami orthography of Hausa. A term with zero extension at the position of a short vowel can be annotated as having the phonological value *e* or *o* without having character status.

[8] `https://www.americannationalcorpus.org/graf-wiki/wiki/WikiStart#GraphModel`, 2009/05/08

[9] This can be compensated by marking the base segmentation differently from alternative segmentations. In the abstract GrAF model, however, this can be represented only by means of labels, i.e., annotations. A more consistent con-

Another problem that arises from the introduction of dummy nodes is their theoretical status, as it is not clear how dummy nodes can be distinguished from annotation structured on a conceptual level. In the PAULA formalization, dummy nodes are not necessary, so that this ambiguity is already resolved in the representation.

References

Thorsten Brants. 2000. *TnT A Statistical Part-of-Speech Tagger.* In Proceedings of the Sixth Conference on Applied Natural Language Processing ANLP-2000. Seattle, WA.

Lou Burnard (ed.). 2007. Reference Guide for the British National Corpus (XML Edition). `http://www.natcorp.ox.ac.uk/XMLedition/URG/bnctags.html`.

Jean Carletta, Stefan Evert, Ulrich Heid, Jonathan Kilgour, Judy Robertson, and Holger Voormann. 2003. *The NITE XML Toolkit: Flexible Annotation for Multi-modal Language Data.* Behavior Research Methods, Instruments, and Computers 35(3), 353-363.

Christian Chiarcos, Stefanie Dipper, Michael Götze, Ulf Leser, Anke Lüdeling, Julia Ritz, and Manfred Stede. 2009. *A Flexible Framework for Integrating Annotations from Different Tools and Tagsets* TAL (Traitement automatique des langues) 49(2).

Oli Christ. 1994. *A modular and flexible architecture for an integrated corpus query system.* COMPLEX'94, Budapest, Hungary.

Stefanie Dipper. 2005. *XML-based Stand-off Representation and Exploitation of Multi-Level Linguistic Annotation.* In Rainer Eckstein and Robert Tolksdorf (eds:): Proceedings of Berliner XML Tage, pages 39-50.

Stefanie Dipper and Michael Götze. 2005. *Accessing Heterogeneous Linguistic Data — Generic XML-based Representation and Flexible Visualization.* In Proceedings of the 2nd Language & Technology Conference 2005, Poznan, Poland, pages 23–30.

Stefanie Dipper, Michael Götze. 2006. ANNIS: Complex Multilevel Annotations in a Linguistic Database. *Proceedings of the 5th Workshop on NLP and XML (NLPXML-2006): Multi-Dimensional Markup in Natural Language Processing.* Trento, Italy.

Jin Guo. 1997. *Critical Tokenization and its Properties*, Computational Linguistic, 23(4), pp.569-596.

ception would encode structural information on the structural level, and only linguistic annotation and metadata on the contents level.

John C. Henderson. 2000. *A DTD for Reference Key Annotation of EDT Entities and RDC Relations in the ACE Evaluations* (v. 5.2.0, 2000/01/05), `http://projects.ldc.upenn.edu/ace/annotation/apf.v5.2.0.dtd` (2009/06/04)

Nancy Ide and Keith Suderman. 2007. *GrAF: A Graph-based Format for Linguistic Annotations.* In Proceedings of the Linguistic Annotation Workshop,held in conjunction with ACL 2007, Prague, June 28-29, 1-8.

Esther König and Wolfgang Lezius. 2000. *A description language for syntactically annotated corpora.* In: Proceedings of the COLING Conference, pp. 1056-1060, Saarbrücken, Germany.

Mitchell P. Marcus, Beatrice Santorini, and Mary Ann Marcinkiewicz. 1993. *Building a large annotated corpus of English: the Penn treebank.* Computational Linguistics 19, pp.313-330.

Christoph Müller and Michael Strube. 2006. *Multi-Level Annotation of Linguistic Data with MMAX2.* In: S. Braun et al. (eds.), Corpus Technology and Language Pedagogy. New Resources, New Tools, New Methods. Frankfurt: Peter Lang, 197–214.

Georg Rehm, Oliver Schonefeld, Andreas Witt, Christian Chiarcos, and Timm Lehmberg. 2009. *SPLICR: A Sustainability Platform for Linguistic Corpora and Resources.* In: Text Resources and Lexical Knowledge. Selected Papers the 9th Conference on Natural Language Processing (KONVENS 2008), Berlin, Sept. 30 – Oct. 2, 2008. Mouton de Gruyter.

Helmut Schmid. 2002. *Tokenizing & Tagging.* In Lüdeling, Anke and Kytö, Merja (Hrsg.) Corpus Linguistics. An International Handbook. (HSK Series). Mouton de Gryuter, Berlin

Thomas Schmidt. 2004. Transcribing and Annotating Spoken Language with Exmaralda. *Proceedings of the LREC-workshop on XML Based Richly Annotated Corpora.* Lisbon, Portugal. Paris: ELRA.

Manfred Stede, Heike Bieler, Stefanie Dipper, and Arthit Suriyawongkul. 2006. SUMMaR: Combining Linguistics and Statistics for Text Summarization. *Proceedings of the 17th European Conference on Artificial Intelligence (ECAI-06).* pp 827-828. Riva del Garda, Italy.

Ralph Weischedel, Sameer Pradhan, Lance Ramshaw and Linnea Micciulla. 2006. OntoNotes Release 1.0. Linguistic Data Consortium, Philadelphia.

Annotating Subordinators in the Turkish Discourse Bank

Deniz Zeyrek[a,0], **Ümit Turan**[b], **Cem Bozsahin**[a], **Ruket Çakıcı**[a],
Ayışığı Sevdik-Çallı[a], **Işın Demirşahin**[a], **Berfin Aktaş**[a], **İhsan Yalçınkaya**[a], **Hale Ögel**[a]
[a] Middle East Technical University, Ankara, Turkey
[b] Anadolu University, Eskişehir, Turkey

Abstract

In this paper we explain how we annotated subordinators in the Turkish Discourse Bank (TDB), an effort that started in 2007 and is still continuing. We introduce the project and describe some of the issues that were important in annotating three subordinators, namely *karşın*, *rağmen* and *halde*, all of which encode the coherence relation *Contrast-Concession*. We also describe the annotation tool.

1 Introduction

The Turkish Discourse Bank (TDB) is a project initiated by the joint effort of a group of researchers in Turkey. The project builds on an existing corpus, namely the METU Turkish Corpus (MTC) (Say et al., 2002), and extends it to a discourse level resource by following the principles of the PDTB (Prasad et al., 2007) in annotating discourse connectives and their arguments. The 2-million-word MTC contains 520 continuous texts from various genres written between 1991-2000.

From a semantic perspective, we take discourse connectives as predicates that take as their arguments tensed or untensed clauses with abstract object interpretations. Abstract objects are propositions, facts, events, situations, etc. (Asher, 1993). Connectives themselves may be realized explicitly or implicitly (Halliday, 1985; Prasad et al., 2007). Explicit connectives are simple or complex lexical items that encode a discourse relation, while implicit connectives can be inferred from related text spans that have coherence relations. The TDB project aims to annotate explicit connectives only.

In Turkish, discourse connectives are identified with three syntactic categories (Zeyrek and Webber, 2008): (a) Coordinating conjunctions (b) Subordinators (c) Discourse adverbials (or anaphoric connectives). All these discourse connectives have two and only two arguments, which are conveniently labeled as ARG1 and ARG2.[1] ARG2 is always the argument that syntactically hosts the connective.

The ARG1/ARG2 organization of discourse connectives is consistent with the following observations in discourse: Sentences in discourse are coherently related, and therefore when explicit discourse connectives are used, if they are really discourse connectives, they are bound to set up a relation between a consequent clause and its antecedent. (Note that the ARG2 designation does not imply that ARG2 is consequent or antecedent.) In certain cases presupposition needs a mediator, viz. the discourse connective. Nonconnectival discourse relations are certainly possible, but connective-engendered discourse relations are claimed to be more specific about their semantics, e.g. they bring about presuppositional meaning (van der Sandt, 1992; Webber et al., 1999).

In this regard, the ARG1/ARG2 classification is unlike syntactic subcategorization, which is a lexical property of functors (e.g. verbs) which are not necessarily presuppositional and hence they can differ in arbitrary ways (ditransitive, transitive, unergative, unaccusative etc.).

2 The Data

The MTC is preprocessed to obtain the raw texts keeping the title, author, publishing date and the text type information at the beginning of each file. Stand-off annotation is done on the textual rendering of the MTC.

To enable the data to be viewable universally without losing any character information, the file format (originally xcs) was converted to text, and the character encoding (originally Turkish-ISO-

[0]Corresponding author: dezeyrek@metu.edu.tr

[1]Whether or not discourse connectives in any language take more than two arguments is an open question that needs to be established in further research.

Proceedings of the Third Linguistic Annotation Workshop, ACL-IJCNLP 2009, pages 44–47,
Suntec, Singapore, 6-7 August 2009. ©2009 ACL and AFNLP

Text type	File Count	%	S1	%	S2	%	S3	%	S4	%
Novel	123	15.63%	31	15.74%	30	15.23%	31	15.82%	31	15.74%
Short story	114	14.49%	28	14.21%	29	14.72%	28	14.29%	29	14.72%
Research /Monograph	49	6.23%	13	6.60%	12	6.09%	12	6.12%	12	6.09%
Article	38	4.83%	9	4.57%	10	5.08%	9	4.59%	10	5.08%
Travel	19	2.41%	5	2.54%	5	2.54%	4	2.04%	5	2.54%
Interview	7	0.89%	2	1.02%	2	1.02%	2	1.02%	1	0.51%
Memoir	18	2.29%	4	2.03%	5	2.54%	5	2.55%	4	2.03%
News	419	53.24%	105	53.30%	104	52.79%	105	53.57%	105	53.30%
TOTAL	**787**		**197**		**197**		**196**		**197**	

Table 1: File count and percentage information according to text type for the preprocessed MTC and its subcorpora. (S:Subcorpus)

8859-9) was converted to the UTF-8. Finally, the processed MTC data were divided into four subcorpora by keeping the text type distribution, file count and word count as equal as possible in each subcorpus. The text type distribution, file count and word percentage information in each subcorpus are given in Table 1. In the project, we plan to annotate subcorpus 1.

3 Subordinating Conjunctions in Turkish: A Brief Overview

Subordinators have two subtypes. Converbs are suffixes attached directly to verb roots. For example, the suffix *-(y)ArAk* 'by (means of)' requires as its ARG2 a nominalized adverbial clause as in (1). Complex subordinators, e.g. *rağmen* 'despite, although', *karşın* 'although', *halde* 'despite, along with', *için* causal 'since', purposive 'so as to', etc. mostly take case-marked nominalized clauses as their ARG2.

(1) Hükümet ... **uyum paketini** onaylayarak ... *Erdoğan'n önündeki engellerden birini kaldırdı.*
By approving **the adaptation package ...**, the government *alleviated one of the obstacles for Erdoğan ...*

In this paper, we will not deal with converbs. We will also not deal with connectives taking as their ARG2 a finite clause because none of these subtypes have been annotated yet. We will focus on three postpositions taking a nominalized clause as ARG2, namely *rağmen*, *karşın* and *halde*, all of which encode the *Contrast-Concession* relation. In the PDTB, such clauses were not annotated as arguments. However, in Turkish, they are so common as arguments of subordinators that we would have missed an important property of Turkish discourse if we did not annotate them. In the rest of the paper, we provide examples taken from the MTC. We underline the connective, show ARG2 in bold letters and render ARG1 in italics.

3.1 The minimality principle

As in the PDTB, the minimality principle is invoked, according to which clauses, parts of clauses or sentences that are minimally necessary and sufficient for the discourse relation engendered by the connective are annotated as ARG1 or ARG2 (Prasad et al., 2007). Any other text span that is perceived to be important for the interpretation of the discourse relation can be selected as supplementary information in addition to ARG1 or ARG2.

3.2 Morphological properties of the arguments and their relative ordering

In Turkish, subordinate clauses are essentially nominalizations, which may be formed by *-DIK* or *-mA* suffixes (the factive nominal and the action nominal, respectively (Kornfilt, 1997)).

Two of the connectives, i.e. *rağmen* and *karşın* expect action nominals, the person agreement suffix, and the dative suffix *-(y)A* on their ARG2. On the other hand, the connective *halde* expects a factive nominal and the person agreement suffix. In the examples below, we show these suffixes with glosses on the English translations.

The arguments of subordinators are necessarily adjacent and mostly exhibit the ARG2-ARG1 order because Turkish is a left-branching language and subordinate clauses are on the left in canonical order. ARG2 can be postposed for backgrounding purposes or to express new and unexpected information, as in (2).

(2) ... aynı annesine oldu]ugu gibi ona da, *kimseye ba/uglanmayanlar kolayca bağlanıyordu*; üstelik **o öyle bir bağımlılık talep etmediği** halde.
... just as it happened to her mother, *people who can't easily commit themselves to anyone would*

easily commit themselves to her, although **she would not ask-FACTN-AGR for such a commitment.**

3.3 Issues in annotating the arguments

One of the challenges we have faced so far is the question of how to annotate connectives which are themselves a converb suffix (e.g. *-(y)ArAk*, as in (1)) or postpositions that choose a case-marked ARG2 as in (2). In both cases, we decided to annotate ARG2 by selecting the clause without separating the suffixes. In this way, we would not interfere with the annotators' intuitions since we would not be demanding them to have conscious knowledge of the morphological constraints on the arguments. This style of annotation was welcomed by the annotators. When all the annotations are completed, we plan to separate the suffixes with a morphological parser to provide a full view of the morphology of the arguments.

Another issue was how to annotate shared subjects in subordinate clauses. Turkish allows subject pro-drop and in complex sentences, the shared subject is shown by the person agreement suffix on the verb of the consequent clause. To capture this fact, we chose to exclude shared subjects from the annotation of the arguments. This style of annotation conforms to the minimality principle. As illustrated in (3), the subject, *Neriman*, which appears in its canonical clause-initial position in ARG2 is not selected because the verb of the subsequent clause carries the person agreement suffix.

(3) Neriman **yatak odasında sigara içilmesini istemediği** halde *şimdilik sigaraya ses çıkarmıyor.*
Although Neriman **does not want-FACTN-AGR people to smoke in her bedroom**, *(she) doesn't say-AGR anything for the moment.*[2]

If the subject is not shared, it is included in the annotation, even if it causes discontinuity. As it is illustrated in (4), ARG2 intervenes in ARG1 by separating it from its subject.

(4) *Rukiye,* **kendisinden üç yaş ufak olmasına** rağmen, *erkek kardeşini kendi oğlu sanıyordu, ...*
Rukiye, although **(he) is-ACTN-AGR-DAT three years younger than herself**, *thought-AGR that her brother was her son...*

[2]The pronoun is in parentheses to reflect pro-drop. The following abbreviations are used on the translations to show the morphological characteristics of the clauses: ACTN: Action nominal, FACTN: Factive nominal, AGR: Person agreement suffix, DAT: Dative case, ABL: Ablative case. NOM: Nominative case.

Example (5) shows that two nominalized clauses can be selected as the arguments of the subordinator *karşın* leaving out the shared subject. In this example, the subject is shown between square brackets for clarity. Note that, ARG1 is also a nominalized clause since it is embedded under the attribution verb *söyle* - 'say'.[3]

(5) ... [herkes yaratılan toplumsal değerden verdiği emek oranında pay alacak biçimindeki sosyalist iktisat ilkesinin] **aslında çok eşitlikçi gibi gözükmesine** karşın *eşitsizliği engelleyemeyeceğini*, ... söyler
... says that ... despite **(it) looks-ACTN-AGR-DAT quite egalitarian**, [the socialist principle, stating that everyone gets a share proportional to his labor] *will not prevent-ACTN-AGR inequality* ...

Finally, in annotating adjuncts, we follow the same principle we followed in annotating shared subjects. For instance in (6), the adjunct *yemekte* 'at dinner' is not annotated since it is shared by the arguments of the connective *rağmen.*

(6) *Gül* de yemekte **kilo aldırmasına** rağmen *Şam tatlılarından çok hoşlandığını* ifade etti.
At dinner, *Gül-NOM*, also said that although **(they$_i$) are-ACTN-AGR-DAT fattening**, *(he) likes Damascus deserts-ABL$_i$ very much.*

4 The Annotation Process

Before the annotation procedure started, a set of annotation guidelines were prepared. The guidelines include the basic principles, such as what discourse connectives are, where in the discourse one can find ARG1 and ARG2, how to annotate shared subjects, adjuncts, etc. Rather than being strict rules, the guidelines are aimed at being general principles guiding the annotators in their decision of selecting the text span that is minimally sufficient for interpreting the discourse relation encoded by the connective.

The annotation cycle consisted of 1) annotating a connective by at least three different people 2) measuring the agreement among them with the inter-anotator agreement tool 3) resolving the disagreements with an anonymous decision.

4.1 The annotation tool

We have an XML-based infrastructure for annotation. It aims to produce searchable and trackable data. Stand-off annotation has well-known advantages such as the ability to see layers separately, or

[3]In the PDTB, attribution is not taken as a discourse relation but it is annotated. Attribution is not annotated in the TDB.

	Overall			Annotator1			Annotator2			Annotator3		
Conn.	ARG1	ARG2	Overall	ARG1	ARG2	Overall	ARG1	ARG2	Overall	ARG1	ARG2	Overall
rağmen	0.37	0.343	0.444	0.476	0.493	0.538	0.810	0.889	0.83	0.591	0.550	0.660
karşın	0.394	0.546	0.364	0.771	0.781	0.724	0.677	0.833	0.71	0.677	0.62	0.676
halde	0.749	0.826	0.758	0.957	1	0.978	0.772	0.826	0.758	-	-	-

Table 2: Textspan inclusion agreement among three annotators for three subordinators with minimum success prob. >0.05. The first column shows the overall agreement among the three annotators. Other columns show the agreement of one annotator with the agreed/gold standard annotations. For *halde*, 2 annotators performed a common annotation (given as Annotator1) and a third annotator annotated it separately (given as Annotator2).

to distribute annotation without data due to licensing constraints. To this list we can add the empirical necessity that, the crossing links in a single layer of same kind of annotation might not be easy to do inline. They can be done inline using SGML OCCURS checks, but they are easier to annotate in stand-off mode.

The tool has a regular expression mode in which the annotator can use his/her knowledge of Turkish word structure to collect similarly inflected words without morphological analysis. For example, -ArAk$, in which the uppercase forms represent metaphonemes, will bring words ending with the allomorphs of the converb suffix due to vowel harmony: *erek, arak* etc.

5 Conclusion

The TDB project is a first attempt in creating an annotated resource for written Turkish discourse. The annotation process is still continuing. In this paper, the emphasis was on a small number of connectives, namely three postpositions, which form a subclass of subordinators. The paper described the role of certain morpho-syntactic facts in interpreting the coherence relation between two clauses, and how these facts were reflected in the annotations.

Three subjects separately annotated each of the subordinators on the annotation tool, and interrater reliability was calculated. The statistics were obtained from Cochran's Q test to the ARG1 and ARG2 spans. The annotation data were encoded with 1 if the character is in the span and 0 if it is not. The encoded data were put to the Q test. All the results were above the minimum success probability (>0.05), showing that the annotations were consistent (see Table 2). We will run another Cochran experiment in which we will test whether the annotators agree on ARG1/ARG2 boundaries, rather than just word inclusion in the text spans as above.

Given the distribution of agreements, Cochran provides the number of subjects who must agree so that a text span can be reliably considered an ARG1 or ARG2. This we believe is important to report with the final product (to be made public soon), so that its gold standard can be assessed by the community.

Acknowledgments

We thank TUBITAK for financial support. We also thank our two anonymous reviewers for their insightful comments.

References

Nicholas Asher. 1993. *Reference to Abstract objects in Discourse*. Kluwer Academic Publishers.

Michael A. K. Halliday. 1985. *An Introduction to Functional Linguistics*. Edward Arnold Publishers Ltd.

Jaklin Kornfilt. 1997. *Turkish*. Routledge, London.

Rashmi Prasad, Eleni Miltsakaki, Nikhil Dinesh, Alan Lee, Aravind Joshi, Livio Robaldo, and Bonnie Webber. 2007. The penn discourse treebank 2.0. annotation manual. Technical report, Institute for Research in Cognitive Science, University of Pennsylvania, March.

Bilge Say, Deniz Zeyrek, Kemal Oflazer, and Umut Özge. 2002. Development of a corpus and a treebank for present-day written turkish. In *Proceedings of the Eleventh International Conference of Turkish Linguistics*.

Rob van der Sandt. 1992. Presuppositon projection as anaphora resolution. *Journal of Semantics*, 9:333–377.

Bonnie Webber, Alistair Knott, Matthew Stone, and Aravind Joshi. 1999. Discourse relations: A structural and presuppositional account using lexicalised tag. In *Proceedings of the 37th Annual Meeting of the Association for Computational Linguistics*, pages 41–48, College Park, Maryland, USA.

Deniz Zeyrek and Bonnie Webber. 2008. A discourse resource for turkish: Annotating discourse connectives in the metu turkish corpus. In *The 6th Workshop on Asian Language Resources, The Third International Joint Conference on Natural Language Processing (IJNLP)*, Hyderabad,India, January.

Annotation of Events and Temporal Expressions in French Texts

André Bittar
Université Paris Diderot — ALPAGE
30 rue du Château des Rentiers
75013 Paris
France
andre.bittar@linguist.jussieu.fr

Abstract

We present two modules for the recognition and annotation of temporal expressions and events in French texts according to the TimeML specification language. The Temporal Expression Tagger we have developed is based on a large coverage cascade of finite state transducers and our Event Tagger on a set of simple heuristics applied over local context in a chunked text. We present results of a preliminary evaluation and compare them with those obtained by a similar system.

1 Introduction

TimeML (Pustejovsky et al., 2003) is a specification language for the annotation and normalization of temporal information in natural language texts. The annotation scheme allows for the annotation of events (<EVENT>), the tagging of temporal expressions and the normalization of their values (<TIMEX3>), as well as the annotation of temporal, aspectual and subordinating relations which may exist among them (<TLINK>, <ALINK> and <SLINK>, respectively). The linguistic markers of these relations can also be marked up (<SIGNAL>). A set of resources, including automatic and manual annotation tools and several reference corpora have been developed around the TimeML language. Evita (Saurí et al., 2005) is an application for automatically recognizing and annotating events in texts, based primarily on symbolic methods and linguistic data (input is a chunked text), although with some integration of statistical data. Its creators report precision of 74.03% and recall of 87.31% for an overall F-score of 80.12% for the task of event identification. GUTime (Mani and Wilson, 2000) annotates temporal expressions according to the TimeML schema and normalizes their values. The system achieves F-scores of 85% and 82% for identification and normalization of temporal expressions, respectively. Further information is available on the TimeML project website[1].

2 A System for TimeML Annotation in French

(Parent et al., 2008) provide the description and evaluation of a system for the TimeML annotation of events and temporal expressions in French texts. The processing of temporal expressions is carried out on a text having undergone a part-of-speech tagging, morphological analysis and shallow syntactic analysis. The system functions by application of a cascade of 90 rules applied over 20 levels. Contrary to the Evita system developed for English, the event detection module relies on a full dependency parse as input for the event recognition task. The authors claim an advantage over chunker-based approaches with respect to the annotation of markable adjectives due to the fact that the dependency relation between copula verb and predicative adjective is available. The authors provide evaluation results according to grammatical category over a development corpus, made up of 35 biographical texts and 22 sports articles, and an evaluation ("unseen") corpus, consisting of an unspecified number of news articles from the website of the École Polytechnique de Montréal. The evaluation results, by grammatical category and global figures, are given in Table 1.

	Development corpus			Evaluation corpus		
Cat	Prec	Rec	F-sc	Prec	Rec	F-sc
Noun	61.5	40.0	48.4	54.7	53.7	54.2
Verb	94.1	97.3	95.7	65.6	90.9	76.2
Adj	66.7	77.8	71.8	N/A	N/A	N/A
Global	86.8	80.6	83.5	62.5	77.7	69.3

Table 1: Evaluation results according to corpora

The system performs best on the annotation of

[1] http://www.timeml.org

Proceedings of the Third Linguistic Annotation Workshop, ACL-IJCNLP 2009, pages 48–51,
Suntec, Singapore, 6-7 August 2009.

event verbs and encounters the most difficulties in the annotation of event nominals. Adjectives are relatively well processed over the development corpus, but no adjectives were annotated by the human annotator in the evaluation corpus, so no results were calculated. As for the annotation of temporal expressions, precision is 83% and recall 79%, for an F-score of 81% over an evaluation corpus containing 544 human-annotated temporal expressions and an F-score of 50% for the normalization of values. These figures are comparable to those cited for GUTime for English.

3 Annotation Modules

In this section, we describe an annotation system, similar to that of (Parent et al., 2008) described above, although based on a rich cascade of finite state transducers and a shallow syntactic analysis, as opposed to a full dependency parse. The system is made up principally of two modules, the first tagging temporal expressions (section 3.1), the second identifying and annotating event expressions (section 3.2).

3.1 Temporal Expression Tagger

This module carries out the tagging and normalization of temporal expressions. The module consists of a large-coverage set of finiste state transducers developed with the Unitex[2] corpus processor. The transducers in this large-coverage grammar, applied to raw text, recognize patterns of dates, times, duration and frequency and tag expressions with the appropriately typed `<TIMEX3>`. A transducer matching expressions **not** to be marked up was also created. This transducer tags with the label `<GARBAGE>` expressions such as phone numbers, which could otherwise match numerical dates. The ambiguous word *été* (*been/summer*), when preceded by an adverb or the auxiliary verb *avoir* is tagged as `<GARBAGE>`, as it has its verb rather than noun reading in this context. Other expressions tagged as `<GARBAGE>` include the common expression *les 35 heures* (*the French 35 hour week*) and names of streets containing a date, such as *la place du 13 Mai*, etc. The normalization script, written in Perl, calculates the standard values of temporal expressions, including underspecified deictic expressions, and removes annotations on items marked `<GARBAGE>`. The script consists of a set of substitution functions for each type of temporal expression tagged by the transducers. Each function converts the content of the expression into a TimeML standard value and inserts it in the `value` attribute of each `<TIMEX3>` tag. This module is available for download at http://www.linguist.univ-paris-diderot.fr/~abittar. This approach differs from that of (Parent et al., 2008) in that it relies almost entirely on lexical processing.

An evaluation was carried out on a subset of the corpus used to evaluate the similar module described in section 2. Our corpus consists of the 45 news articles from the Agence France Press used in the training and test sets described by (Parent et al., 2008). Figures for the evaluation are given in Table 2. The column labeled "Loose" represents the number of matches which cover an incomplete span of the expression, for example *un mois* (*one month*) instead of *un mois et demi* (*a month and a half*). The column "Strict" is for exact matches. The "Value" column represents the correctly normalized values for the temporal expressions detected, calculated over strict matches.

	Human	Found	Loose	Strict	Value
Number	592	575	508	484	317
Precision	-	-	85.8	84.2	55.0
Recall	-	-	88.4	81.8	44.9
F-score	-	-	87.1	83.0	49.4

Table 2: Evaluation results for the Temporal Expression Tagger

These figures are much in line with those of the system described in (Parent et al., 2008). Performance is slightly lower on loose matches (F-score 87.1 versus 91.0), but we achieve better results on strict matches (F-score 83.0 versus 81.0). This could be explained by the fact that we did not develop our grammar on the same type of source text, but shows that the grammar has a good coverage of the variants of each type of expression.

Sources of noise include age values tagged as durations, e.g. *M. Dupont, 58 ans* (*Mr. Dupont, 58 years old*) (11 errors), and numerical values taken to be years, e.g. *l'astéroïde 2001 UU92* (*Asteroid 2001 UU92*) (8 errors). Silence occurs mostly on coordinated date expressions or sequences, e.g. *les 4, 5 et 6 février* (*the 4th, 5th and 6th of February*) (11 errors) or expressions taking a

[2] Unitex is a graphical corpus processing program, available for download under GNU General Public Licence at http://www-igm.univ-mlv.fr/~unitex/

"vague" normalized value, e.g. *dans le passé* (*in the past*) (15 errors).

Results for the normalization of values for temporal expressions are practically identical to the other system for French. The majority of errors produced by our system (97 out of 167) are due to the fact that our normalization script does not yet fully deal with underspecified weekday expressions, such as *jeudi soir* (*Thursday evening*). In the hand-annotated corpus these expressions are fully resolved, with year, month and day values specified, e.g. `2002-01-15TEV`, whereas we provide a correct, but not completely resolved value, which specifies the day of the week, e.g. `2002-WXX-4TEV`. Excluding this difference in processing boosts precision to 73.6 and recall to 60.1 (F-score 66.85) for the normalization of values. We are currently working on fully normalizing these values.

3.2 Event Tagger

This module tags event expressions with the `<EVENT>` tag and classifies the events according to the ontology defined for TimeML. It also detects negative polarity contexts, as well as any aspectual or modal properties of certain verbal constructions. Input is a text having undergone part-of-speech tagging, an inflectional morphological analysis and shallow syntactic analysis, carried out by Macaon, a modular processing pipeline for French[3]. The Event tagger consists of several levels of processing - a layer of lexical processing, basically a lexical lookup for nouns and verb classes, and a layer of contextual processing consisting in the application of heuristics for detecting and eliminating event candidates and classifying them. This module relies on certain lexical resources. For the detection of event nominals, a lexicon containing nouns with at least one event interpretation is used. Many of the entries in this lexicon are ambiguous as they may also have a non-event interpretation. For example, *repas* (*meal*) has an object interpretation as well as an event reading. This highlights the need for disambiguation of nominals. The noun lexicon is based on the VerbAction lexicon (Hathout et al., 2002) which provided 9 200 unique deverbal noun lemmas. We further enriched the lexicon through semi-automated search engine queries, such as *X a eu lieu* (*X took place*) and *lors du/de la/des X* (*during the X*), where X is likely to be an event nominal. An initial application of this method yielded 769 unique noun lemmas which were not in VerbAction - mostly rare or non-deverbal nouns, such as *anticoagulothérapie* (*anticoagulation therapy*) and *anniversaire* (*birthday*). The noun lexicon is of comparable size to that used in Evita.

We created by hand a verb lexicon which is used to perform classification of verbal events. It contains 200 lemmas for verbs in 6 of the 7 TimeML event classes[4]. Verbs were initially added to the lexicon by translating those proposed in the TimeML classifcation for English. The list of verbs was enriched by querying the dictionary of synonyms at the Université de Caen[5]. The lexicon is small for the time being and will need to be increased to ensure better coverage for classification. Like the noun lexicon, the lexicon of verbs contains ambiguities as certain verbs may belong to different classes or may not have an event reading in certain contexts. For example, the verb *expliquer* (*to explain*) belongs to the class `REPORTING` when it introduces a complementizer phrase in *que* (*that*) headed by an event (*Max a expliqué qu'il avait commis une erreur - Maca explained that he had made a mistake*). This is the class attributed by the lexicon. However, when it has a human subject and an event in object position (*Le manager a expliqué le renouvellemetn de l'équipe - the manager explained the renewal of the team*), it must be annotated with the class `I_ACTION`. Finally, if this verb has events in both subject and object position (*Le réchauffement climatique explique la fonte des calottes glacières - global warming explains the melting of the ice caps*), it is to be annotated with the class `CAUSE`. The system is thus confronted with the non-trivial problem of word sense disambiguation to identify the correct readings of nouns and verbs in the text. Initially, we tackle this problem for verbs with a number of heuristics, applied to local chunk context, for each of the TimeML verb classes in the lexicon. A total of 16 heuristics are used for choosing candidates for markup with the `<EVENT>` tag and 30 heuristics for classifying the events and determining values for the `aspect`, `modality` and `polarity` attributes. For example, in the case of the verb *expliquer* given above, the

[3]Macaon is freely available for download at http://pageperso.lif.univ-mrs.fr/~alexis.nasr/macaon/.

[4]As the class OCCURRENCE is the default class, it has no entries in the lexicon

[5]http://www.crisco.unicaen.fr/cgi-bin/cherches.cgi

heuristics include a search for the complementizer *que* in the chunk after the verb and a search for an event nominal chunk directly to the left of the verb chunk (approximation of subject position). Further heuristics are used to eliminate verbs and nouns which do not have an event reading. For example, event nominal chunks which do not have a determiner, such as in *prisonier de guerre* (*prisoner of war*), are not considered as candidates as they do not denote event instances, but rather event types, and cannot be attributed a specific temporal localisation. A set of heuristics is used to detect predicative adjectives, like in *Jean était malade* (*Jean was sick*), which are potential candidates for markup with the `<EVENT>` tag. For example, if the preceding verb is a copula, the adjective is flagged as a markable.

To evaluate our event tagger we used a corpus of 30 hand-annotated news articles from the newspaper *Le Monde*. The corpus was split into a development set of 20 documents (11 224 tokens, 1 187 `EVENT` tags) and a test set of 10 documents (5 916 tokens, 583 `EVENT` tags). Overall, the corpus contains 1 205 verbal, 471 nominal, 62 adjectival and 18 prepositional phrase `EVENT` tags.

	Development corpus			Evaluation corpus		
Category	Prec	Rec	F-sc	Prec	Rec	F-sc
Noun	50.2	94.5	72.4	54.0	95.1	74.5
Verb	87.7	92.3	90.0	86.5	91.1	88.8
Adjective	60.0	72.4	66.2	46.0	82.1	64.1

Table 3: Evaluation results for the Event Tagger

The results shown in Table 3 are fairly homogenous over both the development and test sets. The detection of event verbs performs slightly lower than that of the other system for French, although the evaluations were carried out on different corpora. For nominals, our system makes a vast improvement on the performance of the other system described in this paper (an F-score of 74.5 versus 54.2 over the respective test sets). The large-coverage lexicon of event nominals allows for a good recall, although precision remains low as more disambiguation is required to filter out nominals with non-event readings. Performance on adjectival events is lower than the other system, although not as bad as might have been expected. This is likely due to the difference in depth of syntactic analysis available to each system.

4 Conclusion

We have presented a comparative evaluation of two systems for the TimeML annotation of events and temporal expressions in French texts. Results show that a lexical approach to annotating temporal expressions performs generally just as well as an approach based on a shallow syntactic analysis. For event detection, the benefits of a full dependency parse are apparent, especially for the detection of markable adjectives, although comparable performance can be obtained with a chunked text as input. The benefits of a large-coverage lexicon for identifying event nominals are evident, although without effective disambiguation techniques precision remains very low. This is one point which requires particular attention and more elaborate guidelines for the annotation of event nominals would be of great value. Figures from the evaluation give a rough indication of performance across systems, however, a validated reference corpus for French is yet to be developed in order to give more meaningful comparisons. These are issues we are currently addressing.

References

Nabil Hathout, Fiammetta Namer, and Georgette Dal. 2002. An Experimental Constructional Database: The MorTAL Project. In Paul Boucher, editor, *Many Morphologies*, pages 178–209. Cascadilla, Somerville, Mass., USA.

Inderjeet Mani and George Wilson. 2000. Processing of news. In *Proceedings of the 38th Annual Meeting of the Association for Computational Linguistics*, pages 69–76, Hong Kong, October. Association for Computational Linguistics.

Gabriel Parent, Michel Gagnon, and Philippe Muller. 2008. Annotation d'expressions temporelles et d'événements en français. In *Actes de TALN 2008*, Avignon, France, June.

James Pustejovsky, José Casta no, Robert Ingria, Roser Saurí, Robert Gaizauskas, Andrea Setzer, and Graham Katz. 2003. TimeML: Robust Specification of Event and Temporal Expressions in Text. In *Proceedings of IWCS-5, Fifth International Workshop on Computational Semantics*.

Roser Saurí, Robert Knippen, Marc Verhagen, and James Pustejovsky. 2005. Evita: A Robust Event Recognizer for QA Systems. In *Proceedings of HLT/EMNLP 2005*, pages 700–707.

Designing a Language Game for Collecting Coreference Annotation

Barbora Hladká and **Jiří Mírovský** and **Pavel Schlesinger**
Charles University in Prague
Institute of Formal and Applied Linguistics
e-mail: {hladka, mirovsky, schlesinger@ufal.mff.cuni.cz}

Abstract

PlayCoref is a concept of an on-line language game designed to acquire a substantial amount of text data with the coreference annotation. We describe in detail various aspects of the game design and discuss features that affect the quality of the annotation.

1 Introduction

Creating a collection of high quality data is resource-demanding regardless of the area of research and type of the data. This fact has encouraged a formulation of an alternative way of data collection, "Games With a Purpose" methodology (GWAP), (van Ahn and Dabbish, 2008). The GWAP methodology exploits the capacity of Internet users who like to play on-line games. The games are designed to generate data for applications that either have not been implemented yet, or have already been implemented with a performance lower than human. The players work simply by playing the game - the data are generated as a by-product of the game. The more enjoyable the game is, the more users play it and the more data is acquired.

The GWAP methodology was first used for online games with images (van Ahn and Dabbish, 2004) and later with tunes (Law et al., 2007),[1] in which the players try to agree on a caption of the image/tune. The popularity of these games is enormous and generates a huge amount of data. *Onto games* (Siorpaes and Hepp, 2008) brought another type of input data to GWAP – video and text.[2]

The situation with text is slightly different. One has to read a text in order to identify its topics. Reading texts takes more time than observing images and the longer text, the worse. Since the game must be of a dynamic character, it is unimaginable that the players would spend minutes reading an input text. Therefore, it must be opened to the players 'part' by 'part'.

So far, besides the Onto games, two more games with texts have appeared: *What did Shannon say?*[3], the goal of which is to help the speech recognizer with difficult-to-recognize words, and *Phrase Detectives*[4] (Kruschwitz, Chamberlain, Poesio, 2009), the goal of which is to identify relationships between words and phrases in a text. No information about their popularity has been published yet.

Motivated by the GWAP portal, the LGame portal[5] dedicated to language games has been established. The LGame portal has been opened with the *Shannon game*, a game of intentionally hidden words in the sentence, where players guess them, and the *Place the Space* game, a game of word segmentation.

2 Coreference

Coreference occurs when several referring expressions in a text refer to the same entity (e.g. person, thing, fact). A *coreferential pair* is marked between subsequent pairs of the referring expressions. A sequence of coreferential pairs referring to the same entity in a text forms a *coreference chain*. The coreferential pairs and the coreference chains cover only the identity relation.

Many projects for various languages on the coreference annotation by linguists are running. The annotated data serve as a basis for further linguistic study of coreference, and most importantly also to train and test procedures for automatic coreference resolution, which is a task that

[1] www.gwap.org
[2] www.ontogame.org
[3] lingo.clsp.jhu.edushannongame.html
[4] www.phrasedetectives.org
[5] www.lgame.cz

Proceedings of the Third Linguistic Annotation Workshop, ACL-IJCNLP 2009, pages 52–55,
Suntec, Singapore, 6-7 August 2009.

many other applications can benefit from, e.g. text summarization, question answering, and information retrieval.

Manual annotation is costly and time consuming. We propose a design of the PlayCoref game – to appear at the LGame portal – as an alternative way of the coreference annotation collection, and most importantly, of a substantially larger volume than any expert annotation can ever achieve.

3 The PlayCoref Game

3.1 Game Design

We prepare the game for Czech and English first. However, PlayCoref can be played in any language.

The game is designed for two players. The game starts with several first sentences of the document displayed in the players' sentence window. According to the restrictions put on the members of the coreferential pairs, parts of the text are unlocked (i.e. they are active) while the other parts are locked (i.e. they are inactive); both of them are graphically distinguished. In our case, only nouns and selected pronouns are unlocked. The players mark coreferential pairs between the individual unlocked words in the text (no phrases are allowed). They mark the coreferential pairs as undirected links.

During the session, the number of words the opponent has linked into the coreferential pairs is displayed to the player. The number of sentences with at least one coreferential pair marked by the opponent is displayed to the player as well. Revealing more information about the opponent's actions would affect the independency of the players' decisions.

If the player finishes pairing all the related words in the visible part of the document (visible to him), he asks for the next sentence of the document. It appears at the bottom of the player's sentence window. The player can remove pairs created before at any time and can make new pairs in the sentences read so far. The session goes on this way until the end of the session time. More than one document can be present in the session.

After the session, the players' scores are calculated and displayed.

Instructions for the Players Instructions for the players must be as comprehensible and concise as possible. To mark a coreferential pair, no linguistic knowledge is required, thus no extensive annotation guidelines need to be formulated. It is all about the text comprehension ability.

3.2 Game Data

Any textual data can be used in the game, but the following pre-processing steps are necessary.

Tagging Most importantly, the morphological tagging (usually preceded by tokenization) is required to recognize part-of-speech categories (and sub-part-of-speech categories), in order to lock/unlock individual words for the game. For most languages, tagging is a well solved problem (e.g. for Czech: the MORČE tagger[6], for English: TnT tagger[7]).

Text Parts Locking In the game, we work with coreferential links between the individual words only. The coreferential pairs that link larger text parts consisting of clauses or even several sentences are disregarded. Their marking requires linguistic knowledge and extensive training.

Our research shows that pronouns that are usually members of such "undesirable" links can be detected automatically in advance (at least in Czech). They will get locked, so the players will not consider them at all during the sessions.

Automatic Coreference Resolution According to the way we calculate the players scores (see below), an automatic procedure for coreference resolution is required. If this procedure works on a different layer than the surface layer, further automatic processing of the data may be needed.

4 Data Quality

4.1 Players' Score

We want to obtain a large volume of data so we must first attract the players and motivate them to play the game more and more. As a reward for their effort we present scoring. We hope that the players' appetite to win, to confront with their opponents and to place well in the long-term top scores tables correlates with our research aims and objectives.

Our goal is to ensure the highest quality of the annotation. The scoring function should reflect the game data quality and thus motivate the players to produce the right data. An agreement with

[6] ufal.mff.cuni.cz/morce

[7] www.coli.uni-saarland.de/~thorsten/tnt/

the manual expert annotation would be a perfect scoring function. But the manual annotation is not available for all languages and above all, it is not our goal to annotate already annotated data.

An automatic coreference resolution procedure serves as a first approximation for the scoring function. Since the procedure does not work for "100%", we need to add another component. We suppose that most of the players will mark the coreferential pairs reliably. Then an agreement between the players' pairs indicates correctness, even if the pair differs from the output of automatic coreference resolution procedure. Therefore, the inter-player agreement will become the second component of the scoring function. To motivate the players to ask for more parts of the text (and not only "tune" links in the initially displayed sentences), the third component of the scoring function will award number of created coreferential links.

The players get points for their coreferential pairs according to the equation $pts_A = w_1 * ICA(A, acr) + w_2 * ICA(A, B) + w_3 * N(A)$ where A and B are the players, acr is an automatic coreference resolution procedure, ICA stands for the inter-coder agreement that we can simultaneously express either by the F-measure or Krippendorff's α (Krippendorf, 2004), N is a contribution of the number of created links, and weights $0 \leq w_1, w_2 \leq 1$, $w_1, w_2, w_3 \in R$ (summing to 1) are set empirically.

The score is calculated at the end of the session and no running score is being presented during the session. From the scientific point of view, the scores serve for the long term quality control of the players' annotation.

4.2 Interactivity Issues

The degree of a player-to-player interactivity contributes to the attractiveness of the game. From the player's point of view, the more interactivity, the better. For example, knowing both his and the opponent's running score would be very stimulating for the mutual competitiveness. From the linguistics' point of view, once any kind of interaction is allowed, statistically pure independency between the players' decisions is lost. A reasonable trade-off between the interactivity and the independency must be achieved. Interactivity that would lead to cheating and decreasing the quality of the game data must be avoided.

Allowing the players to see their own running score would lead to cheating. The players might adjust their decisions according to the changes in the score. Another possible extension of interactivity that would lead to cheating is highlighting words that the opponent used in the coreferential pairs. The players might then wait for the opponent's choice and again, adjust their decisions accordingly. Such game data would be strongly biased. However, we still believe that a slight idea of what the opponent is doing can boost inter-coder agreement and yet avoid cheating. Revealing the information about the opponent's number of pairs and number of sentences with at least one pair offers not zero but low interactivity, yet it will not harm the quality of the data.

4.3 Post-Processing

The players mark the coreferential links undirected. This strategy differs from the general conception of coreference being understood as either the anaphoric or cataphoric relation depending on the "direction" of the link in the text. We believe that the players will benefit from this simplification and so will the data quality. After the session, the coreference chains are automatically reconstructed from the coreferential pairs.

4.4 Evaluation

Data with manually annotated coreference will be used to measure the game data quality. We will also study how much the scoring function suffers from the difference between the output of the automatic coreference resolution procedure and the manual annotation (gold standard). For Czech, we will use the data from PDT 2.0, for English from MUC-6.

PDT 2.0 [8] contains the annotation of grammatical and pronominal textual coreference. Nominal textual coreference is being annotated in PDT 2.0 in an ongoing project (Nedoluzhko, 2007). Since the PDT 2.0 coreference annotation operates on the so-called tectogrammatical layer (layer of meaning) and PlayCoref plays on the surface layer, the coreferential pairs must be projected to the surface first. The process consists of several steps and only a part of the coreferential pairs is actually projectable to the surface (links between nodes that have no surface counterpart get lost).

[8] `ufal.mff.cuni.cz/pdt2.0`

MUC-6 [9] operates on the surface layer. This data can be used in a much more straightforward way. The coreferential pairs are marked between nouns, noun phrases, and pronouns and no projection is needed. The links with noun phrases are disregarded.

Evaluation Methods For the game data evaluation, well established methods for calculating an inter-annotator agreement in the coreference annotation will be employed. These methods consider a coreference chain to be a set of words and they measure the agreement on the membership of the individual words in the sets (Passonneau, 2004). Weighted agreement coefficients such as Krippendorf's α (Krippendorf, 2004) need to be used - sets of words can differ only partially, which does not mean a total disagreement.

5 Further Work

Acquisition Evaluation Process The quality of the game annotation undergoes standard evaluation. Apart from collecting, assuming the game reaches sufficient popularity, long-term monitoring of the players' outputs can bring into question new issues concerning the game data quality: How much can we benefit from presenting a document into more sessions? Should we prefer the output of more reliable and experienced players during the evaluation? Should we omit the output of 'not-so-reliable' players?

Named Entity Recognition The step of the named entity recognition will be applied in the subsequent stages of the project. Multi-word expressions that form a named entity (e.g. "Czech National Bank") will be presented to the players as a single unit of annotation. We also plan to implement a GWAP for named entity recognition.

6 Conclusion

We have presented the concept of the PlayCoref game, a proposed language game that brings a novel approach to collecting coreference annotation of texts using the enormous potential of Internet users. We have described the design of the game and discussed the issues of interactivity of the players and measuring the player score – issues that are crucial both for the attractiveness of the game and for the quality of the game data. The game can be applied on any textual data in any language, providing certain basic tools also discussed in the paper exist. The GWAPs are open-ended stories so until the game is released, it is hard to say if the players will find it attractive enough. If so, we hope to collect a large volume of data with coreference annotation at extremely low costs.

[9] `cs.nyu.edu/faculty/grishman/muc6.html`

Acknowledgments

We gratefully acknowledge the support of the Czech Ministry of Education (grants MSM-0021620838 and LC536), the Czech Grant Agency (grant 405/09/0729), and the Grant Agency of Charles University in Prague (project GAUK 138309).

References

Klaus Krippendorf. 2004. Content Analysis: An Introduction to Its Methodology, second edition, chapter 11, Sage, Thousand Oaks, CA.

Udo Kruschwitz, Jon Chamberlain, Massimo Poesio. 2009. (Linguistic) Science Through Web Collaboration in the ANAWIKI project. In *Proceedings of the WebSci'09: Society On-Line*, Athens, Greece, in press.

Lucie Kučová, Eva Hajičová. 2005. Coreferential Relations in the Prague Dependency Treebank. In *Proceedings of the 5th International Conference on Discourse Anaphora and Anaphor Resolution*, San Miguel, Azores, pp. 97–102.

Edith. L. M. Law et al. 2007. Tagatune: A game for music and sound annotation. In *Proceedings of the Music Information Retrieval Conference*, Austrian Computer Soc., pp. 361–364.

Anna Nedoluzhko. 2007. Zpráva k anotování rozšířené textové koreference a bridging vztahů v Pražském závoslostním korpusu (Annotating extended coreference and bridging relations in PDT). Technical Report, UFAL, MFF UK, Prague, Czech Republic.

Rebecca J. Passonneau. 2004. Computing Reliability for Coreference. *Proceedings of LREC*, vol. 4, pp. 1503–1506, Lisbon.

Katharina Siorpaes and Martin Hepp. 2008. Games with a purpose for the Semantic Web. *IEEE Intelligent Systems Vol. 23, number 3*, pp. 50–60.

Luis van Ahn and Laura Dabbish. 2004. Labelling images with a computer game. In *Proceedings of the SIGHI Conference on Human Factors in Computing Systems, ACM Press*, New York, pp. 319–326.

Luis van Ahn and Laura Dabbish. 2008. Designing Games with a Purpose. *Communications of the ACM*, vol. 51, No. 8, pp. 58–67.

Marc Vilain et al. 1995. A Model-Theoretic Coreference Scoring Scheme. *Proceedings of the Sixth Message Understanding Conference*, pp. 45–52, Columbia, MD.

Explorations in Automatic Image Annotation using Textual Features

Chee Wee Leong
Computer Science & Engineering
University of North Texas
cheeweeleong@my.unt.edu

Rada Mihalcea
Computer Science & Engineering
University of North Texas
rada@cs.unt.edu

Abstract

In this paper, we report our work on automatic image annotation by combining several textual features drawn from the text surrounding the image. Evaluation of our system is performed on a dataset of images and texts collected from the web. We report our findings through comparative evaluation with two gold standard collections of manual annotations on the same dataset.

1 Introduction

Despite the usefulness of images in expressing ideas, machine understanding of the meaning of an image remains a daunting task for computers, as the interplay between the different visual components of an image does not conform to any fixed pattern that allows for formal reasoning of its semantics. Often, the machine interpretation of the concepts present in an image, known as *automatic image annotation*, can only be inferred by its accompanying text or co-occurrence information drawn from a large corpus of texts and images (Li and Wang, 2008; Barnard and Forsyth, 2001). Not surprisingly, humans have the innate ability to perform this task reliably, but given a large database of images, manual annotation is both labor-intensive and time-consuming.

Our work centers around the question : Provided an image with its associated text, can we use the text to reliably extract keywords that relevantly describe the image ? Note that we are not concerned with the generation of keywords for an image, but rather their *extraction* from the related text. Our goal eventually is to automate this task by leveraging on texts which are naturally occurring with images. In all our experiments, we only consider the use of nouns as annotation keywords.

2 Related Work

Although automatic image annotation is a popular task in computer vision and image processing, there are only a few efforts that leverage on the multitude of resources available for natural language processing to derive robust linguistic based image annotation models. Most of the work has posed the annotation task as a classification problem, such as (Li and Wang, 2008), where images are annotated using semantic labels associated to a semantic class.

The most recent work on image annotation using linguistic features (Feng and Lapata, 2008) involves implementing an extended version of the continuous relevance model that is proposed in (Jeon et al., 2003). The basic idea underlying their work is to perform annotation of a test image by using keywords shared by similar training images. Evaluation of their system performance is based on a dataset collected from the news domain (BBC). Unlike them, in this paper, we attempt to perform image annotation on datasets from unrestricted domains. We are also interested in extending the work pursued in (Deschacht and Moens, 2007), where *visualness* and *salience* are proposed as important textual features for discovering named entities present in an image, by extracting other textual features that can further improve existing image annotation models.

3 Data Sets

We use 180 images collected from the Web, from pages that have a single image within a specified size range (width and height of 275 to 1000 pixels). 110 images are used for development, while the remaining 70 are used for test. We create two different gold standards. The first, termed as *Intuitive annotation standard* ($GS_{intuition}$), presents a user with the image in the absence of its associated text, and asks the user for the 5 most relevant annotations. The second, called *Contextual annotation standard* ($GS_{context}$), provides the user with a list of candidates[1] for annotation, with the user free to choose any of the candidates deemed relevant to describe the image. The user, however, is not con-

[1]Union of candidates proposed by all systems participating in the evaluation, including the baseline system

Proceedings of the Third Linguistic Annotation Workshop, ACL-IJCNLP 2009, pages 56–59,
Suntec, Singapore, 6-7 August 2009.

strained to choose any candidate word, nor is she obligated to choose a specified number of candidates. For each image I in the evaluation set, we invited five users to perform the annotation task per gold standard. The agreement is 7.78% for $GS_{intuition}$ and 22.27% for $GS_{context}$, where we consider an annotation that is proposed by three or more users as one that is being agreed upon. The union of their inputs forms the set $GS_{intuition}(I)$ and $GS_{context}(I)$ respectively. We do not consider image captions for use as a gold standard here due to their absence in many of the images – a random sampling of 15 images reveals that 7 of them lack captions. Contrary to their use as a proxy for annotation keywords in (Feng and Lapata, 2008; Deschacht and Moens, 2007), where evaluation is performed on datasets gleaned from authoritative news websites, most captions in our dataset are not guaranteed to be noise free. However, they are used as part of the text for generating annotations where they exist.

4 Automatic Image Annotation

We approach the task of automatic image annotation using four methods. Due to the orthogonal nature in their search for keywords, the output for each method is generated separately and later combined in an unsupervised setting. However, all four methods perform their discrimination of words by drawing information exclusively from the text associated to the image, using no image visual features in the process.

4.1 Semantic Cloud (Sem)

Every text describes at least one topic that can be semantically represented by a collection of words. Intuitively, there exists several "clouds" of semantically similar words that form several, possibly overlapping, sets of topics. Our task is to select the dominant topic put forward in the text, with the assumption that such a topic is being represented by the largest set of words. We use an adapted version of the K-means clustering approach, which attempts to find natural "clusters" of words in the text by grouping words with a common centroid. Each centroid is the semantic center of the group of words and the distance between each centroid and the words are approximated by ESA (Gabrilovich and Markovitch, 2007). Further, we perform our experiments with the following assumptions : (1) To maximize recall, we assume that there are only two topics in every text. (2) Every word or collocation in the text must be classified under one of these two topics, but not both. In cases, where there is a tie, the classification is chosen randomly. For each dominant cluster extracted, we rank the words in decreasing order of their ESA distance to the centroid. Together, they represent the gist of the topic and are used as a set of candidates for labeling the image.

4.2 Lexical Distance (Lex)

Words that are lexically close to the picture in the document are generally well-suited for annotating the image. The assumption is drawn from the observation that the caption of an image is usually located close to the image itself. For images without captions, we consider words surrounding the image as possible candidates for annotation. Whenever a word appears multiple times within the text, its occurrence closest to the image is used to calculate the lexical distance. To discriminate against general words, we weigh the Lexical Distance Score (LDS) for each word by its *tf * idf* score as in the equation shown below :

$$LDS(W_i) = tf * idf(W_i)/LS(W_i) \qquad (1)$$

where LS(W_i) is the minimum lexical distance of W_i to the image, and *idf* is calculated using counts from the British National Corpus.

4.3 Saliency (Sal)

To our knowledge, all word similarity metrics provide a symmetric score between a pair of words w_1 and w_2 to indicate their semantic similarity. Intuitively, this is not always the case. In psycholinguistics terms, uttering w_1 may bring into mind w_2, while the appearance of w_2 without any contextual clues may not associate with w_1 at all. Thus, the degree of similarity of w_1 with respect to w_2 should be separated from that of w_2 with respect to w_1. We use a directional measure of similarity:

$$DSim(w_i, w_j) = \frac{C_{ij}}{C_i} * Sim(w_i, w_j) \qquad (2)$$

where C_{ij} is the count of articles in Wikipedia containing words w_i and w_j, C_i is the count of articles containing words w_i, and Sim(w_i, w_j) is the cosine similarity of the ESA vectors representing the two words. The *directional weight* (C_{ij}/C_i) amounts to the degree of association of w_i with respect to w_j. Using the directional inferential similarity scores as directed edges and distinct words as vertices, we obtain a graph for each text. The directed edges denotes the idea of "recommendation" where we say w_1 recommends w_2 if and only if there is a directed edge from w_1 to w_2, with the weight of the recommendation being the directional similarity score. By employing the graph iteration algorithm proposed in (Mihalcea and Tarau, 2004), we can compute the rank of a vertex in the entire graph. The output generated is a sorted list of words in decreasing order of their ranks, which serves as a list of candidates for annotating the image. Note that the top-ranked word must infer some or all of the words in the text.

Table 1: An image annotation example

Sem	**symptoms**, **treatment**, **medical treatment**, **medical care**, **sore throat**, fluids, **cough**, **tonsils**, **strep throat**, **swab**
Lex	**strep throat**, **cotton swab**, lymph nodes, rheumatic fever, **swab**, **strep**, fever, **sore throat**, **lab**, **scarlet fever**
Sal	**strep**, **swab**, nemours, **teens**, ginger ale, grapefruit juice, **sore**, antibiotics, **kids**, fever
Pic	**throat**, runny nose, **strep throat**, **sore throat**, hand washing, orange juice, 24 hours, **medical care**, beverages, lymph nodes
Combined	**treatment**, **cough**, **tonsils**, **swab**, fluids, **strep throat**
Doc Title	**strep throat**
tf * *idf*	**strep**, **throat**, antibiotics, **symptoms**, **child**, **swab**, fever, **treatment**, **teens**, nemours
$\mathrm{GS}_{context}$	medical care, medical treatment, doctor, cotton swab, treatment, tonsils, sore throat, swab, throat, sore, sample, symptoms, throat, cough, medication, bacteria, lab, scarlet fever, strep throat, teens, culture, kids, child, streptococcus, doctor, strep
$\mathrm{GS}_{intuition}$	tongue, depressor, exam, eyes, cartoon, doctor, health, child, tonsils, fingers, hair, mouth, dentist, sample, cloth, curly, tip, examine

4.4 Picturable Cues (Pic)

Some words are more *picturable* than others. For instance, it is easy to find a picture that describes the word *banana* than another word *paradigm*. Clearly, picturable words in the associated text of an image are natural candidates for labeling it. Unlike the work in (Deschacht and Moens, 2007), we employ a corpus-based approach to compute word to word similarity. We collect a list of 200 manually-annotated words[2] that are deemed to be picturable by humans. We use this list of words as our set of seed words, S_{seed}. We then iterate a bootstrapping process where each word in the text is compared to every word in the set of seed words, and any word having a maximum ESA score of greater than 0.95 is added to S_{seed}. Similarly, the maximum ESA score of each word over all S_{seed} words is recorded. This is the picturability score of the word.

5 Experiments and Evaluations

We investigate the performance of each of the four annotation methods individually, followed by a combined approach using all of them. In the individual setting, we simply obtain the set of candidates proposed by each method as possible annotation keywords for the image. In the unsupervised combined setting, only the labels proposed by all individual methods are selected, and listed in reverse order of their combined rankings.

We allow each system to produce a re-ranked list of top k words to be the final annotations for a given image. A system can discretionary generate less (but not more) than k words that is appropriate to its confidence level. Similar to (Feng and Lapata, 2008), we evaluate our systems using precision, recall and F-measure for k=10, k=15 and k=20 words.

For comparison, we also implemented two baselines systems: *tf* * *idf* and *Doc Title*, which simply takes all the words in the title of the web page and uses them as annotation labels for the image. In the absence of a document title, we use the first sentence in the document. The results for $GS_{intuition}$ and $GS_{context}$ are tabulated in Tables 2 and 3 respectively. We further illustrate our results with an annotation example (an image taken from a webpage discussing strep throat among teens) in Table 1. Words in bold matches $GS_{context}$ while those underlined matches $GS_{intuition}$.

6 Discussion

As observed, the system implementing the Semantic Cloud method significantly outperforms the rest of the systems in terms of recall and F-measure using the gold standard $GS_{intuition}$. The unsupervised combined system yields the highest precision at 16.26% (at k=10,15,20) but at a low recall of 1.52%. Surprisingly, the baseline system using *tf* * *idf* performs relatively well across all the experiments using the gold standard $GS_{intuition}$, outperforming two of our proposed methods Salience (Sal) and Picturability Cues (Pic) consistently for all k values. The other baseline, *Doc Title*, records the highest precision at 16.33% at k=10 with a low recall of 3.81%. For k=15 and k=20, the F-measure scored 6.31 and 6.29 respectively, both lower than that scored by *tf* * *idf*.

[2] http://simple.wikipedia.org/wiki/Wikipedia:Basic_English_picture_wordlist

Table 2: Results for Automatic Image Annotation for $GS_{intuition}$. In both Tables 2 and 3, statistically significant results are marked with *(measured against Doc Title, $p<0.05$, paired t-test), $^{\times}$(measured against tf*idf, $p<0.1$, paired t-test), †(measured against tf*idf, $p<0.05$, paired t-test).

	$GS_{intuition}$								
	k=10			k=15			k=20		
	P	R	F	P	R	F	P	R	F
Sem	11.71	**6.25***	**8.15**	11.31	**8.91**$^{*\times}$	**9.97***†	10.36	**9.45**$^{*\times}$	**9.88***†
Lex	9.00	4.80	6.26	7.33	5.86	6.51	7.14	7.62	7.37
Sal	4.57	2.43	3.17	6.28	5.03	5.59	6.38	6.78	6.57
Pic	7.14	3.81	4.97	6.09	4.87	5.41	5.64	6.02	5.82
Combined	16.26	1.52	2.78	**16.26**†	1.52	2.78	**16.26**†	1.52	2.78
Doc Title	**16.33**	3.81	6.18	15.56	3.96	6.31	15.33	3.96	6.29
*tf * idf*	9.71	5.18	6.76	8.28	6.63	7.36	7.14	7.62	7.37

Table 3: Results for Automatic Image Annotation for $GS_{context}$

	$GS_{context}$								
	k=10			k=15			k=20		
	P	R	F	P	R	F	P	R	F
Sem	71.57	**26.20***†	**38.36***†	68.00	**37.34***†	**48.21***†	64.56	**47.17***†	**54.51***†
Lex	61.00	22.23	32.59	58.95	32.37	41.79	56.92	41.68	48.12
Sal	46.42	16.99	24.88	51.14	28.08	36.25	54.59	39.80	46.04
Pic	51.71	21.12	29.99	56.85	31.22	40.31	56.35	41.26	47.64
Combined	**75.60***†	4.86	9.13	**75.60***†	4.86	9.13	**75.60***†	4.86	9.13
Doc Title	32.67	5.23	9.02	32.33	5.64	9.60	32.15	5.70	9.68
*tf * idf*	55.85	20.44	29.93	54.19	29.75	38.41	49.07	35.93	41.48

When performing evaluations using the gold standard $GS_{context}$, significantly higher precision, recall and F-measure values are scored by all the systems, including both baselines. This is perhaps due to the availability of candidates that suggests a form of cued recall, rather than free recall, as is the case with $GS_{intuitive}$. The user is able to annotate an image with higher accuracy e.g. labelling a Chihuahua as a *Chihuahua* instead of a *dog*. Again, the Semantic Cloud method continues to outperform all the other systems in terms of recall and F-measure consistently for k=10, k=15 and k=20 words. A similar trend as observed using the gold standard of $GS_{intuition}$ is seen here, where again our combined system favors precision over recall at all values of k.

A possible explanation for the poor performance of the Saliency method is perhaps due to over-specific words that infer all other words in the text, yet unknown to the knowledge of most human annotators. For instance, the word *Mussolini*, referring to the dictator *Benito Mussolini*, was not selected as an annotation for an image showing scenes of World War II depicting the Axis troops, though it suggests the concepts of *war*, *World War II* and so on. The Pic method is also not performing as well as expected under the two gold annotation standards, mainly due to the fact that it focuses on selecting picturable nouns but not necessarily those that are semantically linked to the image itself.

7 Future Work

The use of the semantic cloud method to generate automatic annotations is promising. Future work will consider using additional semantic resources such as ontological information and encyclopaedic knowledge to enhance existing models. We are also interested to pursue human knowledge modeling to account for the differences in annotators in order create a more objective gold standard.

References

Kobus Barnard and David Forsyth. 2001. Learning the semantics of words and pictures. In *Proceedings of International Conference on Computer Vision*.

Koen Deschacht and Marie-Francine Moens. 2007. Text analysis for automatic image annotation. In *Proceedings of the Association for Computational Linguisticd*.

Yansong Feng and Mirella Lapata. 2008. Automatic image annotation using auxiliary text information. In *Proceedings of the Association for Computational Linguistics*.

Evgeniy Gabrilovich and Shaul Markovitch. 2007. Computing semantic relatedness using wikipedia-based explicit semantic analysis. In *International Joint Conferences on Artificial Intelligence*.

J Jeon, V Lavrenko, and R Manmatha. 2003. Automatic image annotation and retrieval using cross-media relevance models. In *Proceedings of the ACM SIGIR Conference on Research and Development in Information Retrieval*.

Jia Li and James Wang. 2008. Real-time computerized annotation of pictures. In *Proceedings of International Conference on Computer Vision*.

Rada Mihalcea and Paul Tarau. 2004. Textrank: Bringing order into texts. In *in Proceedings of Empirical Methods in Natural Language Processing*.

Human Evaluation of Article and Noun Number Usage: Influences of Context and Construction Variability

John Lee
Spoken Language Systems
MIT CSAIL
Cambridge, MA 02139, USA
jsylee@csail.mit.edu

Joel Tetreault
Educational Testing Service
Princeton, NJ 08541
jtetreault@ets.org

Martin Chodorow
Hunter College of CUNY
New York, NY 10021
martin.chodorow@hunter.cuny.edu

Abstract

Evaluating systems that correct errors in non-native writing is difficult because of the possibility of multiple correct answers and the variability in human agreement. This paper seeks to improve the best practice of such evaluation by analyzing the frequency of multiple correct answers and identifying factors that influence agreement levels in judging the usage of articles and noun number.

1 Introduction

In recent years, systems have been developed with the long-term goal of detecting, in the writing of non-native speakers, usage errors involving articles, prepositions and noun number (Knight and Chander, 1994; Minnen et al., 2000; Lee, 2004; Han et al., 2005; Peng and Araki, 2005; Brockett et al., 2006; Turner and Charniak, 2007). These systems should, ideally, be evaluated on a corpus of learners' writing, annotated with acceptable corrections. However, since such corpora are expensive to compile, many researchers have instead resorted to measuring the accuracy of predicting what a native writer originally wrote in well-formed text. This type of evaluation effectively makes the assumption that there is one correct form of native usage per context, which may not always be the case.

Two studies have already challenged this "single correct construction" assumption by comparing the output of a system to the original text. In (Tetreault and Chodorow, 2008), two human judges were presented with 200 sentences and, for each sentence, they were asked to select which preposition (either the writer's preposition, or the system's) better fits the context. In 28% of the cases where the writer and the system differed, the human raters found the system's prediction to be equal to or better than the writer's original preposition. (Lee and Seneff, 2006) found similar results on the sentence level in a task that evaluated many different parts of speech.

Percentage	Article	Number	Example
42.5%	null	singular	*stone*
22.7%	*the*	singular	*the stone*
17.6%	null	plural	*stones*
11.4%	*a/an*	singular	*a stone*
5.7%	*the*	plural	*the stones*

Table 1: Distribution of the five article-number *constructions* of head nouns, based on 8 million examples extracted from the MetaMetrics Lexile Corpus. The various constructions are illustrated with the noun "*stone*".

2 Research Questions

It is clear that using what the author wrote as the gold standard can underestimate the system's performance, and that multiple correct answers should be annotated. Using this annotation scheme, however, raises two questions that have not yet been thoroughly researched: (1) what is the human agreement level on such annotation? (2) what factors might influence the agreement level? In this paper, we consider two factors: the *context* of a word, and the variability of its usage.

In the two studies cited above, the human judges were shown only the target sentence and did not take into account any constraint on the choice of word that might be imposed by the larger context. For PP attachment, human performance improves when given more context (Ratnaparkhi et al., 1994). For other linguistic phenomena, such as article/number selection for nouns, a larger context window of at least several sentences may be required, even though some automatic methods for exploiting context have not been shown to boost performance (Han et al., 2005).

The second factor, variability of usage, may be

Proceedings of the Third Linguistic Annotation Workshop, ACL-IJCNLP 2009, pages 60–63,
Suntec, Singapore, 6-7 August 2009.

Three years ago John Small, a sheep farmer in the Mendip Hills, read an editorial in his local newspaper which claimed that foxes never killed lambs. **He drove down to the paper's office and presented `[?]`, killed the night before, to the editor.**

	NO-CONTEXT	IN-CONTEXT
lamb:	no	no
a lamb:	yes	yes*
the lamb:	yes	no
lambs:	yes	yes
the lambs:	yes	no

Table 2: An example of a completed annotation item.

expressed as the entropy of the distribution of the word's constructions. Table 1 shows the overall distribution of five article/number constructions for head nouns, i.e. all permissible combinations of number (*singular* or *plural*), and article ("*a/an*", "*the*", or the "*null article*"). A high entropy noun such as "*stone*" can appear freely in all of these, **either as a count noun or a non-count noun**. This contrasts with a low entropy noun such as "*pollution*" which is mostly limited to two construction types ("*pollution*" and "*the pollution*").

In this paper, we analyze the effects of varying context and noun entropy on human judgments of the acceptability of article-number constructions. As a result of this study, we hope to advance the best practice in annotation for evaluating error detection systems. §3 describes our annotation task. In §4, we test the "single correct construction" assumption for article and noun number. In §5, we investigate to what extent context and entropy constrain the range of acceptable constructions and influence the level of human agreement.

3 Annotation Design

3.1 Annotation Scheme

Two native speakers of English participated in an annotation exercise, which took place in two stages: NO-CONTEXT and IN-CONTEXT. Both stages used a common set of sentences, each containing one noun to be annotated. That noun was replaced by the symbol `[?]`, and the five possible *constructions*, as listed in Table 1, were displayed below the sentence to be judged.

In the NO-CONTEXT stage, only the sentence in question and the five candidate constructions (i.e., the bolded parts in Table 2) were shown to the raters. They were asked to consider each of the five constructions, and to select `yes` if it would yield a good sentence *in some context*, and `no` otherwise[1].

	null	*a*	*the*	
			anaphoric	not anaphoric
singular	2	2	2	2
plural	2	n/a	2	2

Table 3: For each noun, two sentences were selected from each configuration of number, article and anaphor.

The IN-CONTEXT stage began after a few days' break. The raters were presented with the same sentences, but including the context, which consisted of the five preceding sentences, some of which are shown in Table 2. The raters were again asked to select `yes` if the choice would yield a good sentence *given the context*, and `no` otherwise. Among the `yes` constructions, they were asked to mark with an asterisk (`yes*`) the construction(s) most likely to have been used in the original text.

3.2 Annotation Example

In Table 2, "*lambs*" are mentioned in the context, but only in the generic sense. Therefore, the `[?]` in the sentence must be indefinite, resulting in `yes` for both "*a lamb*" and "*lambs*". Of these two constructions, the singular was judged more likely to have been the writer's choice.

If the context is removed, then the `[?]` in the sentence could be anaphoric, and so "*the lamb*" and "*the lambs*" are also possible. Finally, regardless of context, the null singular "*lamb*" is not acceptable.

3.3 Item Selection

All items were drawn from the Grade 10 material in the 2.5M-sentence MetaMetrics Lexile corpus. To avoid artificially inflating the agreement level, we excluded noun phrases whose article or number can be predicted with very high confidence, such as proper nouns, pronouns and non-count nouns. Noun phrases with certain words, such as non-article determiners (e.g., *this car*), possessive pronouns (e.g., *his car*), cardinal numbers (e.g., *one car*) or quantifiers (e.g., *some cars*), also fall into this category. Most of these preclude the articles *a* and *the*.

[1]Originally, a third response category was offered to the rater to mark constructions that fell in a grey area between `yes` and `no`. This category was merged with `yes`.

Rater	NO-CONTEXT		IN-CONTEXT	
	yes	no	yes	no
R1	62.4%	37.6%	29.3%	70.7%
R2	51.8%	48.2%	39.2%	60.8%

Table 4: Breakdown of the annotations by rater and by stage. See §4 for a discussion.

	NO-CONTEXT		IN-CONTEXT	
R1:↓ R2:→	yes	no	yes	no
yes	846	302	462	77
no	108	584	260	1041

Table 5: The confusion tables of the two raters for the two stages.

Once these easy cases were filtered out, the head nouns in the corpus were divided into five sets according to their dominant construction. Each set was then ranked according to the entropy of the distribution of their constructions. *Low entropy* typically means that there is one particular construction whose frequency dwarfs the others', such as the singular definite for "*sun*". *High entropy* means that the five constructions are more evenly represented in the corpus; these are mostly generic objects that can be definite or indefinite, singular or plural, such as "*stone*". For each of the five constructions, the three nouns with the highest entropies, and three with the lowest, were selected. This yielded a total of 15 "high-entropy" and 15 "low-entropy" nouns.

For each noun, 14 sentences were drawn according to the breakdown in Table 3, ensuring a balanced representation of the article and number used in the original text, and the presence of anaphoric references[2]. A total of 368 items[3] were generated.

4 Multiple Correct Constructions

We first establish the reliability of the annotation by measuring agreement with the original text, then show how and when multiple correct constructions can arise. All results in this section are from the IN-CONTEXT stage.

Since the items were drawn from well-formed text, each noun's original construction should be marked yes. The two raters assigned yes to the original construction 80% and 95% of the time, respectively. These can be viewed as the upper bound of system performance if we assume there can be only one correct construction. A stricter ceiling can be obtained by considering how often the yes⋆ constructions overlap with the original one[4]. The yes⋆ items overlapped with the original 72% and 83% of the time, respectively. These relatively high figures serve as evidence of the quality of the annotation.

Both raters frequently found more than one valid construction — 18% of the time if only considering yes⋆, and 49% if considering both yes and yes⋆. The implication for automatic system evaluation is that one could potentially underestimate a system's performance by as much as 18%, if not more. For both raters, the most frequent combinations of yes⋆ constructions were {*null-plural,the-plural*}, {*a-singular,the-singular*}, {*a-singular,null-plural*}, and {*the-singular,the-plural*}. From the standpoint of designing a grammar-checking system, a system should be less confident in proposing change from one construction to another within the same construction pair.

5 Sources of Variation in Agreement

It is unavoidable for agreement levels to be affected by how accepting or imaginative the individual raters are. In the NO-CONTEXT stage, Rater 1 awarded more yes's than Rater 2, perhaps attributable to her ability to imagine suitable contexts for some of the less likely constructions. In the IN-CONTEXT stage, Rater 1 used yes more sparingly than Rater 2. This reflects their different judgments on where to draw the line among constructions in the grey area between acceptable and unacceptable.

We have identified, however, two other factors that led to variations in the agreement level: the amount of context available, and the distribution of the noun itself in the English language. Careful consideration of these factors should lead to better agreement.

Availability of Context As shown in Table 4, for both raters, the context sharply reduced the number of correct constructions. The confusion tables

[2]For practical reasons, we have restricted the study of context to *direct anaphoric references*, i.e., where the same head noun has already occurred in the context.

[3]In theory, there should be 420 items, but some of the configurations in Table 3 are missing for certain nouns, mostly the low-entropy ones.

[4]Both raters assigned yes⋆ to an average of 1.2 constructions per item.

for the two raters are shown in Table 5. For the NO-CONTEXT stage, they agreed 78% of the time and the kappa statistic was 0.55. When context is provided, human judgment can be expected to increase. Indeed, for the IN-CONTEXT stage, agreement rose to 82% and kappa to 0.60[5].

Another kind of context — previous mention of the noun — also increases agreement. Among nouns originally constructed with "*the*", the kappa statistics for those with direct anaphora was 0.63, but only 0.52 for those without[6].

Most previous research on article-number prediction has only used features extracted from the target sentence. These results suggest that using features from a wider context should improve performance.

Noun Construction Entropy For the low-entropy nouns, we found a marked difference in human agreement among the constructions depending on their frequencies. For the most frequent construction in a noun's distribution, the kappa was 0.78; for the four remaining constructions, which are much more rare, the kappa was only 0.52[7]. They probably constitute "border-line" cases for which the line between `yes` and `no` was often hard to draw, leading to the lower kappa.

Entropy can thus serve as an additional factor when a system decides whether or not to mark a usage as an error. For low-entropy nouns, the system should be more confident of predicting a frequent construction, but more wary of suggesting the other constructions.

6 Conclusions & Future Work

We conducted a human annotation exercise on article and noun number usage, making two observations that can help improve the evaluation procedure for this task. First, although the context substantially reduces the range of acceptable answers, there are still often multiple acceptable answers given a context; second, the level of human agreement is influenced by the availability of the context and the distribution of the noun's constructions.

These observations should help improve not only the evaluation procedure but also the design of error correction systems for articles and noun number. Entropy, for example, can be incorporated into the estimation of a system's confidence in its prediction. More sophisticated contextual features, beyond simply noting that a noun has been previously mentioned (Han et al., 2005; Lee, 2004), can also potentially reduce uncertainty and improve system performance.

Acknowledgments

We thank the two annotators, Sarah Ohls and Waverely VanWinkle.

References

C. Brockett, W. Dolan, and M. Gamon. 2006. Correcting ESL Errors using Phrasal SMT Techniques. *Proc. ACL*.

N.-R. Han, M. Chodorow, and C. Leacock. 2005. Detecting Errors in English Article Usage by Non-Native Speakers. *Natural Language Engineering*, 1(1):1–15.

K. Knight and I. Chander. 1994. Automated Postediting of Documents. *Proc. AAAI*.

J. R. Landis and G. G. Koch. 1977. The Measurement of Observer Agreement for Categorical Data. *Biometrics* 33:159–174.

J. Lee. 2004. Automatic Article Restoration. *Proc. HLT-NAACL Student Research Workshop*.

J. Lee and S. Seneff. 2006. Automatic Grammar Correction for Second-Language Learners. *Proc. Interspeech*.

G. Minnen, F. Bond, and A. Copestake. 2000. Memory-based Learning for Article Generation. *Proc. CoNLL/LLL*.

J. Peng and K. Araki. 2005. Correction of Article Errors in Machine Translation Using Web-based Model. *Proc. IEEE NLP-KE*.

A. Ratnaparkhi, J. Reynar, and S. Roukos. 1994. A Maximum Entropy Model for Prepositional Phrase Attachment. *Proc. ARPA Workshop on Human Language Technology*.

J. Tetreault and M. Chodorow. 2008. Native Judgments of Non-Native Usage. *Proc. COLING Workshop on Human Judgements in Computational Linguistics*.

J. Turner and E. Charniak. 2007. Language Modeling for Determiner Selection. *Proc. HLT-NAACL*.

[5]This kappa value is on the boundary between "moderate" and "substantial" agreement on the scale proposed in (Landis and Koch, 1977). The difference between the kappa values for the NO-CONTEXT and IN-CONTEXT stages approaches statistical significance, $z = 1.71, p < 0.10$.

[6]The difference between these kappa values is statistically significant, $z = 2.06, p < 0.05$.

[7]The two kappa values are significantly different, $z = 4.35, p < 0.001$.

Stand-off TEI Annotation: the Case of the National Corpus of Polish

Piotr Bański
Institute of English Studies
University of Warsaw
Nowy Świat 4, 00-497 Warszawa, Poland
pkbanski@uw.edu.pl

Adam Przepiórkowski
Institute of Computer Science
Polish Academy of Sciences
Ordona 21, 01-237 Warszawa, Poland
adamp@ipipan.waw.pl

Abstract

We present the annotation architecture of the National Corpus of Polish and discuss problems identified in the TEI stand-off annotation system, which, in its current version, is still very much unfinished and untested, due to both technical reasons (lack of tools implementing the TEI-defined XPointer schemes) and certain problems concerning data representation. We concentrate on two features that a stand-off system should possess and that are conspicuously missing in the current TEI Guidelines.

1 Introduction

The present paper presents the National Corpus of Polish (NCP).[1] The project is a joint undertaking of a consortium consisting of institutions that created their own large corpora of Polish in the past (see (Przepiórkowski et al., 2008) for details); these corpora formed the initial data bank of the corpus. The intended size of the corpus is one billion (10^9) tokens and as such, at the time of completion in 2010, the NCP is going to be one of the largest corpora available, possibly the largest corpus featuring multiple levels of linguistic annotation of various kinds. Currently, a hand-verified one-million-token subcorpus is being completed, and a basic, automatically created 430-million-token demo is available online at http://nkjp.pl/.

The project uses an extended morphosyntactic tagset with several years of practical use behind it in one of the source corpora (cf. http://korpus.pl/) and an open-source query engine with a powerful, regex-based language and a graphical front-end.

Section 2 of this paper talks about the encoding format adopted for the corpus, section 3 presents its general architecture, and section 4 discusses the reasons for, and our implementation of, the suggested NCP enhancements to the TEI Guidelines.

2 The encoding format: stand-off TEI

The Text Encoding Initiative (TEI Consortium, 2007) has been at the forefront of text annotation and resource interchange for many years. It has influenced corpus linguistic practices in at least three related ways. Firstly, the formalism itself, in the mature form, has been used to mark up linguistic corpora, e.g. the British National Corpus. An early application of the TEI, the Corpus Encoding Standard (CES; see http://www.cs.vassar.edu/CES/), together with its XML version, XCES (http://www.xces.org/), have served as *de facto* standards for corpus encoding in numerous projects. Finally, the experience gained in creating and using XCES (together with e.g. the feature-structure markup of the TEI) has served as a foundation for the Linguistic Annotation Format (LAF, Ide and Romary, 2007), within ISO TC37 SC4. LAF promises to provide a standard interchange format for linguistic resources of many diverse kinds and origins.

The relationship between the TEI (especially in its stand-off version) and the LAF is straightforward. Both are implemented in XML, which makes transduction between a rigorous TEI format and the LAF "dump" (pivot) format mostly a matter of fleshing out some data structures.

3 NCP – general architecture

Stand-off annotation is by now a well-grounded data representation technique, pioneered by the CES and continuing to be the foundation of the LAF. In short, it assumes that the source text in the corpus, ideally kept in an unannotated form and in read-only files, is the root of a possibly multi-file system of data descriptions (each description focusing on a distinct aspect of the

[1] The Polish name of the corpus is *Narodowy Korpus Języka Polskiego*, hence the abbreviation NKJP, used in web addresses and namespace identifiers.

Proceedings of the Third Linguistic Annotation Workshop, ACL-IJCNLP 2009, pages 64–67,
Suntec, Singapore, 6-7 August 2009.

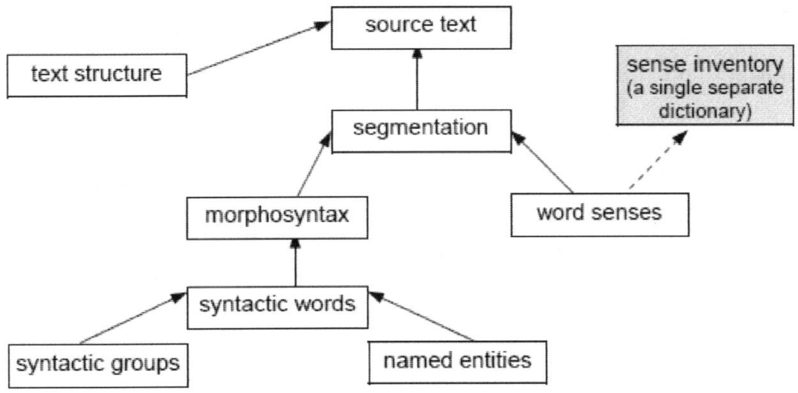

Figure 1: The logical data structure of the NCP

source data). The source text is typically accompanied by a level of primary segmentation, which may be the lowest-level XML layer of annotation. The other files form a possibly multi-leaved and multi-leveled hierarchy referencing either the level of primary segmentation, or higher order levels of description. The NCP follows these guidelines to the extent allowed by the TEI schema.

Each corpus text is kept in a separate directory together with the annotation files that reference it directly or indirectly, and with the header that is included by all these files. Contents of an example directory are shown below.

(1)
```
text.xml
header.xml
ann_morphosyntax.xml
ann_segmentation.xml
ann_structure.xml
```

All of these files contain TEI documents (or, in the case of header.xml, proper subsets thereof). They form a hierarchy of annotation levels, as presented in Figure 1. The text.xml file is the root, referenced by the layer of text structure (providing markup from the paragraph level upwards) and the layer of segmentation. The segmentation layer is further referenced by the layer of morphosyntactic information and word-sense annotation. The morphosyntactic level, in turn, is the basis for the level identifying syntactic words, which constitutes the foundation upon which the levels identifying syntactic chunks and named entities are built.

In text.xml, the normalized source text is divided in paragraph-sized chunks (enclosed in anonymous blocks, <ab>, to be further refined in the text-structure level of annotation).[2] It also includes two headers: the main corpus header, which encodes information relevant to all parts of the corpus, and the local header, which records the information on the particular text and its annotations.

The segmentation file provides what the LAF calls the base segmentation level that is further used as the basis for other kinds of annotation. It is implemented as a TEI document with <seg> elements that contain XInclude instructions (see example (4) in the next section). As such, it may serve both as a separate annotation layer or as a merged structure, after the inclusion directives are resolved. Crucially, in the latter case, which is the default with many parsers, the XPointer indexing information is lost. We shall come back to this issue in section 4.1.

The text-structure layer is defined similarly to the segmentation layer. Other annotation layers replace the mechanism of XInclude with XLink, in the way advocated by the XCES.

The morphosyntactic layer of annotation consists of a series of <seg> elements that contain TEI feature structures (i) providing basic information on the segment, (ii) specifying the possible interpretations as identified by the morphological analyser, and (iii) pointing at the morpho-

[2] Ideally, as mentioned above, the primary text should be stored without markup, and the segmentation layer should constitute the lowest-level XML document. This is exactly what the LAF-encoded American National Corpus does, requiring dedicated tools for merging plain text corpus files with the segmentation documents. Unfortunately, this is where we reach the technological boundary of the XInclude system: it is unable to reference substrings in a plain text file, due to a weakly motivated ban on the concurrent presence of @parse="text" attribute and the @xpointer attribute. We therefore enclose the source text in anonymous blocks (<ab>) that we can easily address with XPointers. An anonymous reviewer agrees that the lack of a single, immutable text file is a serious weakness of this system and notes that being able to derive plain text from markup is no remedy. This may constitute either a case for XLink, or an argument for lifting the @parse/@pointer ban.

syntactic description selected by the disambiguating agent.

The higher-order annotation layers also contain feature structures, which usually point at the selected segments of annotation layers that are one level lower, and identify their function within the given data structure.

4 Enhancements to the TEI stand-off recommendations

In this section, we first illustrate a case where the stand-off annotation system as advocated by the TEI loses information on the boundedness of segments, and then move on to illustrate a different issue stemming from the lack of a neutral bracket-like element in the TEI markup.

4.1 Identification of bound segments

Segmentation of Polish texts is not a trivial matter, partially because of the person-number enclitics – elements that can attach to almost any part of the clause, while being functionally related to the main verb. Segmenting them together with their hosts, apart from being a methodologically bad move, would greatly increase the complexity of the linguistic analysis built on top of such segmentations. The diamond in (2) below marks alternative positions where the 2nd Person Plural clitic (separated by a vertical bar) may appear. All of the resulting sentences have the same interpretation.

(2) Czemu|ście znowu♦ wczoraj♦ Piotra♦ gonili♦?
why|2pl again yesterday Piotr chased.prt
"Why did you chase Piotr yesterday again?"

Yet another group of segmentation problems concerns compounds, right-headed (3a) or coordinative (3b).

(3) a. żółto|czerwony materiał
yellow|red fabric
"yellowish red fabric"
b. żółto-czerwony materiał
"yellow and red fabric"

Inline markup of the above examples preserves information on which segment is bound (attached to the preceding one) or free-standing. This is due to the whitespace intervening between the <seg> elements in this kind of markup.

When, however, stand-off markup using the XInclude mechanism is applied here, complications arise. The segmental level of annotation with unresolved inclusions provides clear hints about the status of segments. This is due to XPointer offsets, as can be seen in (4) below, which is an example assuming that the adjective *żółto-czerwony* is the first word in an <ab> element bearing the @xml:id attribute set to "t1".[3]

(4)
```
<seg xml:id="segm_1.1-seg">
 <xi:include href="text.xml"
 xpointer="string-range(t1,0,5)"/></seg>
<seg xml:id="segm_1.2-seg">
 <xi:include href="text.xml"
 xpointer="string-range(t1,5,1)"/></seg>
<seg xml:id="segm_1.3-seg">
 <xi:include href="text.xml"
 xpointer="string-range(t1,6,8)"/></seg>
```

However, after inclusions are resolved, all of the offset information is lost, because all the @xpointer attributes (indeed, all the <xi:include> elements) are gone and all that remains is a sequence of <seg> elements such as `<seg>żółto</seg><seg>-</seg><seg>czerwony</seg>`.

While, in many cases, information on boundedness could be recovered from the morphosyntactic description of the given segment, this does not resolve the issue because, firstly, a recourse to morphosyntactic annotation layer in order to recover information lost in the segmentation layer is methodologically flawed (in some cases, it is perfectly imaginable that a text is only accompanied by the segmentation layer of annotation and nothing else), and, secondly, morphosyntactic identity will not resolve all such cases. Consider the example of *żółto-czerwony* "yellow and red": the segment *czerwony* here is bound, but both graphically and morphosyntactically identical to the frequent free-standing segment *czerwony* "red".

In order to accommodate such cases, we have defined an additional attribute of the <seg> element, @nkjp:nps, where "nkjp:" is the non-TEI namespace prefix, while "nps" stands for "no preceding space" and its default value is "false". Naturally, this attribute solves issues specific to Polish and similar languages. It can be generalized and become something like @bound={"right", "left", "both"}, and in this shape, get incorporated into the TEI Guidelines.

4.2 Structural disjunction between alternative segmentations

One strategy to handle alternative segmentations, where the choice is between a single segment of

[3]Note that here, string-range() is an XPointer **scheme** defined by the TEI. It is not to be confused with the string-range() **function** of the XPointer xpointer() scheme, defined by the W3C permanent working draft at http://www.w3.org/TR/xptr-xpointer/.

the form <seg>*New York*</seg> and a sequence of two separate segments, <seg>*New*</seg> and <seg>*York*</seg>, is to perform radical segmentation (always segment *New* and *York* separately) and provide an extra layer of alternative segmentation that may link the two parts of the name into a single unit. This is what we do in the creation of the annotation level of syntactic words that may, e.g., need to link the three segments of *żółto-czerwony* above into a single unit, because this is how they function in the syntactic representation.

In some cases, however, radical segmentation may create false or misleading representations, and Polish again provides numerous relevant examples. Sometimes bound segments, such as the person-number clitics illustrated in (2) above, are homophonous with parts of words.

(5)	a.	miał|em had.prt|1sg	vs. miałem fines.instr.sg
	b.	czy|m whether|1sg	vs. czym what.instr
	c.	gar|ście pot.acc|2pl	vs. garście fistful.nom.pl

One may attempt to defend radical segmentation for case (a) on the not-so-innocent assumption that segmenting tools might sometimes reach inside morphological complexes and separate affixes from stems, rather than clitics from their hosts. However, examples (b) and (c) show that this is not a feasible approach here: the Instrumental *czym* in (b) is monomorphemic, and the segmentation of *garście* "fistfuls" into *gar-* and *-ście* is likewise false, because the putative segment division would fall inside the root *garść*.

Thus, radical segmentation is not an available strategy in the case at hand. What we need instead is a way to express the disjunction between a sequence such as <seg>*miał*</seg> <seg>*em*</seg> (cf. (5a)) on the one hand, and the single segment <seg>*miałem*</seg> on the other. It turns out that the TEI has no way of expressing this kind of relationship structurally.

The TEI Guidelines offer the element <choice>, but it can only express disjunction between competing segments, and never between sequences thereof. The Guidelines also offer two non-structural methods of encoding disjunction. The first uses the element <join> (which is an ID-based equivalent of a bracket – it points to the segments that are to be virtually joined) and the element <alt> (which points at encoding alternatives). The other utilizes the @exclude attribute, which, placed in one segment, points at elements that are to be ignored if the segment at hand is valid (the excluded elements, in turn, point back at the excluding segment).

Recall that the intended size of the corpus is one billion segments. Tools that process corpora of this size should not be forced to backtrack or look forward to see what forms a sequence and what the alternative to this sequence is. Instead, we need a simple structural statement of disjunction between sequences. The solution used by the NCP consists in (i) adding an element meant to provide a semantically neutral bracket (<nkjp:paren>) and (ii) including <nkjp:paren> in the content model of <choice>. Note that this representation can be readily converted into the pivot format of the LAF:

(6)
```
<choice>
  <seg>miałem</seg>
  <nkjp:paren>
        <seg>miał</seg>
        <seg nkjp:nps="true">em</seg>
  </nkjp:paren>
</choice>
```

5 Conclusion

We have presented the TEI-P5-XML architecture of the National Corpus of Polish and identified some weak points of the TEI-based stand-off approach: the impossibility of keeping the primary text unannotated in the XInclude system, the loss of information on segment-boundedness, and the absence of a structural statement of disjunction between sequences of segments (this last issue is also due to the lack, among the numerous detailed markup options provided by the TEI, of a semantically neutral bracket-like element whose only role would be to embrace sequences of elements).

We are grateful to the two anonymous LAW-09 reviewers for their helpful comments.

References

Ide, N. and L. Romary. (2007). Towards International Standards for Language Resources. In Dybkjaer, L., Hemsen, H., Minker, W. (eds.), Evaluation of Text and Speech Systems, Springer, 263-84.

Przepiórkowski, A., R. L. Górski, B. Lewandowska-Tomaszczyk and M. Łaziński. (2008). Towards the National Corpus of Polish. In the proceedings of the 6th Language Resources and Evaluation Conference (LREC 2008), Marrakesh, Morocco.

TEI Consortium, eds. 2007. TEI P5: Guidelines for Electronic Text Encoding and Interchange. Version 1.2.0. Last updated on February 1st 2009. TEI Consortium.

Committed Belief Annotation and Tagging

Mona T. Diab
CCLS
Columbia U.
mdiab@cs.columbia.edu

Lori Levin
LTI
CMU
lsl@cs.cmu.edu

Teruko Mitamura
LTI
CMU
teruko+@cs.cmu.edu

Owen Rambow
CCLS
Columbia U.
rambow@ccls.columbia.edu

Vinodkumar Prabhakaram
CS
Columbia U.

Weiwei Guo
CS
Columbia U.

Abstract

We present a preliminary pilot study of belief annotation and automatic tagging. Our objective is to explore semantic meaning beyond surface propositions. We aim to model people's cognitive states, namely their beliefs as expressed through linguistic means. We model the strength of their beliefs and their (the human) degree of commitment to their utterance. We explore only the perspective of the author of a text. We classify predicates into one of three possibilities: committed belief, non committed belief, or not applicable. We proceed to manually annotate data to that end, then we build a supervised framework to test the feasibility of automatically predicting these belief states. Even though the data is relatively small, we show that automatic prediction of a belief class is a feasible task. Using syntactic features, we are able to obtain significant improvements over a simple baseline of 23% F-measure absolute points. The best performing automatic tagging condition is where we use POS tag, word type feature AlphaNumeric, and shallow syntactic chunk information CHUNK. Our best overall performance is 53.97% F-measure.

1 Introduction

As access to large amounts of textual information increases, there is a strong realization that searches and processing purely based on surface words is highly limiting. Researchers in information retrieval and natural language processing (NLP) have long used morphological and (in a more limited way) syntactic analysis to improve access and processing of text; recently, interest has grown in relating text to more abstract representations of its propositional meaning, as witnessed by work on semantic role labeling, word sense disambiguation, and textual entailment. However, there are more levels to "meaning" than just propositional content. Consider the following examples, and suppose we find these sentences in the *New York Times*:[1]

(1) a. GM will lay off workers.

b. A spokesman for GM said GM will lay off workers.

c. GM may lay off workers.

d. The politician claimed that GM will lay off workers.

e. Some wish GM would lay of workers.

f. Will GM lay off workers?

g. Many wonder if GM will lay off workers.

If we are searching text to find out whether GM will lay off workers, all of the sentences in (1) con-

[1] In this paper, we concentrate on written communication, and we use the terms *reader* and *writer*. However, nothing in the approach precludes applying it to spoken communication.

Proceedings of the Third Linguistic Annotation Workshop, ACL-IJCNLP 2009, pages 68–73,
Suntec, Singapore, 6-7 August 2009.

tain the proposition LAYOFF(GM,WORKERS). However, the six sentences clearly allow us very different inferences about whether GM will lay off workers or not. Supposing we consider the *Times* a trustworthy news source, we would be fairly certain with (1a) and (1b). (1c) suggests the *Times* is not certain about the layoffs, but considers them possible. When reading (1d), we know that someone else thinks that GM will lay off workers, but that the *Times* does not necessarily share this belief. (1e), (1f), and (1g) do not tell us anything about whether anyone believes whether GM will lay off workers.

In order to tease apart what is happening, we need to refine a simple IR-ish view of text as a repository of propositions about the world. We use two theories to aid us. The first theory is that in addition to facts about the world (GM will or will not lay off workers), we have facts about people's cognitive states, and these cognitive states relate their bearer to the facts in the world. (Though perhaps there are only cognitive states, and no facts about the world.) Following the literature in Artificial Intelligence (Cohen and Levesque, 1990), we can model cognitive state as beliefs, desires, and intentions. In this paper, we are only interested in beliefs (and in distinguishing them from desires and intentions). The second theory is that communication is intention-driven, and understanding text actually means understanding the communicative intention of the writer. Furthermore, communicative intentions are intentions to affect the reader's cognitive state – his or her beliefs, desires, and/or intentions. This view has been worked out in the text generation and dialog community more than in the text understanding community (Mann and Thompson, 1987; Hovy, 1993; Moore, 1994).

In this paper we are interested in exploring the following: we would like to recognize what the text wants to make us believe about various people's cognitive states, including the speaker's. As mentioned, we are only interested in people's belief. In this view, the result of text processing is not a list of facts about the world, but a list of facts about different people's cognitive states.

This paper is part of an on-going research effort. The goals of this paper are to summarize a pilot annotation effort, and to present the results of initial experiments in automatically extracting facts about people's beliefs from open domain running text.

2 Belief Annotation

We have developed a manual for annotating belief, which we summarize here. For more detailed information, we refer to the cited works. In general, we are interested in the writer's intention as to making us believe that various people have certain beliefs, desires, and intentions. We simplify the annotation in two ways: we are only interetsed in beliefs, and we are only interested in the writer's beliefs. This is not because we think this is the only interesting information in text, but we do this in order to obtain a manageable annotation in our pilot study. Specifically, we annotate whether the writer intends the reader to interpret a stated proposition as the writer's strongly held belief, as a proposition which the writer does not believe strongly (but could), or as a proposition towards which the writer has an entirely different cognitive attitude, such as desire or intention. We do not annotate subjectivity (Janyce Wiebe and Martin, 2004; Wilson and Wiebe, 2005), nor opinion (for example: (Somasundaran et al., 2008)): the nature of the proposition (opinion and type of opinion, statement about interior world, external world) is not of interest. Thus, this work is orthogonal to the extensive literature on opinion detection. And we do not annotate truth: real-world (encyclopedic) truth is not relevant.

We have three categories:

- Committed belief (CB): the writer indicates in this utterance that he or she believes the proposition. For example, *GM has laid off workers*, or, even stronger, *We know that GM has laid off workers.*

  A subcase of committed belief concerns propositions about the future, such as *GM will lay off workers.* People can have equally strong beliefs about the future as about the past, though in practice probably we have stronger beliefs about the past than about the future.

- Non-committed belief (NCB): the writer identifies the propositon as something which he or she could believe, but he or she happens not to have a strong belief in. There are two subcases. First, there are cases in which the writer makes clear that the belief is not strong, for example by using a modal auxiliary:[2] *GM may lay off workers.* Second, in reported speech, the writer is not signaling to us what he or she believes about the reported speech: *The politician claimed that GM will lay off workers.* However, sometimes, we can use the speech act verb to infer the writer's attitude,[3] and we can use our own knowledge

[2]The annotators must distinguish epistemic and deontic uses of modals.

[3]Some languages may also use grammatical devices; for

to infer the writer's beliefs; for example, in *A GM spokesman said that GM will lay off workers*, we can assume that the writer believes that GM intends to lay off workers, not just the spokesman. However, this is not part of the annotation, and all reported speech is annotated as NCB. Again, the issue of tense is orthogonal.

- Not applicable (NA): for the writer, the proposition is not of the type in which he or she is expressing a belief, or could express a belief. Usually, this is because the proposition does not have a truth value in this world (be it in the past or in the future). This covers expressions of desire (*Some wish GM would lay of workers*), questions (Will GM lay off workers? or *Many wonder if GM will lay off workers*, and expressions of requirements (*GM is required to lay off workers* or *Lay off workers!*).

This sort of annotation is part of an annotation of all "modalities" that a text may express. We only annotate belief. A further complication is that these modalities can be nested: one can express a belief about someone else's belief, and one may be strong and the other weak (*I believe John may believe that GM will lay off workers*). At this phase, we only annotate from the perspective of the writer, i.e. what the writer of the text that is being annotated believes.

The annotation units (annotatables) are, conceptually, propositions as defined by PropBank (Kingsbury et al., 2002). In practice, annotators are asked to identify full lexical verbs (whether in main or embedded clauses, whether finite or non-finite). In predicative constructions (*John is a doctor/in the kitchen/drunk*), we ask them to identify the nominal, prepositional, or adjectival head rather than the form of *to be*, in order to also handle small clauses (*I think [John an idiot]*).

The interest of the annotation is clear: we want to be able to determine automatically from a given text what beliefs we can ascribe to the writer, and with what strengths he or she holds them. Across languages, many different linguistic means are used to denote this attitude towards an uttered proposition, including syntax, lexicon, and morphology. To our knowledge, no systematic empirical study exists for English, and this annotation is a step towards that goal.

---

example, in German, the choice between indicative mood and subjunctive mood in reported speech can signal the writer's attitude.

3 Related Work

The work of Roser et al. (2006) is, in many respects, very similar to ours. In particular, they are concerned with extracting information about people's beliefs and the strength of these beliefs from text. However, their annotation is very different from ours. They extend the TimeML annotation scheme to include annotation of markers of belief and strength of belief. For example, in the sentence *The Human Rights Committee regretted that discrimination against women persisted in practice*, TimeML identifies the events associated with the verbs *regret* and *persist*, and then the extension to the annotation adds the mark that there is a "factive" link between the *regret* event and the *persist* event, i.e., if we regret something, then we assume the truth of that something. In contrast, in our annotation, we directly annotate events with their level of belief. In this example, we would annotate *persist* as being a committed belief of the Human Rights Committee (though in this paper we only report on beliefs attributed to the writer). This difference is important, as in the annotation of Roser et al. (2006), the annotator must analyze the situation and find evidence for the level of belief attributed to an event. As a result, we cannot use the annotation to *discover* how natural language expresses level of belief. Our annotation is more primitively semantic: we ask the annotators simply to annotate meaning (does X believe the event takes place), as opposed to annotating the linguistic structures which express meaning. As a consequence of the difference in annotation, we cannot compare our automatic prediction results to theirs.

Other related works explored belief systems in an inference scenario as opposed to an intentionality scenario. In work by (Ralf Krestel and Bergler, 2007; Krestel et al., 2008), the authors explore belief in the context of news media exploring reported speech where they track newspaper text looking for elements indicating evidentiality. The notion of belief is more akin to finding statements that support or negate specific events with different degrees of support. This is different from our notion of committed belief in this work, since we seek to make explicit the intention of the author or the speaker.

4 Our Approach

4.1 Data

We create a relatively small corpus of English manually annotated for the three categories: CB, NCB, NA. The data covers different domains and genres from newswire, to blog data, to email correspondence, to letter correspondence, to transcribed dialogue data. The data comprises 10K words of running text. 70% of the data was doubly annotated comprising 6188 potentially annotatable tokens. Hence we had a 4 way manual classification in essence between NONE, CB, NCB, and NA. Most of the confusions between NONE and CB from both annotators, for 103 tokens. The next point of disagreement was on NCB and NONE for 48 tokens.They disagreed on NCB and CB for 32 of the tokens. In general the interannotator agreements were high as they agreed 95.8% of the time on the annotatable and the exact belief classification.[4] Here is an example of a disagreement between the two annotators, *The Iraqi government has* **agreed** *to let Rep Tony Hall visit the country next week to assess a humanitarian crisis that has festered since the Gulf War of 1991 Hall's office said Monday.* One annotator deemed "agreed" a CB while the other considered it an NCB.

4.2 Automatic approach

Once we had the data manually annotated and revised, we wanted to explore the feasibility of automatically predicting belief states based on linguistic features. We apply a supervised learning framework to the problem of both identifying and classifying a *belief* annotatable token in context. This is a three way classification task where an annotatable token is tagged as one of our three classes: Committed Belief (CB), Non Committed Belief (NCB), and Not Applicable (NA). We adopt a chunking approach to the problem using an Inside Outside Beginning (IOB) tagging framework for performing the identification and classification of belief tokens in context. For chunk tagging, we use YamCha sequence labeling system.[5] YamCha is based on SVM technology. We use the default parameter settings most importantly the kernels are polynomial degree 2 with a c value of 0.5.

We label each sentence with standard IOB tags. Since this is a ternary classification task, we have 7 different tags: B-CB (Beginning of a committed belief chunk), I-CB (Inside of a committed belief chunk), B-NCB (Beginning of non committed belief chunk), I-NCB (Inside of a non committed belief chunk), B-NA (Beginning of a not applicable chunk), I-NA (Inside a not applicable chunk), and O (Outside a chunk) for the cases that are not annotatable tokens. As an example of the annotation, a sentence such as *H*all said he wanted to investigate reports from relief agencies that a quarter of Iraqi children may be suffering from chronic malnutrition. will be annotated as follows: {Hall_O said_B-CB he_O wanted_B-NCB to_B-NA investigate_I-NA reports_O from_O relief_O agencies_O that_O a_O quarter_O of_O Iraqi_O children_O may_O be_O suffering_B-NCB from_O chronic_O malnutrition_O.}

We experiment with some basic features and some more linguistically motivated ones.

CXT: Since we adopt a sequence labeling paradigm, we experiment with different window sizes for context ranging from $-/+2$ tokens after and before the token of interest to $-/+5$.

NGRAM: This is a character n-gram feature, explicity representing the first and last character ngrams of a word. In this case we experiment with up to $-/+4$ characters of a token. This feature allows us to capture implicitly the word inflection morphology.

POS: An important feature is the Part-of-Speech (POS) tag of the words. Most of the annotatables are predicates but not all predicates in the text are annotatables. We obtain the POS tags from the TreeTagger POS tagger tool which is trained on the Penn Treebank.[6]

ALPHANUM: This feature indicates whether the word has a digit in it or not or if it is a non alphanumeric token.

VerbType: We classify the verbs as to whether they are modals (eg. may, might, shall, will, should, can, etc.), auxilliaries (eg. do, be, have),[7] or regular verbs. Many of our annotatables occur in the vicinity of modals and auxilliaries. The list of modals and auxilliaries is deterministic.

Syntactic Chunk (CHUNK): This feature explicitly models the syntactic phrases in which our tokens occur. The possible phrases are shallow syntactic representations that we obtain from the TreeTagger chunker:[8] ADJC (Adjective Chunk), ADVC (Adverbial Chunk), CONJC (Conjunctional Chunk), INTJ (Interjunctional Chunk), LST (numbers 1, 2,3 etc), NC (Noun Chunk), PC (Prepositional Chunk), PRT (off,out,up etc), VC (Verb Chunk).

5 Experiments and Results

5.1 Conditions

Since the data is very small, we tested our automatic annotation using 5 fold cross validation

[4] This interannotator agreement number includes the NONE category.

[5] http://www.tado-chasen.com/yamcha

[6] http://www.ims.uni-stuttgart.de/projekte/corplex/TreeTagger/

[7] We realize in some of the grammar books auxilliaries include modal verbs.

[8] http://www.ims.uni-stuttgart.de/projekte/corplex/TreeTagger/

where 10% of the data is set aside as development data, then 70% is used for training and 20% for testing. The reported results are averaged over the 5 folds for the Test data for each of our experimental conditions.

Our baseline condition is using the tokenized words only with no other features (TOK). We empirically establish that a context size of $-/+3$ yields the best results in the baseline condition as evaluated on the development data set. Hence all the results are yielded from a CXT of size 3.

The next conditions present the impact of adding a single feature at a time and then combining them. It is worth noting that the results reflect the ability of the classifier to identify a token that could be annotatable and also classify it correctly as one of the possible classes.

5.2 Evaluation Metrics

We use $F_{\beta=1}$ (F-measure) as the harmonic mean between (P)recision and (R)ecall. All the presented results are the F-measure. We report the results separately for the three classes CB, NCB, and NA as well as the overall global F measure for any one condition averaged over the 5 folds of the TEST data set.

5.3 Results

In Table 1 we present the results yielded per condition including the baseline TOK and presented for the three different classes as well as the overall F-measure.

All the results yielded by our experiments outperform the baseline TOK. We highlight the highest performing conditions in Table 1: TOK+AlphaNum+POS +CHUNK, TOK+AN+POS and TOK+POS. Even though all the features independently outperform the baseline TOK in isolation, POS is the single most contributing feature. The least contributing factor independently is the AlphaNumeric feature AN. However combining AN with character Ngram NG yields better results than using each of them independently. We note that adding NG to any other feature combination is not helpful, in fact it seems to add noise rather than signal to the learning process in the presence of more sophisticated features such as POS or syntactic chunk information. Adding the verbtype VT explicitly as a feature is not helpful for all categories, it seems most effective with CB. As mentioned earlier we deterministically considered all modal verbs to be modal. This might not be the case for all modal auxilliaries since some of them are used epistemically while others deontically, hence our feature could be introducing an element of noise. Adding syntactic chunk information helps boost the results by a small margin from 53.5 to 53.97 F-measure. All the results seem to suggest the domination of the POS feature and it's importance for such a tagging problem. In general our performance on CB is the highest, followed by NA then we note that NCB is the hardest category to predict. Examining the data, NCB has the lowest number of occurrence instances in this data set across the board in the whole data set and accordingly in the training data, which might explain the very low performance. Also in our annotation effort, it was the hardest category to annotate since the annotation takes more than the sentential context into account. Hence a typical CB verb such as "believe" in the scope of a reporting predicate such as "say" as in the following example *Mary said he believed the suspect with no qualms*. The verb *believed* should be tagged NCB however in most cases it is tagged as a CB. Our syntactic feature CHUNK helps a little but it does not capture the overall dependencies in the structure. We believe that representing deeper syntactic structure should help tremendously as it will model these relatively longer dependencies.

We also calculated a confusion matrix for the different classes. The majority of the errors are identification errors where an annotatable is considered an O class as opposed to one of the 3 relevant classes. This suggests that identifying the annotatable words is a harder task than classification into one of the three classes, which is consistent with our observation from the interannotator disagreements where most of their disagreements were on the annotatable tokens, though a small overall number of tokens, 103 tokens out of 6188, it was the most significant disagreement category. We find that for the TOK+POS condition, CBs are mistagged as un-annotatable O 55% of the time. We find most of the confusions between NA and CB, and NCB and CB, both cases favoring a CB tag.

6 Conclusion

We presented a preliminary pilot study of belief annotation and automatic tagging. Even though the data is relatively tiny, we show that automatic prediction of a belief class is a feasible task. Using syntactic features, we are able to obtain significant improvements over a simple baseline of 23% F-measure absolute points. The best performing automatic tagging condition is where we use POS tag, word type feature AlphaNumeric, and shallow syntactic chunk information CHUNK. Our best overall performance is 53.97% F-measure.

	CB	NA	NCB	Overall F
TOK	25.12	41.18	13.64	30.3
TOK+NG	33.18	42.29	5	34.25
TOK+AN	30.43	44.57	12.24	33.92
TOK+AN+NG	37.17	42.46	9.3	36.61
TOK+POS	54.8	59.23	13.95	**53.5**
TOK+NG+POS	43.15	50.5	**22.73**	44.35
TOK+AN+POS	54.79	58.97	22.64	**53.54**
TOK+NG+AN+POS	43.09	54.98	18.18	45.91
TOK+POS+CHUNK	55.45	57.5	15.38	52.77
TOK+POS+VT+CHUNK	53.74	57.14	14.29	51.43
TOK+AN+POS+CHUNK	55.89	**59.59**	22.58	**53.97**
TOK+AN+POS+VT+CHUNK	**56.27**	58.87	12.9	52.89

Table 1: Final results averaged over 5 folds of test data using different features and their combinations: NG is NGRAM, AN is AlphaNumeric, VT is verbtype

In the future we are looking at ways of adding more sophisticated deep syntactic and semantic features using lexical chains from discourse structure. We will also be exploring belief annotation in Arabic and Urdu on a parallel data collection since these languages express evidentiality in ways that differ linguistically from English. Finally we will explore ways of automatically augmenting the labeled data pool using active learning.

Acknowledgement

This work was supported by grants from the Human Language Technology Center of Excellence. Any opinions, findings, and conclusions or recommendations expressed in this material are those of the authors and do not necessarily reflect the views of the sponsor.

References

Philip R. Cohen and Hector J. Levesque. 1990. Rational interaction as the basis for communication. In Jerry Morgan Philip Cohen and James Allen, editors, *Intentions in Communication*. MIT Press.

Eduard H. Hovy. 1993. Automated discourse generation using discourse structure relations. *Artificial Intelligence*, 63:341–385.

Rebecca Bruce Matthew Bell Janyce Wiebe, Theresa Wilson and Melanie Martin. 2004. Learning subjective language. In *Computational Linguistics, Volume 30 (3)*.

Paul Kingsbury, Martha Palmer, and Mitch Marcus. 2002. Adding semantic annotation to the Penn TreeBank. In *Proceedings of the Human Language Technology Conference*, San Diego, CA.

Ralf Krestel, Sabine Bergler, and René Witte. 2008. Minding the Source: Automatic Tagging of Reported Speech in Newspaper Articles. In European Language Resources Association (ELRA), editor, *Proceedings of the Sixth International Language Resources and Evaluation (LREC 2008)*, Marrakech, Morocco, May 28–30.

William C. Mann and Sandra A. Thompson. 1987. Rhetorical Structure Theory: A theory of text organization. Technical Report ISI/RS-87-190, ISI.

Johanna Moore. 1994. *Participating in Explanatory Dialogues*. MIT Press.

René Witte Ralf Krestel and Sabine Bergler. 2007. Processing of Beliefs extracted from Reported Speech in Newspaper Articles. In *International Conference on Recent Advances in Natural Language Processing (RANLP 2007)*, Borovets, Bulgaria, September 27–29.

Saurí Roser, Marc Verhagen, and James Pustejovsky. 2006. Annotating and Recognizing Event Modality in Text. In FLAIRS 2006, editor, *In Proceedings of the 19th International FLAIRS Conference*, Melbourne Beach, Florida, May 11-13.

Swapna Somasundaran, Janyce Wiebe, and Josef Ruppenhofer. 2008. Discourse level opinion interpretation. In *Proceedings of the 22nd International Conference on Computational Linguistics (Coling 2008)*, pages 801–808, Manchester, UK, August. Coling 2008 Organizing Committee.

Theresa Wilson and Janyce Wiebe. 2005. Annotating attributions and private states. In *Proceedings of the Workshop on Frontiers in Corpus Annotations II: Pie in the Sky*, pages 53–60, Ann Arbor, Michigan, June. Association for Computational Linguistics.

Annotation of Sentence Structure; Capturing the Relationship among Clauses in Czech Sentences

Markéta Lopatková and **Natalia Klyueva** and **Petr Homola**
Charles University in Prague, Institute of Formal and Applied Linguistics
Malostranské nám. 25, 118 00 Prague 1, Czech Republic
{lopatkova,kljueva,homola}@ufal.mff.cuni.cz

Abstract

The goal of the presented project is to assign a structure of clauses to Czech sentences from the Prague Dependency Treebank (PDT) as a new layer of syntactic annotation, a layer of clause structure. The annotation is based on the concept of segments, linguistically motivated and easily automatically detectable units. The task of the annotators is to identify relations among segments, especially relations of super/subordination, coordination, apposition and parenthesis. Then they identify individual clauses forming complex sentences.

In the pilot phase of the annotation, 2,699 sentences from PDT were annotated with respect to their sentence structure.

1 Motivation

Syntactic analysis of natural languages is the fundamental requirement of many applied tasks. Parsers providing automatic syntactic analysis are quite reliable for relatively short and simple sentences. However, their reliability is significantly lower for long and complex sentences, especially for languages with free word order; see, e.g., Zeman (2004) for results for Czech.

The identification of the overall structure of a sentence prior to its full syntactic analysis is a natural step capable to reduce the complexity of full analysis. Such methods brought good results for typologically different languages, see e.g. Jones (1994) for English or Ohno et al. (2006) for Japanese.

The goal of the presented project is to annotate a structure of clauses to Czech sentences from the Prague Dependency Treebank. The main idea is to reuse the already existing language resource and to enrich it with a new layer of annotation, a layer of clause structure.

We exploit a concept of segments, easily automatically detectable and linguistically motivated units, as they were defined by Lopatková and Holan (2009).[1] The annotation captures relationship among segments, especially subordination, coordination, apposition and parenthesis. Based on segment annotation, the annotators identify clauses forming (complex) sentences: they group the segments constituting individual clauses of complex sentences.

Contrary to such well known approaches as e.g. chunking, see Abney (1991) or cascaded parsing, see Abney (1995) or Ciravegna and Lavelli (1999), which group individual tokens into more complex structures as nominal or prepositional phrases, i.e., in a bottom-up direction, the proposed approach aims at determining a hierarchy of sentence parts in a 'top-down' way. Such an approach is quite novel not only for Czech, it has not been reported for other Slavic languages.

Prague Dependency Treebank[2] (PDT), see Hajič et al. (2006) is a large and elaborated corpus with rich syntactic annotation of Czech newspaper texts. As the dependency-based framework has been adopted for PDT, the treebank contains explicit information on mutual relations among individual tokens (words and punctuation marks). However, relations among more complex units, esp. clauses, are not explicitly indicated, see Figure 1.

Syntactic information stored in PDT can be used (at least to some extent) for the identification of individual clauses as well. Let us refer to the experiments described in the papers by Lopatková and Holan (2009) and Krůza and Kuboň (2009). In both papers, the authors designed well-developed procedures for identifying segments and their mu-

[1] We adopt the basic idea of segments introduced and used by Kuboň (2001) and Kuboň et al. (2007). We slightly modify it for the purposes of the annotation task.

[2] http://ufal.mff.cuni.cz/pdt2.0/

Proceedings of the Third Linguistic Annotation Workshop, ACL-IJCNLP 2009, pages 74–81,
Suntec, Singapore, 6-7 August 2009.

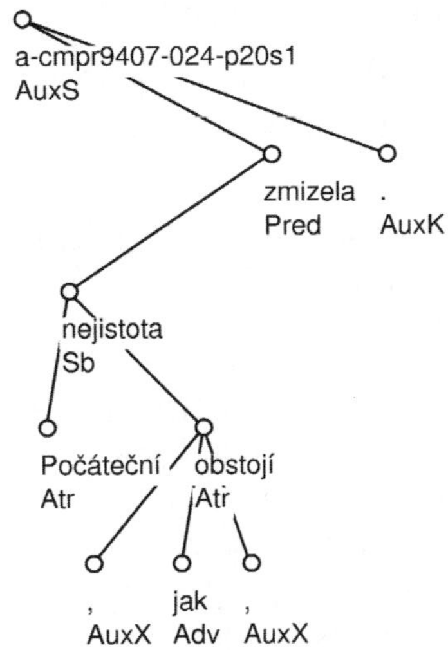

Figure 1: Analytic tree of the sentence *Počáteční nejistota, jak obstojí, zmizela.* 'Initial uncertainty, how it-will-do, vanished.'

tual relationship from the analytical layer of PDT (i.e., layer of surface syntax). However, they either do not identify individual clauses in the complex sentence at all, or their procedural definition of clause does not exactly model what a human would consider as a clause.

The previous experiments brought clear specification of segmentation charts describing the relation among individual segments. The results showed that for further research it is necessary to work with a large set of precisely annotated data. It has turned out that such data cannot be obtained without extensive (semi)manual annotation of a large set of sentences, see Lopatková and Holan (2009) and Krůza and Kuboň (2009).

In this article, we present a project of manual annotation of sentence structure for complex Czech sentences. In Section 2, we introduce the basic concepts, esp. boundaries, segments and segmentation charts. Then we focus on the annotation of basic linguistic phenomena (Section 3). Section 4 brings specification of a data format and an editor used for the annotation. Lastly, basic statistics of the annotated data are presented (Section 5).

2 Boundaries, Segments and Segmentation Charts

The aim of the annotation is to explicitly describe relations among clauses of (complex) Czech sentences. We focus on the annotation of (part of) Czech sentences from PDT. We take advantage of morphological analysis (m-layer) and partially also surface syntactic analysis (a-layer) stored in PDT.

All tokens from PDT are disjunctively divided into two groups – ordinary words and segment boundaries. *Segment boundaries* are tokens and their sequences that divide a sentence into individual units referred to as segments. As segment boundaries, the following tokens are considered:

- punctuation marks: comma, colon, semicolon, question mark, exclamation mark, dash (all types), opening and closing bracket (all kinds), and quotation mark (all types);
- coordinating conjunctions: tokens morphological tag of which starts with the pair `J^` (e.g., *a* 'and', *ale* 'but', *nebo* 'or', *neboť* 'for', *ani* 'nor'), see Hajič (2004).

After the identification of boundaries, the input sentence is partitioned into individual segments – a *segment* is understood as a maximal non-empty sequence of tokens that does not contain any boundary.

This concept of the linear segment serves as a good basis for the identification of clauses, basic linguistically motivated syntactic units. We will see that a single *clause* consists of one or more segments; one or more clauses then create(s) a *complex sentence* (see Section 3).

The definition of segments adopted in this project is based on very strict rules for punctuation in Czech. Generally, beginning and end of each clause must be indicated by a boundary, i.e., sentence boundary (usually fullstop, question mark or exclamation mark), punctuation (mostly comma) or conjunction. This holds for embedded clauses as well. In particular, there are only very few exceptions to a general rule saying that there must be some kind of a boundary between two finite verb forms of meaningful verbs.

Segmentation Charts and Clauses

Relations between clauses, esp. super- or subordination, coordination, apposition or parenthesis, are described by so called *segmentation charts* (one or more, if we allow for ambiguous annotation) – segmentation chart captures the levels of embedding for individual segments, as described below.

The principal idea of the segmentation chart is quite clear – it can be described by the following basic instructions. (In examples, segments are marked by square brackets [and $]_k$, where k is a level of embedding. In addition, individual clauses are marked by brackets { and $\}_j$, where j is an index of a particular clause.)

Main clauses. Segments forming all main clauses[3] of a complex sentence belong to the basic level (level of embedding 0), as in the following sentence.
{[*O studium byl velký zájem*]$_0$}$_1$, {[*v přijímacích pohovorech bylo vybráno 50 uchazečů*]$_0$}$_2$. 'There was a lot of interest in studying, 50 applicants were selected in admission interviews.'

Dependent clauses. Segments forming clauses that depend on clauses at the k-th level obtain level of embedding $k + 1$ (i.e., the level of embedding for subordinated segments is higher than the level of segments forming their governing clause).
{[*Potom zjistíte*]$_0$}$_1$, {[*že vám nikdo nedá vstupní vízum*]$_1$}$_2$. 'Then you realize that nobody gives you entrance visa.'

Coordination and apposition. Segments forming coordinated sentence members and coordinated clauses occupy the same level. The same holds for apposition.
{[*Hra nám jde*]$_0$}$_1$ *a* {[*forma stoupá*]$_0$}$_1$. 'We're getting on well in game and our form improves.'

Parenthesis. Segments forming parenthesis (e.g., sequence of wordforms within brackets) obtain the level of embedding $k + 1$ if the level of their neighboring segments is k .
{[*Návrh mluví o dvou letech u mužů*]$_0$ *(* {[*zvyšuje věk z 60 na 62*]$_1$}$_1$ *) a* [*o čtyřech letech u žen*]$_0$}$_2$. 'The proposal mentions two years for men (it raises the age from 60 to 62) and four years for women.'

Although this basic idea of segmentation charts seems simple, it appears that – working with 'real data' from newspaper corpus – detailed annotation guidelines are necessary for good and consistent annotation of specific linguistic phenomena and especially for their combination. We focus on some of them in the following section.

[3]As a main clauses, such clauses are considered that are *syntactically / formally* independent, see also Section 3.

3 Annotation of Complex Sentences

Segments can be divided into two main groups, mutually independent and mutually related segments.

Mutually independent segments. Mutually independent segments are, e.g., segments forming two dependent clauses, each of them modifying (different) part of the main clause, as segments *do které se zamiloval* 'with whom he felt in love' and *který zazvonil* 'that rang' in the following sentence.
{[*Marie*]$_0$, {[*do které se zamiloval*]$_1$}$_1$, {[*když ji potkal*]$_2$}$_2$, [*zvedla telefon*]$_0$}$_3$, {[*který zazvonil*]$_1$}$_4$. 'Mary, with whom he felt in love when he met her, answered the phone that rang.'

Such segments can have the same level of embedding (as the above mentioned segments) or they can belong to clauses with different levels of embedding (as segments *když ji potkal* 'when he met her' and *který zazvonil* 'that rang').

Mutually related segments. Mutually related segments either belong to different levels of embedding – they are super- or subordinated, we focus on this group in the following Section 3.1, or they have the same level of embedding – this type is described in Section 3.2.

Let us stress here that the segment annotation is based on *formally expressed* structures rather than on their semantic interpretation. For example, we do not interpret text enclosed in brackets – whether it is semantically apposition, sentence member or independent sentence part, see also the discussion in Kuboň et al. (2007). We annotate such text as parenthetical segment(s) on a lower level compared to the neighboring segments.

The annotators have been instructed to *disambiguate annotated* sentences – if more readings of a particular sentence are possible, they should respect the reading rendered in PDT.

3.1 Subordination and Superordination

The super- or subordinated mutually related segments capture primarily **relations between governing and dependent clauses**.

Identification of subordinated status of a particular segment is based on morphological properties of tokens forming this segment, i.e., on the presence of a token with 'subordinating function'.

'Subordinating tokens' are especially of the following types:

- subordinating conjunctions (e.g., *aby* 'in order that', *dokud* 'till', *kdyby* 'if', *protože* 'because', *přestože* 'although', *že* 'that');
- relative/interrogative pronouns and some types of numerals (e.g., *kdo* 'who', *co* 'what', *jaký* 'which', *kolik* 'how many');
- pronominal adverbs (e.g., *kde* 'where', *kdy* 'when', *jak* 'how', *proč* 'why').

In Czech, a subordinating token is usually at the beginning of the segment, as in the following sentence (marked pronoun *který* 'who' serves as subordinating token here).
{[*Klejch*]$_0$, {[*který dal devět ze dvanácti ligových gólů Zlína*]$_1$}$_1$, [*má vydatné pomocníky*]$_0$}$_2$. 'Klejch who scored nine goals out of twelve for Zlín has good helpers.'

A particular subordinated segment can precede or follow its superordinated segment or it can be placed between two superordinated segments (in case of a governing clause with embedded dependent clause, as in the previous example).

In addition to governing and dependent clauses, there are also other constructions that should evidently be captured as subordinated segments, especially:

- Segments representing **direct speech**:
  „{[*Například závod Ejpovice projevil zájem dokonce o 150 pracovníků*]$_1$}$_1$,"{[*uvedl Ladislav Vltavský*]$_0$}$_2$. ' "For example Ejpovice company showed interest in 150 workers," said Ladislav Vltavský.'
- Some types of **parenthesis**, esp. those marked by brackets:
  {[*Guido Reni*]$_0$ ({[*1575 až 1642*]$_1$}$_1$ [*byl vynikající figuralista*]$_0$}$_2$. 'Guido Reni (1575 to 1642) was an outstanding figural painter.' In such cases, parenthetical expressions are captured as separate clauses even if they consist of fragmental expression.

3.2 Segments on the Same Level and Identification of Clauses

We can identify three main groups of structures where segments are mutually related and they share the same level of embedding:

- **segments forming a clause with embedded dependent clause**, as the attributive dependent clause in the following example.
  {[*V případě*]$_0$, {[*že se nedovoláte*]$_1$}$_1$, [*vytočte číslo ve večerních hodinách znovu*]$_0$}$_2$. 'In case that you will not succeed, redial the number again in the evening.'
- coordinated segments (see the corresponding section below);
- others, esp. segments in apposition and some types of parenthesis (see the corresponding section below).

In particular, segments on the same level – unlike the super/subordinated ones – can form a single clause. For the annotators, the important task is to *identify individual clauses*. They group those segments that constitute individual clauses of a complex sentence and thus mark them as a single syntactic unit of a higher level, level of clause structures. (Let us recall that clauses are marked here by brackets { and }$_j$ where j is an index of a particular clause).

Coordination of sentence members and coordination of clauses

The relation of coordination may occur between two (or more) sentence members or between two (or more) clauses, be they main clauses or dependent ones. The syntactic position of coordinated units is 'multiplied', that is, they share the same syntactic relations to other sentence members. The annotators have to identify segments containing coordinated sentence members and put them together into a single clause; coordinated clauses are marked as separate clauses sharing the same level of embedding,[4] as in the following sentence.
{[*Český prezident apeloval na Čechy*]$_0$ *a* [*na Němce*]$_0$}$_1$, {[*aby odpovědně zacházeli s minulostí*]$_1$}$_2$ *a* {[*aby posouvali vpřed dialog*]$_1$ *a* [*spolupráci.*]$_1$}$_3$ 'Czech president appealed to Czechs and Germans that they should treat their history responsibly and improve their mutual dialogue and cooperation.' This complex sentence consists of five segments (marked by [and]), which form three clauses (marked by { and }), namely one main clause (on the zero level) and two coordinated dependent clauses (first embedded level), see also Figure 3.

[4] In PDT, coordination of sentence members and coordination of clauses are not distinguished (at the analytical layer).

Segmentation is purely linear (on segment follows another); after the identification of segments, they are grouped into the clauses. As we have seen, a single clause consists (prototypically) of one or more segments. This is fully true for semantically and syntactically complete sentences, i.e. sentences without ellipses of different kinds.

Let us mention one construction where clauses identified by the annotators (i.e., clauses based on segments) do not conform with the linguistic intuition, namely the case of coordinated clauses sharing one (or more) sentence member(s) or a syntactic particle. We interpret such cases as cases of ellipses, i.e., a shared sentence member or particle is supposed to belong only to one of the clauses and to be elided in the second clause. Thus a shared sentence member or particle is annotated only as a part of one clause.

{[*Neopravuje se*]$_0$}$_1$ *a* {[*neinvestuje*]$_0$}$_2$, {[*peníze stačí jen na běžný provoz*]$_0$}$_1$. 'They do not renovate nor invest, there is enough money only for routine operation.' (The underlined reflexive particle belongs to both verbs *opravovat* 'to renovate' and *investovat* 'to invest' (reflexive passive forms of the verbs); in the segmentation chart, it is marked as a part of the first clause *Neopravuje se* and elided in the second clause *neinvestuje*.)

On the other hand, a basic rule was adopted saying that a single finite verb form indicates a single clause, i.e., verb constitutes (a core of) a sentence[5] (providing that other formal labels as, e.g., brackets do not indicate more levels). This rule implies that if the shared sentence member is a predicate, then the particular segments are joined together into a single clause, as in the following example.

{[*Petr přišel včera*]$_0$ *a* [*babička dneska*]$_0$}$_1$. 'Petr came yesterday and my grandma today.'

Other constructions

Apposition is a construction where the same 'idea' is rendered in different ways (the latter being an explanatory equivalent of the former), both having the same syntactic relation to other sentence members (e.g., a name and a function of particular person, as in the following sentence).

{[*Oznámil to Václav Havel*]$_0$, [*president České republiky*]$_0$}$_1$. 'It was announced by Václav Havel, president of the Czech Republic.'

Following PDT, apposition is treated in the same way as coordination as the members of an apposition are considered to share (multiple) syntactic position in a sentence (like in the case of coordination).

Contrary to PDT, **parenthesis** without explicit/unambiguous formal mark, as e.g. brackets, is annotated as segment(s) on the same level as its/their neighboring segments.

{[*Před smrtí*]$_0$, {[*neznámo proč*]$_0$}$_1$, [*si koupil tramvajenku*]$_0$}$_2$. 'Before dying, nobody knows why, he bought a tram pass.'

Again, parenthetical expressions are captured as separate clauses even if they consist of fragmental expression.

Semi-direct speech, i.e., direct speech without quotation marks (or other formal label(s)) is annotated as segment(s) on the same level as the segment containing a governing verb. The reason is quite evident – there is no formally expressed indication of subordination in the segment(s) creating a semi-direct speech.

{[*Přijde později*]$_0$}$_1$, {[*ohlásil doma Pavel*]$_0$}$_2$. 'I will be late, said Pavel.'

4 Data Format and Editor for Segment Annotation

4.1 PML Data Format

The *Prague Markup Language*[6] (PML), see Pajas and Štěpánek (2006) is an XML-based domain language which has been developed and is used as primary data format for PDT (version 2.0).

The PDT 2.0 data consist of one non-annotated word layer (w-layer) and three layers of annotation: morphological (m-layer), analytical (a-layer) and tectogrammatical (t-layer). In PML, individual layers of annotation can be stacked one over another in a stand-off fashion and linked together as well as with other data resources in a consistent way.

We use two layers in our annotation editor, namely the m-layer and the a-layer. The m-layer provides the word form, lemma and tag for every token. The a-layer represents syntactic relations between tokens, resulting in an analytical tree. For the segment annotation, only information on analytical functions of tokens is used – it helps the annotators in their decisions on the appropriate level of embedding and in disambiguation if more readings of a particular sentence are possible.

[5] The account for this decision lies in the verb-centric character of dependency syntax traditionally used for Czech.

[6] http://ufal.mff.cuni.cz/pdt2.0/doc/pdt-guide/en/html/ch03.html#a-data-formats

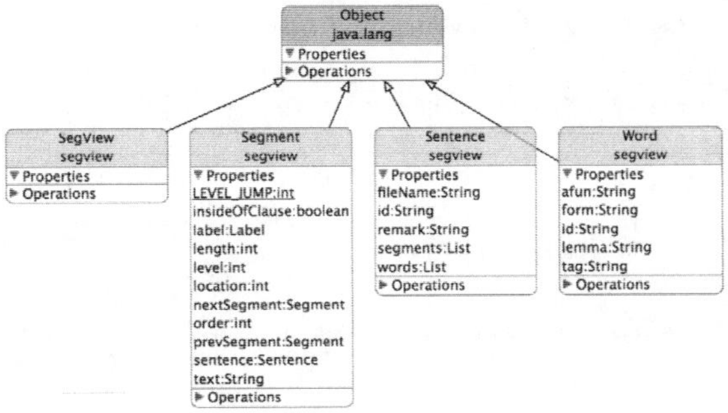

Figure 2: Class hierarchy of SegView annotation editor.

The output of the segment annotation is stored as a new layer of annotation, the seg-layer.

4.2 SegView Annotation Editor

The SegView annotation editor is implemented completely in Java because of its cross-platformity and availability of rich libraries. The presentation layer is implemented in the class *MainWindow* using the standard Swing library. As for the data layer, the editor works with files in the PML format (see Section 4.1). The model representing the core of the implementation comprises three classes: Sentence, Word and Segment, Figure 2.

After launching the editor, the user has the possibility to select multiple files to annotate. After the selection, the program directly reads the files and creates an internal representation with the instances of the three aforementioned classes. The manual annotation is saved in files with the extension `.seg`.

The screenshot of SegView editor is shown in Figure 3.

5 Basic Statistics and Conclusion

We have described the pilot phase of the segment annotation, during which 2,699 sentences from PDT were annotated with respect to their sentence structure.[7] Table 1 summarizes the amount of annotated data and gives statistics on number of processed segments and clauses.

The most frequent annotation patterns are presented in Table 2 showing the most common types of sentences and relation among their clauses (only patterns with more than 100 sentence instances are listed).

[7]We have focused on the sentences from data/full/amw/train2 portion of the PDT data.

# sentences	2,699
# segments	7,975
# clauses	5,003
max segments in clause	27
max clauses in sentence	11
max levels of embedding	4

Table 1: Basic statistics of the annotated texts.

sentences	segments	clauses	max level
783	1	1	0
298	2	1	0
195	2	2	1
148	3	2	1
123	3	1	0
111	2	2	0

Table 2: Distribution of segments and clauses.

The most frequent type of annotated sentence consists of one segment only (and thus one clause), then comes the case where two segments form a single clause. The third position is for sentences with two segments, each forming an individual clause, where one of them depends on the other). The fourth case represents sentences formed by two clauses, one either depending on the other or forming a parenthesis. The fifth and sixth line represent sentences with segments on the same level, e.i., with sentence members in coordination or apposition and with coordinated clauses, respectively. (The most common cases listed in the table represent 61.5% of the annotated sentences; the rest has more complicated structures.)

Future work

We focus on the inter-annotator agreement on a reasonable large set of data now to check the consistency between the human annotators. Then the annotation will continue – the goal is to cover 10% of sentences from PDT with assigned sentence structure.

We expect the use of the manually annotated data for testing tools and hypotheses on possible sentence structures. The proposed amount of data is comparable with the standard PDT testing data. We do not foreseen the use of this set of segmentation charts for training statistically-based tool(s) for an automatic identification of sentence structures.

The set of precisely annotated data allows us to solidly compare and evaluate the already existing automatic segmentation tools processing either the raw texts or syntactically annotated trees, see Krůza and Kuboň (2009) and Lopatková and

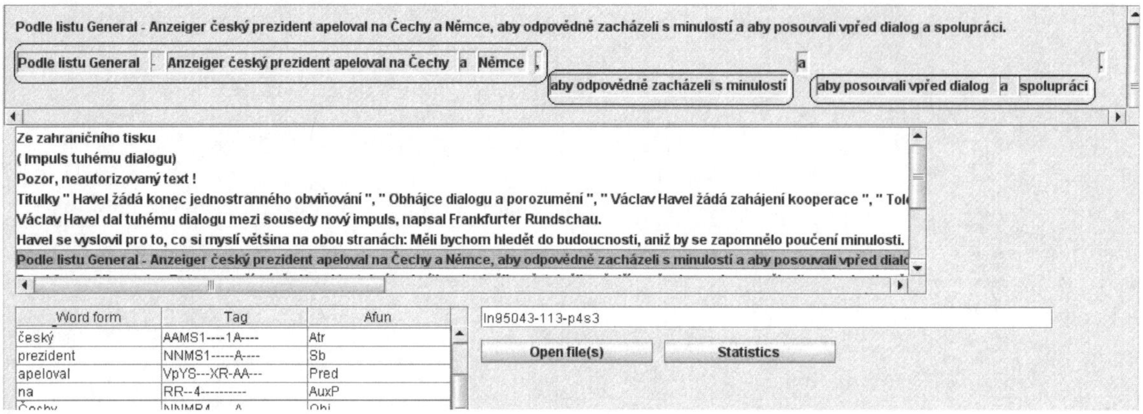

Figure 3: SegView editor: The segmentation chart for sentence ‘According to the General-Anzeiger, Czech president appealed to Czechs and Germans that they should treat their history responsibly and improve their mutual dialogue and cooperation.’ (clauses marked by ellipses).

Holan (2009). These data also allow us to search for systemic differences between the manual and automatic sentence structure annotation. Then the possibility of further improving the tools will be opened.

The use of data with automatically annotated sentence structure in machine translation system among related languages, as in Homola and Kuboň (2008), is also foreseen.

Acknowledgements

This paper presents the results of the grant of the Grant Agency of Czech Republic No. 405/08/0681. The research is carried out within the project of the Ministry of Education, Youth and Sports of Czech Republic No. MSM0021620838.

References

Steven P. Abney. 1991. Parsing By Chunks. In R. Berwick, S. Abney, and C. Tenny, editors, *Principle-Based Parsing*, pages 257–278. Kluwer Academic Publishers.

Steven P. Abney. 1995. Partial Parsing via Finite-State Cascades. *Journal of Natural Language Engineering*, 2(4):337–344.

Fabio Ciravegna and Alberto Lavelli. 1999. Full Text Parsing using Cascades of Rules: An Information Extraction Procedure. In *Proceedings of EACL’99*, pages 102–109. University of Bergen.

Jan Hajič, Eva Hajičová, Jarmila Panevová, Petr Sgall, Petr Pajas, Jan Štěpánek, Jiří Havelka, and Marie Mikulová. 2006. *Prague Dependency Treebank 2.0*. LDC.

Jan Hajič. 2004. *Disambiguation of Rich Inflection (Computational Morphology of Czech)*. Karolinum Press.

Petr Homola and Vladislav Kuboň. 2008. A hybrid machine translation system for typologically related languages. In David Wilson and Chad Lane, editors, *Proceedings of FLAIRS 2008)*, pages 227–228, Coconut Grove, Florida, USA. AAAI Press.

Bernard E. M. Jones. 1994. Exploiting the Role of Punctuation in Parsing Natural Text. In *Proceedings of the COLING’94*, pages 421–425.

Oldřich Krůza and Vladislav Kuboň. 2009. Automatic Extraction of Clause Relationships from a Treebank. In *Computational Linguistics and Intelligent Text Processing - Proceedings of CICLing 2009*, volume 5449 of *LNCS*, pages 195–206. Springer-Verlag.

Vladislav Kuboň, Markéta Lopatková, Martin Plátek, and Patrice Pognan. 2007. A Linguistically-Based Segmentation of Complex Sentences. In D.C. Wilson and G.C.J. Sutcliffe, editors, *Proceedings of FLAIRS Conference*, pages 368–374. AAAI Press.

Vladislav Kuboň. 2001. *Problems of Robust Parsing of Czech*. Ph.D. thesis, Faculty of Mathematics and Physics, Charles University in Prague.

Markéta Lopatková and Tomáš Holan. 2009. Segmentation Charts for Czech – Relations among Segments in Complex Sentences. In A. H. Dediu, A. M. Ionescu, and C. Martín-Vide, editors, *Proceedings of LATA 2009*, volume 5457 of *LNCS*, pages 542–553. Springer-Verlag.

Tomohiro Ohno, Shigeki Matsubara, Hideki Kashioka, Takehiko Maruyama, and Yasuyoshi Inagaki. 2006. Dependency Parsing of Japanese Spoken Monologue Based on Clause Boundaries. In *Proceedings of COLING and ACL*, pages 169–176. ACL.

Petr Pajas and Jan Štěpánek. 2006. XML-Based Representation of Multi-Layered Annotation in the PDT 2.0. In *Proceedings of LREC 2006 Workshop on Merging and Layering Linguistic Information*, pages 40–47. ELRA.

Daniel Zeman. 2004. *Parsing with a Statistical Dependency Model*. Ph.D. thesis, Charles University in Prague, Prague.

Schema and Variation: Digitizing Printed Dictionaries

Christian Schneiker and **Dietmar Seipel**
Department of Computer Science
University of Würzburg, Germany
{schneiker, seipel}@informatik.uni-wuerzburg.de

Werner Wegstein
Department of Computational Philology
University of Würzburg, Germany
werner.wegstein@uni-wuerzburg.de

Abstract

In this paper we show how to exploit typographical and textual features of raw text for creating a fine–grain XML Schema Markup with special focus on capturing linguistic variation in dictionaries. We use declarative programming techniques and context–free grammars implemented in PROLOG.

1 Introduction

In 1996, Cambridge University Press proudly presented an outstanding milestone in electronic publishing: Samuel Johnson: A Dictionary of the English Language on CD–ROM, edited by Anne McDermott; containing the First Edition 1755 and the significantly revised Fourth Edition 1773 (McDermott, 1996). "The Dictionary is not only the first great work of English lexicography but also a literary and historical resource of immense value, and this electronic edition has been prepared to the highest standards by a team of scholars at the University of Birmingham." (Cambridge University Press Catalogue, 2009)

The announcement highlighted all the key *characteristics of electronic texts*: accessability, completeness, use of multi–media environment, searchability and highest standards applied by scholars, i.e. philological reliability and precision, wrapped in leading edge technology (Gärtner/Wisbey, 1974). Today, more than a decade and at least one electronic product life-cycle later, the CD is still on sale – as far as we could find out unchanged – and has not lost anything of its former value.

In the context of *digitizing* the cultural heritage there is even a strong and growing demand for digitizing research tools like dictionaries (cf., e.g., Gallica Digital Library Charter/Chapter: Time period covered). But, in the field of electronic text editing, requirements grow rapidly and standards develop fast. The users of electronic texts today want to search not only for words, phrases, headwords, quotations, and authors of sources. They would like to get access to and search for *variant forms, grammatical categories, usage indicators* and the structuring of the description of *word senses*, etc., not only in single dictionaries, but – perhaps using a grid environment – in fully connected dictionary networks (cf. the dictionary search, possible within the Trier Dictionary Net and as a TextGrid feature). In the context of these new user scenarios, possibly grid–based, usable for collabortive research and secured safely in longterm archive structures, we try to put fine–grain encoding ideas into practise using Joachim Heinrich Campe's dictionary of the German Language as testbed.

This is one of the reasons why TEXTGRID (2009), the first grid project in German e*Humanities*, funded by the Federal Ministry of Education and Research, chose the Campe Dictionary (1811): 6 volumes with altogether about 6.000 pages and about 140.000 entries, published between 1807 and 1813 as one testbed for their TEXTGRID Lab, a Virtual Research Library. It entails a grid–enabled workbench that will process, analyse, annotate, edit and publish text data for academic research and TEXTGRIDRep, a grid repository for long–term storage. Electronic dictionaries are used in a wide field of new research areas such as the growing community of *eHumanities*. One of the main projects for the German humanities is the community project TEXTGRID, which aims to develop a platform for the collaborative editing, annotation, analysis and publication of texts (TEXTGRID, 2009). According to the TEI Consortium (2009), large text corpora from different epochs have to be parsed and annotated for performing further analysis, such as building a meta–lemma list for the project *interdependencies* between *language* and *genomes*.

In general, there are the following important *prerequisites* for state of the art text encoding in the Humanities. The encoding should use international standards, especially XML and related standards, e.g., TEI P5 with

Proceedings of the Third Linguistic Annotation Workshop, ACL-IJCNLP 2009, pages 82–89,
Suntec, Singapore, 6-7 August 2009.

XML Schema. Also the combination of text and image is necessay. The text capture should aim at reference quality for the encoded text. A fine–grain encoding preserving lexicographical and textual variation without blurring (distorting) the content modelling of XML elements is helpful. Finally, a TEI schema (Relax NG) that is flexible enough to encode variation in lexicographical and textual structures without loosening the grip of the constraints is necessary to define clear cut element content.

In this paper, we present an annotation *workflow* using declarative programming techniques for fine–grain text markup, and we apply it for retro–digitizing a printed version of the Campe Dictionary. Our *parsing* and *annotation* toolkit is based on SWI–PROLOG and the XML query and transformation language FNQUERY (Seipel, 2002), which is implemented in SWI–PROLOG. Using PROLOG technology for parsing and annotating is common in natural language processing. It has, e.g., been used within the Jean Paul project at the Berlin–Brandenburg Academy of Sciences (Seipel et al., 2005), where XML transformations based on FNQUERY turned out to be easier to write than XSLT transformations. A frequently applied method in PROLOG programming is to find the proper level of abstraction and to write suitable macros for frequently occurring patterns in the code; PROLOG even allows to design dedicated special–purpose languages (O'Keefe, 1990). Definite clause grammars have been developed as an abstraction for parsing; this has, e.g., been very successful for parsing controlled natural languages (Fuchs et al., 1994; Fuchs et al., 1995; Schwitter, 2008).

Structure of the Paper. The rest of this paper is organized as follows: In Section 2, we sketch the worklflow for capturing text from the printed text corpus and the semi–automatic error correction to produce a source file for our parsing and annotation toolkit. Section 3 gives an overview of the structure of the different entries in the dictionary; we will explain this structure with the lemma "Der Aal", and we will examplify the variation of entries. The next section shows the annotation of the different lemma variants and the parsing of nouns and verbs. In Section 5, we describe the parsing and annotation of the sense block with citations and references, punctuation, linebreaks and hyphenation. The last section gives a conclusion of our work.

2 The Campe Workflow for Text Capture

Since the Campe Dictionary was written in the early 19th century, the text could not be captured with modern methods of optical character recognition (OCR). Thus, in a first step, the whole corpus had to be doubled–keyed in China. This could also avoid unconsciously corrected spelling variants in old German text, which is frequently done by native speakers. Figure 1 shows the typographical layout of an entry in the Campe Dictionary.

The second step in the text capture workflow was the correction of illegible characters according to the context, as well the manual correction of printing errors provided by the publishers. For providing an efficient and easy–to–undo workflow system for these corrections, we decided to use a semi–automatic process: corrections made by human experts could be repeated on the whole context by using regular expressions in a standard POSIX–Regex environment, and automatic corrections could be done by processing the workflow logfiles of other volumes of the Campe Dictionary.

One of the main concerns in this preprocessing steps was the pre–annotation of abbreviatons used by the author such as etc., s. a. and z. b. or even abbreviated author names like C. for Campe. These had to be checked manually and pre–annotated by a parser written in PROLOG, which can also recognize named entities.

After logging all these corrections in UNIX diff files, the base file for the text conversion into XML could be generated.

3 The Structure of Entries

Within the parsing process, the only annotations available so far for structure recognition were the declaration of the different font sizes used by Joachim Heinrich Campe, the numbering of the line and page breaks in the dictionary, and paragraphs; thus, we found a very limited XML structure in the source file which we used for the first basic transformaions.

In most available dictionaries, each entry is encapsulated in its own paragraph, and thus, it could be easily detected. In the following preannotated example, which is the result of the double key process, an entry is annotated with `paragraph` and is followed by an element `W_2`, which shows the lemma of the entry in a larger font; recognizing both elements is necessary, because there could exist other `paragraph` elements which do not represent entries. This preliminary structure, which is not yet according to TEI, is used as the starting point for the annotation process.

```
<paragraph>
   <W_2>Der Aal</W_2>,
   <W_1>
      des -- es, Mz. die -- e
   </W_1>, ...
</paragraph>
```

The following annotation process derives an encoding based on the TEI P5 Guidelines (TEI Consortium, 2009), using a Relax NG Schema. The encoding structure uses elements to markup an entry of a dictionary, which consists of 1) a form block with inflectional and morphological information and 2) a sense block handling semantic description and references, quotations, related entries, usage as well as notes. In the future,

Der Aal, des —es, Mz. die —e, Verkleinerungswort, das Älchen,
des —s, d. Mz. w. d. Ez. 1) Ein langer, runder, schwärzlicher, in
süßem Wasser lebender Fisch mit einer sehr schlüpfrigen Haut, weß=
halb er nicht leicht festgehalten werden kann, (Muraena anguilla
L.). Von diesem letzten Umstande sind die auf Menschen, welche sehr
gewandt sind, übergetragenen Redensarten hergenommen: Er ist
glatt wie ein Aal; ich konnte ihn nicht fassen, er entschlüpfte mir
wie ein Aal. Der bunte Aal oder die Meerschlange, der Meeraal,
Sandaal. S. d. — Älchen, so nennt man die Würmchen, welche sich
in Essig, Kleister rc. erzeugen, s. Essigälchen, Kleisterälchen. 2)
Ein Backwerk aus Butterteige in Gestalt eines Aales. 3) Die fal=
schen Brüche, welche beim Walken in den Tüchern entstehen.

Figure 1: Excerpt from the Campe Dictionary

Der Aal, | des – es, | Mz. die – e,

Verkleinerungswort, das **Älchen,** | des – s, | d. Mz. w. d. Ez.

1)
Ein langer, runder, schwärzlicher, in süßem Wasser lebender Fisch
mit einer sehr schlüpfrigen Haut, weß=
halb er nicht leicht festgehalten werden kann, (***Muraena anguilla L.***).
Von diesem letzten Umstande sind die auf Menschen, welche sehr gewandt
sind, übergetragenen Redensarten hergenommen: Er ist glatt wie ein ***Aal***;
ich konnte ihn nicht fassen, er entschlüpfte mir wie ein ***Aal***. Der bunte ***Aal***
oder die Meerschlange, der ***Meeraal***, ***Sandaal***. S. d. -- ***Älchen***, so nennt
man die Würmchen, welche sich in Essig, Kleister *(etc.)* erzeugen, s.
Essigälchen, ***Kleisterälchen***

2)
Ein Backwerk aus Butterteige in Gestalt eines ***Aales***.

3) Die fal=
schen Brüche, welche beim Walken in den Tüchern entstehen.

Figure 2: Rendering of an Annotated Entry

this encoding will help us to structure the digital world according to semantic criteria and thus provide an essential basis for constructing reliable ontologies. The annotation of the form block and of the sense block will be described in the Sections 4 and 5, respectively. For both, we have to be able to handle many forms of variation.

The Variation Problem. Lexicographical structures, such as in the Campe Dictionay, can have a lot of variation in entry and headword. E.g., volume 1 has 26.940 entries. The morphological structure is as follows: attributes are used to form elements for the encoding of inflectional, lexical and dialect variation [orthographical, ...], as well as variation in usage. In semantical structures, attributes to elements of the sense block are used to encode semantics.

Variation could, e.g., consist of several headwords linked by conjunctions like "oder" and "und"; the additional headwords are usually printed with a smaller font size than the first headword of the entry. The following example shows such a variant with more than one headword and its appropriate inflectional forms. Abbreviations like "d. Mz. w. d. Ez." or "Mz. s. Ez." are defining a plural form with the same notation as the singular. These inflections have to be recognized and annotated; in the following preannotated example, the singluar form element is repeated.

```
<paragraph>
   <W_2>Der Aalstreif</W_2>,
   <W_1>des -- es, Mz. die -- e</W_1>,
   oder <W_1>der Aalstreifen, des
   ^$0002.18 -- s</W_1>,
   d. <W_1>Mz.</W_1> w. d. Ez.
</paragraph>
```

4 Annotating the Form Block in TEI

We use declarative programming in PROLOG and FN-QUERY as a solution for text conversion in general. In the following, we will illustrate and discuss this for nouns and verbs. This reflects our workflow for annotating the Campe Dictionary, but our approach can also be applied to other dictionaries.

4.1 Nouns

The lemma line "Der Aal" is encoded as follows:

```
<form type="lemma">
   <gramGrp>
      <pos value="noun" />
      <gen value="m" />
   </gramGrp>
   <form type="determiner">
      <orth>Der</orth>
   </form>
   <form type="headword">
      <orth>Aal</orth>
   </form>
</form>
```

For the inflected lemma line "Mz. die – e" we would like to obtain the following TEI structure:

```
<form type="inflected">
   <gramGrp>
      <gram type="number">
      <abbr>Mz.</abbr> </gram>
      <case value="nominative"/>
      <number value="plural"/>
   </gramGrp>
   <form type="determiner">
      <orth>die</orth>
   </form>
   <form type="headword">
      <orth>
         <oVar>
            <oRef>-- e</oRef>
         </oVar>
      </orth>
   </form>
</form>
```

The Parsing Workflow in PROLOG. A sequence "Xs" of form elements is read using the new PROLOG predicate "sequence", which we have implemented. This is a compact way of specifying lists of tokens of the same type (in our case form).

```
campe_parse_headword(Xs) -->
   sequence('*', form, Xs).
```

In standard PROLOG, we would have to encode this in a more verbous way using recursion. In addition, the rule above uses the *definite clause grammar (*DCG*)* notation ("-->") of PROLOG (Gazdar, 1989; O'Keefe, 1990).

For handling complex specifications, a more compact grammar formalism than standard DCG's is needed (Abramson, 1989; Sperberg–McQueen, 2003). For parsing text, we have mainly used an additional grammar formalism ("==>"), which we have developed, the so–called *extended definite clause grammars* (EDCG's); the technical details of EDCG's are described in Schneiker et al. (2009). The following EDCG rules can derive an XML structure that is very close to the TEI for the inflected lemma line above. The rules almost look like the rules of a context–free grammar. A form element consists of a grammar determiner followed by a form headword.

```
form ==>
   grammar_determiner,
   form_headword.
```

A grammar determiner is either a gram element followed by a determiner, or simply a determiner. The alternative is encoded by ";", which stands for "or" in PROLOG. The cut "!" freezes the first alternative, if we detect a gram element; i.e., then a simple determiner is not allowed.

```
grammar_determiner ==>
   ( gram, !, determiner
   ; determiner ).
```

Tokens from the input strean are read using the list notation "[...]". A gram element can only be of the form "Mz.", and a determiner is a token "X", that is a campe determiner. The bracket notation "{...}" does not read from the input stream; instead, it is used for expressing test conditions on the tokens.

```
gram ==> ['Mz.'].
determiner ==> [X],
   { campe_is_determiner(X) }.
```

Finally, a form headword is an orth element, which itself must be the sequence '--' followed by any other token. The wildcard for arbitrary tokens is the anonymous variable "_" of PROLOG.

```
form_headword ==> orth.
orth ==> ['--', _].
```

The 6 EDCG rules above form an EDCG grammar, which can be applied to the stream of input tokens. Thus, we obtain the following XML structure; the tag names are generically taken from the EDCG rules. At this stage, the most important and complicated steps of the parsing have been done. In some further steps of fine tuning, the desired TEI structure can be obtained using XSLT or the FNTRANSFORM component of FNQUERY.

```
<form>
   <grammar_determiner>
      <gram>Mz.</gram>
      <determiner>die</determiner>
   </grammar_determiner>
   <form_headword>
      <orth>   e</orth>
   </form_headword>
</form>
```

Finally, sequences of campe headwords can be parsed using the PROLOG predicate "campe_parse_headword".

Visualization of EDCG Rules. EDCG's could be easily visualized using derivation trees (Figure 3); each non–terminal is shown in an ellipse, the terminals are denoted by rectangles, representing the leaves of the

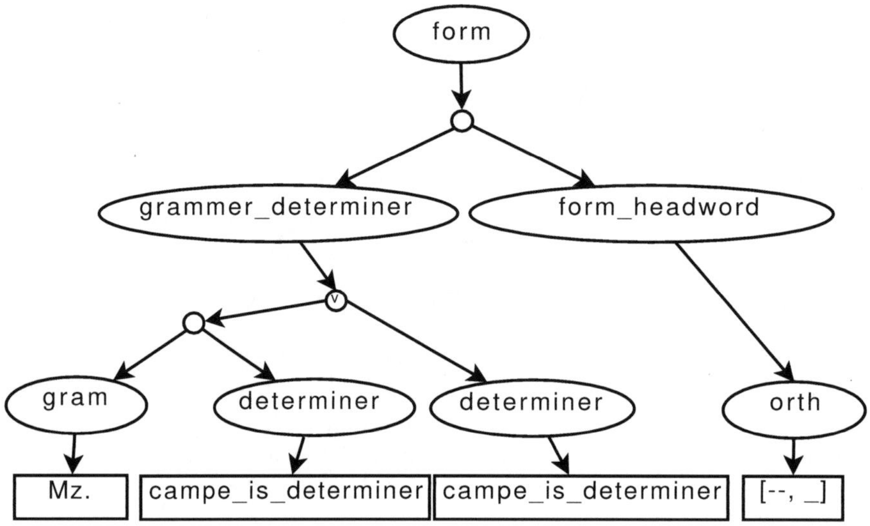

Figure 3: Visualization of the EDCG-rules for parsing forms

tree. Nodes could be either emtpy circles for conjunctions – the "," in the EDCG's – or circles with a "∨" for a logical disjunctions – denoted by ";" in PROLOG.

Handling of Variation. *Grammar* formalisms like DCG's or EDCG's can very well handle variation. The different alternatives can be represented using multiple rules for an XML element or by the alternative construct ";" within a single rule. Moreover, since our grammar formalisms are very compact and thus easily readable, it is possible for the implementer to understand even larger sets of rules and to keep track of the complex structures.

Finally, when several ways of parsing a sequence of tokens are possible, the *backtracking* mechanism of PROLOG explores all alternatives, and it can return all possible results. If later inconsistencies make previous choices of parsing rules impossible, then PROLOG goes back to the last choice point and explores the next alternative. In other programming languages, backtracking has to be implemented explicitely, whereas it is implicit in PROLOG. This overhead makes backtracking more difficult to handle in other programming languages.

4.2 Verbs

Each verb could have additional information about its corresponding part of speech. This information is highlighted with a roman font type in the Campe Dictionary and 8 groups could be isolated:

v. ↦ "verb",
imp. ↦ "impersonal",
intr. ↦ "intransitive",
ntr. ↦ "neuter",
rec. ↦ "reciprocal",
regelm. ↦ "regular",
trs. ↦ 'transitive",
unregelm. ↦ "irregular"

In our base file, we find two different variants of pre–annotated `pos` elements depending on the current processing stage:

```
<A>v.</A>
<A>trs.</A>
<A>unregel.</A>
```

or

```
<hi _>v.</hi>
<hi _>trs.</hi>
<hi _>unregel.</hi>
```

where "_" stands for the attribute/value pair "rend="roman"", which would be annotated as follows:

```
<gramGrp>
   <pos value="verb">
      <abbr>
         <hi rend="roman">v. </hi>
      </abbr>
   </pos>
   <subc value="transitive">
      <abbr>trs.</abbr>
   </subc>
   <subc value="irregular">
      <abbr>unregelm.</abbr>
   </subc>
</gramGrp>
```

Inflected forms are possible for verbs, too.

5 Annotating the Sense Block in TEI

Lists in the sense block can have many different forms and a complex nesting structure, like different sense blocks, citations, hyphenations, references and different font types.

For annotating these sequences and variation, we frequently use the predicate `sequence` of the DDK. Moreover, for parsing lists, we make extensive use of PROLOG's backtracking feature.

5.1 Structuring the Sense Block

The sense block could have a complex nesting structure for defining different meanings of a lemma. In a printed dictionary, often arabic or roman numbers a used for creating a fine–grained structure.

```
<W_2>Abängsten und Abängstigen</W_2>,
<abbr><A>v.</A></abbr>
I) <abbr><A>trs.</A></abbr>
1) Sehr ängsten oder ...
2) Durch Angstmachen zu etwas ...
II) <abbr><A>rec.</A></abbr> ...
<W_1>Das Abängsten,
<lb n="0003.91" /> Abängstigen.
Die Abängstung, Abängstigung</W_1>.
```

Each sense could be part of another subsense, or a new sense could be created. Using PROLOG's backtracking feature, we can find a suitable interpretation of such a structure and annotate it in XML:

```
<sense n="I">
   <lbl type="ordering">I)</lbl> ...
   <sense n="1">
      <lbl type="ordering">1)</lbl> ...
   </sense>
   <sense n="2">
      <lbl type="ordering">2)</lbl> ...
   </sense>
</sense>
```

PROLOG is very well–suited for parsing such nested structures. In general, roman or arabic numbering could be used for a listing at any depth. E.g., the text

```
1)...2)...1)...2)...3)
```

could be structured as a list "`1,2(1,2,3)`" with two elements, where the second element has three subelements, or as a list "`1,2(1,2),3`" with three elements, where the second element has two subelements. Both alternatives can be generated by backtracking. But, if we extend the text by "`...3)`", then our PROLOG approach correctly structures the above prefix in the first way; otherwise there would be two consecutive top–list elements with the same numbering.

5.2 Citations and References

Citations and cross references to other entries are used all over the text corpus.

Citations. Often, citations could be recognized by bible citations and names of authers like *Lessing* or *Richter*, which are often pre–annotated in a larger font size.

```
Um Geld zu fischen, Geld! Um Geld,
^$0004.71 Geld einem Juden
<W_1>abzubangen</W_1>, Geld!
<W_1>Lessing</W_1>.
```

These citations are annotated with a `cit` tag containing the citation as a `quote` tag and the corresponding author in `bibl` and `author`.

```
<cit type="quote">
   <quote> ... </quote>
   <bibl>
      <author n="#Lessing">
         <hi rend="spaced">Lessing</hi>
      </author>
   </bibl>
</cit>
```

References. Cross references to other entries of the Campe Dictionary are usally marked with "S.", "Siehe da" or "s.a." in the sense block.

```
<W_1>Die Abberufung</W_1>. S. d.

<W_1>
   s. Essigälchen, Kleisterälchen
</W_1>
```

These references are annoated with `xr` containing an `lbl` tag with an attribute for marking it as a reference. The target of this references is annotated with `ref` and the corresponding entries as the `target` attribute.

```
<xr>
   <lbl type="reference">s.</lbl>
   <ref target=
   "Essigälchen, Kleisterälchen">
      Essigälchen
      <c type="$,">,</c>
      Kleisterälchen
   </ref>
</xr>
```

5.3 Punctuation

For annotating punctuation in a lemma, which can appear between single headwords, the DCG predicate `campe_punctuation` is used: for each token we check if it is a punctuation mark, and – if so – annotate it with a `c` tag. The meta–predicate `sequence` used in the DCG predicate `campe_punctuations` parses such a list of elements.

```
campe_punctuations(Xs) -->
   sequence('*',
      campe_punctuation, Xs).
```

```
campe_punctuation(X) -->
   ( [A],
     { is_punctuation(A), X = c:[A] }
   ; [X] ).
```

5.4 Linebreaks and Hyphenations

Linear structures like linebreaks and hyphenations are parsed using a combination of FnQuery and DCG's. A linebreak is annotated as an `lb` element; e.g., `^$0001.24` becomes `<lb n="0001.24" />`. In the base file, each hyphenation is labeled with an equals sign as a separator followed by a line break element.

```
auf Muenzen das Zei=
<lb n="0001.24" />
chen der ersten Stadt
```

The hyphenation itself should not be visual later in the rendered representation of the XML document, so we have removed the delimiter symbol and defined this syllable division as an attribute `rend` of the surrounding <w> element. [1]

```
auf Muenzen das
<w rend="Zei-chen">
   Zei=
   <lb n="0001.24"/>
   chen
</w>
der ersten Stadt
```

This sequence could be parsed easily with standard DCG rules in Prolog. The predicate `create_hyphenation_element` creates the hyphenation XML element with the required attribute and content.

```
campe_hyphenations(Xs) -->
   sequence('*',
     campe_hyphenation, Xs).

campe_hyphenation(X) -->
   ( campe_hyphenation_element(X)
   ; [X] ).
```

The difference between standard DCG's (operator ”-->”) and the new EDCG formalism (operator ”==>”) proposed by us is that EDCG's are more compact and more readable, since they hide the output arguments for the derived syntax tree and produce a generic XML structure instead.

5.5 Font Types

The different font types in the Campe Dictionary, like the roman font family or larger fonts sizes for headwords and inflected forms, are pre–annotated in the capturing process.

[1] We would like to remark that for a better text processing an additional attribute is required. This attribute has to represent the correct spelling of the hyphenated word without any delimiter symbol

For transforming these annotations according to our TEI schema, we used our transforming technology FnTransform which is implemented in Prolog. These transformations could also be processed using XSLT stylesheets.

6 Conclusions and Future Work

For retro–digitizing old printed German dictionaries, we have presented a workflow for parsing and annotating these text corpora according to the *Text Encoding Initiative*. With declarative programming techniques like EDCG's and FnQuery, a fast and reliable parser could be implemented. Combined with transformation languages like FnTransform and XSLT, we are able to handle different types of *variation*, such as different types of entries, inflected forms, lemma variants, and flexible XML schemas. To exemplify these annotations, we have processed the Campe Dictionary with 6 volumes and over 140.000 different entries. The techniques, which we have applied to the German Campe Dictionary, could be used for handling other types of text copora as well, and of course also other languages like English or French.

In a current project, a web interface for a free community access is implemented for our toolkit as a *streaming editor*. With this editor, an easy to use graphical user interface gives access to a huge platform for parsing and annotating text corpora for the *eHumanities*, with the ability to reuse the already implemented parser for handling other text corpora. The declarative toolkit DDK, which includes all of the described frameworks, is available on the web.

A subject of future work will be the implementation of an XSLT preprocessor in Prolog to provide a native interface for handling EDCG's within XSLT; the path language XPath is already implemented in our XML toolkit FnQuery.

References

Abramson, H.; Dahl, V.: *Logic Grammars.* Springer, 1989

Blümm, M. (ed.): *Die textsortenspezifische Kernkodierung für Dokumente in TEI P5, TextGrid 2007, 2009.* http://www.textgrid.de/fileadmin/TextGrid/reports/Textsortenspezifische_Kernkodierung_2009.pdf, accessed 30.04.2009

Cambridge University Press Catalogue, *A Dictionary of the English Language on CD–ROM.* http://www.cambridge.org/catalogue/catalogue.asp?isbn=9780521557658, accessed 30.04.2009

Campe, Joachim Heinrich: *Wörterbuch der deutschen Sprache.* 5 Volumes, Braunschweig 1807–1811

Covington, M.A.: *GULP 3.1: An Extension of Prolog for Unification–Based Grammar.* Research

Report AI–1994–06, Artificial Intelligence Center, University of Georgia, 1994

DEREKO: *The German Reference Corpus Project.* http://www.ids-mannheim.de/kl/projekte/korpora/, 2009

FUCHS, N.E.; FROMHERZ, M.P.J.: *Transformational Development of Logic Programs from Executable Specifications – Schema Based Visual and Textual Composition of Logic Programs.* Beckstein, C.; Geske, U. (eds.), Entwicklung, Test und Wartung deklarativer KI–Programme, GMD Studien Nr. 238, Gesellschaft für Informatik und Datenverarbeitung, 1994

FUCHS, N.E.; SCHWITTER, R.: *Specifying Logic Programs in Controlled Natural Language.* Proc. Workshop on Computational Logic for Natural Language Processing (CLNP), 1995

GÄRTNER, K.; WISBEY, R.: *Die Bedeutung des Computers für die Edition altdeutscher Texte.* Kritische Bewahrung. Beiträge zur deutschen Philologie. Festschrift für Werner Schröder zum 60. Geburtstag. Hg. von Ernst–Joachim Schmidt, Berlin, 1974

GAZDAR, G.; MELLISH, C. *Natural Language Processing in Prolog. An Introduction to Computational Linguistics.* Addison–Wesley, 1989

HAUSMANN, F.J.; REICHMANN, O.; WIEGAND, H.E.; ZGUSTA, L. (eds.): *Wörterbücher / Dictionaries / Dictionnaires – Ein internationales Handbuch zur Lexikographie / An International Encyclopedia of Lexicography / Encyclopédie internationale de lexicographie.* Vol. 1 1989; Vol. 2 1990; Vol. 3 1991; Berlin et. al.

HIRAKAWA, H.; ONO, K.; YOSHIMURA, Y.: *Automatic Refinement of a POS Tagger Using a Reliable Parser and Plain Text Corpora.* Proc. 18th International Conference on Computational Linguistics (COLING), 2000

LANDAU, S.: *Dictionaries. The Art and Craft of Lexicography.* 2nd Edition, Cambridge, 2001

LLOYD, J.: *Practical Advantages of Declarative Programming.* CSLI Lecture Notes, Number 10, 1987

MCDERMOTT, A. (ed.): *Samuel Johnson. A Dictionary of the English Language on CD–ROM.* The First and Fourth Edition. Introduction and CD, Cambridge, 1996

O'KEEFE, R.A.: *The Craft of Prolog.* MIT Press, 1990

PEREIRA, F.C.N.; SHIEBER, S.M: *Prolog and Natural Language Analysis.* Lecture Notes, CSLI, Number 10, 1987

SCHNEIKER, C.; SEIPEL, D.; WEGSTEIN, W.; PRÄTOR, K.: *Declarative Parsing and Annotation of Electronic Dictionaries.* Proc. 6th International Workshop on Natural Language Processing and Cognitive Science (NLPCS), 2009

SCHWITTER, R.: *Working for Two: a Bidirectional Grammer for a Controlled Natural Language.* Proc. 28th International Conference on Artificial Intelligence (AI), 2008

SEIPEL, D.: *Processing* XML*–Documents in Prolog.* Proc. 17th Workshop on Logic Programmierung (WLP), 2002

SEIPEL, D.; PRÄTOR, K.: XML *Transformations Based on Logic Programming.* Proc. 18th Workshop on Logic Programming (WLP), 2005

SPERBERG–MCQUEEN, C. M.: *Logic Grammars and XML Schema.* Proc. Conference on Extreme Markup Languages, 2003.

TEI CONSORTIUM (eds.): TEI *P5: Guidelines for Electronic Text Encoding and Interchange.* 2 Vols. Oxford/Providence/Charlotteville/Nancy, 2008 http://www.tei-c.org/release/doc/tei-p5-doc/en/html/index.html, accessed 30.04.2009

TEXTGRID: *A Modular Platform for Collaborative Textual Editing – a Community Grid for the Humanities.* http://www.textgrid.de, 2009

Syntactic annotation of spoken utterances: A case study on the Czech Academic Corpus

Barbora Hladká and Zdeňka Urešová

Charles University in Prague
Institute of Formal and Applied Linguistics
{hladka, uresova}@ufal.mff.cuni.cz

Abstract

Corpus annotation plays an important role in linguistic analysis and computational processing of both written and spoken language. Syntactic annotation of spoken texts becomes clearly a topic of considerable interest nowadays, driven by the desire to improve automatic speech recognition systems by incorporating syntax in the language models, or to build language understanding applications. Syntactic annotation of both written and spoken texts in the Czech Academic Corpus was created thirty years ago when no other (even annotated) corpus of spoken texts has existed. We will discuss how much relevant and inspiring this annotation is to the current frameworks of spoken text annotation.

1 Motivation

The purpose of annotating corpora is to create an objective evidence of the real usage of the language. In general, it is easier to annotate written text – speech must be recorded and transcribed to process it whilst texts are available "immediately"; moreover, written texts usually obey standard grammar rules of the language in questions, while a true transcript of spoken utterances often does not.

The theoretical linguistic research considers the language to be a system of layers (e.g. the Government and Binding theory (Chomsky, 1993), the Functional-Generative Description of the language (Sgall, Hajičová, Panevová 1986)). In order to be a valuable source of linguistic knowledge, the corpus annotation should respect this point of view. The morphological and syntactic layers of annotation represent a standard in today's text corpora, e.g. the Penn Treebank, the family of the Prague Dependency Treebanks, the Tiger corpus for German, etc. Some corpora contain a semantic annotation, such as the Penn Treebank enriched by PropBank and Nombank, the Prague Dependency Treebank in its highest layer, the Penn Chinese or the the Korean Treebanks. The Penn Discourse Treebank contains discourse annotation.

It is desirable that syntactic (and higher) annotation of spoken texts respects the written-text style as much as possible, for obvious reasons: data "compatibility", reuse of tools etc.

A number of questions arise immediately: How much experience and knowledge acquired during the written text annotation can we apply to the spoken texts? Are the annotation instructions applicable to transcriptions in a straightforward way or some modifications of them must be done? Can transcriptions be annotated "as they are" or some transformation of their inner structure into a written text structure must precede the annotation? The Czech Academic Corpus will help us to find out the answers.

2 Introduction

The first attempts to syntactically annotate spoken texts date back to the 1970s and 1980s when the Czech Academic Corpus – CAC (Králík, Uhlířová, 2007) and the Swedish Talbanken (Nilsson, Hall, Nivre, 2005) appeared. Talbanken was annotated with partial phrase structures and grammatical functions, CAC with dependency-based structures and analytical functions. Thus both corpora can be regarded as belonging to the pioneers in corpus linguistics, together with the paper-only "Quirk corpus" (Svartvik, Quirk, 1980; computerized later as the London-Lund Corpus).[1]

[1] When these annotation projects began in the 1960s, there were only two computerized manually annotated corpora available: the Brown Corpus of American Eng-

Proceedings of the Third Linguistic Annotation Workshop, ACL-IJCNLP 2009, pages 90–98,
Suntec, Singapore, 6-7 August 2009.

During the last twenty years the work on creating new treebanks has increased considerably and so CAC and Talbanken have been put in a different light, namely with regard to their internal formats and annotation schemes. Given that, transformation of them became necessary: while the Talbanken's transformation concerned only the internal format, transformation of CAC concerned both internal format and annotation scheme.

Later, more annotated corpora of spoken texts have appeared, like the British Component of the International Corpus of English (ICE-GB, Greenbaum, 1996), the Fisher Corpus for English (Cieri *et al.*, 2004), the Childes database[2], the Switchboard part of the Penn Treebank (Godfrey *et al.*, 1992), Corpus Gesproken Nederlands (Hoekstra *et al.*, 2001) and the Verbmobil corpora.[3] The syntactic annotation in these corpora is mostly automatic using tools trained on written corpora or on a small, manually annotated part of spoken corpora.

The aim of our contribution is to answer the question whether it is possible to annotate speech transcriptions syntactically according to the guidelines originally designed for text corpora. We will show the problems that arise in extending an explicit scheme of syntactic annotation of written Czech into the domain of spontaneous speech (as found in the CAC).

Our paper is organized as follows. In Section 3, we give a brief description of the past and present of the Czech Academic Corpus. The compatibility of the original CAC syntactic annotation with a present-day approach adopted by the Prague Dependency Treebank project is evaluated in Section 4. Section 5 is the core of our paper. We discuss phenomena typical for spoken texts making impossible to annotate them according to the guidelines for written texts. We explore a trade-off between leaving the original annotation aside and annotating from scratch, and an upgrade of the original annotation. In addition, we briefly compare the approach adopted for Czech and those adopted for other languages.

lish and the LOB Corpus of British English. Both contain written texts annotated for part of speech. Their size is 1 mil. tokens.

[2] `http://childes.psy.cmu.edu/grasp/`

[3] `http://verbmobil.dfki.de/`

3 The Czech Academic Corpus: past and present (1971-2008)

The idea of the Czech Academic Corpus (CAC) came to life between 1971 and 1985 thanks to the Department of Mathematical Linguistics within the Institute of Czech Language. The discussion on the concept of academic grammar of Czech, i.e. on the concept of CAC annotation, finally led to the traditional, systematic, and well elaborated concept of morphology and dependency syntax (Šmilauer, 1972). By the mid 1980s, a total of 540,000 words of CAC were morphologically and syntactically manually annotated.

The documents originally selected for the CAC are articles taken from a range of media. The sources included newspapers and magazines, and transcripts of spoken language from radio and TV programs, covering administrative, journalistic and scientific fields.

The original CAC was on par with it peers at the time (such as the Brown corpus) in size, coverage, and annotation; it surpassed them in that it contained (some) syntactic annotation. CAC was used in the first experiments of statistical morphological tagging of Czech (Hajič, Hladká, 1997).

After the Prague Dependency Treebank (PDT) has been built (Hajič *et al.*, 2006), a conversion from the CAC to the PDT format has started. The PDT uses three layers of annotation: morphological, syntactic and "tectogrammatical" (or semantic) layers (henceforth m-layer, a-layer and t-layer, respectively).

The main goal was to make the CAC and the PDT compatible at the m-layer and the a-layer, and thus to enable integration of the CAC into the PDT. The second version of the CAC presents such a complete conversion of the internal format and the annotation schemes. The overall statistics on the CAC 2.0 are presented in Table 1.

Annotation transformation is visualized in Figure 1. In the areas corresponding to the corpora, the morphological annotation is symbolized by the horizontal lines and syntactical annotation by the vertical lines.

Conversion of the originally simple textual comma-separated values format into the Prague Markup Language (Pajas, Štěpánek, 2005) was more or less straightforward.

Morphological analysis of Czech in the CAC and in the PDT is almost the same, except that the morphological tagset of CAC is slightly more detailed. Semi-automatic conversion of the original morphological annotation into the Czech positional morphological tagset was executed in compliance with the morphological annotation of PDT (Hana *et al.*, 2005). Figure 1 shows that morphological annotation conversion of both written and spoken texts was done.

The only major problem in this conversion was that digit-only tokens and punctuation were omitted from the original CAC since they were deemed linguistically "uninteresting", which is certainly true from the point of view of the original CAC's purpose to give quantitative lexical support to a new Czech dictionary. Since the sources of the CAC documents were no longer available, missing tokens had to inserted and revised manually.

Syntactic conversion of CAC was more demanding than the morphological one. In a pilot study, (Ribarov *et al.*, 2006) attempt to answer a question whether an automatic transformation of the CAC annotation into the PDT format (and subsequent manual corrections) is more effective than to leave the CAC annotation aside and process the CAC's texts by a statistical parser instead (again, with subsequent manual correction). In the end, the latter variant was selected (with regrets). No distinction in strategy of written and spoken texts annotation transformation was made. However, spoken texts were eventually excluded from the CAC 2.0 (Figure 1). Reasons for this are explained in detail in the following two sections.

4 Syntax in the CAC and the PDT

4.1 Syntactic annotation in the CAC

The syntactic analysis of Czech in the CAC and in the PDT is very much alike, but there are phenomena in which the CAC syntactic annotation scenario differs from the PDT, even though both corpora are based on the same linguistic theory (Šmilauer, 1969), i.e. on the dependency grammar notion common to the "Prague school" of linguists since the 1930s.

However, the syntactic annotation differs between the two corpora. The CAC works with a single syntactic layer, whereas the PDT works with two independent (although interlinked) syntactic layers: an analytical (syntactic) one and a tectogrammatical one (a-layer and t-layer, respectively). In this paper, we are referring to the a-layer of the PDT in our comparisons unless specifically noted for those elements of the tectogrammatical annotation that do have some counterpart in the CAC.

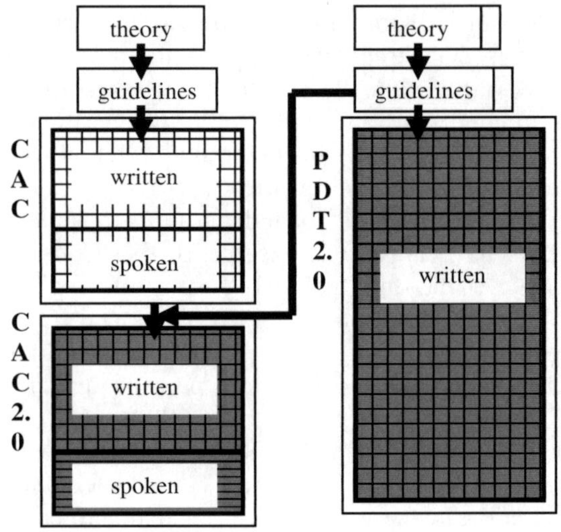

Figure 1 Overall scheme of the CAC conversion

Style	form[4]	#docs	#sntncs (K)	#tokens (K)
Journalism	w	52	10	189
Journalism	s	8	1	29
Scientific	w	68	12	245
Scientific	s	32	4	116
administrative	w	16	3	59
administrative	s	4	2	14
Total	w	135	25	493
Total	s	44	7	159
Total	**w&s**	**180**	**32**	**652**

Table 1 Size of the CAC 2.0 parts

The CAC annotation scheme makes a substantial distinction between two things: surface syntactic relations within a single clause as well as syntactic relations between clauses in a complex sentence. These two types of syntactic information are captured by two types of syntactic tags.

(a) Word-level (intra-clausal) syntactic tag is a 6-position tag assigned to every non-auxilliary ("autosemantic") word within a single clause, representing the intra-clausal dependency relations.

(b) Clause-level (intra-sentential) syntactic tag is a 8-position tag assigned to the first token of each clause in a complex sentence, representing the status (and possible dependency) of the given clause within the given (complex) sentence.

[4] Either written (w) or spoken (s) texts.

The CAC thus annotates not only dependency relations within a single clause but also dependency relations within a complex sentence.

A description of the 6-position and the 8-position tags is given in Tables 2 and 3, respectively. (Ribarov *et al.*, 2006) gives a detailed description.

4.2 Syntactic annotation in the PDT

The PDT a-layer annotates two main things: a *dependency structure* of the sentence and *types* of these dependencies.

Representation of a structure of the sentence is rendered in a form of a dependency tree, the nodes of which correspond to the tokens (words and punctuation) that form the sentence. The type of dependency (subject, object, adverbial, complement, attribute, etc.) is represented by a node attribute called an "analytical function" (`afun` for short; the most frequent values of this attribute are listed in Table 4).

4.3 CAC vs. PDT

Comparing the CAC and the PDT syntactic annotation scenarios, we can see that the annotation of the major syntactic relations within a sentence is very similar, from similar adaptations of the theoretical background down to the high-level corpus markup conventions. For example, in both corpora the predicate is the clausal head and the subject is its dependent, unlike the descriptions we can find in the traditional Czech syntactic theory (Šmilauer, 1969). Another (technical) similarity can be found in the way the dependency types are encoded. In both corpora, the dependency type label is stored at the dependent. No confusion arises since the link from a dependent to its governor is unique.

However, the list of differences is actually quite long. Some are minor and technical: for example, in the PDT an "overarching" root of the sentence tree (marked `AuxS`) is always added, so that all other nodes appear as if they depend on it. Some differences are more profound and are described below.

We are not going to list all the differences in individual syntactic labels - they can be found easily by confronting Tables 2 and 4, but we would like to draw the readers' attention to the main dissimilarities between the CAC's and the PDT's syntactic annotation scenarios.

Punctuation

The first difference can be observed at first glance: in CAC no punctuation marks can be found (as mentioned in Section 3). While some might question whether punctuation should ever be part of syntax, in computational approaches punctuation is certainly seen as a very important part of written-language syntax and is thus taken into account in annotation (for important considerations about punctuation in spoken corpora, see Section 5).

Digits

CAC leaves out digital tokens, even though they are often a valid part of the syntactic structure and can plausibly get various syntactic labels as we can see in the PDT annotation, where nothing is left out of the syntactic tree structure.

Prepositions and function words

The next most significant difference is in the treatment of prepositions (or function words in general, see also the next paragraphs on conjunctions and other auxiliaries). Whereas CAC neither labels them nor even includes them in the dependency tree, PDT at the a-layer, reflecting the surface shape of the sentence, makes them the head of the autosemantic nodes they "govern" (and labels them with the `AuxP` analytical function tag). The CAC way of annotation (rather, non-annotation) of prepositions is, in a sense, closer to the annotation scenario of the underlying syntactic layer (the t-layer) of the PDT, It is also reflected in the adverbial types of labels (column 2 in Table 2) – these would all be labeled only as `Adv` at the (surface-syntactic) a-layer of the PDT, but at the (deep) t-layer, they get a label from a mix of approx. 70 functional, syntactic and semantic labels. Unfortunately, only seven such labels are used in the CAC, resulting in loss of information in some cases (adverbials of aim, accompaniment, attitude, beneficiary, etc.); the same is true for certain subtypes of time and location adverbials, since they are not distinguished in terms of direction, location designation (*on/under/above/next to* and many other), duration, start time vs. end time, etc.

Conjunctions

Further, subordinating as well as coordinating conjunctions get only a sentential syntactic tag in the CAC (if any), i.e. they are labeled by the 9-position tag but not by the word-level, intra-clausal syntactic tag. In PDT, subordinating and coordinating conjunctions get assigned the analytical function value `AuxC` and `Coord`, respectively, and they are always included in the syntactic tree. For subordinating conjunctions, the CAC approach is again in some ways similar to the annotation scenario of the tectogrammatical layer of PDT – dependencies between clauses are annotated but the set of labels is much smaller than that of t-layer of the PDT, again resulting in a loss of information. For coordination and apposition, the difference is structural; while CAC marks an a coordination element with a specific label (value '1' in the column 6 of a word-level tag and the same value in column 8 of the clause-level tag, see Tables 2 and 3), PDT makes a node corresponding to the coordination (apposition) a virtual head of the members of the coordination or apposition (whether phrasal or clausal). CAC thus cannot annotate hierarchy in coordination and apposition without another loss of information, while PDT can.

Reflexive particles

In CAC, reflexive particles *se/si* are often left unannotated, while PDT uses detailed labels for all occurrences. Lexicalized reflexives (`AuxT` in the PDT), particles (`AuxO`) and reflexive passivization (`AuxR`) and also certain (yet rare) adverbial usages (`Adv`) are not annotated in the CAC at all. The only case where CAC annotates them is in situations where they can be considered objects (accusative or dative case of the personless reflexive pronoun *sebe*).

Analytic verb forms

In CAC, no syntactic relation is indicated for auxiliary verbs, loosing the reference to the verb they belong to; in the PDT, they are put as dependents onto their verb, and labeled `AuxV` to describe their function.

Special adverbs and particles

In PDT, there are also syntactic labels for certain type of "special" adverbials and particles, such as *raději* [*better*], *zřejmě* [*probably*], *také* [*also*], *přece* [*surely*], *jedině* [*only*]. In CAC, dependencies and syntactic tags for these tokens are missing.

Other differences in both syntactic scenarios will be described in the next section since they are related to spoken language annotation.

5 CAC syntactic annotation of spoken utterances

Current Czech syntactic theory is based almost entirely on written Czech but spoken language often differs strikingly from the written one (Müllerová, 1994).

In the CAC guidelines, only the following word-level markup specifically aimed at the spoken utterance structure is described:

- non-identical reduplication of a word (value '7' in column 6),
- identical reduplication of a word (value '8' in column 6),
- ellipsis (value '9' or '0' in column 6).

Let's take this spoken utterance from CAC:

CZ: *A to jsou trošku, jedna je, jedna má světlou budovu a druhá má tmavou budovu, ony jsou umístěny v jednom, v jednom areále, ale ta, to centrum, patřilo té, bylo to v bloku Univerzity vlámské, a já jsem se ptala na univerzitě, na, v Univerzitě svobodné, že, no a to přeci oni nevědí, to nanejvýš, to prostě jedině, když je to Univerzita vlámská, tak o tom oni přece nemohou nic vědět, a nic.*

(Lit.: *And they are a bit, one is, one has a light building and the second has a dark building, they are placed in one, in one campus, but the, the center, it belonged to the, it was in a bloc of the Flemish University, and I asked at the University, in, at the Free University, that, well, and that surely they don't know, it at most, it simply only, if it is the Flemish University, so they surely cannot know anything, and nothing.*)

Words *jsou* [*are*] and *ta* [*the*] represent a non-identical reduplication of a word; that is why they have been assigned the value '7' (as described above), while *je* [*is*], *jednom* [*one*], *to* [*the*] and *nic* [*nothing*] represent an identical reduplication of a word, i.e. they get the value '8' ("identical reduplication of a word"). The description does not quite correspond to what a closer look at the data reveals: '7' is used to mark a reparandum (part of the sentence that was corrected by the speaker later), while '8' is used to mark the part that replaces the reparandum (cf. also the "EDITED" nonterminal and the symbols "[", "+" and "\" in the Penn Treebank Switchboard annotation (Godfrey *et al.*, 1992). Ellipsis (the value '9') was assigned to the words *trošku* [*a bit*] and *té* [*to the*].

However, our sample sentence contains more phenomena typical for spoken language than CAC attempts to annotate, for example:

- unfinished sentences (fragments), with apparent ellipsis: *A to je trošku...* [*And they are a bit...*],
- false beginnings (restarts): *jedna je, jedna má* [*one is, one has*],
- repetition of words in the middle of sentence: *jsou umístěny v jednom, jednom areále* [*they are placed in one, in one campus*],
- redundant and ungrammatically used words: *ony jsou umístěny v jednom..., univerzitě, na,v Univerzitě svobodné,...* [*, they are placed in one... at the University, in, at the Free University,*],
- redundant deictic words: *...ale ta, to centrum...* [*...but the, the center...*],
- intonation fillers: *no* [*well*],
- question tags: *na Univerzitě svobodné, že* [*at the Free University, that*],
- redundant conectors: *když je to Univerzita vlámská, tak to o tom* [*if it is the Flemish University, so they surely cannot know anything*],
- broken coherence of utterance, „teared“ syntactic scheme of proposition: *ale ta, to centrum, bylo to v bloku* [*but the, the center, it belonged to the, it was in a bloc*],
- syntactic errors, anacoluthon: *přeci nemohu nic vědět, a nic.* [*surely (I) cannot know anything, and nothing*].

The CAC syntactic scenario does not cover these phenomena in the guidelines (and tag tables), and even if some of them would easily fall in the reparandum/repair category (such as the phrase *jedna je, jedna má* [*one is, one has*]), which is seemingly included, it does not annotate them as such. Moreover, these are just some of the spoken language phenomena, taken from just one random utterance; a thorough look at the spoken part of the CAC reveals that most of the well-known spoken language phenomena, e.g. grammatically incoherent utterances, grammatical additions spoken as an afterthought, redundant co-references or phrase-connecting errors (Shriver, 1994, Fitzgerald, 2009), are present in the texts but left unnoticed.

In comparison, however, the PDT covers none of these typical spoken structures in the text annotation guidelines (the main reason being that it does not contain spoken material in the first place). Thus, at the surface-syntactic layer (the a-layer) of the PDT, there are only limited means for capturing such spoken phenomena.

For example, words playing the role of fillers could get the analytical function `AuxO` designed mostly for a redundant (deictic or emotive) constituent.

Many phenomena typical for spoken language would get, according to the PDT guidelines, the analytical function `ExD` (Ex-Dependent), which just "warns" of such type of incomplete utterance structure where a governing word is missing, i.e. it is such ellipsis where the dependent is present but its governing element is not.

In Figure 2, we present an attempt to annotate the above spoken utterance using the standard PDT guidelines. The "problematic" nodes, for which we had to adopt some arbitrary annotation decisions due to the lack of proper means in the PDT annotation guidelines, are shown as dark squares. For comparison, we have used dashed line for those dependency edges that were annotated in the CAC by one of the spoken-language specific tags (values '7', '8', '9' in the column 6 of the original annotation, see above at the beginning of Sect. 5),

Most of the square-marked nodes do correspond well to the PDT labels for special cases which are used for some of the peripheral language phenomena (`ExD`, `Apos` and its members, several `AuxX` for extra commas, `AuxY` for particles etc.).

It can also be observed that the dashed lines (CAC spoken annotation labels) correspond to some of the nodes with problematic markup in the PDT, but they are used only in clear cases and therefore they are found much more sparingly in the corpus.

6 Conclusion

Courage of the original CAC project's team deserves to be reminded. Having the experience with the present spoken data processing, we do appreciate the initial attempts with the syntactic annotation of spoken texts.

Given the main principles of the a-layer of PDT annotation (no addition/deletion of tokens, no word-order changes, no word corrections), one would have to introduce arbitrary, linguistically irrelevant rules for spoken material annotation with a doubtful use even if applied consistently to the corpus. Avoiding that, transcriptions currently present in the CAC could not be syntactically annotated using the annotation guidelines of the PDT.

However, in the future, we plan to complete the annotation of the spoken language transcriptions, using the scheme of the so-called "speech reconstruction" project (Mikulová *et al.*, 2008), running now within the framework of the PDT (for both Czech and English)[5]. This project will enable to use the text-based guidelines for syntactic annotation of spoken material by introducing a separate layer of annotation, which allows for "editing" of the original transcript and transforming it thus into a grammatical, comprehensible text. The "edited" layer is in addition to the original transcript and contains explicit links between them at the word granularity, allowing in turn for observations of the relation between the original transcript and its syntactic annotation (made "through" the edited text) without any loss. The scheme picks up the threads of the speech reconstruction approach developed for English by Erin Fitzgerald (Fitzgerald, Jelinek, 2008). Just for a comparison see our sample sentence (analyzed in Sect. 5) transformed into a reconstructed sentence (The bold marking means changes, and parentheses indicate elements left out in the reconstructed sentence.).

CZ*: A* ***(to)*** *jsou trošku* ***rozdílné,(jedna je,)*** *jedna má světlou budovu a druhá má tmavou budovu.****(, ony)*** *Jsou umístěny* ***(v jednom,)*** *v jednom areále, ale* ***(ta,)*** *to centrum* ***(, patřilo té,)*** *bylo* ***(to)*** *v bloku Univerzity vlámské****(,)*** *a já jsem se ptala na* ***(univerzitě, na, v)*** *Univerzitě svobodné.****(, že, no a to přeci oni nevědí, to nanejvýš, to prostě jedině,) K****dyž je to Univerzita vlámská, tak o tom oni přece nemohou nic vědět* ***(, a nic).***

(Lit.: *And they are a bit* ***different****, one has a light building and the second has a dark building. They are placed in one campus, but the center* ***(, it belonged to the, it)*** *was in a bloc of the Flemish University, and I asked at the* ***(University, in, at the)*** *Free University.****(, that, well, and that surely they don't know, it at most, it simply only,) I****f it is the Flemish University, so they surely cannot know anything****(, and nothing)***.)

[5] http://ufal.mff.cuni.cz/pdtsl

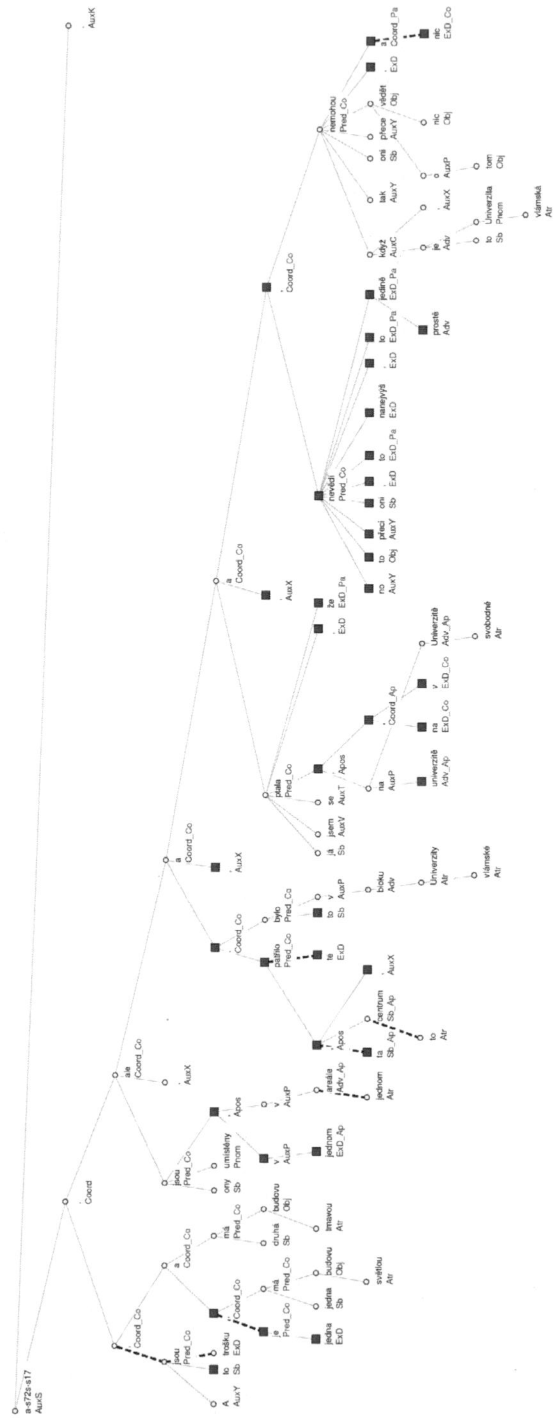

Figure 2. A syntactic annotation attempt (PDT-guidelines based) at the sample CAC sentence. The dashed edges are the only ones containing some spoken-language specific CAC annotation, the others correspond as close as possible to the PDT annotation scenario. Square-shaped nodes mark the problematic parts (phenomena with no explicit support in the PDT guidelines).

Dependency relation		Dependency subtypes	Governor			Other	
			Direction		Offset		
1		2	3		4 5	6	
Tag	Desc.		Tag	Desc.		Tag	Desc.
1	Subject	Values specific to the dependency relation (see column 1)	+	Right	Distance between words (two digit string: for ex. 01 denotes neighboring word)	1-6	Coordination types
2	Predicate		-	Left		7,8	Repetitions (for the spoken part)
3	Attribute					9, 0	Ellipses
4	Object						
5	Adverbial						
6	Clause core						
7	Trans. type						
8	Independent clause member						
9	Parenthesis						

Table 2 Main word-level syntactic tags in the Czech Academic Corpus

Clause ID	Clause Type		Subordination (dep.) type		Governing clause/word		Clausal relation	
					Gov. noun	Gov. clause		
1 2	3		4		5	6 7	8	
	Tag	Desc.	Tag	Desc.			Tag	Desc.
Two-digit id (unique within a sentence: for ex. 91 denotes the first sentence	1	Simple			One-digit relative position of a noun modified by the clause Attributive clauses only	Two-digit id of the governing clause	1	Coordination
	2	Main					2	Parenthesis
	3	Sub-ordinated	1	Subject			3	Direct Speech
			2	Predicate			5	Parenthesis in direct speech
			3	Attribute			6	Introductory clause
			4	Object			8	Parenthesis, introductory clause
			5	Local			!	Structural error
			...	....			...	etc.

Table 3 Clause-level syntactic tags in the Czech Academic Corpus

Analytic function	Description
`Pred`	Predicate
`Sb`	Subject
`Obj`	Object
`Adv`	Adverbial
`Atr`	Attribute
`Pnom`	Nominal predicate, or nom. part of predicate with copula *to be*
`AuxV`	Auxiliary verb *to be*
`Coord`	Coordination node
`Apos`	Apposition (main node)
`AuxT`	Reflexive tantum
`AuxR`	Reflexive,neither Obj nor AuxT (passive reflexive)
`AuxP`	Primary preposition, parts of a secondary preposition
`AuxC`	Conjunction (subordinate)
`AuxO`	Redundant or emotional item, 'coreferential' pronoun
`ExD`	A technical value for a node depending on a deleted item (ellipsis with dependents)
`Aux.., Atv(V),..`	Other auxiliary tags, verbal complements, other special syntactic tags

Table 4 Dependency relation tags in the Prague Dependency Treebank

Acknowledgement

We gratefully acknowledge the support of the Czech Ministry of Education through the grant No. MSM-0021620838 and ME 838 and the Grant Agency of Charles University in Prague through the grant No. GAUK 52408/2008.

We wish to thank Jan Hajič, whose comments stimulated us to make our paper better. We are grateful to Petr Pajas for Figure 2 presenting a wide dependency tree.

References

Christopher Cieri, David Miller, Kevin Walker. 2004. The Fisher Corpus: a Resource for the Next Generations of Speech-to-Text. In *Proceedings of the 4th LREC*, Lisbon, Portugal, pp. 69-71.

John J. Godfrey, Edward C. Holliman, Jane McDaniel. 1992. SWITCHBOARD: Telephone speech corpus for research and development, IEEE ICASSP, pp. 517-520.

Erin Fitzgerald. 2009. *Reconstructing spontaneous speech*. PhD thesis, Baltimore, Maryland.

Erin Fitzgerald, Frederick Jelinek. 2008. Linguistic resources for reconstructing spontaneous speech text. In *LREC Proceedings*, Marrakesh, Morocco, pp. 1–8.

Sidney Greenbaum (ed.). 1996. *Comparing English Worldwide: The International Corpus of English*. Oxford: Clarendon Press.

Jan Hajič, Barbora Hladká. 1997. Tagging of inflective languages: a comparison. In *Proceedings of ANLP'97*, Washington, DC, pp. 136--143.

Jan Hajič et al. 2006. *The Prague Dependency Treebank 2.0,* (Linguistic Data Consortium, Philadelphia, PA, USA), Cat. No. LDC2006T01.

Jiří Hana, Daniel Zeman, Jan Hajič, Hana Hanová, Barbora Hladká, Emil Jeřábek. 2005. *Manual for Morphological Annotation*. TR-2005-27, Ústav formální a aplikované lingvistiky, MFF UK.

Heleen Hoekstra, Michael Moortgat, Ineke Schuurman, Ton van der Wouden 2001. Syntactic Annotation for the Spoken Dutch Corpus Project. In Daelemans, W.; Simaan, K.; Veenstra. J.; Zavrel, J. (eds.): *Computational Linguistics in the Netherlands* 2000. Amsterdam/New York, Rodopi, pp. 73-87.

Noam Chomsky. 1993. *Lectures on Government and Binding: The Pisa Lectures.* Holland: Foris Publications, 1981. Reprint. 7th Edition. Berlin and New York: Mouton de Gruyter.

Jan Králík, Ludmila Uhlířová. 2007. The Czech Academic Corpus (CAC), its history and presence, In *Journal of quantitative linguistics*. 14 (2-3): 265-285.

Marie Mikulová. 2008. *Rekonstrukce standardizovaného textu z mluvené řeči v Pražském závislostním korpusu mluvené češtiny. Manuál pro anotátory.* TR-2008-38, Institute of Formal and Applied Linguistics, MFF UK.

Olga Müllerová. 1994. *Mluvený text a jeho syntaktická výstavba*. Academia, Praha.

Jens Nilsson, Johan Hall, Joakim Nivre. 2005. MAMBA meets TIGER: Reconstructing a Treebank from Antiquity. In *Proceedings of NODALIDA 2005 Special Session on Treebanks for Spoken and Discourse*, Copenhagen Studies in Language 32, Joensuu, Finland, pp. 119-132

Petr Pajas, Jan Štěpánek. 2005. *A Generic XML-based Format for Structured Linguistic Annotation and its Application to the Prague Dependency Treebank 2.0.* TR-2005-29, Institute of Formal and Applied Linguistics, MFF UK.

Kiril Ribarov, Alevtina Bémová, Barbora Hladká. 2006. When a statistically oriented parser was more efficient than a linguist: A case of treebank conversion, In *Prague Bulletin of Mathematical Linguistics*, 1 (86):21-38.

Petr Sgall, Eva Hajičová, Jarmila Panevová. 1986. *The meaning of the sentence in its semantic and pragmatic aspects*, ed. by J. Mey. Reidel, Dordrecht; Academia, Praha.

Elisabeth Shriberg. 1994. *Preliminaries to a Theory of Speech Disfluencies*. PhD thesis, University of California, Berkeley.

Jan Svartvik and Randolph Quirk. 1980. *A Corpus of English Conversation*. Lund.

Vladimír Šmilauer. 1972. *Nauka o českém jazyku*. Praha.

Vladimír Šmilauer. 1969. *Novočeská skladba.* Státní pedagogické nakladatelství. Praha.

High-Performance High-Volume Layered Corpora Annotation

Tiago Luís and David Martins de Matos
L^{2}F - INESC-ID
R. Alves Redol 9, Lisboa, Portugal
{tiago.luis,david.matos}@l2f.inesc-id.pt

Abstract

NLP systems that deal with large collections of text require significant computational resources, both in terms of space and processing time. Moreover, these systems typically add new layers of linguistic information with references to another layer. The spreading of these layered annotations across different files makes them more difficult to process and access the data. As the amount of input increases, so does the difficulty to process it. One approach is to use distributed parallel computing for solving these larger problems and save time.

We propose a framework that simplifies the integration of independently existing NLP tools to build language-independent NLP systems capable of creating layered annotations. Moreover, it allows the development of scalable NLP systems, that executes NLP tools in parallel, while offering an easy-to-use programming environment and a transparent handling of distributed computing problems. With this framework the execution time was decreased to 40 times less than the original one on a cluster with 80 cores.

1 Introduction

Linguistic information can be automatically created by NLP systems. These systems are composed by several NLP tools that are typically executed in a pipeline, where each tool performs a processing step. Therefore, each tool uses the results produced by the previous processing steps and produces new linguistic information that can be later used by other tools. The addition of new layers of linguistic information (layered annotations) by NLP tools makes the processing and access to data difficult due to the spreading of the layered annotations across different files. Moreover, whenever these tools are integrated, several problems related with information flow between them may arise. A given tool may need an annotation previously produced by another tool but some of the information in annotation can be lost in conversions between the different tool data formats, because the expressiveness of each format may be different and not completely convertible into other formats.

Besides tool integration problems, there is also another problem related with the data-intensive nature of NLP and the computation power needed to produce the linguistic information. The wealth of annotations has increased the amount of data to process. Therefore, the processing of this linguistic information is a computation-heavy process and some algorithms continue to take a long time (hours or days) to produce their results. This kind of processing can benefit from distributed parallel computing but it may create other problems, such as fault tolerance to machine failures. Because some NLP algorithms can take long time to produce their results, it is important to automatically recover from these failures, in order not to lose the results of computations already performed. Task scheduling is also a problem due to data-intensive nature of NLP. Data-driven scheduling (based on data location) improves performance because it reduces bandwidth usage.

Our framework aims to simplify the integration of independently developed NLP tools, while providing an easy-to-use programming environment, and transparent handling of distributed computing problems, such as fault tolerance and task scheduling, when executing the NLP tools in parallel. Moreover, NLP systems built on top of the framework are language-independent and produce layered annotations. We also measured the gains that can be achieved with the parallel execution of NLP

Proceedings of the Third Linguistic Annotation Workshop, ACL-IJCNLP 2009, pages 99–107,
Suntec, Singapore, 6-7 August 2009.

tools and the merging of the layered annotations.

Section 2 discusses related work, Section 3 present the framework's architecture and a detailed description of its components, Section 4 shows the integrated tools, Section 5 explains how the information produced by tools is merged, and Section 6 presents the achieved results. Finally, Section 7 presents concluding remarks.

2 Related Work

GATE (Cunningham et al., 2002) is one of the most used framework for building NLP systems. However, it does not provide a controller for parallel execution, it only supports the execution of applications on different machines over data shared on the server (Bontcheva et al., 2004). However, this solution cannot be applied in a large-scale distributed environment because the shared repository becomes a bottleneck in computation due to the accesses from all the machines making computations.

UIMA (Ferrucci and Lally, 2004) is also used to build NLP systems, and this framework supports replication of pipeline components to improve throughput on multi-processor or multi-machine platforms. However, we did not find any published results regarding the parallel execution. The UIMA framework has been successfully leveraged (Egner et al., 2007) with Condor[1], a manager of loosely coupled compute resources, allowing the parallel execution of multiple instances of the NLP system built with UIMA. The Condor scheduler allows to solve problems where there is no communication between tasks and complicates the development of parallel applications when this interaction is needed, like in our case, where it is necessary to merge multiple layers of annotations. Also, the Condor does not move computations closer to their input data, like the MapReduce approach.

The MapReduce paradigm has already been successfully adopted by the Ontea semantic annotator (Laclavík et al., 2008). We think that GATE and UIMA frameworks could also benefit with the MapReduce. For example, the NLTK (Loper and Bird, 2002) adopted this paradigm, and already have implementations of some algorithms like term frequency-inverse document frequency (tf-idf) or expectation-maximization (EM).

There are already tools for merging of layered annotations, like the ANC tool (Ide and Suderman, 2006). However, we did not find any approach to this task in a scalable manner.

Concerning the parallel programming approaches, Message Passing Interface (MPI) (Gropp, 2001) continues to be widely used in parallel programming and therefore there are currently many libraries built based on this programming model. However, this approach provides very low level routines that are difficult to use and make for obscure algorithm implementation, making code reuse and maintenance difficult and time consuming. MPI programming can be difficult because it is necessary to divide the problem among processes with separate address spaces and coordinate these processes with communication routines.

MapReduce (Dean and Ghemawat, 2008) forces the programmer to consider the data parallelism of the computation. Also, this framework automatically schedules and distributes data to tasks. The simple API provided by the system allows programmers to write simple serial programs that are run in a distributed way, while hiding several parallel programming details. Therefore, this framework is accessible to a wide range of developers and allows them to write their applications at a higher level of abstraction than the MPI approach.

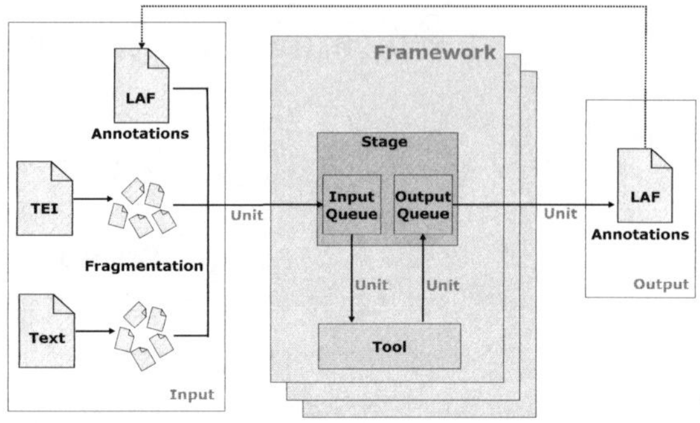

Figure 1: Framework architecture.

3 Framework Architecture

Our framework aims to simplify the integration of independently developed NLP tools, while executing the NLP tools in a parallel manner. Our architecture is composed by: Stage, Tool, and Unit (see Figure 1). Stages represent phases in the annotation process of the NLP system. They can be interconnected in order to form an NLP system. The

[1] http://www.cs.wisc.edu/condor/

Tool interacts with the existing NLP tool and can receive as input an annotation previously created or a text file (structured or unstructured). The text files received are divided into sets of independent Units. Units are used to represent the input file fragmentation (each fragment is represented by a Unit). These independent Units are then processed in parallel. Previously created annotations are already divided, since they correspond to an annotation that refers the corresponding input fragment.

Tools are wrapped in Stage components. Stages have two queues: an input and an output queue of Units. Stages are responsible for consuming input queue Units, pass them to the Tool and, after their processing, put the result on output queue. These queues allow multithreaded consumption and production of the Units.

The framework was implemented using the MapReduce (Dean and Ghemawat, 2008) paradigm due to its scalability when dealing with large data volumes. The Hadoop[2] framework (described in the next section) was used as the base for implementation. The next sections describe the representation format used for annotations, the input accepted, and the framework components in more detail.

3.1 Hadoop

Hadoop is a MapReduce implementation written in Java. One of the main advantages of using the MapReduce paradigm is task scheduling. When dealing with large datasets in a distributed manner, bandwidth to data becomes a problem. The MapReduce paradigm and the Hadoop Distributed File System (HDFS) allows to reduce bandwidth consumption because tasks are scheduled close to their inputs whenever possible.

Another advantage is fault tolerance and task synchronization handling. These problems, inherent to distributed systems, are transparently solved by the Hadoop framework, facilitating programming of distributed applications.

The MapReduce framework operates exclusively on key/value pairs, i.e., the framework views the input to the job as a set of key/value pairs and produces a set of key/value pairs as the output of the job. These key and value elements can be any user defined data type.

The main tasks of MapReduce are the map and the reduce task. The map task produces a set of intermediate key/value pairs from input key/value pairs. Each map is an individual task that runs on a machine. The reduce phase creates a smaller set of key/value pairs from a set of intermediate values that have the same key. Since different mappers can output the same key, the framework groups reducer input key/value pairs with the same key. This grouping capability is used to merge annotations produced by different tools and that are related with each other, as shown is the Section 5.

[2]http://hadoop.apache.org/core/

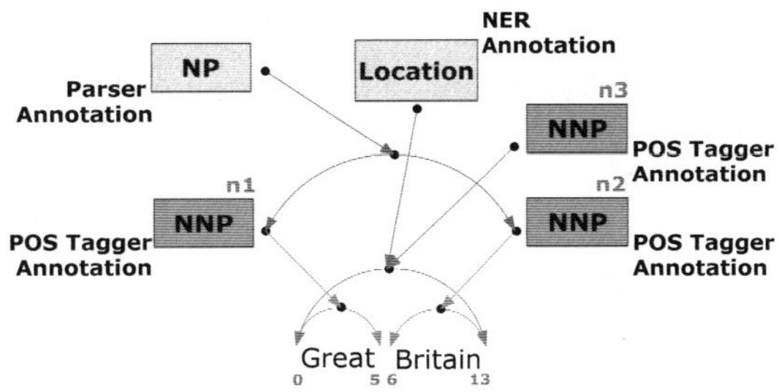

Figure 2: Graph-based model annotation example.

3.2 Representation Format

In order to represent linguistic information generated by the tools, we chose the Linguistic Annotation Framework (LAF) (Ide and Romary, 2006) format, that uses a graph model to store annotations.

An annotation can be viewed as a set of linguistic information items that are associated with some data (a part of a text or speech signal, for example), called primary data. Primary data objects are represented by locations in the input. These locations can be the offset of a character comprising a sentence or word, in the case of a text input, or a point at which a given temporal event begins or ends, in the case of a speech signal input. As such, primary data objects have a simple structure. However, it is possible to build more complex data objects, composed by sets of contiguous or noncontiguous locations. Primary data objects are used to build segmentations over data. A segmentation represents a list of ordered segments, where each segment represents a linguistic element. A segment is represented by an edge between virtual nodes located between each character in the primary data (see Figure 2). It is possible to define multiple segmentations over the same primary data, and multiple annotations may refer to the same segmentation.

An annotation is defined as a label and a feature structure. A feature structure is itself a graph in

```
<laf>
    <edgeSet>
        <edge id="e1" from="0" to="5"/>
        <edge id="e2" from="6" to="13"/>
    </edgeSet>
    <nodeSet>
        <node id="n1" edgesTo="e1">
            <fs type="segment">
                <f name="SEGMENT" value="Great"/>
                <f name="POS" value="NNP"/>
            </fs>
        </node>
        <node id="n2" edgesTo="e2">
            <fs type="segment">
                <f name="SEGMENT" value="Britain"/>
                <f name="POS" value="NNP"/>
            </fs>
        </node>
        <node id="n3" edgesTo="e1 e2">
            <fs type="segment">
                <f name="SEGMENT" value="Great Britain"/>
                <f name="POS" value="NNP"/>
            </fs>
        </node>
    </nodeSet>
</laf>
```

Figure 3: Morphosyntactic LAF annotation example.

```
<TEI.2 lang="en" >
    <teiHeader>
    ...
    </ teiHeader >
    <text lang="en" >
    ...
        <p id="p16" >Great</p>
        ...
        <p id="p29" >Britain</p>
        ...
    </text>
</TEI.2>                                TEI file
```

↓

```
<laf addressing="XPointer" >
    <edgeSet>
        <edge id="e1"
            from="xpointer(id("p16")/text()/point[position()=0])"
            to="xpointer(id("p16")/text()/point[position()=5])"/>
        <edge id="e2"
            from="xpointer(id("p29")/text()/point[position()=0])"
            to="xpointer(id("p29")/text()/point[position()=7])"/>
    </edgeSet>
    <nodeSet>
    ...
    </nodeSet>
</laf>                                  LAF annotation
```

Figure 4: TEI file LAF annotation example.

which nodes are labeled with feature/value pairs or other feature structures. Hence, a morphosyntactic annotation is represented by a graph in which nodes are labeled with feature/value pairs. These pairs contain the morphosyntactic information. Figure 3 shows how the two possible segmentations in the POS tagger annotation in Figure 2 can be represented: the segment "Great Britain" has a total of 13 characters; the edges use the character offsets to delimit the segment; the nodes built on top of these edges contain the morphosyntactic information, such as the POS, and the text pointed to by the segment. As shown in the third node (with identifier "n3"), it is possible to have a node referring to multiple edges. A node can also refer to other nodes to add other kinds of linguistic information, such as dependencies between segments or syntactic annotations.

3.3 Input

Currently, the Tools integrated in our framework can process three kinds of input files: structured and unstructured text, and previously created annotations. The structured text format currently supported is TEI (Text Encoding Initiative)[3]. Both structured and unstructured text are fragmented into a set of Units. The division is currently paragraph-based, in the case of the unstructured text, and on XML textual elements, in the case of the TEI input. However, it is possible to create Units with other user-defined granularity.

In order to make references to locations in the TEI input, we adopted the XPointer[4] format (see Figure 4). Assuming that each text element in the TEI file has a unique identifier, the XPointer of the start and end tag will refer this identifier and the word character offset.

3.4 Unit

When processing large files, with several gigabytes, it is not efficient to process them in serial mode due to memory constraints. Therefore, we divide them into sets of Units that are processed independently.

Each Unit is associated with a portion of the input file and contains the linguistic information generated by a tool in a stage. The Unit has a unique identifier, a set of dependencies (contains information about other Units that the Unit depends on), the identifier of the Stage that produced the unit and the annotation (linguistic information produced by Tool). Besides these elements, it also has a common identifier that is shared across the layered annotations that are related with each other.

[3] `http://www.tei-c.org/`

[4] `http://www.w3.org/TR/xptr/`

3.5 Stage

Stages represent a phase in the annotation process. Each Stage has two queues: an input and an output queue of Units. This component is responsible for consuming input units, pass them to the Tool and, after their processing, putting them on the output queue. The Units in the output queue can later be used by another Stage (by connecting the output queue to the input queue of the next stage) or written to a file.

An NLP system can be composed of several Stages that are responsible for a specific annotation task. The framework allows the composition of various Tools to form a complete NLP system: each Tool receives the information produced by the Tools in the previous Stages and produces a Unit with the annotation created with references to the previous ones. This information is maintained in memory, along the created tool pipeline, and is only written to disk at the end of the NLP system.

3.6 Tool

Tools are responsible for specific linguistic tasks. Currently, these Tools include (without limitation) Tokenizers and Classifiers. Tokenizers receive the input text and produce segmentations (list of segments) that refer to the input, i.e., divide the input sentences into words. Classifiers produce sets of classifications for a given segmentation. These classifications can be, for example, the grammar class of each word. These tools accept two kinds of inputs: an input text or a previously created annotation with a segmentation.

In order to add new tools, it is necessary to extend the previous classes and add the necessary code in order to add the information produced by the existing NLP tool in the LAF format.

Because the framework is written in Java, and the tools could have been developed in a different language, such as C++ or Perl, it was necessary to find a way to interact with other programming languages. Hence, an existing tool can be integrated in various ways. If a tool provides an API, we currently provide an Remote Procedure Call (RPC) mechanism with the Thrift[5] software library. If the API can be used in a C/C++ program, it is also possible to use the existing tool API with Java Native Interface (JNI) (Liang, 1999). The framework also supports tools that can only be executed from the command line.

[5]`http://incubator.apache.org/thrift/`

4 Applications

The tools that have been integrated can be divided into two classes: those capable of producing first level annotations and those capable of producing second level annotations. The first level tools produce morphosyntactic annotation from an input text. Second level tools receive morphosyntactic information as input and produce morphosyntactic annotations. To show the language independence of the framework, we integrated tools from four different languages: Arabic, Japanese, English, and Portuguese. One of the tools capable of analyzing Arabic texts is AraMorph (Buckwalter, 2002), a Java-based Arabic morphological analyzer. For the Japanese language we chose Chasen (Matsumoto et al., 1999), a morphological analyzer capable of processing Japanese texts. The Stanford POS Tagger (Toutanova, 2000; Toutanova et al., 2003) is only being used to process English texts but it can be easily adapted (by changing its input dictionary) to process other languages, like Chinese or German. For processing Portuguese, we chose the Palavroso morphological analyzer (Medeiros, 1995). The morphological analyzers previously described produce first level annotations, i.e., they receive text as input and produce annotations.

Besides these tools, we also integrated types of tools for testing second level annotations: RuDriCo (Paulo, 2001) and JMARv (Ribeiro et al., 2003). RuDriCo is a post-morphological analyzer that rewrites the results of a morphological analyzer. RuDriCo uses declarative transformation rules based on pattern matching. JMARv is a tool that performs morphosyntactic disambiguation (selects a classification from the possible classifications in each segment from the input sequence). The two previous tools were used for processing Portuguese morphosyntactic information, but can be easily adapted to process other languages. For example, JMARv could be used to disambiguate AraMorph classifications and RuDriCo could translate Chasen's Japanese POS information into other formats.

5 Merging Layered Annotations

The stand-off annotation provided by the LAF format allows to add new layers of linguistic information by creating a tree whose nodes are references to another layer. This approach offers many advantages, like the possibility to distribute the an-

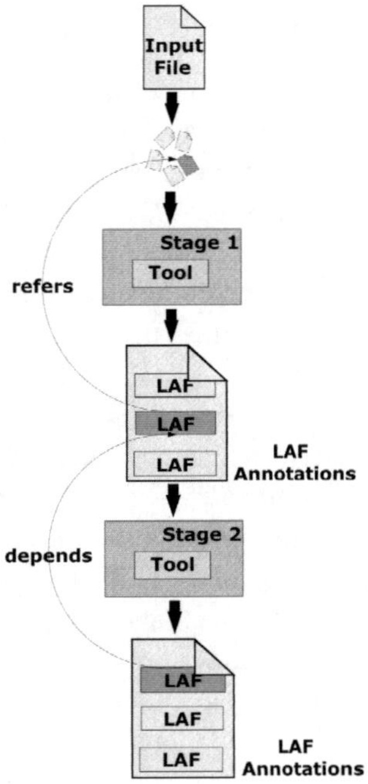

Figure 5: Illustration of the dependencies between annotation layers.

Figure 6: Codification of the layered annotations dependencies.

notations without the source text, and the possibility to annotate discontinuous segments of text. However, these layers, although separate, depend on each other, and their information can be difficult to access, because these layers can be spread across different files. There is a naïve approach to do this merge, that consists in loading all annotations from all files to memory and then resolve their dependencies. However, these dependencies can be dispersed across several large files (see Figure 5. Thus, the machine memory constraints become a problem for this solution.

Therefore, we propose a novel solution to solve the merging problem in a efficient manner using the MapReduce programming paradigm. The grouping capability offered by the Hadoop framework – a Java implementation of the MapReduce paradigm – allows to efficiently merge the annotations produced by the different tools, i.e., the layered annotations. This operation is performed as follows:

Map - this phase produces key/value pairs with a key equal to the identifier that is shared by annotations that depend on one another (see Figure 6). Thus, all related annotations are grouped by the framework after this phase.

Reduce - before the creation of the new annotation, merge the previously created annotations. This merging process creates a single annotation that contains all the annotations that were combined. This unified annotation is then passed to the Tool. The Tool processes the annotation and produces another one sharing a common identifier. The new annotation is written at the end of this phase.

The serialization of the intermediate key and value elements from a pair in a binary format allows us to reduce bandwidth usage due to the more compact representation of the key and value compared to the LAF (XML-based format representation of the input file).

6 Results

The tests were performed on a cluster with 20 machines. Each machine had an Intel Quad-Core Q6600 2.4 GHz processor, 8 GB of DDR2 RAM at 667 MHz and was connected to a gigabit ethernet.

To measure the amount of achieved parallelism, we used the speedup formula shown in Equation 1: T_s is the execution time of the sequential algorithm; T_p is the execution time of the parallel algorithm. Speedup refers to how much a parallel solution is faster than the corresponding sequential solution.

$$S = \frac{T_s}{T_p} \tag{1}$$

The Hadoop framework was installed on all machines and each one was configured to run 4 map and 4 reduce tasks simultaneously. The Hadoop uses HDFS as storage. This file system was configured to split each file into 64 MB chunks. These blocks are replicated across the machines in the

Data [MB]	Stanford POS Tagger Serial Time [s]
1	308
2	606
5	1531
10	3055
20	6021
50	15253

Table 1: Serial processing time of the Stanford POS Tagger

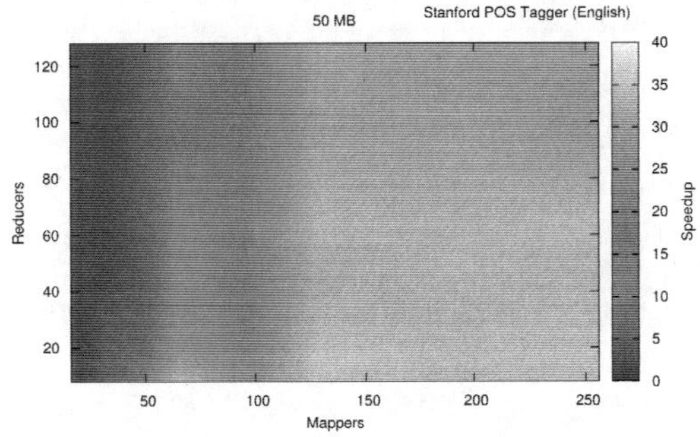

Figure 7: Stanford POS Tagger speedup results

cluster in order to tolerate machine failures. We used a HDFS replication factor of three.

To test the system, we used the speedup formula and selected the Stanford POS Tagger. Table 1 shows the serial execution time of the Stanford POS Tagger. This time corresponds to the standalone execution of the tool (without being integrated in the framework) on a single computer, for various sizes of input data (from 1 MB to 50 MB). Input and output were read/written from/to the local disk.

In addition to the previous tool, we also tested JMARv in order to assess the impact of annotation merging at execution time. Unlike the other tools, this tool receives annotations as input.

We must also consider the setup time for Hadoop. When executing the tools on top of Hadoop, it is necessary to store the input data on HDFS. However, these files are, in many cases, rarely updated. Therefore, they are perfect for the write-once read-many nature of HDFS and the copy times of the input data files were not considered (the HDFS write speed was around 22 MB/s).

Section 6.1 shows the speedups achieved with the Stanford POS Tagger, and Section 6.2 the annotation merging results, with the JMARv tool.

6.1 Stanford POS Tagger Results

Figure 7 shows the speedup values when considering various values for the number of mappers and reducers, without any compression of the final output, for an input of 50 MB. The large standalone times show that this tool is computationally heavy. With this tool it was possible to achieve a speedup value of approximately 40.

The horizontal progression of the speedup is explained by the heavy computation performed by the tool. Since processing from the Stanford POS Tagger is performed in mappers, the increase in the number of mappers improves speedup values.

The execution time of this tool is around 400 seconds, on the yellow (light gray) portion of Figure 7 and 1700 seconds on the dark blue (black) portions. On the intermediate values the execution time is approximately 1000 seconds.

The top right corner of the graph shows a small speedup decrease. This can be explained by the large number of queued map and reduce tasks.

Input [MB]	Compressed		Uncompressed	
	Output [MB]	Time [s]	Output [MB]	Time [s]
1	3	56	24	57
2	6	66	48	67
5	15	91	119	94
10	31	140	238	140
20	62	235	476	226
50	155	534	1192	529

Table 2: Stanford POS tagger output compression evaluation with a fixed number of 64 mappers and 64 reducers.

6.1.1 Compression Evaluation

Table 2 shows how output compression influences execution times values. As shown in Table 2, this tool produces, approximately, an output 24 times larger than the input, without compression, and 3 times larger with compression. However, output compression does not improve execution times due to heavy computation performed by the tool. Hence, processing time dominates output writing time.

6.2 Annotation Merging Results

Unlike the previous tool, JMARv does not process text as input. This tool receives an annotation as input that, in this case, was previously created by Palavroso.

In order to test the parallel annotation merging on top of Hadoop, we measured three kinds of times: Palavroso execution time with output cre-

	Palavroso	Palavroso + JMARv	JMARv
Time [s]	171 s	323 s	179 s

Table 3: Annotation merging time evaluation with a fixed number of 64 mappers and 64 reducers, for an input of 100 MB of text.

ation time, execution time of JMARv with the previously written Palavroso output and the time of Palavroso and JMARv executed in a pipeline (intermediate data is maintained in memory and the output produced is only written to disk after the execution of the two tools). The results are presented in Table 3. The first column shows the execution time of the Palavroso tool. The second column shows the time of Palavroso and JMARv execution in a pipeline. Finally, the last column shows the execution time of JMARv with the previously created Palavroso output.

In order to execute JMARv after Palavroso, it was necessary to handle about 8 GB of output produced by the previous tool (already stored on disk). However, these results show that running JMARv with this amount of data is practically the same as running both tools in pipeline with the original input (100 MB) and only write their output at the end.

7 Conclusions

This framework allowed us to build scalable NLP systems that achieve significant speedups: in the case of computation heavy tools, speedups reached values of approximately 40. In this case, an increase on the number of map tasks improves speedups, because processing time dominates the output writing time.

In addition, the framework supports a wide range of linguistic annotations, thanks to the adoption of LAF. The integration of tools does not consider any aspect related with the parallel execution on top of the Hadoop. Thus, the programmer focuses only on representing the linguistic information produced by the tool for a given input text or previously created annotations. In addition, the programming ease offered by the Hadoop framework allows to focus only on the problem we are solving, i.e., linguistic annotation. All the problems inherent to distributed computing are transparently solved by the platform. The MapReduce sort/grouping capabilities has been used to efficiently merge layered annotations produced by tools integrated in the framework. Regarding future work, on the linguistic part, we plan to integrate tools that produce syntactic annotations (the LAF format already supports these annotations). This linguistic information can be merged with the current tree by simply adding more nodes above the nodes that contain the morphosyntactic annotations. Also, this work did not focus on information normalization. The Data Category Registry (DCR) (Wright, 2004) could be explored in the future, in order to improve interoperability between linguistic resources.

Finally, the creation of NLP systems can be simplified by an XML parametrization. This way it is possible to compose a tool pipeline by simply editing an XML file. An graphical environment for visualization and editing of LAF annotations is also useful.

Our code is available at `http://code.google.com/p/anota/`.

Acknowledgments

This work was supported by the partnership between Carnegie Mellon University and Portugal's National Science and Technology Foundation (FCT – Fundação para a Ciência e a Tecnologia).

References

Kalina Bontcheva, Valentin Tablan, Diana Maynard, and Hamish Cunningham. 2004. Evolving gate to meet new challenges in language engineering. *Nat. Lang. Eng.*, 10(3-4):349–373.

Tim Buckwalter. 2002. Buckwalter Arabic Morphological Analyzer Version 1.0. Linguistic Data Consortium, catalog number LDC2002L49, ISBN 1-58563-257-0.

H. Cunningham, D. Maynard, K. Bontcheva, and V. Tablan. 2002. Gate: A framework and graphical development environment for robust nlp tools and applications. In *Proceedings of the 40th Annual Meeting of the ACL.*

Jeffrey Dean and Sanjay Ghemawat. 2008. MapReduce: simplified data processing on large clusters. *Commun. ACM*, 51(1):107–113, January.

Michael Thomas Egner, Markus Lorch, and Edd Biddle. 2007. Uima grid: Distributed large-scale text analysis. In *CCGRID '07: Proceedings of the Seventh IEEE International Symposium on Cluster Computing and the Grid*, pages 317–326, Washington, DC, USA. IEEE Computer Society.

David Ferrucci and Adam Lally. 2004. Uima: an architectural approach to unstructured information processing in the corporate research environment. *Nat. Lang. Eng.*, 10(3-4):327–348.

William Gropp. 2001. Learning from the Success of MPI. In Burkhard Monien, Viktor K. Prasanna, and Sriram Vajapeyam, editors, *HiPC*, volume 2228 of *Lecture Notes in Computer Science*, pages 81–94. Springer.

Nancy Ide and Laurent Romary. 2006. Representing linguistic corpora and their annotations. In *Proceedings of the Fifth Language Resources and Evaluation Conference (LREC*.

Nancy Ide and Keith Suderman. 2006. Merging layered annotations. In *Proceedings of Merging and Layering Linguistic Information*, Genoa, Italy.

Michal Laclavík, Martin Šeleng, and Ladislav Hluchý. 2008. Towards large scale semantic annotation built on mapreduce architecture. In *ICCS '08: Proceedings of the 8th international conference on Computational Science, Part III*, pages 331–338, Berlin, Heidelberg. Springer-Verlag.

Sheng Liang. 1999. *Java Native Interface: Programmer's Guide and Reference*. Addison-Wesley Longman Publishing Co., Inc., Boston, MA, USA.

Edward Loper and Steven Bird. 2002. Nltk: the natural language toolkit. In *Proceedings of the ACL-02 Workshop on Effective tools and methodologies for teaching natural language processing and computational linguistics*, pages 63–70, Morristown, NJ, USA. Association for Computational Linguistics.

Yuji Matsumoto, Akira Kitauchi, Tatsuo Yamashita, Y. Hirano, Hiroshi Matsuda, and Masayuki Asahara, 1999. *Japanese morphological analysis system ChaSen version 2.0 manual 2nd edition*. Nara Institute of Science and Technology, technical report naist-istr99009 edition.

Jos Carlos Medeiros. 1995. Processamento morfolgico e correco ortogrfica do portugułs. Master's thesis, Insituto Superior Tcnico – Universidade Tcnica de Lisboa, Portugal.

Joana Lcio Paulo. 2001. PAsMo - Ps Analisador Morfolgico. Master's thesis, Insituto Superior Tcnico – Universidade Tcnica de Lisboa, Portugal.

Ricardo Ribeiro, Nuno J. Mamede, and Isabel Trancoso. 2003. Using Morphossyntactic Information in TTS Systems: comparing strategies for European Portuguese. In *Computational Processing of the Portuguese Language: 6th International Workshop, PROPOR 2003, Faro, Portugal, June 26-27, 2003. Proceedings*, volume 2721 of *Lecture Notes in Computer Science*. Springer.

Kristina Toutanova, Dan Klein, Christopher D. Manning, and Yoram Singer. 2003. Feature-rich part-of-speech tagging with a cyclic dependency network. In *Proceedings of HLT-NAACL 2003*, pages 252–259.

Kristina Toutanova. 2000. Enriching the knowledge sources used in a maximum entropy part-of-speech tagger. In *Proceedings of EMNLP/VLC 2000*, pages 63–70.

S. E. Wright. 2004. A global data category registry for interoperable language resources. In *Proceedings of the Fourth Language Resources and Evaluation Conference – LREC 2004*, pages 123–126. ELRA European Language Resources Association.

The Coding Scheme for Annotating Extended Nominal Coreference and Bridging Anaphora in the Prague Dependency Treebank

Anna Nedoluzhko, Jiří Mírovský, Petr Pajas
Charles University in Prague
Institute of Formal and Applied Linguistics
{nedoluzko, mirovsky, pajas}@ufal.mff.cuni.cz

Abstract

The present paper outlines an ongoing project of annotation of the extended nominal coreference and the bridging anaphora in the Prague Dependency Treebank. We describe the annotation scheme with respect to the linguistic classification of coreferential and bridging relations and focus also on details of the annotation process from the technical point of view. We present methods of helping the annotators – by a pre-annotation and by several useful features implemented in the annotation tool. Our method of the inter-annotator agreement is focused on the improvement of the annotation guidelines; we present results of three subsequent measurements of the agreement.

1 Introduction

The Prague Dependency Treebank (PDT 2.0) is a large collection of linguistically annotated data and documentation (Hajič et al., 2006). In PDT 2.0, Czech newspaper texts are annotated on three layers. The most abstract (tectogrammatical) layer includes the annotation of coreferential links of two types: grammatical coreference (typically within a single sentence) and textual coreference (for pronominal and zero anaphora). The current paper focuses on the present annotation of extended textual coreference, where the anaphoric expression is neither personal pronoun, nor zero. Also the annotation of bridging anaphora on PDT is discussed.

In the last few years, a number of annotation schemes have been released, three of which are to be shortly presented here. The MUC is considered to be the most standard annotation scheme (Hirschman, 1997) and it is used in more than one application (MUC-6, MUC-7, ACE). The advantage of this scheme is its simplicity and a very detailed linguistically oriented coding scheme. It has been however criticized for its vague interpretation of the notion of coreference and for the limited coverage of relations (only identical relation between nouns is annotated). One of the most well known later approaches is MATE (Poesio, 2004) and its extension on the GNOME corpus. The project is meant to be multi-functional. The annotation scheme was primarily developed for dialog acts analyses, but may be easily adapted for any other investigation. In the extended GNOME scheme, the identical coreference is annotated along with some bridging relations, such as ELEMENT, SUBSET, POSSession and OTHER for underspecified relations. In PoCoS (Krasavina and Chiarchos, 2007), a two layer coreference annotation scheme was suggested: the Core Layer is general and reusable, while the Extended Layer supports a wider range of specific extensions.

In this document, we present the application of coreference annotation on a slavonic language (Czech). Czech has no definite article, so in many cases, an anaphoric relation cannot be easily identified. That's why we concentrated solely on coreference, i.e. on the case when two expressions denote the same entity. Anaphoric relation between non-coreferential objects is annotated separately, together with some other types of bridging anaphora (see 2.1).

2 Methods of coreference and bridging anaphora annotation

Subject to annotation are pairs of coreferring expressions, the preceding expression is called antecedent, the subsequent one is called anaphor.

The (mostly manual) annotation of the extended coreference and bridging anaphora proceeds basically in one phase. Unlike MUC/MATE/PoCoS projects, where annotation is divided into two phases (identifying elements that can come in coreference relation (so called "markables") and establishing anaphoric relation), we do not make preliminary annotation of "markables". Realizing the disadvantage of difficult agreement comparison, we still think that to separate identifying "markables" is unnecessary in case of a language without grammatical category of definiteness.

Proceedings of the Third Linguistic Annotation Workshop, ACL-IJCNLP 2009, pages 108–111,
Suntec, Singapore, 6-7 August 2009.

2.1 The annotation scheme

For the time being, we annotate textual coreference and bridging anaphora. In what follows, we briefly present the classification of these two types of context-dependences.

The cases where anaphor is a personal, demonstrative or zero pronoun are already annotated in PDT. In the present annotation, the most cases of anaphoric expressions are expressed by NP with nominal head, in some cases also by pronominal demonstrative adverbs (*there, then* etc.), adjectives (by named entities (e.g. *Germany – German*) and possessive forms)), numerals or verbs (*own – ownership*), see ex. (1).

Textual coreference is further classified into two types – coreference of NPs with specific or generic coreference. This decision is made on the basis of the expectation, that generic coreferential chains have different anaphoric rules from the specific ones. Into this group, there is also included a big number of abstract nouns, whose coreference is not quite clear in every particular case. So, the generic type of textual coreference serves as the ambiguity group too.

In **bridging anaphora** we distinguish PART, SUBSET and FUNCT traditional relations (see e.g. Clark 1977), CONTRAST for coherence relevant discourse opposites (e.g. *<u>People</u> don't chew, it's <u>cows</u> who chew*) and further underspecified group REST, which is used for capturing bridging references – potential candidates for a new bridging group (e.g. location – resident, relatives, event – argument and some others).

2.2 Annotation Principles

In order to develop maximally consistent annotation scheme, we follow a number of basic principles. Some of them are presented below:

Chain principle: coreference relations in text are organized in ordered chains. The most recent mention of a referent is marked as antecedent. This principle is controlled automatically (see 3.1.2). Chain principle does not concern bridging anaphora.

Principle of the **maximum length of coreferencial chains** also concerns only the case of coreference. It says that in case of multiple choice, we prefer to continue the existing coreference chain, rather than to begin a new one. To satisfy this principle, grammatical coreferential chains are being continued by textual ones, and already annotated textual coreferences are continued by currently annotated non-pronominal links in turn.

The principle of **maximal size of an anaforic expression**: subject to annotation is always the whole subtree of the antecedent/anaphor. This principle is partially directed by the dependency structure of tectogrammatical trees and may be sometimes counter-intuitive. See ex. (1):

> (1) Henry's brother Nicholas has owned the Hall for 27 years. On Nicholas' death, it passed into the ownership of his nephew, Yarburgh Greame

The principle of **cooperation with the syntactic structure of a given dependency tree**: we do not annotate relations, which are already caught up by the syntactic structure of the tectogrammatical tree. So, unlike most schemes, we do not annotate predication and apposition relations.

Preference of coreference over bridging anaphora: in case of multiple choice, we prefer coreference.

3 The Tool and Data Format

The primary format of PDT 2.0 is called PML. It is an abstract XML-based format designed for annotation of treebanks. For editing and processing data in PML format, a fully customizable tree editor TrEd has been implemented (Pajas & Štěpánek 2008).

TrEd can be easily customized to a desired purpose by extensions that are included into the system as modules. In this section, we describe some features of an extension that has been implemented for our purposes.

The data scheme used in PDT 2.0 has been slightly extended to support the annotation of the extended textual coreference (that has – unlike the originally annotated textual coreference – a type) and the bridging anaphora (that has not been annotated before and also has a type). Technically, various kinds of non-dependency relations between nodes in PDT 2.0 use dedicated referring attributes that contain unique identifiers of the nodes they refer to.

3.1 Helping the Annotators

We employ two ways of helping the annotators in their tedious task. First, we pre-annotate the data with highly probable coreference relations. The annotators check these links and can remove them if they are wrong. This approach has proved to be faster than letting the annotators annotate the data from scratch. Second, we have implemented several supporting features into the annotation tool (the TrEd extension) that help during the annotation process.

3.1.1 Pre-Annotation

We use a list of pairs of words that with a high probability form a coreferential pair in texts. Most of the pairs in the list consist of a noun and a derived adjective, which are different in Czech, e.g. Praha – pražský (in English: Prague – Prague, like in the sentence: *He arrived in Prague and found the Prague atmosphere quite casual*). The rest of the list is formed by pairs consisting of an abbreviation and its one-word expansion, e.g. ČR – Česko (similarly in English: USA – States). The whole list consists of more than 6 thousand pairs obtained automatically from the morphological synthesizer for Czech, manually checked and slightly extended.

3.1.2 Annotation

Several features have been implemented in the annotation tool to help with the annotation.

Manual pre-annotation: If the annotator finds a word in the text that appears many times in the document and its occurrences seem to corefer, he can create a coreferential chain out of these words by a single key-stroke. All nodes that have the same tectogrammatical lemma (t_lemma) become a part of the chain.

Finding the nearest antecedent: The annotation instructions require that the nearest antecedent is always selected for the coreferential link. The tool automatically re-directs a newly created coreferential arrow to the nearest one (in the already existing coreferential chain) if the annotator selects a farther antecedent by mistake. However, the rule of the nearest antecedent can be broken in less clear situations. For example, if there are three coreferential words in the text, A, B and C (ordered from left to right), and the annotator connects A and C (overlooking B), and later realizes that B is also coreferential with A and creates the arrow from B to A, the tool reconnects the C→A arrow to C→B. Thus, the chain C→B→A is correctly created.

Preserving the coreferential chain: If the annotator removes an arrow and a coreferential chain is thus interrupted, the tool asks the annotator whether it should re-connect the chain.

Text highlighting: The annotation of the extended textual coreference and the bridging anaphora is performed on the tectogrammatical layer of PDT. However, the annotators prefer to work on the surface form of the text, using the tectogrammatical trees only as a supporting depiction of the relations. After selecting a word in the sentences (by clicking on it), the tool determines to which node in the tectogrammatical trees the word belongs. Then, the projection back to the surface is performed and all words on the surface that belong to the selected node are highlighted. Only one word of the highlighted words is a lexical counterpart of the tectogrammatical node (which is usually the word the annotator clicked on – only in cases such as if the annotator clicks on a preposition or other auxiliary word, the lexical counterpart of the corresponding tectogrammatical node differs from the word clicked on). Using this information, also all words in the sentences that have the same t_lemma (again, we use only the lexical counterparts) as the selected word, are underlined. Words that are connected with the selected word via a coreferential chain are highlighted in such colors that indicate whether the last connecting relation in the chain was textual or grammatical. Moreover, all words that are connected via a bridging anaphora with any word of this coreferential chain, are highlighted in a specific color.

4 Application and Evaluation

The annotation of the extended textual coreference and the bridging anaphora started in November 2008. Two annotators work on different texts (each document is annotated only by one annotator), except for a small overlap used for measuring the inter-annotator agreement.

As of April 2009, about one fifth of PDT 2.0 data has been annotated. The detailed numbers are summed in Table 1:

number of annotated documents	611
total number of sentences	9,425
total number of words	157,817
total number of tectogrammatical nodes (excl. the technical root)	127,954
number of newly annotated co-referring nodes (bridging relations and textual coreference)	16,874
number of co-referring nodes including the textual coreference originally annotated in PDT 2.0	20,532
% of co-referring nodes	16 %

Table 1. Annotation statistics

Figure 1 presents the proportion of types of coreferential and bridging relations in the currently annotated part of PDT[1]. TK_0 is used for textual coreference of specific NPs, TK_NR for textual coreference of non-specific NPs, other abbreviations are believed to be self-explaining.

[1] Including the originally annotated textual coreference in PDT 2.0.

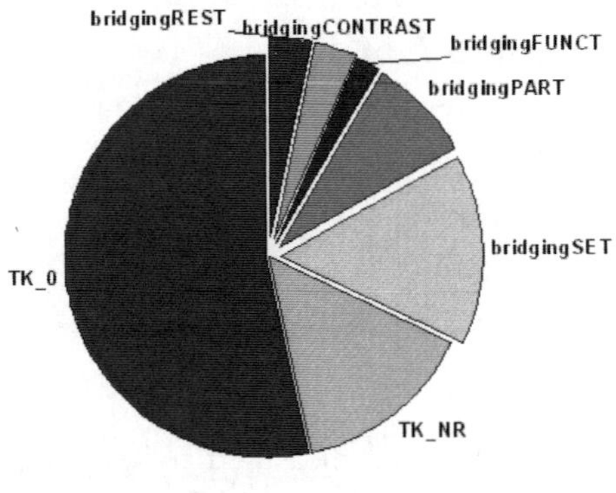

Figure 1. Types of relations

Inter-annotator agreement: For the purposes of checking and improving the annotation guidelines, we require a more strict inter-annotator agreement than agreement on sets (for coreference), often used in other projects (e.g. Passoneau 2004). For both the extended textual coreference and the bridging anaphora, we use F_1-measure for the agreement on the antecedent, and Cohen's κ (Cohen 1960) for the agreement on the type of the link. In Table 2, the results of the three performed measurements of the inter-annotator agreement are presented:

	arrows TC (F_1)	arrows TC + types (F_1)	TC types only (κ)	arrows bridging (F_1)	arrows bridging + types (F_1)	bridging types only (κ)
1st measurement (40 sent.)	0.76	0.67	0.54	0.49	0.42	0.79
2nd measurement (40 sent.)	0.64	0.41	0.33	0.52	0.52	1
3rd measurement (100 sent.)	0.80	0.68	0.67	0.59	0.57	0.88

Table 2. Evaluation of the inter-annotator agreement

5 Conclusion

We have presented the annotation scheme and principles for the extended textual coreference and the bridging anaphora in PDT 2.0.

Pre-annotation and features of the annotation tool that help the annotators have been described in detail. We have presented basic statistics about the annotation completed so far and results of first measurements of the inter-annotator agreement (which are difficult to compare to other approaches, as we do not use "markables").

Improvement of the inter-annotator agreement is in our focus for the upcoming stage of the project. The experience shows that the agreement is greatly affected by parameters of the text as a whole. Short texts are generally far less demanding for their interpretation than longer ones, texts with many abstract and general notions allow more possibilities of interpretation and so on. Frequent problems causing inter-annotator disagreement are of two types - different understanding of the content and inaccuracy of the coding scheme. The first case is hardly to be solved entirely. The problems of the second type are being worked on: we prepare the detailed classification of the inter-annotator disagreement and regularly specify the annotation guidelines.

Acknowledgment

We gratefully acknowledge the support of the Czech Ministry of Education (grant MSM-0021620838), the Czech Grant Agency (grant 405/09/0729), the European Union (project Companions – FP6-IST-5-034434), and the Grant Agency of the Academy of Sciences of the Czech Republic (project 1ET101120503).

References

Clark, H. 1977. Bridging. In Johnson-Laird and Wason, editors, *Thinking: Readings in Cognitive Science.* Cambridge. 411-420.

Cohen, J. 1960. A coefficient of agreement for nominal scales. Educational and Psychological Measurement, 20(1), 37-46.

Hajič, J. et al. 2006. Prague Dependency Treebank 2.0.CD-ROM, Linguistic Data Consortium, LDC Catalog No.: LDC2006T01, Philadelphia.

Hirschman, L. 1997. MUC-7 coreference task definition. Version 3.0.

Krasavina, O. and Ch. Chiarcos. 2007. PoCoS – Potsdam Coreference Scheme. Proc. of ACL 2007, Prague, Czech Republic

Kučová L. and E. Hajičová. 2004. Coreferential Relations in the Prague Dependency Treebank. In 5th Discourse Anaphora and Anaphor Resolution Colloquium. Ediçôes Colibri.

Pajas, P. and J. Štěpánek 2008. Recent advances in a feature-rich framework for treebank annotation. In The 22nd Interntional Conference on Computational Linguistics – Proceedings of the Conference. Manchester, pp. 673-680.

Passonneau, R. 2004. Computing Reliability for Coreference. In Proceedings of LREC, vol. 4, Lisbon, pp. 1503-1506.

Poesio, M. 2004 The MATE/GNOME Proposals for Anaphoric Annotation, Revisited. Proc. of SIGDIAL.

Timed Annotations — Enhancing MUC7 Metadata by the Time It Takes to Annotate Named Entities

Katrin Tomanek and **Udo Hahn**
Jena University Language & Information Engineering (JULIE) Lab
Friedrich-Schiller-Universität Jena, Germany
{katrin.tomanek|udo.hahn}@uni-jena.de

Abstract

We report on the re-annotation of selected types of named entities from the MUC7 corpus where our focus lies on recording the time it takes to annotate these entities given two basic annotation units – sentences *vs.* complex noun phrases. Such information may be helpful to lay the empirical foundations for the development of cost measures for annotation processes based on the investment in time for decision-making per entity mention.

1 Introduction

Manually supplied annotation metadata is at the heart of (semi)supervised machine learning techniques which have become very popular in NLP research. At their flipside, they create an enormous bottleneck because major shifts in the domain of discourse, the basic entities of interest, or the text genre often require new annotation efforts. But annotations are costly in terms of getting well-trained and intelligible human resources involved.

Surprisingly, cost awareness has not been a primary concern in most of the past linguistic annotation initiatives. Only recently, annotation strategies (such as Active Learning (Cohn et al., 1996)) which strive for minimizing the annotation load have gained increasing attention. Still, when it comes to the empirically plausible assessment of annotation costs even proponents of Active Learning make overly simplistic and empirically questionable assumptions, e.g., the uniformity of annotation costs over the number of linguistic units (e.g., tokens) to be annotated.

We here consider the time it takes to annotate a particular entity mention as a natural indicator of effort for named entity annotations. In order to lay the empirical foundations for experimentally grounded annotation cost models we couple common named entity annotation metadata with a time stamp reflecting the time measured for decision making.[1]

Previously, two studies – one dealing with POS annotation (Haertel et al., 2008), the other with named entity and relation annotation (Settles et al., 2008) – have measured the time needed to annotate sentences on small data sets and attempted to learn predictive models of annotation cost. However, these data sets do not meet our requirements as we envisage a large, coherent, and also well-known newspaper entity corpus extended by annotation costs on a fine-grained level. Especially size and coherence of such a corpus are not only essential for building accurate cost models but also as a reference baseline for cost-sensitive annotation strategies. Moreover, the annotation level for which cost information is available is crucial because document- or sentence-level data might be too coarse for several applications. Accordingly, this paper introduces MUC$7_{\mathcal{T}}$, our extension to the entity annotations of the MUC7 corpus (Linguistic Data Consortium, 2001) where time stamps are added to two levels of annotation granularity, *viz.* sentences and complex noun phrases.

2 Corpus Annotation

2.1 Annotation Task

Our annotation initiative constitutes an extension to the named entity annotations (ENAMEX) of the English part of the MUC7 corpus covering *New York Times* articles from 1996. ENAMEX annotations cover three types of named entities, *viz.* PERSONS, LOCATIONS, and ORGANIZATIONS. We instructed two human annotators, both advanced students of linguistics with good English language skills, to re-annotate the MUC7 corpus for the ENAMEX subtask. To be as consistent as possi-

[1] These time stamps should not be confounded with the annotation of temporal expressions (TIMEX in MUC7, or even more advanced metadata using TIMEML for the creation of the TIMEBANK (Pustejovsky et al., 2003)).

Proceedings of the Third Linguistic Annotation Workshop, ACL-IJCNLP 2009, pages 112–115,
Suntec, Singapore, 6-7 August 2009.

ble with the existing MUC7 annotations, the annotators had to follow the original guidelines of the MUC7 named entity task. For ease of re-annotation, we intentionally ignored temporal and number expressions (TIMEX and NUMEX).

MUC7 covers three distinct document sets for the named entity task. We used one of these sets to train the annotators and develop the annotation design, and another one for our actual annotation initiative which consists of 100 articles reporting on airplane crashes. We split lengthy documents (27 out of 100) into halves to fit on the annotation screen without the need for scrolling. Furthermore, we excluded two documents due to over-length which would have required overly many splits. Our final corpus contains 3,113 sentences (76,900 tokens) (see Section 3.1 for more details).

Time-stamped ENAMEX annotation of this corpus constitutes MUC$7_{\mathcal{T}}$, our extension of MUC7. Annotation time measurements were taken on two syntactically different *annotation units* of single documents: *(a)* complete sentences and *(b)* complex noun phrases. The annotation task was defined such as to assign an entity type label to each token of an annotation unit. Sentence-level annotation units where derived by the OPENNLP[2] sentence splitter. The use of complex noun phrases (CNPs) as an alternative annotation unit is motivated by the fact that in MUC7 the syntactic encoding of named entity mentions basically occurs through nominal phrases. CNPs were derived from the sentences' constituency structure using the OPENNLP parser (trained on PENNTREEBANK data) to determine top-level noun phrases. To avoid overly long phrases, CNPs dominating special syntactic structures, such as coordinations, appositions, or relative clauses, were split up at discriminative functional elements (e.g., a relative pronoun) and these elements were eliminated. An evaluation of our CNP extractor on ENAMEX annotations in MUC7 showed that 98.95% of all entities where completely covered by automatically identified CNPs. For the remaining 1.05% of the entity mentions, parsing errors were the most common source of incomplete coverage.

2.2 Annotation and Time Measurement

While the annotation task itself was "officially" declared to yield only annotations of named entity mentions within the different annotation units, we were primarily interested in the time needed for these annotations. For precise time measurements, single *annotation examples* were shown to the annotators, one at a time. An annotation example consists of the chosen MUC7 document with one annotation unit (sentence or CNP) selected and highlighted. Only the highlighted part of the document could be annotated and the annotators were asked to read only as much of the context surrounding the annotation unit as necessary to make a proper annotation decision. To present the annotation examples to annotators and allow for annotation without extra time overhead for the "mechanical" assignment of entity types, our annotation GUI is controlled by keyboard shortcuts. This minimizes annotation time compared to mouse-controlled annotation such that the measured time reflects only the amount of time needed for taking an annotation decision.

In order to avoid learning effects at the annotators' side on originally consecutive syntactic subunits, we randomly shuffled all annotation examples so that subsequent annotation examples were not drawn from the same document. Hence, annotation times were not biased by the order of appearance of the annotation examples.

Annotators were given blocks of either 500 CNP- or 100 sentence-level annotation examples. They were asked to annotate each block in a single run under noise-free conditions, without breaks and disruptions. They were also instructed not to annotate for too long stretches of time to avoid tiring effects making time measurements unreliable.

All documents were first annotated with respect to CNP-level examples within 2-3 weeks, with only very few hours per day of concrete annotation work. After completion of the CNP-level annotation, the same documents had to be annotated on the sentence level as well. Due to randomization and rare access to surrounding context during the CNP-level annotation, annotators credibly reported that they had indeed not remembered the sentences from the CNP-level round. Thus, the time measurements taken on the sentence level do not seem to exhibit any human memory bias.

Both annotators went through all annotation examples so that we have double annotations of the complete data set. Prior to coding, they independently got used to the annotation guidelines and were trained on several hundred examples. For the annotators' performance see Section 3.2.

[2] http://opennlp.sourceforge.net

3 Analysis

3.1 Corpus Statistics

Table 1 summarizes statistics on the time-stamped MUC7 corpus. About 60% of all tokens are covered by CNPs (45,097 out of 76,900 tokens) showing that sentences are made up from CNPs to a large extent. Still, removing the non-CNP tokens markedly reduces the amount of tokens to be considered for entity annotation. CNPs cover slightly less entities (3,937) than complete sentences (3,971), a marginal loss only.

sentences	3,113
sentence tokens	76,900
chunks	15,203
chunk tokens	45,097
entity mentions in sentences	3,971
entity mentions in CNPs	3,937
sentences with entity mentions	63%
CNPs with entity mentions	23%

Table 1: Descriptive statistics of time-stamped MUC7 corpus

On the average, sentences have a length of 24.7 tokens, while CNPs are rather short with 3.0 tokens, on the average. However, CNPs vary tremendously in their length, with the shortest ones having only one token and the longest ones (mostly due to parsing errors) spanning over 30 (and more) tokens. Figure 1 depicts the length distribution of sentences and CNPs showing that a reasonable portion of CNPs have less than five tokens, while the distribution of sentence lengths almost follows a normal distribution in the interval $[0, 50]$. While 63% of all sentences contain at least one entity mention, only 23% of CNPs contain entity mentions. These statistics show that CNPs are generally rather short and a large fraction of CNPs does not contain entity mentions at all. We may hypothesize that this observation will be reflected by annotation times.

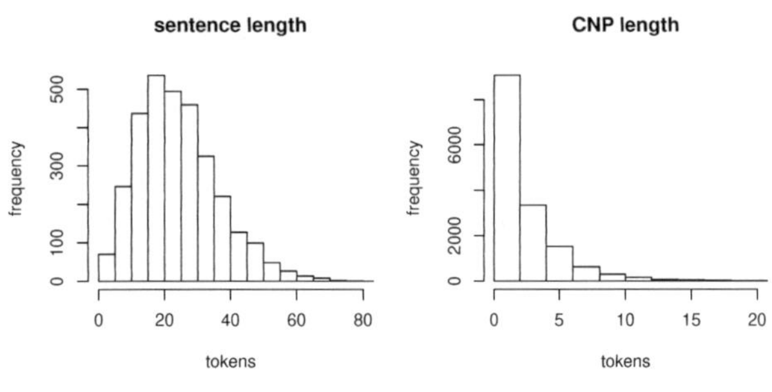

Figure 1: Length distribution of sentences and CNPs

3.2 Annotation Performance

To test the validity of the guidelines and the general performance of our annotators A and B, we compared their annotation results on 5 blocks of sentence-level annotation examples created during training. Annotation performance was measured in terms of Cohen's kappa coefficient κ on the token level and entity-segment F-score against MUC7 annotations. The annotators achieved $\kappa_A = 0.95$ and $\kappa_B = 0.96$, and $F_A = 0.92$ and $F_B = 0.94$, respectively.[3] Moreover, they exhibit an inter-annotator agreement of $\kappa_{A,B} = 0.94$ and an averaged mutual F-score of $F_{A,B} = 0.90$. These numbers reveal that the task is well-defined and the annotators have sufficiently internalized the annotation guidelines to produce valid results.

Figure 2 shows the annotators' scores against the original MUC7 annotations for the 31 blocks of sentence-level annotations (3,113 sentences) which range from $\kappa = 0.89$ to $\kappa = 0.98$. Largely, annotation performance is similar for both annotators and shows that they consistently found a block either rather hard or easy to annotate. Moreover, annotation performance seems stationary – no general trend in annotation performance over time can be observed.

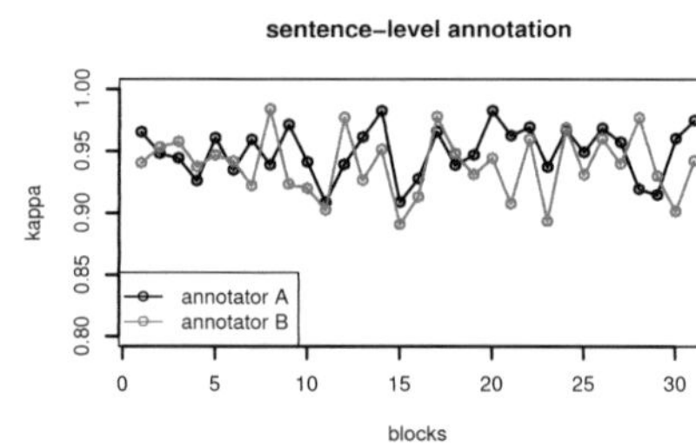

Figure 2: Average kappa coefficient per block

3.3 Time Measurements

Figure 3 shows the average annotation time per block (CNPs and sentences). Considering the CNP-level annotations, there is a learning effect for annotator B during the first 9 blocks. After that, both annotators are approximately on a par regarding the annotation time. For sentence-level annotations, both annotators again yield similar annotation times per block, without any learning effects. Similar to annotation performance,

[3]Entity-specific F-scores against MUC7 annotations for A and B are 0.90 and 0.92 for LOCATION, 0.92 and 0.93 for ORGANIZATION, and 0.96 and 0.98 for PERSON, respectively.

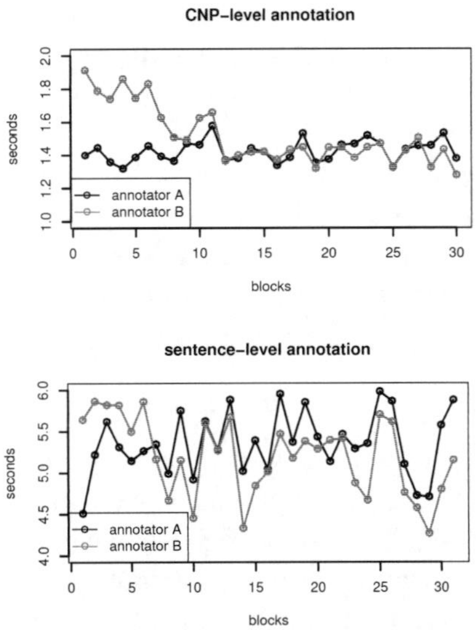

Figure 3: Average annotation times per block

analysis of annotation time shows that the annotation behavior is largely stationary (excluding first rounds of CNP-level annotation) which allows single time measurements to be interpreted independently of previous time measurements. Both, time and performance plots exhibit that there are blocks which were generally harder or easier than other ones because both annotators operated in tandem.

3.4 Easy and Hard Annotation Examples

As we have shown, inter-annotator variation of annotation performance is moderate. Intra-block performance, in contrast, is subject to high variance. Figure 4 shows the distribution of annotator A's CNP-level annotation times for block 20. A's average annotation time on this block amounts to 1.37 seconds per CNP, the shortest time being 0.54, the longest one amounting 10.2 seconds. The figure provides ample evidence for an extremely skewed time investment for coding CNPs.

A preliminary manual analysis revealed CNPs with very low annotation times are mostly short and consist of stop words and pronouns only, or are otherwise simple noun phrases with a surface structure incompatible with entity mentions (e.g., all tokens are lower-cased). Here, humans can quickly exclude the occurrence of entity mentions which results in low annotation times. CNPs which took desparately long (more than 6 seconds) were outliers indicating distraction or loss of concentration. Times between 3 and 5 seconds were basically caused by semantically complex CNPs.

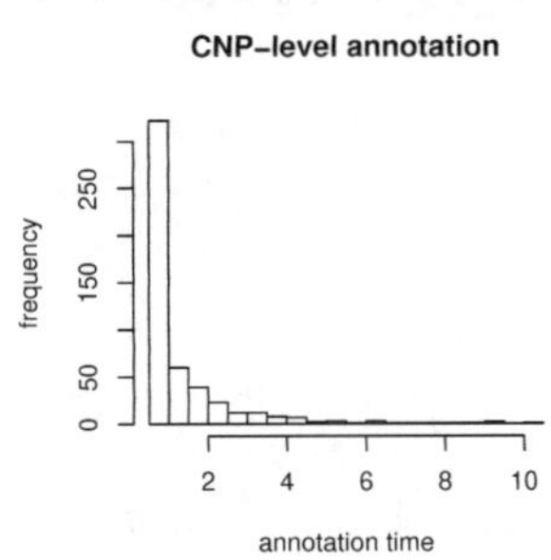

Figure 4: Distribution of annotation times in one block

4 Conclusions

We have created a time-stamped version of MUC7 entity annotations, MUC7$_{\mathcal{T}}$, on two levels of annotation granularity – sentences and complex noun phrases. Especially the phrase-level annotations allow for fine-grained time measurement. We will use this corpus for studies on (time) cost-sensitive Active Learning. MUC7$_{\mathcal{T}}$ can also be used to derive or learn accurate annotation cost models allowing to predict annotation time on new data. We are currently investigating causal factors of annotation complexity for named entity annotation on the basis of MUC7$_{\mathcal{T}}$.

Acknowledgements

This work was funded by the EC within the BOOTStrep (FP6-028099) and CALBC (FP7-231727) projects. We want to thank Oleg Lichtenwald (JULIE Lab) for implementing the noun phrase extractor for our experiments.

References

David A. Cohn, Zoubin Ghahramani, and Michael I. Jordan. 1996. Active learning with statistical models. *Journal of Artificial Intelligence Research*, 4:129–145.

Robbie Haertel, Eric Ringger, Kevin Seppi, James Carroll, and Peter McClanahan. 2008. Assessing the costs of sampling methods in active learning for annotation. In *Proceedings of the ACL-08: HLT, Short Papers*, pages 65–68.

Linguistic Data Consortium. 2001. Message Understanding Conference 7. LDC2001T02. FTP file.

James Pustejovsky, Patrick Hanks, Roser Saurí, Andrew See, Robert Gaizauskas, Andrea Setzer, Dragomir Radev, Beth Sundheim, David Day, Lisa Ferro, and Marcia Lazo. 2003. The TIMEBANK corpus. In *Proceedings of the Corpus Linguistics 2003 Conference*, pages 647–656.

Burr Settles, Mark Craven, and Lewis Friedland. 2008. Active learning with real annotation costs. In *Proceedings of the NIPS'08 Workshop on Cost Sensitive Learning*, pages 1–10.

Transducing Logical Relations from Automatic and Manual GLARF

Adam Meyers[†], Michiko Kosaka[‡], Heng Ji[⋆], Nianwen Xue[⋄],
Mary Harper[▽], Ang Sun[†], Wei Xu[†] and Shasha Liao[†]
[†] New York Univ., [‡]Monmouth Univ., [⋄]Brandeis Univ,, [⋆]City Univ. of New York, [▽]Johns Hopkins Human Lang. Tech. Ctr. of Excellence & U. of Maryland, College Park

Abstract

GLARF relations are generated from treebank and parses for English, Chinese and Japanese. Our evaluation of system output for these input types requires consideration of multiple correct answers.[1]

1 Introduction

Systems, such as treebank-based parsers (Charniak, 2001; Collins, 1999) and semantic role labelers (Gildea and Jurafsky, 2002; Xue, 2008), are trained and tested on hand-annotated data. Evaluation is based on differences between system output and test data. Other systems use these programs to perform tasks unrelated to the original annotation. For example, participating systems in CONLL (Surdeanu et al., 2008; Hajič et al., 2009), ACE and GALE tasks merged the results of several processors (parsers, named entity recognizers, etc.) not initially designed for the task at hand. This paper discusses differences between hand-annotated data and automatically generated data with respect to our GLARFers, systems for generating Grammatical and Logical Representation Framework (GLARF) for English, Chinese and Japanese sentences. The paper describes GLARF (Meyers et al., 2001; Meyers et al., 2009) and GLARFers and compares GLARF produced from treebank and parses.

2 GLARF

Figure 1 includes simplified GLARF analyses for English, Chinese and Japanese sentences. For each sentence, a GLARFer constructs both a Feature Structure (FS) representing a constituency analysis and a set of 31-tuples, each representing up to three dependency relations between pairs of words. Due to space limitations, we will focus on the 6 fields of the 31-tuple represented in Figure 1. These include: (1) a functor (**func**); (2) the depending argument (**Arg**); (3) a surface (**Surf**) label based on the position in the parse tree with no regularizations; (4) a logic1 label (L1) for a relation that reflects grammar-based regularizations of the surface level. This marks relations for filling gaps in relative clauses or missing infinitival subjects, represents passives as paraphrases as actives, etc. While the general framework supports many regularizations, the relations actually represented depends on the implemented grammar, e.g., our current grammar of English regularizes across passives and relative clauses, but our grammars of Japanese and Chinese do not currently.; (5) a logic2 label (**L2**) for Chinese and English, which represents PropBank, NomBank and Penn Discourse Treebank relations; and (6) Asterisks (*) indicate *transparent* relations, relations where the functor inherits semantic properties of certain special arguments (*CONJ, *OBJ, *PRD, *COMP).

Figure 1 contains several transparent relations. The interpretation of the *CONJ relations in the Japanese example, include not only that the nouns *[zaisan]* (*assets*) and *[seimei]* (*lives*) are conjoined, but also that these two nouns, together form the object of the Japanese verb *[mamoru]* (*protect*). Thus, for example, semantic selection patterns should treat these nouns as possible objects for this verb. Transparent relations may serve to neutralize some of the problematic cases of attachment ambiguity. For example, in the English sentence *A number of phrases with modifiers are not ambiguous*, there is a transparent *COMP relation between *numbers* and *of* and a transparent *OBJ relation between *of* and *phrases*. Thus, high attachment of the PP *with modifiers*, would have the same interpretation as low attachment since *phrases* is the underlying head of *number of*

[1]Support includes: NSF IIS-0534700 & IIS-0534325 Structure Alignment-based MT; DARPA HR0011-06-C-0023 & HR0011-06-C-0023; CUNY REP & GRTI Program. This work does not necessarily reflect views of sponsors.

Proceedings of the Third Linguistic Annotation Workshop, ACL-IJCNLP 2009, pages 116–120,
Suntec, Singapore, 6-7 August 2009.

1. E glis : *A n e of phra e with m difie s a e t a ig u*				
S f	**L**	**L**	**Fu c**	**Arg**
SB		A1	are	num er
ADV	*ADV	NE	re	no
PRD	*PRD	A2	are	am iguo s
	SB		am iguo s	num er
Q-PO	Q-PO		num er	a
CO	*CO	A1	num er	o
W TH	*W TH		num er	w th
O	*O		o	phrases
O	O		w th	m fiers
2. C ines : 汉语中．关联词和被动句也有很明显的特点。				
I hin e con u tion a pa sive e e e a so ha e e y obviou fe u e .				
ADV	ADV		有/have	中/in
SB	SB	A0	有/have	和/and

system output. For this paper, we evaluate solely on the logic1 relations (the second column in figure 1.) Figure 2 lists our results for all three languages, based on treebank and parser input.

As in (Meyers et al., 2009), we generated 4-tuples consisting of the following for each dependency: (A) the logic1 label (SBJ, OBJ, etc.), (B) its transparency (True or False), (C) The functor (a single word or a named entity); and (D) the argument (a single word or a named entity). In the case of conjunction where there was no lexical conjunction word, we used either punctuation (commas or semi-colons) or the placeholder *NULL*. We then corrected these results by hand to produce the answer key–an answer was correct if all four members of the tuple were correct and incorrect otherwise. Table 2 provides the **Prec**ision, **Rec**all and **F**-scores for our output. The **F-T** columns indicates a modified F-score derived by ignoring the +/-Transparent distinction (resulting changes in precision, recall and F-score are the same).

For English and Japanese, an expert native speaking linguist corrected the output. For Chinese, several native speaking computational linguists shared the task. By checking compatibility of the answer keys with outputs derived from different sources (parser, treebank), we could detect errors and inconsistencies. We processed the following corpora. English: 86 sentence article (wsj_2300) from the Wall Street Journal PTB test corpus (WSJ); 46 sentence letter from Good Will (LET), the first 100 sentences of a switchboard telephone transcript (TEL) and the first 100 sentences of a narrative from the Charlotte Narrative and Conversation (NAR). These samples are taken from the PTB WSJ Corpus and the SIGANN shared subcorpus of the OANC. The filenames are: 110CYL067, NapierDianne and sw2014. Chinese: a 20 sentence sample of text from the Penn Chinese Treebank (CTB) (Xue et al., 2005). Japanese: 20 sentences from the Kyoto Corpus (KYO) (Kurohashi and Nagao, 1998)

5 Running the GLARFer Programs

We use Charniak, UMD and KNP parsers (Charniak, 2001; Huang and Harper, 2009; Kurohashi and Nagao, 1998), JET Named Entity tagger (Grishman et al., 2005; Ji and Grishman, 2006) and other resources in conjunction with language-specific GLARFers that incorporate hand-written rules to convert output of these processors into a final representation, including logic1 structure, the focus of this paper. English GLARFer rules use Comlex (Macleod et al., 1998a) and the various NomBank lexicons (`http://nlp.cs.nyu.edu/meyers/nombank/`) for lexical lookup. The GLARF rules implemented vary by language as follows. **English:** correcting/standardizing phrase boundaries and part of speech (POS); recognizing multiword expressions; marking subconstituents; labeling relations; incorporating NEs; regularizing infinitival, passives, relatives, VP deletion, predicative and numerous other constructions. **Chinese:** correcting/standardizing phrase boundaries and POS, marking subconstituents, labeling relations; regularizing copula constructions; incorporating NEs; recognizing dates and number expressions. **Japanese:** converting to PTB format; correcting/standardizing phrase boundaries and POS; labeling relations; processing NEs, double quote constructions, number phrases, common idioms, light verbs and copula constructions.

6 Discussion

Naturally, the treebank-based system outperformed parse-based system. The Charniak parser for English was trained on the Wall Street Journal corpus and can achieve about 90% accuracy on similar corpora, but lower accuracy on other genres. Differences between treebank and parser results for English were higher for LET and NAR genres than for the TEL because the system is not currently designed to handle TEL-specific features like disfluencies. All processors were trained on or initially designed for news corpora. Thus corpora out of this domain usually produce lower results. LET was easier as it consisted mainly of short simple sentences. In (Meyers et al., 2009), we evaluated our results on 40 Japanese sentences from the JENAAD corpus (Utiyama and Isahara, 2003) and achieved a higher F-score (90.6%) relative to the Kyoto corpus, as JENAAD tends to have fewer long complex sentences.

By using our answer key for multiple inputs, we discovered errors and consequently improved the quality of the answer keys. However, at times we were also compelled to *fork* the answer keys–given multiple correct answers, we needed to allow different answer keys corresponding to different inputs. For English, these items represent approximately 2% of the answer keys (there were a total

	Treebank				Parser			
ID	**% Prec**	**% Rec**	**F**	**F-T**	**% Prec**	**% Rec**	**F**	**F-T**
WSJ	$\frac{1238}{1491}$ = 83.0	$\frac{1238}{1471}$ = 84.2	83.6	87.1	$\frac{1164}{1452}$ = 80.2	$\frac{1164}{1475}$ = 78.9	79.5	81.8
LET	$\frac{419}{451}$ = 92.9	$\frac{419}{454}$ = 92.3	92.6	93.3	$\frac{390}{434}$ = 89.9	$\frac{390}{454}$ = 85.9	87.8	87.8
TEL	$\frac{478}{627}$ = 76.2	$\frac{478}{589}$ = 81.2	78.6	82.2	$\frac{439}{587}$ = 74.8	$\frac{439}{589}$ = 74.5	74.7	77.4
NAR	$\frac{817}{1013}$ = 80.7	$\frac{817}{973}$ =84.0	82.3	84.1	$\frac{724}{957}$ = 75.7	$\frac{724}{969}$ = 74.7	75.2	76.1
CTB	$\frac{351}{400}$ = 87.8	$\frac{351}{394}$ = 89.1	88.4	88.7	$\frac{352}{403}$ = 87.3	$\frac{352}{438}$ = 80.4	83.7	83.7
KYO	$\frac{525}{575}$ = 91.3	$\frac{525}{577}$ = 91.0	91.1	91.1	$\frac{493}{581}$ = 84.9	$\frac{493}{572}$ = 86.2	85.5	87.8

Figure 2: Logic1 Scores

■ igu ty	**orp**	**T e an**	**arse**
1 Tok nization	NAR	*2 + + ou ,* *2 + + nt*	2 hou , 2 cent
2. Tok nization	NAR	*c n't = c n + 't*	*c n't = c + 't*
3. P efix?	K O	大 *big + framework*	*the big pic u e*
4. E cod ng of zero	CTB	二０００年*/y ar 2000*	二000 年*/y ar 2000*
5. Attachment (relativ)	E	*thou ands [f people]* *[ho fac obstac es]*	*thou ands of [eople* *[ho fac obstac es]]*
6. Attachment (P	E	*give a gift* *[o G odwill]*	*give [gift [o* *G odwill]]*
7 Conj Scope	TE	*[earls or [eads of* *some sort of nec ac]]*	*[earls or beads] of* *some sort of nec ac]*
8 Mod mbigu ty	K O	Relativ Clau e *bu inesses that are varied*	Ad ectiv l Mod fier *variou bu inesses*
9. P S ambigu ty 进口 export = N or V	CTB	进口 十亿 *Exportation of 5 billion*	进口 十亿 *Exported 5 billion*

Figure 3: Examples of Answer Key Divergences

of 74 4-tuples out of a total of 3487). Figure 3 lists examples of answer key divergences that we have found: (1) alternative tokenizations; (2) spurious differences in attachment and conjunction scope; and (3) ambiguities specific to our framework.

Examples 1 and 2 reflect different treatments of hyphenation and contractions in treebank specifications over time. Parsers trained on different treebanks will either keep hyphenated words together or separate more words at hyphens. The Treebank treatment of *can't* regularizes so that (*can* need not be differentiated from *ca*), whereas the parser treatment makes maintaining character offsets easier. In example 3, the Japanese parser recognizes a single word whereas the treebank divides it into a prefix plus stem. Example 4 is a case of differences in character encoding (zero).

Example 5 is a common case of spurious attachment ambiguity for English, where a transparent noun takes an *of* PP complement–nouns such as *form*, *variety* and *thousands* bear the feature *transparent* in the NOMLEX-PLUS dictionary (a NomBank dictionary based on NOMLEX (Macleod et al., 1998b)). The relative clause attaches either to the noun *thousands* or *people* and, therefore, the subject gap of the relative is filled by either *thousands* or *people*. This ambiguity is spurious since there is no meaningful distinction between these two attachments. Example 6 is a case of attachment ambiguity due to a support construction (Meyers et al., 2004). The recipient of the gift will be *Goodwill* regardless of whether the PP is attached to *give* or *gift*. Thus there is not much sense in marking one attachment more correct than the other. Example 7 is a case of conjunction ambiguity–the context does not make it clear whether or not the pearls are part of a necklace or just the beads are. The distinction is of little consequence to the understanding of the narrative.

Example 8 is a case in which our grammar handles a case ambiguously: the prenominal adjective can be analyzed either as a simple noun plus adjective phrase meaning *various businesses* or as a noun plus relative clause meaning *businesses that are varied*. Example 9 is a common case in Chinese where the verb/noun distinction, while unclear, is not crucial to the meaning of the phrase – under either interpretation, 5 billion was exported.

7 Concluding Remarks

We have discussed challenges of automatic annotation when transducers of other annotation schemata are used as input. Models underlying different transducers approximate the original annotation in different ways, as do transducers trained on different corpora. We have found it necessary to allow for multiple *correct* answers, due to such differences, as well as, genuine and spurious ambiguities. In the future, we intend to investigate automatic ways of identifying and handling spurious ambiguities which are predictable, including examples like 5,6 and 7 in figure 3 involving transparent functors.

References

E. Charniak. 2001. Immediate-head parsing for language models. In *ACL 2001*, pages 116–123.

M. Collins. 1999. *Head-Driven Statistical Models for Natural Language Parsing*. Ph.D. thesis, University of Pennsylvania.

D. Gildea and D. Jurafsky. 2002. Automatic Labeling of Semantic Roles. *Computational Linguistics*, 28:245–288.

R. Grishman, D. Westbrook, and A. Meyers. 2005. Nyu's english ace 2005 system description. In *ACE 2005 Evaluation Workshop*.

J. Hajič, M. Ciaramita, R. Johansson, D. Kawahara, M. A. Martí, L. Màrquez, A. Meyers, J. Nivre, S. Padó, J. Štěpánek, P. Straňák, M. Surdeanu, N. Xue, and Y. Zhang. 2009. The CoNLL-2009 shared task: Syntactic and semantic dependencies in multiple languages. In *CoNLL-2009*, Boulder, Colorado, USA.

Z. Huang and M. Harper. 2009. Self-training PCFG Grammars with Latent Annotations across Languages. In *EMNLP 2009*.

H. Ji and R. Grishman. 2006. Analysis and Repair of Name Tagger Errors. In *COLING/ACL 2006*, Sydney, Australia.

S. Kurohashi and M. Nagao. 1998. Building a Japanese parsed corpus while improving the parsing system. In *Proceedings of The 1st International Conference on Language Resources & Evaluation*, pages 719–724.

C. Macleod, R. Grishman, and A. Meyers. 1998a. COMLEX Syntax. *Computers and the Humanities*, 31:459–481.

C. Macleod, R. Grishman, A. Meyers, L. Barrett, and R. Reeves. 1998b. Nomlex: A lexicon of nominalizations. In *Proceedings of Euralex98*.

A. Meyers, M. Kosaka, S. Sekine, R. Grishman, and S. Zhao. 2001. Parsing and GLARFing. In *Proceedings of RANLP-2001*, Tzigov Chark, Bulgaria.

A. Meyers, R. Reeves, and Catherine Macleod. 2004. NP-External Arguments: A Study of Argument Sharing in English. In *The ACL 2004 Workshop on Multiword Expressions: Integrating Processing*, Barcelona, Spain.

A. Meyers, M. Kosaka, N. Xue, H. Ji, A. Sun, S. Liao, and W. Xu. 2009. Automatic Recognition of Logical Relations for English, Chinese and Japanese in the GLARF Framework. In *SEW-2009 at NAACL-HLT-2009*.

M. Surdeanu, R. Johansson, A. Meyers, L. Márquez, and J. Nivre. 2008. The CoNLL-2008 Shared Task on Joint Parsing of Syntactic and Semantic Dependencies. In *Proceedings of the CoNLL-2008 Shared Task*, Manchester, GB.

M. Utiyama and H. Isahara. 2003. Reliable Measures for Aligning Japanese-English News Articles and Sentences. In *ACL-2003*, pages 72–79.

N. Xue, F. Xia, F. Chiou, and M. Palmer. 2005. The Penn Chinese Treebank: Phrase Structure Annotation of a Large Corpus. *Natural Language Engineering*.

N. Xue. 2008. Labeling Chinese Predicates with Semantic roles. *Computational Linguistics*, 34:225–255.

Using Parallel Propbanks to enhance Word-alignments

Jinho D. Choi
Dept. of Computer Science
Univ. of Colorado at Boulder
choijd@colorado.edu

Martha Palmer
Dept. of Linguistics
Univ. of Colorado at Boulder
mpalmer@colorado.edu

Nianwen Xue
Dept. of Computer Science
Brandeis University
xuen@brandeis.edu

Abstract

This short paper describes the use of the linguistic annotation available in parallel PropBanks (Chinese and English) for the enhancement of automatically derived word alignments. Specifically, we suggest ways to refine and expand word alignments for verb-predicates by using predicate-argument structures. Evaluations demonstrate improved alignment accuracies that vary by corpus type.

1 Introduction

Since verbs tend to be the roots of dependency relations in a sentence (Palmer et al., 2005), when it comes down to translations, finding correct mappings between verbs in a source and a target language is very important. Many machine translation systems (Fraser and Marcu, 2007) use word-alignment tools such as GIZA++ (Och and Ney, 2003) to retrieve word mappings between a source and a target language. Although GIZA++ gives well-structured alignments, it has limitations in several ways. First, it is hard to verify if alignments generated by GIZA++ are correct. Second, GIZA++ may not find alignments for low-frequent words. Third, GIZA++ does not account for any semantic information.

In this paper, we suggest a couple of ways to enhance word-alignments for predicating expressions such as verbs[1]. We restricted the source and the target language to Chinese and English, respectively. The goal is to use the linguistic annotation available in parallel PropBanks (Xue and Palmer, 2009) to refine and expand automatic word-alignments. First, we check if the alignment for each Chinese predicate, generated by GIZA++, is also a predicate in English (Section 3). If it is, we verify if the alignment is correct by matching their arguments (Section 4.1). If it is not, we find an English predicate that has the maximum argument matching with the Chinese predicate (Section 4.2). Finally, we evaluate the potential of the enhanced word-alignments for providing a significant improvement over the GIZA++ baseline.

[1]Throughout the paper, all predicates refer to verbs.

2 Parallel Corpus

We used the 'English Chinese Translation Treebank' (ECTB), a parallel English-Chinese corpus. In addition to the treebank syntactic structure, the corpus has also been annotated with semantic role labels in the standard PropBank style of Arg0, Arg1, etc., based on verb specific frame file definitions (Xue and Palmer, 2009). The corpus is divided into two parts: the Xinhua Chinese newswire with literal English translations (4,363 parallel sentences) and the Sinorama Chinese news magazine with non-literal English translations (12,600 parallel sentences). We experimented with the two parts separately to see how literal and non-literal translations affect word-alignments.

3 Predicate Matching

For preprocessing, we ran GIZA++ on ECTB to get word-alignments between Chinese and English. Then, for each Chinese predicate, we checked if it is aligned to an English predicate by using the gold-standard parallel Propbanks. Table 1 shows how many Chinese predicates were aligned to what kind of English words.

Only (45.3%-Xinhua, 19.1%-Sinorama) of Chinese predicates were aligned to words that are predicates in English. It is true that not all Chinese verbs are supposed to be translated to verbs in English, but that does not account for the numbers in Table 1. We therefore assume that there are opportunities to enhance word-alignments for Chinese and English predicates.

Proceedings of the Third Linguistic Annotation Workshop, ACL-IJCNLP 2009, pages 121–124,
Suntec, Singapore, 6-7 August 2009. ©2009 ACL and AFNLP

Alignment	Xinhua	Sinorama
Ch.pred → En.pred	5,842	7,643
Ch.pred → En.be	386	1,229
Ch.pred → En.else	2,489	8,726
Ch.pred → En.none	4,178	22,488
Total	12,895	40,086

Table 1: Results of predicate matching (Ch: Chinese, En: English, pred: predicates, be: be-verbs, else: non-verbs, none: no word). The numbers indicate the amount of verb-tokens, not verb-types.

4 Argument Matching

For Chinese predicates aligned to English predicates, we can verify the alignments by 'Top-down argument matching': given Chinese and English predicates that are aligned, check if their arguments are also aligned (arguments are found from parallel Propbanks). The intuition is that if the predicates are correctly aligned across the languages, their arguments should be aligned as well.

For Chinese predicates not aligned to any English words, we can find their potential English alignments by 'Bottom-up argument matching': given a set of arguments for a such Chinese predicate, find some English predicate whose set of arguments has the most words aligned to words in the Chinese arguments. If the words in the arguments are mostly aligned (above a certain threshold) across the languages, we suspect that the predicates should be aligned as well.

4.1 Top-down Argument Matching (T-D)

Given a Chinese predicate p_c aligned to an English predicate p_e, let S_c and S_e be a set of arguments for p_c and p_e, respectively. For each $ca_i \in S_c$, we match it with some $ea_j \in S_e$ that has the most words aligned to words in ca_i. If such ea_j exists, we count the number of aligned words, say $|ca_i \cap ea_j|$; otherwise, the count is 0. Once the matchings are done, we average the proportions of the counts and if the average is above a certain threshold, we consider the alignment is correct.

Let us look at the example in Table 2. After the preprocessing, a Chinese predicate '设立' is aligned to an English predicate 'set up' by GIZA++. '设立' has two arguments, Ch.Arg0 and Ch.Arg1, retrieved from the Chinese Propbank. For each Chinese argument, we search for some argument of 'set' (from the English Propbank) that has the most words aligned. For instance, words in Ch.Arg0, '这些 城市', are aligned to 'those municipalities' by GIZA++ so Ch.Arg0 finds En.Arg0 as the one maximizes word-interscetions (similar for Ch.Arg1 and En.Arg1). In this case, the argument matchings for all pairs of arguments are 100%, so we consider the alignment is correct.

– Chinese Sentence –
: 同时 还 批准 这些 城市 设立 十四 个 边境 经济 合作区
- **Predicate**: 设立.01 → set up
- **Ch.Arg0**: 这些 城市 → those municipalities
- **Ch.Arg1**: 十四 个 边境 经济 合作区 → fourteen border economic cooperation zones

– English Sentence –
: At the same time it also sanctioned those municipalities to set up fourteen border economic cooperation zones
- **Predicate**: set.03 (set up)
- **En.Arg0**: those municipalities
- **En.Arg1**: fourteen border economic cooperation zones

Table 2: Parallel sentences labelled with their semantic roles

Table 3 shows the average argument matching scores for all pairs of Chinese and English predicates. For each pair of predicates, 'macro-average' measures the proportion of word-intersections for each pair of Chinese and English arguments (with the most words aligned) and averages the proportions whereas 'micro-average' counts word-intersections for all pairs of arguments (each pair with the most words aligned) and divides it by the total number of words in Chinese arguments.

- S_c = a set of Chinese arguments, $ca_i \in S_c$
- S_e = a set of English arguments, $ea_j \in S_e$
- Macro average argument matching score $= \frac{1}{|S_c|} \sum_{\forall ca_i} (\frac{argmax(|ca_i \cap ea_j|)}{|ca_i|})$
- Micro average argument matching score $= \frac{\sum_{\forall ca_i} argmax(|ca_i \cap ea_j|)}{\sum_{\forall ca_i} |ca_i|}$

	Xinhua	Sinorama
Macro Avg.	80.55%	53.56%
Micro Avg.	83.91%	52.62%

Table 3: Average argument matching scores for top-down argument matching

It is not surprising that Xinhua's scores are higher because the English sentences in Xinhua are more literally translated than ones in Sinorama so that it is easier to find correct alignments in Xinhua.

4.2 Bottom-Up Argument Matching (B-U)

A large portion of Chinese predicates are aligned to no English words. For such Chinese predicate, say p_c, we check to see if there exists an English predicate within the parallel sentence, say p_e, that is not aligned to any Chinese word and gives the maximum micro-average score (Section 4.1) compare to all other predicates in the English sentence. If the micro-average score is above a certain threshold, we align p_c to p_e.

The thresholds we used are 0.7 and 0.8. Thresholds below 0.7 assumes too many alignments that are incorrect and ones above 0.8 assumes too few alignments to be useful. Table 4 shows the average argument matching scores for alignments found by bottom-up argument matching.

	Xinhua		**Sinorama**	
Thresh.	**0.7**	**0.8**	**0.7**	**0.8**
Macro	80.74	83.99	77.70	82.86
Micro	82.63	86.46	79.45	85.07

Table 4: Average argument matching scores in percentile for bottom-up argument matching

5 Evaluations

Evaluations are done by a Chinese-English bilingual. We used a different English-Chinese parallel corpus for evaluations. There are 100 parallel sentences, 365 Chinese verb-tokens, and 273 Chinese verb-types in the corpus. We tested word-alignments, refined and expanded by our approaches, on verb-types rather than verb-tokens to avoid over-emphasizing multiple appearances of a single type. Furthermore, we tested word-alignments from Xinhua and Sinorama separately to see how literal and non-literal translations affect the outcomes.

5.1 Refining word-alignment

We used three kinds of measurements for comparisons: term coverage, term expansion, and alignment accuracy. 'Term coverage' shows how many source terms (Chinese verb-types) are covered by word-alignments found in each corpus. Out of 273 Chinese verb-types in the test corpus, (79-Xinhua, 129-Sinorama) were covered by word-alignments generated by GIZA++. 'Term expansion' shows how many target terms (English verb-types) are suggested for each of the covered source terms. There are on average (1.77-Xinhua, 2.29-Sinorama) English verb-types suggested for each covered Chinese verb-type. 'Alignment accuracy' shows how many of the suggested target terms are correct. Among the suggested English verb-types, (83.35%-Xinhua, 57.76%-Sinorama) were correct on average.

The goal is to improve the alignment accuracy with minimum reduction of the term coverage and expansion. To accomplish the goal, we set a threshold for the T-D's macro-average score: for Chinese predicates aligned to English predicates, we kept only alignments whose macro-average scores meet or exceed a certain threshold. The thresholds we chose are 0.4 and 0.5; lower thresholds did not have much effect and higher thresholds threw out too many alignments. Table 5 shows the results of three measurements with respect to the thresholds (Note that all these alignments were generated by GIZA++).

	Xinhua			**Sinorama**		
TH	**TC**	**ATE**	**AAA**	**TC**	**ATE**	**AAA**
0.0	**79**	**1.77**	83.35	**129**	**2.29**	57.76
0.4	76	1.72	83.54	93	1.8	65.88
0.5	76	1.68	**83.71**	62	1.58	**78.09**

Table 5: Results for alignment refinement (TH: threshold, TC: term coverage, ATE: average term expansion, AAA: average alignment accuracy in percentage). The highest score for each measurement is marked as bold.

As you can see, thresholds did not have much effect on alignments found in Xinhua. This is understandable because the translations in Xinhua are so literal that it was relatively easy for GIZA++ to find correct alignments; in other words, the alignments generated by GIZA++ were already very accurate. However, for alignments found in Sinorama, the average alignment accuracy increases radically as the threshold increases. This implies that it is possible to refine word-alignments found in a corpus containing many non-literal translations by using T-D.

Notice that the term coverage for Sinorama decreases as the threshold increases. Considering how much improvement it made for the average alignment accuracy, we suspect that it filtered out mostly ones that were incorrect alignments.

5.2 Expanding word-alignment

We used B-U to expand word-alignments for Chinese predicates aligned to no English words. We decided not to expand alignments for Chinese predicates aligned to non-verb English words because GIZA++ generated alignments are more accurate than ones found by B-U in general.

There are (22-Xinhua, 20-Sinorama) additional verb-types covered by the expanded-alignments. Note that these alignments are already filtered by the micro-average score (Section 4.2). To refine the alignments even more, we set a threshold on the macro-average score as well. The thresholds we used for the macro-average score are 0.6 and 0.7. Table 6 shows the results of the expanded-alignments found in Xinhua and Sinorama.

	Mac - 0.7			**Mac - 0.8**		
	TC	**ATE**	**AAA**	**TC**	**ATE**	**AAA**
Mic	**Xinhua**					
0.0	**22**	**4.27**	50.38	**20**	3.35	57.50
0.6	21	3.9	54.76	18	**3.39**	**63.89**
0.7	19	3.47	**55.26**	17	3.12	61.76
Mic	**Sinorama**					
0.0	**37**	**3.59**	**18.01**	**29**	**3.14**	**14.95**
0.6	31	3.06	15.11	27	2.93	14.46
0.7	21	2.81	11.99	25	2.6	11.82

Table 6: Results for expanded-alignments found in Xinhua and Sinorama (Mac: threshold on macro-average score, Mic: threshold on micro-average score)

The average alignment accuracy for Xinhua is encouraging; it shows that B-U can expand word-alignments for a corpus with literal translations. The average alignment accuracy for Sinorama is surprisingly low; it shows that B-U cannot function effectively given non-literal translations.

6 Summary and Future Works

We have demonstrated the potential for using parallel Propbanks to improve statistical verb translations from Chinese to English. Our B-U approach shows promise for expanding the term-coverage of GIZA++ alignments that are based on literal translations. In contrast, our T-D is most effective with non-literal translations for verifying the alignment accuracy, which has been proven difficult for GIZA++.

This is still a preliminary work but in the future, we will try to enhance word-alignments by using automatically labelled Propbanks, Nombanks (Meyers et al., 2004), Named-entity tagging, and test the enhancement on bigger corpora. Furthermore, we will also evaluate the integration of our enhanced alignments with statistical machine translation systems.

Acknowledgments

Special thanks to Daniel Gildea, Ding Liu (University of Rochester) who provided word-alignments, Wei Wang (Information Sciences Institute at University of Southern California) who provided the test-corpus, and Hua Zhong (University of Colorado at Boulder) who performed the evaluations. We gratefully acknowledge the support of the National Science Foundation Grants IIS-0325646, Domain Independent Semantic Parsing, CISE-CRI-0551615, Towards a Comprehensive Linguistic Annotation, and a grant from the Defense Advanced Research Projects Agency (DARPA/IPTO) under the GALE program, DARPA/CMO Contract No. HR0011-06-C-0022, subcontract from BBN, Inc. Any contents expressed in this material are those of the authors and do not necessarily reflect the views of the National Science Foundation.

References

Alexander Fraser and Daniel Marcu. 2007. Measuring word alignment quality for statistical machine translation. *Computational Linguistics*, 33(3):293–303.

A. Meyers, R. Reeves, C. Macleod, R. Szekely, V. Zielinska, B. Young, and R. Grishman. 2004. The nombank project: An interim report. In *HLT-NAACL 2004 Workshop: Frontiers in Corpus Annotation*, pages 24–31.

Franz Josef Och and Hermann Ney. 2003. A systematic comparison of various statistical alignment models. *Computational Linguistics*, 29(1):19–51.

Martha Palmer, Daniel Gildea, and Paul Kingsbury. 2005. The proposition bank: An annotated corpus of semantic roles. *Computational Linguistics*, 31(1):71–106.

Nianwen Xue and Martha Palmer. 2009. Adding semantic roles to the chinese treebank. *Natural Language Engineering*, 15(1):143–172.

WordNet and FrameNet as Complementary Resources for Annotation

Collin F. Baker
International Computer Science Institute
1947 Center St., Berkeley, California 94704
collinb@icsi.berkeley.edu

Christiane Fellbaum
Princeton University
Princeton, NJ 08540-5233
fellbaum@princeton.edu

Abstract

WordNet and FrameNet are widely used lexical resources, but they are very different from each other and are often used in completely different ways in NLP. In a case study in which a short passage is annotated in both frameworks, we show how the synsets and definitions of WordNet and the syntagmatic information from FrameNet can complement each other, forming a more complete representation of the lexical semantic of a text than either could alone. Close comparisons between them also suggest ways in which they can be brought into alignment.

1 Background and motivation

FrameNet and WordNet are two lexical databases that are widely used for NLP, often in conjunction. Because of their complementary designs they are obvious candidates for alignment, and an exploratory research project within the larger context of the semantic annotation of the the American national Corpus is currently underway. We give specific illustrative examples of annotations against both resources, highlighting their different contributions towards a rich semantic analysis.

WordNet (WN):[1] (Fellbaum, 1998), is a large electronic lexical database of English. Originally conceived as a full-scale model of human semantic organization, it was quickly embraced by the Natural Language Processing (NLP) community, a development that guided its subsequent growth and design. WordNet has become the lexical database of choice for NLP and has been incorporated into other language tools, including VerbNet (Kipper et al., 2000) and OntoNotes (Hovy et al., 2006). Numerous on-line dictionaries, including Google's "define" function, rely significantly on WordNet.

WordNet's coverage is sometimes criticized as being too fine-grained for automatic processing, though its inventory is not larger than that of a standard collegiate dictionary. But the present limitation of automatic WSD cannot be entirely blamed on existing systems; for example, Fellbaum and Grabowski (1997) have shown that humans, too, have difficulties identifying context-appropriate dictionary senses. One answer is clearly that meanings do not exist outside contexts. Furthermore, although WN does contain "sentence frames" such as "Somebody —-s something" for a transitive verb with a human agent, it provides little syntagmatic information, except for what can be gleaned from the example sentences. WordNet's great strength is its extensive coverage, with more than 117,000 synonym sets (**synsets**), each with a definition and relations to other synsets covering almost all the general vocabulary of English.

FrameNet (FN):[2] (Fontenelle, 2003) is a lexical resource organized not around words *per se*, but **semantic frames** (Fillmore, 1976): characterizations of events, relations, and states which are the conceptual basis for understanding groups of word senses, called **lexical units (LUs)**. Frames are distinguished by the set of roles involved, known as **frame elements (FEs)**. Much of the information in the FrameNet lexicon is derived by annotating corpus sentences; for each LU, groups of sentences are extracted from a corpus, sentences which collectively exemplify all of the lexicographically relevant syntactic patterns in which the LU occurs. A few examples of each pattern are annotated; annotators not only mark the target word which **evokes** the frame in the mind of the hearer, but also mark those phrases which are syntactically related to the target word and express its frame elements. FrameNet is much smaller than WordNet, covering roughly 11,000 LUs, but contains very rich syntagmatic information about the combinatorial possibilities of each LU.

Given these two lexical resources with different strengths, it seems clear that combining WN and FN annotation will produce a more complete semantic representation of the meaning of a text than either could alone. What follows is intended as an example of how they can usefully be combined.

2 Case Study: Aegean History

The text chosen for this study is a paragraph from the American National Corpus[3] (Ide et al., 2002), from the Berlitz travel guide to Greece, discussing the history of

[1] http://wordnet.princeton.edu

[2] http://framenet.icsi.berkeley.edu

[3] http://www.americannationalcorpus.org

Proceedings of the Third Linguistic Annotation Workshop, ACL-IJCNLP 2009, pages 125–129,
Suntec, Singapore, 6-7 August 2009.

Greece, specifically the Aegean islands after the fall of Byzantium to the Crusaders. Although brief, its three sentences provide ample material to demonstrate some of the subtlety of both WN and FN annotation:

(1) While Byzantine land was being divided, there was no one in control of the seas, so pirates raided towns on many of the islands. (2) To counter this, the populations moved from their homes on the coast and built settlements inland, out of sight of the raiding parties. (3) This created a pattern seen today throughout the Aegean of a small port (skala) *which serves an inland settlement or* chora, *making it easier to protect the island from attack.*

Below, we present three tables containing the annotation of both the WordNet synsets for each open class (content) word in the text[4] and the FrameNet frames and the fillers of the frame elements in each sentence. We also provide brief notes on some interesting features of the semantics of each sentence.

2.1 Discussion of Sentence 1, shown in Table 1 on page 4 :

(2) Information about what the land was separated into is not given in the sentence nor clear from the context, so the PARTS FE has been annotated as "indefinite null instantiated" (INI). Clearly this is an intentional action, but because the verb is passive, the agent can be (and is) omitted, so the AGENT FE is marked as "constructionally null instantiated" (CNI).[5]

(4) In addition to FEs and their phrase types and grammatical functions, FrameNet annotates a limited set of syntactic facts: here, *in* is annotated as at "support preposition", allowing *control* to function as an adjectival, and *was* as a copula, allowing *no one* to fill the External syntactic position of *in control*.

(5) Since FN is based on semantic frames, annotation of nouns is largely limited to those which express events (e.g. *destruction*), relations (*brother*), or states (*height*). For the most part, nouns denoting artifacts and natural kinds evoke relatively uninteresting frames, and hence relatively few of them have been included in FN. However, there are three such instances in this sentence, *seas*, *islands* (9), and *towns* (12); In all three cases, the frame-evoking noun also **denotes** the filler of the FE LOCALE.

(6) At the top level of organization, *so* evokes the Causation frame. Actually, it is misleading to simply annotate *control of the seas* in the frames Be_in_control and Natural_features; here, we regard *seas* as metonymic for "ship traffic on the seas", but neither the FN annotation nor the WN definition indicates this.

(7) The noun *pirates* evokes the very rich frame of Piracy, and also denotes the filler of the FE PERPETRATOR, but that is the only FE filled in in that frame. Instead, *pirates* actually fills the ASSAILANT FE of the Attack frame, (8); the main idea is about the raids, not the piratical acts on the seas that the same people have a habit of committing. Note that the WN definition takes the view that raiding coastal towns **is** a typical part of piracy.

(10) Political_locales roughly corresponds to "Geopolitical entity" in named entity recognition.

Despite the relatively fine level of detail of the annotations, there are still many important semantic features of the sentence not represented in FrameNet or WordNet. For example, there is no treatment of negation *cum* quantification, no representation of the fact that *there was no one in control* should mean that Be_in_control is not happening.

2.2 Discussion of Sentence 2, shown in Table 2 on page 5:

The two highest level predicates in this sentence are *moved* (2) and *built* (6), in the frames Motion and Building respectively; since they are conjoined, the phrase *to counter this* fills the FE PURPOSE in both frames. [6] In (2) the GOAL FE of the Motion is marked as definite null instantiation (DNI), because, although it is not expressed in the VP headed by *moved*, it is recoverable from context (i.e. the second VP).

(4) Note that FN puts this sense of *home* in the Buildings frame[7], but WN has a less specific definition. (6) *Coast* is a Relational_natural_feature because it is defined in relation to another natural feature; a coast has to be the coast **of** some land mass, although here the land mass is DNI. (9) *Inland* both evokes a Locative_relation and denotes the GROUND FE. (10) FN and WN agree on a sense of *sight* denoting the range of vision. (11) WN's example sentence for *raid* is precisely about pirates.

2.3 Discussion of Sentence 3 shown in Table 3 on page 5:

(2) The concept of "pattern" is very slippery–the arrangement of port and inland settlement is both spatial and temporal in terms of building practices over centuries. (3) This sense of *see* can refer to the area in which something is seen, the time, or the conditions under which it can be seen; these are subsumed by the FE STATE. (4) *Today* expresses a Temporal_collocation and denotes the LANDMARK. (Repetitions of the words *settlement* and *island* have been omitted.) The interrelation among (7), (10), (11) and (12) is rather complex: the arrangement in which the port serves the settlement has the making easier as a result. The arrangement is also the CAUSE FE of *making*. *Easier* in the Difficulty frame requires an EX-

[4]Note that for reasons of space, many WN examples have been omitted.

[5]In fact, the previous sentence describes the sack of Constantinople by the Crusaders, so they can be inferred to be the dividers of the lands, as well.

[6]This is a **peripheral** FE, common to all frames which inherit from the Intentionally_act frame.

[7]Not to be confused with the Building frame, in (7).

PERIENCER FE which is not specified here (thus INI) and an ACTIVITY FE, *to protect*. The FE PROTECTION (which can be a person, a thing, or an activity) is marked CNI, because it is the external argument of the infinitive.

3 Towards an alignment of WordNet and FrameNet

We hope these examples have shown that finding related WN and FN senses can contribute to text understanding. Fellbaum and Baker (2008) discuss the respective strengths and weaknesses of WN and FN as well as their complementary advantages that could be fruitfully exploited aligning the two resources. Work of this type is actually underway; researchers are semi-automatically annotating selected lemmas in the American National Corpus with both FN frames and WN senses. The lemmas are chosen so as to reflect the part of speech distribution in text and to represent a spectrum of frequency and polysemy. A preliminary group of instances are manually tagged by trained annotators, and then the teams working on WN and FN annotation discuss and resolve discrepancies among the taggers before the remaining tokens are annotated.

Three cases sum up the annotation and alignment process:

(1) In the very unlikely case that a synset and a frame contain exactly the same set of lexemes, their correspondence is simply recorded.

(2) In the more common case in which all the words in a synset are a subset of those in the frame, or all the words in a frame are a subset of those in the synset, this fact is also recorded.

(3) In case two synsets are subsets of the LUs of one frame, we will record this and note that it as a possible candidate for collapsing the synsets, respectively.

FN and WN are two comprehensive but complementary lexical resources. Both WN's paradigmatic and FN's syntagmatic approach to lexical semantics are needed for a rich representation of word meaning in context. We have demonstrated how text can be annotated against both resources to provide the foundation for deep language understanding and, as an important by-product, help to align the word senses of these widely-used resources. Of course, these examples were manually annotated, but automatic systems for word-sense disambiguation (largely based on WordNet) and FrameNet role labeling (Johansson and Nugues, 2007; Coppola et al., 2008) are improving rapidly. The project just described is intended to provide more gold-standard annotation (both WN and FN) to help train automatic systems for both WN and FN annotation, which are clearly related tasks e.g. (Pradhan et al., 2007; Erk, 2005).

Acknowledgment

We gratefully acknowledge support from the National Science Foundation (#IIS-0705199) for the work reported here.

References

Bonaventura Coppola, Alessandro Moschitti, Sara Tonelli, and Giuseppe Riccardi. 2008. Automatic framenet-based annotation of conversational speech. In *Proceedings of IEEE-SLT 2008*, pages 73–76, Goa, India, December.

Katrin Erk. 2005. Frame assignment as word sense disambiguation. In *Proceedings of IWCS 6*, Tilburg.

Christiane Fellbaum and Collin F. Baker. 2008. Can WordNet and FrameNet be made "interoperable"? In Jonathan Webster, Nancy Ide, and Alex Chengyu Fang, editors, *Proceedings of The First International Conference on Global Interoperability for Language Resources*, pages 67–74, Hong Kong. City University.

Christiane Fellbaum and J. Grabowski. 1997. Analysis of a hand-tagging task. In *Proceedings of the ACL/Siglex workshop*. Association for Computational Linguistics.

Christane Fellbaum, editor. 1998. *WordNet. An electronic lexical database*. MIT Press, Cambridge/Mass.

Charles J. Fillmore. 1976. Frame semantics and the nature of language. *Annals of the New York Academy of Sciences*, 280:20–32.

Thierry Fontenelle, editor. 2003. *International Journal of Lexicography–Special Issue on FrameNet*, volume 16. Oxford University Press.

Eduard H. Hovy, Mitch Marcus, Martha Palmer, Sameer Pradhan, Lance Ramshaw, and Ralph-Weischedel. 2006. OntoNotes: The 90% solution. In *Proceedings of HLT-NAACL 2006*, New York.

Nancy Ide, Randi Reppen, and Keith Suderman. 2002. The American National Corpus: More than the web can provide. In *Proceedings of the Third Language Resources and Evaluation Conference (LREC)*, pages 839–44, Las Palmas, Canary Islands, Spain.

Richard Johansson and Pierre Nugues. 2007. LTH: Semantic structure extraction using nonprojective dependency trees. In *Proceedings of the Fourth International Workshop on Semantic Evaluations (SemEval-2007)*, pages 227–230, Prague, Czech Republic, June. Association for Computational Linguistics.

Karin Kipper, Hoa Trang Dang, and Martha Palmer. 2000. Class-based construction of a verb lexicon. In *Seventeenth National Conference on Artificial Intelligence*, Austin, TX. AAAI-2000.

Sameer Pradhan, Edward Loper, Dmitriy Dligach, and Martha Palmer. 2007. Semeval-2007 task-17: English lexical sample, srl and all words. In *Proceedings of the Fourth International Workshop on Semantic Evaluations (SemEval-2007)*, pages 87–92, Prague, Czech Republic, June. Association for Computational Linguistics.

1. Frame: Political_locales: [CONTAINER_POSSESSOR Byzantine] [LOCALE **LAND**] WN: (adj) *Byzantine* (of or relating to or characteristic of the Byzantine Empire or the ancient city of Byzantium) (n) domain, demesne, *land* (territory over which rule or control is exercised) "his domain extended into Europe"; "he made it the law of the land"
2. Frame: Separating: [WHOLE Byzantine land] was being **DIVIDED** [AGENT CNI] [PARTS INI] WN: (v) *divide*, split, split up, separate, dissever, carve up (separate into parts or portions) "divide the cake into three equal parts"; "The British carved up the Ottoman Empire after World War I")
3. Frame: Existence: [TIME While Byzantine land was being divided], **THERE WAS** [ENTITY no one in control of the seas]
4. Frame: Be_in_control: there [was COPULA] [CONTROLLING_ENTITY no one] [in SUPPORT] **CONTROL** [DEPENDENT_ENTITY of the seas] WN: (n) *control* (power to direct or determine) "under control")
5. Frame: Natural_features: [LOCALE **SEAS**] WN: (n) *sea* (a division of an ocean or a large body of salt water partially enclosed by land)
6. Frame: Causation: [CAUSE While Byzantine land was being divided, there was no one in control of the seas], **SO** [EFFECT pirates raided towns on many of the islands]
7. Frame: Piracy: [PERPETRATOR **PIRATES**] WN: (n) *pirate*, buccaneer, sea robber, sea rover (someone who robs at sea or plunders the land from the sea without having a commission from any sovereign nation)
8. Frame: Attack: [ASSAILANT pirates] **RAIDED** [VICTIM towns on many of the islands] WN: (v) foray into, *raid* (enter someone else's territory and take spoils) "The pirates raided the coastal villages regularly")
9. Frame: Political_locales: [LOCALE **TOWNS**] [RELATIVE_LOCATION on many of the islands]. WN: (n) town (an urban area with a fixed boundary that is smaller than a city)
10. Frame: Locative_relation: [FIGURE towns] **ON** [GROUND many of the islands]
11. Frame: Quantity: [QUANTITY **MANY**] [INDIVIDUALS of the islands]
12. Frame: Natural_features: [LOCALE **ISLANDS**] WN: (n) *island* (a land mass (smaller than a continent) that is surrounded by water)

Table 1: FN/WN Annotation of sentence 1

1. Frame: Thwarting: To **COUNTER** [ACTION this], [PREVENTING_CAUSE the populations moved ... raiding parties] WN:(v) anticipate, foresee, forestall, *counter* (act in advance of; deal with ahead of time)
2. Frame: Aggregate: [AGGREGATE **POPULATIONS**] WN: (n) *population* (the people who inhabit a territory or state) "the population seemed to be well fed and clothed"
3. Frame: Motion: [PURPOSE To counter this], [THEME the populations] **MOVED** [SOURCE from their homes on the coast] [GOAL DNI] WN: (v) *move* (change residence, affiliation, or place of employment)
4. Frame: Buildings: [BUILDING **HOMES**] [PLACE on the coast] WN: (n) *home*, place (where you live at a particular time) "deliver the package to my home"
5. Frame: Locative_relation: [FIGURE their homes] **ON** [GROUND the coast]
6. Frame: Relational_natural_features: [FOCAL_FEATURE **COAST**] [RELATIVE_LOCATION DNI] WN: (n) seashore, *coast*, seacoast, sea-coast (the shore of a sea or ocean)
7. Frame: Building: [PURPOSE To counter this], [AGENT the populations] ... **BUILT** [CREATED_ENTITY settlements] [PLACE inland], [PLACE out of sight of the raiding parties]. WN: (v) construct, *build*, make (make by combining materials and parts)
8. Frame: Locale_by_use: [LOCALE **SETTLEMENTS**] WN: (n) village, small town, *settlement* (a community of people smaller than a town)
9. Frame: Locative_relation: built [FIGURE settlements] [GROUND **INLAND**] WN: (adv) inland (towards or into the interior of a region) "the town is five miles inland"
10. Frame: Range: ... out of [DISTANCE **SIGHT**] [PARTICIPANT of the raiding parties] WN: (n) *sight*, ken (the range of vision) "out of sight of land"
11. Frame: Attack: **RAIDING** [ASSAILANT parties] WN: (v) foray into, *raid* (enter someone else's territory and take spoils) "The pirates raided the coastal villages regularly"
12. Frame: Aggregate: [AGGREGATEPROPERTY raiding] [AGGREGATE **PARTIES**] WN: (n) *party*, company (a band of people associated temporarily in some activity) "they organized a party to search for food"

Table 2: FN/WN Annotation of sentence 2

1. Frame: Creating: [CAUSE This] **CREATED** [CREATED_ENTITY a pattern seen today ... from attack]. WN: (v) create (bring into existence) "He created a new movement in painting"
2. Frame: Pattern: **PATTERN** [DESCRIPTOR seen today throughout the Aegean] [ENTITIES of a small port (skala) which serves an inland settlement or chora] WN: (n) practice, pattern (a customary way of operation or behavior) "they changed their dietary pattern"
3. Frame: Perception_experience: [PHENOMENON a pattern] **SEEN** [TIME today] [STATE throughout the Aegean] [PHENOMENON of a small port ... from attack]. [PERCEIVER_PASSIVE CNI] WN: (v) witness, find, see (perceive or be contemporaneous with) "You'll see a lot of cheating in this school"
4. Frame: Temporal_collocation: [TRAJECTOR_EVENT a pattern seen] [LANDMARK_EVENT **TODAY**] [TRAJECTOR_EVENT throughout the Aegean... attack] WN: (n) today (the present time or age) "the world of today" (n) Aegean, Aegean Sea (an arm of the Mediterranean between Greece and Turkey...)
5. Frame: Dimension: [DIMENSION **SMALL**] [OBJECT port] WN: (adj) small, little (limited or below average in number or quantity or magnitude or extent)
6. Frame: Locale_by_use: [DESCRIPTOR small] [LOCALE **PORT**] WN: (n) port (a place (seaport or airport) where people and merchandise can enter or leave a country)
7. Frame: Assistance: [HELPER a small port (skala)] [HELPER which] **SERVES** [BENEFITED_PARTY an inland settlement or chora], [RESULT making it easier to protect the island from attack] WN: (v) service, serve (be used by; as of a utility) "The sewage plant served the neighboring communities"
8. Frame: Locative_relation: [GROUND **INLAND**] [FIGURE settlement]
10. Frame: causation: [CAUSE a small port (skala) which serves an inland settlement or chora], **MAKING** it [EFFECT easier to protect the island from attack.] [AFFECTED DNI] WN: chora: not in WordNet (v) *make*, get (give certain properties to something) "This invention will make you a millionaire"
11. Frame: Difficulty: **EASIER** [ACTIVITY to protect the island from attack]. [EXPERIENCER INI] WN: (adj) easy (posing no difficulty; requiring little effort) "an easy job"; "an easy victory"
12. Frame: Protecting: [PROTECTION CNI] **PROTECT** [ASSET the island] [DANGER from attack] WN: (v) protect (shield from danger, injury, destruction, or damage) "Weatherbeater protects your roof from the rain"
14. Frame: Attack: from **ATTACK**. [ASSAILANT DNI] WN: (n) attack, onslaught, onset, onrush ((military) an offensive against an enemy (using weapons)) "the attack began at dawn"

Table 3: FN/WN Annotation of sentence 3

Annotating language errors in texts: investigating argumentation and decision schemas

Camille ALBERT, Laurie BUSCAIL
Marie GARNIER, Arnaud RYKNER
LLA, Université Toulouse le Mirail
31000 TOULOUSE France
mhl.garnier@gmail.com

Patrick SAINT-DIZIER
IRIT-CNRS, 118, route de Narbonne,
31062 TOULOUSE France
stdizier@irit.fr

Abstract

In this short paper, we present annotations for tagging grammatical and stylistic errors, together with attributes about the nature of the correction which are then interpreted as arguments. A decision model is introduced in order for the author to be able to decide on the best correction to make. This introduces an operational semantics for tags and related attributes.

1 Aims and Situation

Non-native English speaking authors producing documents in English often encounter lexical, grammatical and stylistic difficulties that make their texts difficult for native speakers to understand. As a result, the professionalism and the credibility of these texts is often affected. Our main aim is to develop procedures for the correction of those errors which cannot (and will not in the near future) be treated by the most advanced text processing systems such as those proposed in the Office Suite, OpenOffice and the like. In the type of errors taken into consideration, several levels are often intertwinned: morphology, lexicon, grammar, style, textual structure, domain usages, context of production, target audience, etc..

While we attempt to correct errors, it turns out that, in a large number of cases, (1) there may be ambiguities in the analysis of the nature of errors, (2) errors can receive various types and levels of corrections depending on the type of document, reader, etc., and (3) some corrections cannot be successfully done without an interaction with the author. To achieve these aims we need to produce a model of the cognitive strategies deployed by human experts (e.g. translators correcting texts, teachers) when they detect and correct errors. Our observations show that it is not a simple and straightforward strategy, but that error diagnosis and corrections are often based on a complex analytical and decisional process. Since we want our system to have a didactic capacity, in order to help writers understand their errors, we propose an analysis of error diagnosis based on argumentation theory, outlining arguments for or against a certain correction and their relative strength paired with a decision theory.

The modelling of correction strategies is based on the annotation of a large variety of types of documents in English produced by a large diversity of French speakers. Annotations allow us to identify and categorize errors as well as the parameters at stake (e.g. category change, length of new corrected segment) at stake when making corrections. This is carried out by bilingual correctors in collaboration with didacticians. Those parameters are a priori neutral in the annotation schemas. We then define a preference model that assigns polarity (positive, negative) and a weight to each of these parameters, together with additional parameters among which the target reader, the type of document, etc. An argumentation model that considers these parameters as weighted arguments, for or against a certain correction, can thus be introduced. Paired with a decision model, optimal corrections can be proposed to the author, together with explanations. This approach confers a formal interpretation to our annotation schema.

Works on the correction of grammatical errors made by human authors (Brockett, 2006), (Han et al. 2005), (Lee et al. 2006), (Tetreau et al 2008), (Writer's v. 8.2) recently started to appear. The approach presented here, which is still preliminary, is an attempt to include some didactic aspects into the correction by explaining to the user the nature of her/his errors, whether grammatical or stylistic, while weighing the pros and cons of a correction, via argumentation and decision theories (Boutiler et ali. 1999), (Amgoud et ali. 2008). Persuasion aspects also matter within the didactical perspective (e.g. Persuation Technology sym-

Proceedings of the Third Linguistic Annotation Workshop, ACL-IJCNLP 2009, pages 130–133,
Suntec, Singapore, 6-7 August 2009.

posiums), (Prakken 2006).

In this document, we present the premisses of an approach to correcting complex grammar and style errors, which allow us to evaluate difficulties, challenges, deadlocks, etc. Annotations are used here for the development of an application.

2 The annotated corpus

The documents analyzed range from spontaneous short productions, with little control and proofreading, such as personal emails or posts on forums, to highly controlled documents such as publications or professional reports. We also consider personal web pages and wiki texts. Within each of these types, we also observed variation in the control of the quality of the writing. For example, emails sent to friends are less controlled than those produced in a professional environment, and even in this latter framework, messages sent to the hierarchy or to foreign colleagues receive more attention than those sent to close colleagues. Besides the level of control, other parameters, such as style, are taken into consideration (e.g. oral vs. academic). Therefore, the different corpora we have collected form a certain continuum over several parameters (control, orality, etc.); they allow us to observe a large variety of language productions.

More details on the elaboration of corpora, definition of attributes and their stability, and annotation scenarios can be found in (Albert et al., 2009).

3 The Annotation System

Let us now briefly introduce the annotation schema we have developed. It is an ongoing effort which is gradually evaluated by real users. This schema is an attempt to reflect, in a factual and declarative way, the different parameters taken into consideration by didacticians and human translators when detecting and correcting errors. It contains several groups of tags which are given below. The values for each attribute are based on a granularity level evaluated by the didacticians of our group. They are still preliminary and require evaluation and revisions. Their structure has been designed so that they can be used in an argumentation framework.

(a) Error delimitation and characterization:
<error-zone> tags the group of words involved in the error. The zone is meant to be as minimal as possible. This tag has several attributes:
comprehension: from 0 to 4 (0 being worse): indicates if the segment is understandable, in spite of the error,
agrammaticality: from 0 to 2: indicates how ungrammtical the error is.
categ: main category of the error: lexical, syntactic, stylistic, semantic, textual,
source: calque (direct copy), overcorrection, etc.

(b) Delimitation of the correction:
<correction-zone> tags the text fragment involved in the correction. It is equal or larger than the error zone.

(c) Characterization of a given correction:
Each correction is characterized by a tag <correction> and associated attributes, positively oriented ones are underlined:
surface: size of the text segment affected by the correction: <u>minimal</u>, average, maximal,
grammar: indicates, whenever appropriate, if the correction proposed is the standard one as suggested by grammar rules; values are: <u>by-default</u>, alternative, unlikely,
meaning: indicates if the meaning has been altered: yes, somewhat, <u>no</u>,
var-size: is an integer that indicates the <u>increase</u>/decrease in number of words of the correction w.r.t. the original fragment,
change: indicates if the changes in the correction are syntactic, lexical, stylistic, semantic or textual,
comp: indicates if the proposed correction is a text fragment which is easy to understand or not; values are: <u>yes</u>, average, no,
fix: indicates, when mentioned, that the error is very specific to that string of words and that the correction is idiosyncratic and cannot be extended to any other such structure.
qualif: indicates the certainty level of the annotator and didacticians, it qualifies the certainty of the error detection and of the proposed correction separetely,
correct: gives the correction.

An example is the N N construction (for the sake of readability, we do not consider longer N chains), with erroneous segments like: *the meaning utterance* or *goal failure*:

It is difficult to characterize <correction-zone>
<error-zone comprehension="2"
agrammaticality="1"
categ="syntax" source="calque">
the meaning utterance
<correction qualif="high" grammar="by-default"

surface= "minimal" meaning= "not altered" Var-size="+2" change="synt" comp="yes"
correct= "**the meaning of the utterance**">
</correction>
<correction qualif="high" grammar="unlikely"
surface= "minimal" meaning= "somewhat" Var-size="0"
change="lexical+synt" comp="average"
correct= "**the meaningful utterance**">
</correction>
</error-zone> </correction-zone> **without a context**.

These tags are relatively simple and intuitive. After some basic training, 2 independent annotators covered about 25 pages (emails and reports) so that we can measure the stability of the annotations and the annotators comprehension and agreement/disagreement. Results are not easy to analyze in a simple way since annotators disagree on some error existence and nature. In about 20% of the cases we observed such forms of disagreement. Beside this observation, annotations turn out to be quite convenient, although, for each error, a considerable analysis effort is required for its analysis. Annotating texts is very much time consuming, in particular when there are several possibilities of corrections.

4 From annotations to correction rules

Our corpus (texts, emails) has been annotated following the above schema. Several steps are required in order to reach the correction rule stage of drafting rules of corrections. The approach is still exploratory, and needs further elaborations and evaluations. This is achieved through a gradual and manually controlled machine learning strategy. As a result, we get 23 main categories of errors based on the elements involved in the grammatical and stylistic aspects, e.g.: incorrect argument structure, incorrect adverb position, incorrect embedded clause construction, incorrect coordination, incorrect paragraph start.

To define a correction rule, the segment of words in the error zone first gets a morphosyntactic tagging, so that it can be easily identified as an erroneous pattern in any circumstance. All the errors that have the same erroneous pattern are grouped to form a single correction procedure. In that same category (named 'incorrect N N constructions'), another pattern is [N(+plural) N] (e.g. *horses carriage*), and it results in a different correction rule.

Concerning the pattern 'Det N N', when all the corresponding errors are grouped, another type of correction is found that corresponds to the inversion (the predicate meaning → the meaning of the predicate). Informally, a correction rule is defined as the union of all the corrections found for that particular pattern:
(1) merge all corrections which are similar, i.e. where the position of each word in the erroneous segment is identical to the one it has in the correction; the values of the different attributes of the <correction> tag are averaged,
(2) append all corrections which have a different correction following the word to word criterion above, and also all corrections for which the attribute 'fix' is true.
(3) tag the corrections with all the appropriate morphosyntactic details,
(4) remove the text segments or keep them as examples.

For the above example, we get the following rule:
<correction-rule>
<error-zone comprehension="2" agrammaticality="1"
categ="syntax" source="calque"
pattern="[Det N(1) N(2)"]>
<correction qualif="high" grammar="by-default"
surface= "minimal" meaning= "not altered" Var-size="+2"
change="synt" comp="yes"
web-correct= "[Det N(1) of the N(2)]" >
</correction>
<correction qualif="high" grammar="unlikely"
surface= "minimal"
meaning= "somewhat" Var-size="0"
change="lexical+synt" comp="average"
correct="[Det Adj(deriv(N(1)) N(2)]"
exemple="the meaningful utterance">
</correction>
<correction qualif="high" grammar="by-default"
surface= "minimal"
meaning= "not altered" Var-size="+2"
change="synt" comp="yes"
web-correct= "[Det N(2) of the N(1)]" >
</correction> </error-zone> </correction-rule>

We observe here several competing solutions: when we have a segment like *the meaning predicate* we have no information as to the noun order and the type of preposition to insert (however, 'of' is the most frequent one). In this example, the best solution is to use the web as a corpus. The attribute web-correct is a shortcut for a function that triggers a web search: the instanciated pattern is submitted to a search engine to evaluate its occurence frequency. The most frequent one is adopted. Other rules contain e.g. interactions with the user to get a missing argument or to correct a pronoun.

The form: *pattern → correct (or) web-correct* is a rewriting rule that operates the correction under constraints given in the 'correct' attribute and under didactic constraints given in the associated attributes. Several corrections from the same rule or from different rules may be competing. This is a very frequent situation, e.g.: the position of the adverb which may equally be either before the main verb, or at the beginning, or at the end of the sentence. A correction rule is $active$ for a given correction iff all the constraints it contains in the 'correct' attribute are met.

5 Using argumentation to structure the correction space

Our goal, within an 'active didactics' perspective, consists in identifying the best corrections and proposing them to the writer together with explanations, so that he can make the most relevant decisions. Classical decision theory must be paired with argumentation to produce explanations. In our framework, argumentation is based on the attributes associated with the tags of the correction rules. This view confers a kind of operational semantics to the tags and attributes we have defined.

Formally, a decision based on practical arguments is represented by a vector **(D, K, G, R)** defined as follows:
(1) D is a vector composed of decision variables associated with explanations: the list of the different decisions which can be taken into consideration, including no correction. The final decision is then made by the writer,
(2) K is a structure of stratified knowledge, possibly inconsistent. Stratifications encode priorities (e.g. Bratman, 1987, Amgoud et al. 2008). K includes, for example, knowledge about readers (e.g. in emails they like short messages, close to oral communication), grammatical and stylistic conventions or by-default behaviors, global constraints on texts or sentences. Each strata is associated with a weight $w_K \in [0, 1]$
(3) G is a set of goals, possibly inconsistent, that correspond to positive attributes Ai to promote in a correction. These goals depend on the type of document being written. For example, for emails, we may have the following goals: (meaning: no, comp: yes, grammar: by-default). These goals may have different weights. The form of a goal is:
$(attribute - name, value, weight)$
where weight is: $w_{Ai} \in [0, 1]$.
(4) R is a set of rejections: i.e. criteria that are not desired, e.g., for emails: (surface: not(minimal), change: style, semantic, textual). Format is the same as for G. R and G have an empty intersection. These rejections may also have weights.
Some attributes may remain neutral (e.g. var-size) for a given type of document or profile.

The global scenario for correcting an error is as follows: while checking a text, when an error pattern (or more if patterns are ambiguous) is activated, the corrections proposed in the <correction> tag are activated and a number of them become active because the corresponding 'correct' attribute is active. Then, the attributes in each of the correction, which form arguments, are integrated in the decision process. Their weight in G or R is integrated in a decision formula; these weights may be reinforced or weakened via the knowledge and preferences given in K. For each correction decision, a *meta-argument* that contains all the weighted pros and cons is produced. This meta-argument is the motivation and explanation for realizing the correction as suggested. It has no polarity.

References

Amgoud, L., Dimopoulos, Y., Moraitis, P., Making decisions through preference-based argumentation. In Proceedings of the International Conference on Principles of Knowledge Representation and Reasoning (KR08), AAAI Press, 2008.

Bratman, M., Intentions, plans, and practical reason. Harvard University Press, Massachusetts, 1987.

Brockett et al. (2006) Correcting ESL Errors Using Phrasal SMT Techniques, Proc of COLING/ACL

Han et al., Detecting Errors in English Article Usage by Non-native Speakers, NLE, 2005

Lee, H., Seneff, A., Automatic Grammar Correction for Second-language Learners, Proc of InterSpeech, 2006

Prakken, H., Formal systems for persuasion dialogue, Knowledge Engineering Review, 21:163188, 2006.

Tetreault, M., Chodorow, C. Native Judgments of Non-native Usage, Proc of COLING Workshop on Human Judgements in Comp. Ling, 2008.

Developing Novel Multimodal and Linguistic Annotation Software

Podlasov A., O'Halloran K., Tan S., Smith B., Nagarajan A.
Multimodal Analysis Lab, IDMI, National University of Singapore
9 Prince George's Park, Singapore
{idmpa,k.ohalloran,sabinetan,idmbas,idmarun}@nus.edu.sg

Abstract

In this paper we present a collaborative work between computer and social scientists resulting in the development of annotation software for conducting research and analysis in social semiotics in both multimodal and linguistic aspects. The paper describes the proposed software and discusses how this tool can contribute for development of social semiotic theory and practice.

1 Introduction

Despite the advances that have been achieved in the conceptualization of multimodal theories for analysing language, images and other semiotic resources, many frameworks and models for the transcription and analysis of multimodal data continue to rely on 'low-tech', manual and computer-assisted, technologies. A construct preferred by many researchers for analyzing and representing the interplay of semiotic resources in multimodal data is the *Table*, as exemplified by a range of transcription templates (Baldry & Thibault, 2006). Although tables can be effective for recording which specific semiotic modes and resources are co-deployed at a given moment in the text, they essentially remain bounded by the confines of the printable page.

Besides being laborious to create, page-based analysis severely limits the researchers' ability to effectively capture and portray the complex interplay of semiotic modes and resources as they unfold on a larger scale, especially in the case of dynamic video texts and interactive digital media sites (O'Halloran, 2009). In addition, the analysis will necessarily be restricted to manual transcription and annotation techniques, which often involve a complexity of symbolic notations and abbreviations which may be difficult to learn and comprehend (e.g. Thibault, 2000).

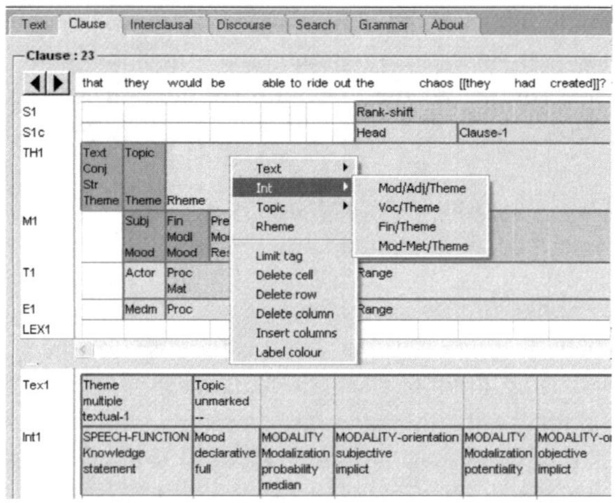

Figure 1. Systemics 1.0 interface.

We propose that the study of meaning-bearing phenomena requires a collaborative effort between social and computer scientists. Social semiotic study clearly can benefit from theoretical concepts and analytical approaches beyond those traditionally developed for typical social science data, and which draw upon the rich variety of computational techniques developed within computational science. This collaborative approach proved to be productive in development of the *Systemics 1.0* (Judd & O'Halloran, 2002) software for research and teaching *Systemic Functional Linguistics* (SFL) (O'Halloran, 2003). *Systemics 1.0* provides a default systemic functional grammar which can be used to manually code the linguistic analysis from pull-down menus, see Figure 1. The results of the analysis are stored in a data-base format which makes it relatively simple to extract linguistic patterns through relational data base searches. The default grammar can be changed to suit user requirements, so that the software is used for teaching and research purposes. The success of the re-

Proceedings of the Third Linguistic Annotation Workshop, ACL-IJCNLP 2009, pages 134–137,
Suntec, Singapore, 6-7 August 2009. ©2009 ACL and AFNLP

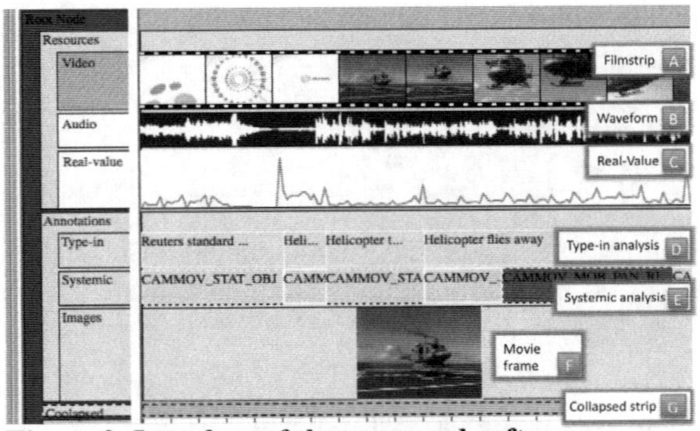

Figure 2. Interface of the proposed software.

search collaboration which resulted in *Systemics 1.0* gives strong motivation to consider computer-based approaches for the more general case of multimodal studies which involves, along with linguistic analysis, analyses of various meaning-bearing phenomena such as gaze, gesture, intonation *etc* (e.g. Bateman, 2008; O'Halloran 2009)

In this paper we report on an ongoing interdisciplinary collaboration between computer scientists and social scientists taking place in Multimodal Analysis Lab, National University of Singapore in the frame of the *Events in the World* project. The project aims at developing an interactive platform for manual, computer-assisted and automatic annotation, analysis and representation of multimedia data for social semiotic and SFL research. The project involves a range of researchers working together to develop the software interface and operational functionalities. The respective roles of the interdisciplinary research team are evolving out of a close collaboration, and the researchers are learning new approaches, perspectives and knowledge which are resulting in new ways of thinking about multimodal phenomena, annotation and analysis.

2 Proposed system

The purpose of the proposed software is to provide social semioticians with the technical means to improve their efficiency and capabilities for studying and annotating multimedia texts, as well as accessing, visualizing and sharing analyses.

2.1 Multimedia resources

Along with supporting standard multimedia resources like video, audio and imagery files, the proposed system supports *real-value resources* to facilitate the use of real-time numerical data in semiotic analysis. Any parameter can be measured during the main media acquisition process or calculated off-line.

2.2 The interface

The interface of the software follows a graphical point-and-click paradigm and is designed to provide easy and straightforward interaction for the user. At the moment of publication, the proposed software is oriented more to the analysis of dynamic time-stamped data, therefore, the main interface window is organized in a partiture-like layout with the horizontal axis corresponding to time. The application's GUI during a sample annotation of a news video clip (© Reuters 2008) is illustrated in Figure 2.

The annotation is organized into strips – containers for semantically grouped annotation elements, which are rendered with respect to the time scale, see Figure 2, D and E. Several strips can be embedded within another strip, which allows hierarchical organization of the annotation data (see Figure 2, 'Annotations' strip with embedded (D) 'Type-in', (E) 'Systemic' and (F) 'Images' strips). A strip can be 'collapsed' (wrapped) in case its display is not needed at any particular time, which is a useful feature when the analysis becomes overloaded with details (see Figure 2, G).

Resources are rendered in the main annotation window in a similar strip-like way. A movie resource control (Figure 2, A) is drawn as a strip of frames enabling interaction with the Movie Viewer tool window. Sound resource control can be drawn as waveform (Figure 2, B). At the moment of publication this control is not interactive and used for display only. Real-value resource control is rendered as a graph (Figure 2, C). Time stamped nodes with associated text or categorical information remain the main tool for annotation and analysis. The node control is rendered as a rectangle and provides the interface for manipulating its position (modifying timestamps) and displaying the associated data, which is text (Figure 2, D) or categorical association (Figure 2, E) using the Systems Browser tool (Figure 3). The software allows rendering of static image resources. The annotation control representing the image also belongs to a strip in order to follow the general partiture-like organization. The software also allows extraction of frames from the video for annotation in a manner similar to images (see Figure 2, F).

2.3 Categorical analysis

By categorical (systemic) analysis we understand a process of associating time stamped annotation controls (nodes) with choices from a system of

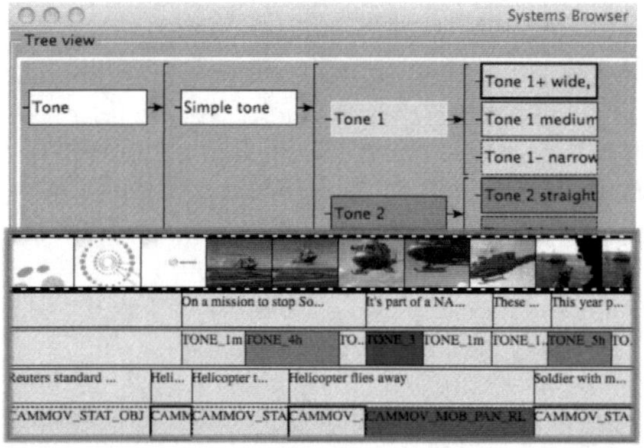

Figure 3. Systems Browser tool window and sample camera movement and tone analysis (superimposed).

categories describing the phenomena semiotically or by other theoretical means. The *Systems Browser* tool window provides the interface to create and manipulate those systems, as well as use them for annotation. Figure 3 illustrates two simple categorical systems: describing camera motion – eg. stationary or mobile camera; the type of tracking (pan, tilt or zoom); and tone choices in speech (cf Halliday 1967). The application allows not only to define the semiotic system itself, but also to associate textual information with every choice, which makes it a helpful interactive glossary for the analyst. Besides that, it allows associating different style attributes of the particular choice: fill color, outline color and dash style, etc. As the user makes systemic choices, the system uses text and style attributes to make the selections visible.

This becomes an important feature of the proposed software. The analysis becomes visible not only textually, but also graphically. In Figure 3 we superimposed the annotation strips with analyzed camera movement and tone for a sample video clip. The filmstrip itself does not visualize the dynamics of the camera in the clip, nor the soundtrack identify tone or other language choices. On the other hand, systemic analysis using style attributes gives a graphical perspective on such choices, so that it is easier to observe and pick up outliers, patterns or points of interest, especially when compared to the traditional page-based annotation. This is especially important when one has to deal with dozen of strips each having hundreds of nodes.

2.4 Overlays

Images and video frames are not dynamic resources and, therefore, are annotated and analyzed by graphical and textual means. Still, textual annotation often needs to be associated with a particular location in the image. Therefore, the proposed software provides a basic graphical annotation tool window – *Overlay Editor*, see Figure 4 - shown also in the thumbnail image in the main interface, giving the analyst the ability to glance over the whole annotation.

Figure 4. Overlay Editor tool window.

2.5 Visualization

Visualization of the data is especially important in cases when there are multiple analyses of the same text presented or there is a large corpus of texts being analyzed. In terms of the former, visualizations may be useful in picturing correlations, interactions and collaborations between different systems operating concurrently in the multimodal text: *e.g.* linguistic aspects, gaze, gesture, intonation, *etc.* In terms of the latter, visualizations may reveal patterns and departures from patterns within a text. At the moment of publication, the annotation data is visualized by the means of style attributes of systemic choices. However, the architecture allows for more sophisticated visualization techniques to be implemented in future.

2.6 Automation

Generally, the proposed system is designed for the human analyst and, therefore, assumes manual annotation as a default way of producing the analysis data. Nevertheless, the current state-of-art in computer science allows many annotation tasks to be semi- or fully automated. When considering techniques to automate semiotic research, one must keep in mind that the proposed software is designed for use by social semioticians, who study media in many different ways. Therefore, when considering automation techniques we assume that the technique must be general enough to be useful for broad class of applications. For example, one can consider *automatic shot boundary-detection*, *automatic face recognition* and more general *object tracking* as technologies, which may be employed for automation. Current state-of-the-art algorithms in *automatic speech recognition* may also be considered since many important multimedia genres, like news or studio TV broadcasts, public presentations, and similar, contain clearly spoken speech which is realistic to recognize.

2.7 Templates and collaboration

Different analytical domains – *e.g.* speech and gesture - and theoretical perspectives require different organization of the annotation document and the use of different semiotic systems. The proposed system allows organizing of predefined templates for different analytical purposes. The template is realized as a standalone file where the required structures are defined. The user is provided with a wizard dialog to select the template, which is then imported into the current annotation document.

2.8 Limitations

The scope of proposed functionalities is broad and, therefore, complete coverage is challenging. A main limitation for the proposed software is the ability to automate the analysis. It is very unrealistic to consider that human analyst can be removed from the process of annotation, since the domain itself, which is social semiotics, is fundamentally human-oriented. Therefore, we consider that semiotic analysis will remain manual to a large extent, and the automation will be employed mostly for routine and technically implementable tasks.

3 Conclusions

In this paper we present a collaborative work between computer and social scientists developing a software platform facilitating research in social semiotics. The proposed software is used for annotation and analysis of multimodal data supporting different media types simultaneously (video, sound, images, text and real-value data) and it provides intuitive GUI for entering the analysis. It supports innovative categorized (systemic) analysis and provides the library of predefined analytical systems developed in the literature together with the ability to create and customize new systems. In addition, the software provides the interface for graphical analysis of imagery data and provides functions for data visualization.

The project contributes to social semiotics by providing a specialized domain-oriented software tool which significantly increases the productivity of the analyst resulting in more extensive studies and better-grounded theories. The proposed visualization interface makes it easier to see data patterns, outliers and recognize points of interest. The ability to customize descriptive systems facilitates experimentation and promotes the development of theoretical frameworks in social semiotics. Unified frameworks for annotation of different media types encourage cross-domain analysis and integration of research from different fields. Though the project is still at the development stage, the obtained results and feedback from practicing social semioticians are promising.

Acknowledgments

This work was supported by the Singapore National Research Foundation (NRF) Interactive Digital Media R&D Program, under research Grant NRF2007IDM-IDM002-066 awarded by the Media Development Authority (MDA) of Singapore.

References

A. Baldry, P. J. Thibault, Multimodal Transcription and Text Analysis, Equinox, London, 2006.

Tan, S. 2005. A Systemic Functional Approach to the Analysis of Corporate Television Advertisements. MA Thesis, Department of English Language and Literature, National University of Singapore.

P. J. Thibault, “The Multimodal Transcription of a Television Advertisement: Theory and Practice”, in Anthony Baldry (ed.) Multimodality and Multimediality in the Distance Learning Age, pp. 311-385, Palladino Editore, Campobasso, Italy, 2000.

K. L. O'Halloran, “Multimodal Analysis and Digital Technology”, In A. Baldry and E. Montagna (eds.), Interdisciplinary Perspectives on Multimodality: Theory and Practice, Proceedings of the Third International Conference on Multimodality, Palladino, Campobasso, 2009.

Halliday, M. A. K. (1967). *Intonation and Grammar in British English.* The Hague; Paris: Mouton.

K. L. O'Halloran, “Systemics 1.0: Software for Research and Teaching Systemic Functional Linguistics”, RELC Journal, vol. 34(2), pp. 157-178, 2003.

Bateman, J. (2008). Multimodality and Genre: A Foundation for the Systematic Analysis of Multimodal Documents. Hampshire: Palgrave Macmillan.

Judd, K. & O'Halloran, K. L. (2002) *Systemics 1.0.* Singapore: Singapore University Press.

Unsupervised Detection of Annotation Inconsistencies Using Apriori Algorithm

Václav Novák **Magda Razímová**
Institute of Formal and Applied Linguistics
Charles University in Prague
Czech Republic
{novak,razimova}@ufal.mff.cuni.cz

Abstract

We present a new method for automated discovery of inconsistencies in a complex manually annotated corpora. The proposed technique is based on Apriori algorithm for mining association rules from datasets. By setting appropriate parameters to the algorithm, we were able to automatically infer highly reliable rules of annotation and subsequently we searched for records for which the inferred rules were violated. We show that the violations found by this simple technique are often caused by an annotation error. We present an evaluation of this technique on a hand-annotated corpus PDT 2.0, present the error analysis and show that in the first 100 detected nodes 20 of them contained an annotation error.

1 Introduction

Complex annotation schemes pose a serious challenge to annotators caused by the number of attributes they are asked to fill. The annotation tool can help them in ensuring that the values of all attributes are from the appropriate domain but the interplay of individual values and their mutual compatibility are at best described in annotation instructions and often implicit. Another source of errors are idiomatic expressions where it is difficult for the annotator to think about the categories of a word which often exists only as a part of the idiom at hand.

In our approach, detection of annotation inconsistencies is an instance of anomaly detection, which is mainly used in the field of intrusion detection. Traditionally, the anomaly detection is based on distances between feature vectors of individual instances. These methods are described in Section 2. Our new method presented in Section 3 uses the data-mining technique Apriori (Borgelt and Kruse, 2002) for inferring high-quality rules, whose violation indicates a possible annotator's mistake or another source of inconsistency. We tested the proposed method on a manually annotated corpus and described both the data and the experimental results in Section 4. We conclude by Section 5.

2 Related Work

Unsupervised anomaly detection has been shown to be viable for intrusion detection (Eskin et al., 2002). The unsupervised techniques rely on feature vectors generated by individual instances and try to find outliers in the vector space. This can be done using clustering (Chimphlee et al., 2005), Principle Component Analysis (Hawkins, 1974), geometric methods (Eskin et al., 2002) and more (Lazarevic et al., 2003).

The difference between our method and previous work lies mainly in the fact that instead using vector space of features, we directly infer annotation rules. The manual annotation is always based on some rules, some of which are contained in the annotation manual but many others are more or less implied. These rules will have their confidence measured in the annotated corpus equal to 1 or at least very close (see Section 3 for definition of confidence). In our approach we learn such rules and detect exceptions to the most credible rules. The rules are learned using the common Apriori algorithm (Borgelt and Kruse, 2002). Previously, rules have been also mined by GUHA algorithm (Hájek and Havránek, 1978), but not in the anomaly detection context.

3 Method Description

Our process of anomaly detection comprises two steps: rules mining and anomaly search.

Proceedings of the Third Linguistic Annotation Workshop, ACL-IJCNLP 2009, pages 138–141,
Suntec, Singapore, 6-7 August 2009. ©2009 ACL and AFNLP

3.1 Rules Mining

The association rules mining was originally designed for market basket analysis to automatically derive rules such as "if the customer buys a toothpaste and a soap, he is also likely to buy a toothbrush". Every check-out $\mathbf{x} = (x_1, x_2, \ldots, x_N)$ is modeled as a draw from an unknown probability distribution Φ, where N is the total number of items available at the store and x_i is the number of items of type i contained in the shopping cart. Further, we define event $E_j = \{\mathbf{x} | x_j > 0\}$, i.e., the event that the shopping cart contains the item j.

In this model, we define a rule $A = (L, R)$ as a tuple where the left side L and the right side R are sets of events E_j. For instance suppose that the toothpaste, toothbrush and soap have indices 1, 2 and 3, respectively. Then the example rule mentioned above can be written as $A_{\text{example}} = (\{E_1, E_3\}, \{E_2\})$, or alternatively $\{E_1, E_3\} \Rightarrow \{E_2\}$. For every rule $A = (L, R)$ we define two important measures: the **support** $s(A)$ and the **confidence** $c(A)$:

$$s((L,R)) = P\left(\bigcap_{l \in L}(l) \cap \bigcap_{r \in R}(r)\right) \quad (1)$$

$$c((L,R)) = P\left(\bigcap_{r \in R}(r) \middle| \bigcap_{l \in L}(l)\right) \quad (2)$$

In our example the support is the probability that a cart contains a toothpaste, a toothbrush and a soap. The confidence is the probability that a cart contains a toothbrush given the cart contains both a toothpaste and a soap.

The input of the Apriori algorithm (Borgelt and Kruse, 2002) consists of a sample from the probability distribution Φ, the threshold of the estimated confidence, the threshold of the estimated support and the maximum size of rules. Using this data the Apriori algorithm lists all rules satisfying the required constraints.

In the context of market basket analysis the confidence is rarely anywhere close to one, but in the case of linguistic annotation, there are rules that are always or almost always followed. The confidence of these rules is very close or equal to one. The Apriori algorithm allows us to gather rules that have the confidence close to one and a sufficient support.

3.2 Anomaly Search

After extracting the highly confident rules we select the rules with the highest support and find the annotations where these rules are violated. This provides us with the list of anomalies. The search is linear with the size of the data set and the size of the list of extracted rules.

4 Experiments

4.1 Data and Tools

The experiments were carried out using the *R* statistical analysis software (R Development Core Team, 2006) using the *arules* library (Borgelt and Kruse, 2002). The dataset used was full manually annotated data of Prague Dependency Treebank 2.0 (PDT 2.0). PDT 2.0 data were annotated at three layers, namely *morphological*, *analytical* (shallow dependency syntax) and *tectogrammatical* (deep dependency syntax; (Hajič et al., 2006)). The units of each annotation layer were linked with corresponding units of the preceding layer. The morphological units were linked directly with the original text. The annotation at the tectogrammatical layer was checked automatically for consistency with the annotation instructions (Štěpánek, 2006), however, using our technique, we were still able to automatically find errors. The experimental dataset (full PDT 2.0 data annotated at all three layers) contained 49,431 sentences or 833,195 tokens.

4.2 Experimental Setup and Error Analysis

In our experimental setup, every check-out (i.e., every draw from the probability distribution Φ) contains all attributes of one tectogrammatical node and its governor. The attributes extracted from the nodes are listed in Table 1. Thus every check-out has exactly 52 items, 26 coming from the node in question and 26 coming from its governor.

This being input to the Apriori algorithm, we set the maximal size of rules to 3, minimal support to 0.001 and minimal confidence to 0.995. When the rules were extracted, we sorted them according to the descending confidence and stripped all rules with confidence equal to 1. Using the remaining rules, we searched the corpus for the violations of the rules (starting from the top one) until we found first 100 suspicious nodes. We manually analyzed these 100 positions and found out that 20

Attribute	Description
functor	semantic values of deep-syntactic dependency relations
is_dsp_root	root node of the sub-tree representing direct speech
tfa	contextual boundness
is_generated	element not expressed in the surface form of the sentence
is_member	member of a coordination or an apposition
is_name_of_person	proper name of a person
is_parenthesis	node is part of a parenthesis
is_state	modification with the meaning of a state
sentmod	sentential modality
subfunctor	semantic variation within a particular functor
aspect	aspect of verbs
degcmp	degree of comparison
deontmod	an event is necessary, possible, permitted etc.
dispmod	relation (attitude) of the agent to the event
gender	masculine animate, masculine inanimate, feminine or neuter
indeftype	types of pronouns (indefinite, negative etc.)
iterativeness	multiple/iterated events
negation	a negated or an affirmative form
number	singular or plural
numertype	types of numerals (cardinal, ordinal etc.)
person	reference to the speaker/hearer/something else
politeness	polite form
resultative	event is presented as the resulting state
sempos	semantic part of speech
tense	verbal tense (simultaneous, preceding or subsequent events)
verbmod	verbal mood (indicative, conditional or imperative)

Table 1: Attributes of tectogrammatical nodes used as the input to the rule mining algorithm. Their complex interplay can hardly be fully prescribed in an annotation manual.

of them constitute an annotation error. Examples of extracted rules follow.

$$\begin{array}{ll} & \textit{is\_parenthesis:1} \\ \& & \textit{governor:functor:PAR} \\ \Rightarrow & \textit{governor:is\_parenthesis:1} \end{array} \quad (3)$$

Rule 3 states that if a tectogrammatical node has the attribute *is_parenthesis* set to 1 (i.e., the node is part of a parenthesis) and at the same time the governor of this node in the tectogrammatical tree has its *functor* set to *PAR* (it is the root node of nodes which are parenthesis in a sentence), the governor's *is_parenthesis* attribute is also set to 1. Using this rule we detected 6 nodes in the corpus where the annotator forgot to fill the value 1 in the *is_parenthesis* attribute. There were no false positives and this automatically extracted rule is likely to be added to the consistency checking routines in the future.

$$\begin{array}{ll} & \textit{functor:RSTR} \\ \& & \textit{gender:nr} \\ \Rightarrow & \textit{number:nr} \end{array} \quad (4)$$

Rule 4 states that *RSTR* nodes (mostly attributes of nouns) with *nr* gender (indeterminable gender) also have indeterminable *number*. Our procedure located a node where the annotator correctly determined the *number* as *sg* but failed to recognize the gender (namely, masculine inanimate) of the node.

$$\begin{array}{ll} & \textit{is\_member:1} \\ \& & \textit{dispmod:nil} \\ \Rightarrow & \textit{tense:nil} \end{array} \quad (5)$$

Rule 5, stating that for nodes with *is_member* set to 1 the *nil* value (which means that none of the defined basic values is suitable) of the *dispmod* attribute implicates the *nil* value of the *tense*, is an example of a rule producing false positives.

Due to the data sparsity problem, there are not so many nodes satisfying the premises and in most of them the *nil* value were simply filled in their *tense* attribute. However, there are (rather rare) transgressive verb forms in the corpus for which the correct annotation violates this rule. Many of them were found by this procedure but they are more anomalies in the underlying text rather than anomalies in the annotation. An interesting point to note is that there were several rules exhibiting this behavior with different first premises (e.g., *gender:anim & governor:dispmod:nil* ⇒ *governor:tense:nil*). The more general rule (*dispmod:nil* ⇒ *tense:nil*) would not get enough confidence, but by combining it with other unrelated attributes, the procedure was able to find rules with enough confidence, although not very useful ones.

$$\begin{array}{ll} & \textit{resultative:res0} \\ \& & \textit{governor:degcmp:pos} \\ \Rightarrow & \textit{governor:sempos:adj.denot} \end{array} \qquad (6)$$

Rule 6 is an example of a successful rule. It states that nodes that govern a non-resultative node and have the positive degree of comparison are always denominating semantic adjectives (i.e., common adjectives such as *black* or *good*). Using this rule we detected a node where the annotators correctly determined the semantic part of speech as *adj.quant.grad* (quantificational semantic adjective) but failed to indicate *degcmp:comp*.

5 Conclusion and Future Work

We have described a fast method for automatic detection of inconsistencies in a hand-annotated corpus using easily available software tools and evaluated it showing that in top 100 suspicious nodes there were an error in 20 cases. This method seem to work best for high-quality annotation where the errors are rare: in our experiments the rules had to achieve at least 99.5% confidence to be included in the search for violations. However, it can also point out inconsistencies in the annotation instructions by revealing the suspicious data points. We have shown the typical rules and errors revealed by our procedure.

The method can be generalized for any manually entered categorical datasets. The rules can take values from multiple data entries (nodes, words, etc.) into account to capture the dependency in the annotation. Other rule-mining techniques such as GUHA (Hájek and Havránek, 1978) can be used instead of Apriori.

Acknowledgement

This work was supported by Czech Academy of Science grants 1ET201120505 and 1ET101120503; by Ministry of Education, Youth and Sports projects LC536 and MSM0021620838.

References

Christian Borgelt and Rudolf Kruse. 2002. Induction of Association Rules: Apriori Implementation. In *Proceedings of 15th Conference on Computational Statistics (Compstat)*, pages 395–400, Heidelberg, Germany. Physica Verlag.

W. Chimphlee, Abdul Hanan Abdullah, Mohd Noor Md Sap, S. Chimphlee, and S. Srinoy. 2005. Unsupervised Clustering methods for Identifying Rare Events in Anomaly Detection. In *Proceedings of the 6th International Enformatika Conference (IEC2005)*, Budapest, Hungary, October 26-28.

E. Eskin, A. Arnold, M. Prerau, L. Portnoy, and S. Stolfo. 2002. A geometric framework for unsupervised anomaly detection: Detecting intrusions in unlabeled data. In *Data Mining for Security Applications*. Kluwer.

Petr Hájek and Tomáš Havránek. 1978. *Mechanizing Hypothesis Formation; Mathematical Foundations for a General Theory*. Springer-Verlag, Berlin, Heidelberg, New York.

Jan Hajič, Jarmila Panevová, Eva Hajičová, Petr Sgall, Petr Pajas, Jan Štěpánek, Jiří Havelka, Marie Mikulová, Zdeněk Žabokrtský, and Magda Ševčíková-Razímová. 2006. Prague Dependency Treebank 2.0. CD-ROM, Linguistic Data Consortium, LDC Catalog No.: LDC2006T01, Philadelphia, Pennsylvania.

D. M. Hawkins. 1974. The Detection of Errors in Multivariate Data Using Principal Components. *Journal of the American Statistical Association*, 69(346):340–344.

A. Lazarevic, A. Ozgur, L. Ertoz, J. Srivastava, and V. Kumar. 2003. A comparative study of anomaly detection schemes in network intrusion detection. In *Proceedings of SIAM International Conference on Data Mining*.

R Development Core Team, 2006. *R: A Language and Environment for Statistical Computing*. R Foundation for Statistical Computing, Vienna, Austria. ISBN 3-900051-07-0.

Jan Štěpánek. 2006. Post-annotation Checking of Prague Dependency Treebank 2.0 Data. In *Proceedings of the 9th International Conference, TSD 2006*, number 4188 in Lecture Notes in Computer Science, pages 277–284. Springer-Verlag Berlin Heidelberg.

Towards a Methodology for Named Entities Annotation

Karën Fort
INIST / LIPN
2 allée du Parc de Brabois,
54500 Vandoeuvre-lès-Nancy, France
karen.fort@inist.fr

Maud Ehrmann
XRCE
6 Chemin de Maupertuis,
38240 Meylan, France
Ehrmann@xrce.xerox.com

Adeline Nazarenko
LIPN, Université Paris 13 & CNRS
99 av. J.B. Clément,
93430 Villetaneuse, France
nazarenko@lipn.univ-paris13.fr

Abstract

Today, the named entity recognition task is considered as fundamental, but it involves some specific difficulties in terms of annotation. Those issues led us to ask the fundamental question of what the annotators should annotate and, even more important, for which purpose. We thus identify the applications using named entity recognition and, according to the real needs of those applications, we propose to semantically define the elements to annotate. Finally, we put forward a number of methodological recommendations to ensure a coherent and reliable annotation scheme.

1 Introduction

Named entity (NE) extraction appeared in the middle of the 1990s with the MUC conferences (*Message Understanding Conferences*). It has now become a successful Natural Language Processing (NLP) task that cannot be ignored. However, the underlying corpus annotation is still little studied. The issues at stake in manual annotation are crucial for system design, be it manual design, machine learning, training or evaluation. Manual annotations give a precise description of the expected results of the target system. Focusing on manual annotation issues led us to examine what named entities are and what they are used for.

2 Named Entities Annotation: practice and difficulties

Named entity recognition is a well-established task (Nadeau and Sekine, 2007). One can recall its evolution according to three main directions. The first corresponds to work in the "general" field, with the continuation of the task defined by MUC for languages other than English, with a revised set of categories, mainly with journalistic corpora[1]. The second direction relates to work in "specialized" domains, with the recognition of entities in medicine, chemistry or microbiology, like gene and protein names in specialized literature[2]. The last direction, spanning the two previous ones, is disambiguation.

For each of those evaluation campaigns, corpora were built and annotated manually. They are generally used to develop automatic annotation tools. "To Develop" is to be understood in a broad sense: the goal is to describe what automatic systems should do, to help writing the symbolic rules they are based on, to learn those rules or decision criteria automatically, and, finally, to evaluate the results obtained by comparing them with a gold standard. The annotation process brings into play two actors, an annotator and a text. The text annotation must follow precise guidelines, satisfy quality criteria and support evaluation.

In the general field, the MUC, CoNLL and ACE evaluation campaigns seem to have paid attention to the process of manual NE annotation, with the definition of annotation guidelines and the calculation of inter-annotator (but not intra-annotator) agreement, using a back-and-forth process between annotating the corpus and defining the annotation guidelines. Nevertheless, some aspects of the annotation criteria remained problematic, caused mainly by "different interpretations of vague portions of the guidelines" (Sundheim, 1995). In the fields of biology and medicine, texts from specialized databases (PubMed and MedLine[3]) were annotated. Annotation guidelines

[0]This work was partly realised as part of the Quaero Programme, funded by OSEO, French State agency for innovation.

[1]See the evaluation campaigns MET, IREX, CoNNL, ACE, ESTER and HAREM (Ehrmann, 2008, pp. 19-21).

[2]See the evaluation campaigns BioCreAtIvE (Kim et al., 2004) and JNLPBA (Hirschman et al., 2005).

[3]www.ncbi.nlm.nih.gov/pubmed, http://medline.cos.com

Proceedings of the Third Linguistic Annotation Workshop, ACL-IJCNLP 2009, pages 142–145,
Suntec, Singapore, 6-7 August 2009. ©2009 ACL and AFNLP

were vague about the annotation of NEs [4], and few studies measured annotation quality. For the GENIA (Kim et al., 2003), PennBioIE (Kulick et al., 2004) or GENETAG (Tanabe et al., 2005) corpora, no inter- or intra-annotator agreement is reported. If NE annotation seems a well-established practice, it involves some difficulties.

As regards general language corpora, those difficulties are identified (Ehrmann, 2008). The first one relates to the choice of annotation categories and the determination of what they encompass. Indeed, beyond the "universal" triad defined by the MUC conferences (ENAMEX, NUMEX and TIMEX), the inventory of categories is difficult to stabilize. For ENAMEX, although it may be obvious that the name of an individual such as *Kofi Annan* is to be annotated using this category, what to do with *the Kennedys*, *Zorro*, *the Democrats* or *Santa Claus*? For the other categories, it is just as difficult to choose the granularity of the categories and to determine what they encompass. Another type of difficulty relates to the selection of the mentions to be annotated as well as the delimitation of NE boundaries. Let us consider the NE "Barack Obama" and the various lexemes that can refer to it: *Barack Obama*, *Mr Obama*, *the President of the United States*, *the new president*, *he*. Should we annotate proper nouns only, or also definite descriptions that identify this person, even pronouns which, contextually, could refer to this NE? And what to do with the various attributes that go with this NE (*Mr* and *president*)? Coordination and overlapping phenomena can also raise problems for the annotators. Finally, another difficulty results from phenomena of referential plurality, with homonyms NEs (*Java* place and *Java* language) and metonyms (*England* as a geographical place, a government or sport team).

Our experience in microbiology shows that these difficulties are even more acute in specialized language. We carried out an annotation experiment on an English corpus of PubMed notices. The main difficulty encountered related to the distinction required between proper and common nouns, the morphological boundary between the two being unclear in those fields where common nouns are often reclassified as "proper nouns", as is demonstrated by the presence of these names in nomenclatures (*small, acid-soluble spore protein A* is an extreme case) or acronymisation phenomena (one finds for example *across the outer membrane (OM)*). In those cases, annotators were instructed to refer to official lists, such as Swiss-Prot[5], which requires a significant amount of time. Delimiting the boundaries of the elements to be annotated also raised many questions. One can thus choose to annotate *nifh messenger RNA* if it is considered that the mention of the state *messenger RNA* is part of the determination of the reference, or only *nifh*, if it is considered that the proper noun is enough to build the determination. Selecting semantic types was also a problem for the annotators, in particular for mobile genetic elements, like plasmids or transposons. Indeed, those were to be annotated in taxons but not in genes whereas they are chunks of DNA, therefore parts of genome. A particularly confusing directive for the annotators was to annotate the acronym *KGFR* as a proper noun and the developed form *keratinocyte growth Factor receptor* as a common noun. This kind of instruction is difficult to comprehend and should have been documented better.

These problems result in increased annotation costs, too long annotation guidelines and, above all, a lot of indecision for the annotators, which induces inconsistencies and lower-quality annotation. This led us to consider the issue of what the annotators must annotate (semantic foundations of NE) and, above all, why.

3 What to Annotate?

3.1 Various Defining Criteria

Ehrmann (2008) proposes a linguistic analysis of the notion of NE, which is presented as an NLP "creation". In the following paragraphs, we take up the distinction introduced in LDC (2004): NE are "mentions" refering to domain "entities", those mentions relate to different linguistic categories: proper nouns ("Rabelais"), but also pronouns ("he"), and in a broader sense, definite descriptions ("the father of Gargantua"). Several defining criteria for NE can be identified.

Referential Unicity One of the main characteristics of proper nouns is their referential behaviour: a proper noun refers to a unique referential entity, even if this unicity is contextual. We consider that this property is essential in the usage of NEs in NLP.

[4](Tanabe et al., 2005) notes that "a more detailed definition of a gene/protein name, as well as additional annotation rules, could improve inter-annotator agreement and help solve some of the tagging inconsistencies".

[5]http://www.expasy.org/sprot/

Referential Autonomy NEs are also autonomous from the referential point of view. It is obvious in the case of proper nouns, which are self-sufficient to identify the referent, at least in a given communication situation (*Eurotunnel*). The case of definite descriptions (*The Channel Tunnel operator*) is a bit different: they can be used to identify the referent thanks to external knowledge.

Denominational Stability Proper nouns are also stable denominations. Even if some variations may appear (*A. Merkel/Mrs Merkel*), they are more regular and less numerous than for other noun phrases[6].

Referential Relativity Interpretation is always carried out relatively to a domain model, that can be implicit in simple cases (for example, a country or a person) but has to be made explicit when the diversity in entities to consider increases.

3.2 Different Annotation Perspectives

The defining criteria do not play the same role in all applications. In some cases (indexing and knowledge integration), we focus on referential entities which are designated by stable and non-ambiguous descriptors. In those cases, the NEs to use are proper nouns or indexing NEs and they should be normalized to identify variations that can appear despite their referential stability. For this type of application, the main point is not to highlight all the mentions of an entity in a document, but to identify which document mentions which entity. Therefore, precision has to be favored over recall. On the other hand, in the tasks of information extraction and domain modelling, it is important to identify all the mentions, including definite descriptions (therefore, coreference relations between mentions that are not autonomous enough from a referential point of view are also important to identify).

As it is impossible to identify the mentions of all the referential entities, the domain model defines which entities are "of interest" and the boundary between what has to be annotated or not. For instance, when a human resources director is interested in the payroll in the organization, s/he thinks in terms of personnel categories and not in terms of the employees as individuals. This appears in the domain model: the different categories of persons (technicians, engineers, etc.) are modelled as instances attached to the concept CAT-OF-EMPLOYEES and the individuals are not represented. On the opposite, when s/he deals with employees' paychecks and promotion, s/he is interested in individuals. In this case, the model should consider the persons as instances and the categories of personnel as concepts.

Domain modelling implies making explicit choices where texts can be fuzzy and mix points of view. It is therefore impossible to annotate the NEs of a text without refering to a model. In the case of the above experiment, as it is often the case, the model was simply described by a list of concepts: the annotators had to name genes and proteins, but also their families, compositions and components.

4 Annotation methodology

Annotation guidelines As the targeted annotation depends on what one wants to annotate and how it will be exploited, it is important to provide annotators with guidelines that explain what must be annotated rather than how it should be annotated. Very often, feasibility constraints overcome semantic criteria,[7] which confuses annotators. Besides, it is important to take into consideration the complexity of the annotation task, without excluding the dubious annotations or those which would be too difficult to reproduce automatically. On the contrary, one of the roles of manual annotation is to give a general idea of the task complexity. The annotators must have a clear view of the target application. This view must be based on an explicit reference model, as that of GENIA, with precise definitions and explicit modelling choices. Examples can be added for illustration but they should not replace the definition of the goal. It is important that annotators understand the underlying logic of annotation. It helps avoiding misunderstandings and giving them a sense of being involved and committed.

Annotation tools Although there exists many annotation tools, few are actually available, free, downloadable and usable. Among those tools are Callisto, MMAX2, Knowtator or Cadixe[8] which was used in the reported experiment. The features

[6] *A contrario*, this explains the importance of synonyms identification in domains where denominations are not stable (like, for instance, in genomics).

[7] "In [src homology 2 and 3], it seems excessive to require an NER program to recognize the entire fragment, however, 3 alone is not a valid gene name." (Tanabe et al., 2005).

[8] http://callisto.mitre.org, http://mmax2.sourceforge.net, http://knowtator.sourceforge.net, http://caderige.imag.fr

and the annotation language expressivity must be adapted to the targeted annotation task: is it sufficient to type the textual segments or should they also be related? is it possible/necessary to have concurrent or overlapping annotations? In our experiment on biology, for instance, although the annotators had the possibility to mention their uncertainty by adding an attribute to the annotations, they seldom did so, because it was not easy to do using the provided interface.

Annotation evaluation Gut and Bayerl (2004) distinguishes the inter-annotator agreement, which measures the annotation stability, and the intra-annotation agreement that gives an idea on how reproducible an annotation is. The inter- and intra-annotator agreements do not have to be measured on the whole corpus, but quite early in the annotation process, so that the annotation guidelines can be modified. Another way to evaluate annotation relies on annotator introspection. Annotators are asked to auto-evaluate the reliability of their annotations and their (un)certainty attributes can be used afterwards to evaluate the overall quality of the work. Since we did not have several annotators working independently on our biology corpus, we asked them to indicate the uncertainty of their annotations on a carefully selected sample corpus. 25 files were extracted out of the 499 texts of our corpus (5%). This evaluation required only few hours of work and it enabled to better qualify and quantity annotation confidence. The annotators declared that around 20% of the total number of annotation tags were "uncertain". We observed that more than 75% of these uncertain tags were associated to common nouns of type *bacteria* and that uncertainty was very often (77%) linked to the fact that distinguishing common and proper nouns was difficult.

More generally, a good annotation methodology consists in having several annotators working independently on the same sample corpus very early in the process. It allows to quickly identify the disagreement causes. If they can be solved, new recommendations are added to the annotation guidelines. If not, the annotation task might be simplified and the dubious cases eliminated.

5 Conclusion and Prospects

In the end, two main points must be considered for a rigorous and efficient NE annotation in corpus. First, as for the content, it is important to focus, not on *how* to annotate, but rather on *what* to annotate, according to the final application. Once specified what is to be annotated, one has to be cautious in terms of methodology and consider from the very beginning of the campaign, the evaluation of the produced annotation.

We intend to apply this methodology to other annotation campaigns of the project we participate in. As those campaigns cover terminology and semantic relations extraction, we will have to adapt our method to those applications.

References

Maud Ehrmann. 2008. *Les entités nommées, de la linguistique au TAL : statut théorique et méthodes de désambiguïsation*. Ph.D. thesis, Univ. Paris 7.

Ulrike Gut and Petra Saskia Bayerl. 2004. Measuring the reliability of manual annotations of speech corpora. In *Proc. of Speech Prosody*, pages 565–568, Nara, Japan.

Lynette Hirschman, Alexander Yeh, Christian Blaschke, and Alfonso Valencia. 2005. Overview of biocreative: critical assessment of information extraction for biology. *BMC Bioinformatics*, 6(1).

J.-D. Kim, T. Ohta, Y. Tateisi, and J. Tsujii. 2003. Genia corpus–a semantically annotated corpus for bio-textmining. *Bioinformatics*, 19:180–182.

Jin-Dong Kim, Tomoko Ohta, Yoshimasa Tsuruoka, Yuka Tateisi, and Nigel Collier. 2004. Introduction to the bio-entity recognition task at JNLPBA. In *Proc. of JNLPBA COLING 2004 Workshop*, pages 70–75.

Seth Kulick, Ann Bies, Mark Liberman, Mark Mandel, Ryan McDonald, Martha Palmer, Andrew Schein, and Lyle Ungar. 2004. Integrated annotation for biomedical information extraction. In *HLT-NAACL 2004 Workshop: Biolink*. ACL.

LDC. 2004. ACE (Automatic Content Extraction) english annotation guidelines for entities. Livrable version 5.6.1 2005.05.23, Linguistic Data Consortium.

David Nadeau and Satoshi Sekine. 2007. A survey of named entity recognition and classification. *Linguisticae Investigaciones*, 30(1):3–26.

B. Sundheim. 1995. Overview of results of the MUC-6 evaluation. In *Proc. of the 6th Message Understanding Conference*. Morgan Kaufmann Publishers.

Lorraine Tanabe, Natalie Xie, Lynne Thom, Wayne Matten, and John Wilbur1. 2005. Genetag: a tagged corpus for gene/protein named entity recognition. *Bioinformatics*, 6.

Online Search Interface for the *Sejong* Korean-Japanese Bilingual Corpus and Auto-interpolation of Phrase Alignment

Sanghoun Song
Korea Univ.
Anam-dong, Sungbuk-gu, Seoul,
South Korea
sanghoun@gmail.com

Francis Bond
NICT Language Infrastructure Group
2-2-2 Hikaridai, Seika-cho,
Soraku-gun, Kyoto, Japan
bond@ieee.org

Abstract

A user-friendly interface to search bilingual resources is of great help to NLP developers as well as pure-linguists. Using bilingual resources is difficult for linguists who are unfamiliar with computation, which hampers capabilities of bilingual resources. NLP developers sometimes need a kind of workbench to check their resources. The online interface this paper introduces can satisfy these needs. In order to implement the interface, this research deals with how to align Korean and Japanese phrases and interpolates them into the original bilingual corpus in an automatic way.

1 Introduction

Bilingual or multilingual corpora are significant language resources in various language studies, such as language education, comparative linguistics, in particular, NLP. What holds the key position in bilingual resources is how to align linguistic units between two languages. In this context, three fundamental questions about how to harness bilingual resources can be raised; (i) which linguistic unit or level should correspond to those in the corresponding language? (ii) which method should be employed for alignment? (iii) which environments should be prepared for users?

This paper covers these matters related to bilingual resources and their use. The language resource that this paper handles is the *Sejong Korean-Japanese Bilingual Corpus* (henceforth SKJBC).[1] The original version of the SKJBC, constructed in a XML format, aligns sentence by sentence or paragraph by paragraph. This research re-organizes and re-aligns the original version using GIZA++ (Och and Ney, 2003) and *Moses* (Koehn et al. 2007), and interpolates the aligning information into each original file automatically. Turning to the interface, this research converts the whole data into a database system (MySQL) to guarantee data integrity. Building on the database, this research implements an online search system accessible without any restrictions; dubbed NARA[2].

2 The SKJBC

The SKJBC had been constructed as a subset of the *Sejong* project[3] which had been carried out from 1998 to 2007, sponsored by the Korean government. The SKJBC is divided into two parts; one is the raw corpus annotated only with sentence aligning indices, the other is the POS-tagged corpus, in which the tag set for Korean complies with the POS-tagging guideline of the *Sejong* project, and the morphological analysis for Japanese is based on *ChaSen* (Matsumoto et al., 1999). This paper is exclusively concerned with the latter, because it is highly necessary for the phrase alignment to make use of well-segmented and well-refined data. Table 1 illustrates the basic configuration of the SKJBC.

Since the prime purpose of the *Sejong* project was to build up balanced corpora, the SKJBC consists of various genres, as shown in Figure 1. This makes a clear difference from other bilingual resources where the data-type is normally homogeneous (e.g. newspapers). Moreover, since it had been strictly prohibited to manipulate the

[1] The SKJBC is readily available for academic and research purposes only. For information on license conditions and others, please contact the *National Academy of Korean Language* (http://www.korean.go.kr/eng/index.jsp).

[2] The name, NARA, has meanings in both Korean and Japanese. It is a local name in Japan; it also means 'a country' in Korean. Since the name can properly stands for this research's goal, the name has been used as a project title.

[3] http://www.sejong.or.kr/eindex.php

Proceedings of the Third Linguistic Annotation Workshop, ACL-IJCNLP 2009, pages 146–149,
Suntec, Singapore, 6-7 August 2009.

original source for any reasons, the data in SKJBC fully reflect on the real usage of Korean. These characteristics, however, sometimes work against computational implementation. Bi-texts do not always correspond to each other sentence by sentence; we can find out that there are a number of cases that a sentence matches two or more sentences in the other language or the corresponding sentences might be non-existent. In other words, it is almost impossible to align all the sentences only one-to-one. These cases eventually produce the multiple-to-multiple alignment, unless annotators discard or separate them artificially. No artificial manipulation was allowed under construction, the SKJBC contains quite a few pairs in a multiple-to-multiple relation.

	Korean		Japanese	
	type	token	type	token
document	50 (KoJa : 38, JaKo : 12)			
sentence		4,030		4,038
word	21,734	43,534	10,452	93,395
morpheme	9,483	101,266	10,223	

Table 1. Configuration of the SKJBC

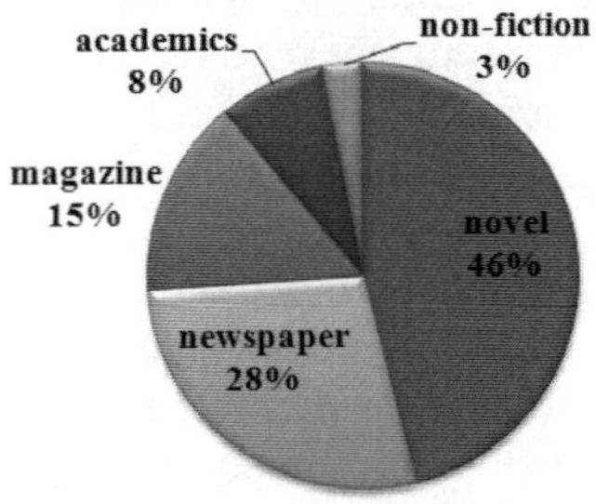

Figure 1. Composition of the SKJBC

3 Alignment

This section is connected with the first question raised in section 1; the proper level of alignment. Most bilingual corpora, including the SKJBC, have been constructed sentence by sentence despite shortcomings, because it costs too much time and effort to annotate word or phrase correspondence by hand (Abeillé, 2003). To annotate more specified alignment between two languages is to enhance the utility value of the resource; this research, first of all, considers how to align at the level of word and phrase.

Multiple Alignments: Because of the problem mentioned in the previous section, the pairs which do not match in a one-to-one relation were excluded from the target of alignment. Throughout a preliminary experiment, it was born out that, if they remained, they led to a worse result. After casting them away, the number of target sentences is 3,776, which account for about 86 percent of the whole data.

Word vs. Phrase: To make the units equivalent as far as possible is the crucial factor in aligning as accurately as possible. One of the main issues that should be taken into account in aligning Korean and Japanese phrases is word boundary. Though Korean and Japanese share lots of features, the boundary of word or phrase is inconsistent with each other. The general concept to segment words in Korean is the so-called *ejeol*, tantamount to word-spacing, whereas that in Japanese is *bunsetsu*, what we say. The difference stems from the different writing style; Korean inserts spacing between words, while Japanese seldom uses spacing. Consequently, each word in Korean is virtually equivalent to a phrasal unit in Japanese, as given in (1-2).

(1) 웃었다 웃/VV+었/EP+다/EF
wus-ess-ta
laugh-PAST-DC 'laughed'

(2) 笑っ 笑う/VIN
た た/AU
warat-ta
laugh-PAST 'langhed'

The first line (i.e. *ejeol*) in (1) for Korean corresponds to the first and second line (i.e. *bunsetsu*) in (2). Hence, it is the most suitable choice to align Korean morphemes (e.g. 웃 *wus*) and Japanese *bunsetsu* (e.g. 笑っ *warat*).

On the other hand, there is a clear cut between lemmatized lexical forms and surface forms in Japanese, (e.g. 笑う and 笑っ in the above, respectively), whereas there is none in Korean. In order to prevent the result from being biased, this paper establishes two training sets (i.e. lemmatized and surface forms) for alignment.

Word Sense Disambiguation (WSD): Other than the above issues, it is also needed to consider WSD. For example, a Korean word 삶 *salm* has two meanings; one is 'life' as a nominal expression, the other is 'boil' as a verbal lexeme, which correspond to 生 *sei*, 煮る *niru*, respectively. This research, therefore, makes training data composed of each morpheme plus its POS tag, such as '삶/NNG' and '生/NCPV'.

4 Auto-interpolation

Turning to the second question, this part covers how to align and annotate. Were it not for automatic processing, it would be painstaking work to construct bilingual resources even line by line. One popular toolkit to align linguistic units between two languages in an unsupervised way is GIZA++.

Even though GIZA++ yields fairly good 'word' alignment, much remains still to be done. For instance, those who want to study two or more languages from a comparative stance are certain to need syntactic data which offer more information about language diversity than plain word-mapping. Besides, Statistical Machine Translation (SMT) commonly runs under the phrase-based model. This research employs the *Moses* toolkit to establish phrase tables. The baseline of this research is the factorless one with a five-gram language model.

In order to measure the accuracy of alignment, this research uses the BLEU scoring (Papineni et al., 2002) which has been widely used for evaluating SMT, under the hypothesis that the BLEU score denotes how well-established the phrase table is. For the evaluation purpose, 500 sentences were selected from the SKJBC at random, and tested within each SMT baseline, as given in Table 2.

	KoJa	JaKo
lemmatized	72.72	71.37
surface	72.98	72.83
surface + tag	70.55	68.26

Table 2. BLEU Score

```
(3) <link xtargets="1.1.p8.s4 ; 1.1.p14.s3">
    <phr xtargets="w1 w2 w3 w4 ; w1 w2 w3 w4">
    <wrd xtargets="w3 ; w1">
    <wrd xtargets="w5 ; w5">
    </link>
(4) <s id=1.1.p8.s4>
    그래야      kulaya              'then'
            <w id=w1>그러/VV</w>      kule
            <w id=w2>ㅓ야/EC</w>      yeya
    자유롭지.   caywulop-ci         'be free'
            <w id=w3>자유롭/VA</w>    caywulop 'free'
            <w id=w4>지/EF</w>        ci
            <w id=w5>./SF</w>
    </s>
(5) <s id=1.1.p14.s3>
    <w id=w1>自由</w>     自由/NG   jiyuu   'freedom'
    <w id=w2>だ</w>       だ/AU     da
    <w id=w3>から</w>     から/PJC  kara
    <w id=w4>ね</w>       ね/PEN    ne
    <w id=w5>。</w>       。/SYF
    </s>
```

Korean and Japanese are typologically very similar. In particular, they have very similar word order, which makes them easy to align using *GIZA++* and *Moses*. Therefore, we could expect the baselines to perform well, and Table 2 proves it. Table 2 indicates the baselines using Japanese surface forms are slightly better than those using lemmatized forms. The next step is to confirm whether or not the baselines with POS tags decrease performance. The last line in Table 2 implies it is not the case, there is a slight decline.

Building on the last baselines, this research interpolates word and phrase aligning information into the original XML files as presented in (3-5), which means 'Then, you will be free'. Figure 2 represents how the online interface this paper proposes handles (3-5).

Figure 2. Sample of Online Interface

5 Online Search Interface

Last but maybe the most important is a user-friendly interface. Those who have a solid background in computation could take advantage of computational surroundings (e.g. *Moses*). Most linguists, however, are not aware of how to use bilingual data so well. It might look uneasy or even vague for them to harness bilingual resources for their current research. That means, no matter how good the bilingual resource is or no matter how well-trained the word or phrase table is, unless there is an available interface, the resource becomes no more than a very restricted one for a small number of people. Bilingual resources are not NLP-dominated ones, admitting NLP developers employ them most widely. They are also useful in doing comparative language research, making learning materials, or even human translation. Since one of the easiest interface in these days would be web-browsers, this research provide a web-interface; NARA (*ver.* 2).[4]

The interface of NARA system looks like a common search site (e.g. Google). A simple search option takes a position on the front side, assuming most of users are unfamiliar with linguistic terms. On the other hand, advanced search mode, as given in Figure 3, offers more specialized search options. One can search by tag, morpheme, or word with specific sub-options, such as matching type. One can also select the result format such as word, sentence, or span. In order to compare the search result in various ways, there are some configuration options, such as search direction (i.e. KoJa or JaKo), genre, source language, etc.

[4] http://corpus.mireene.com/nara.php

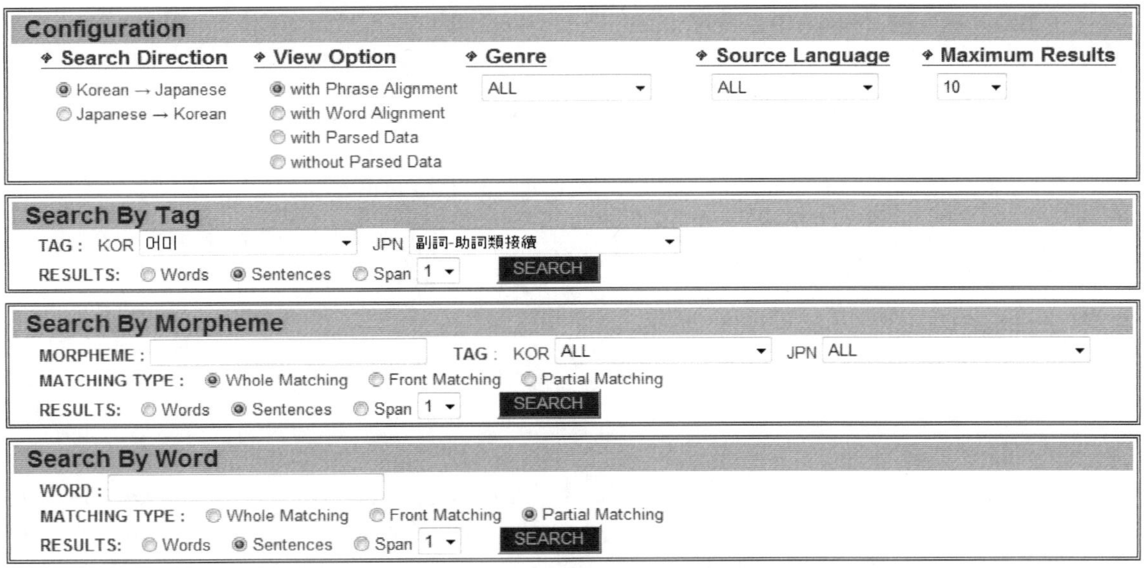

Figure 3. Screenshot of Advanced Search Mode

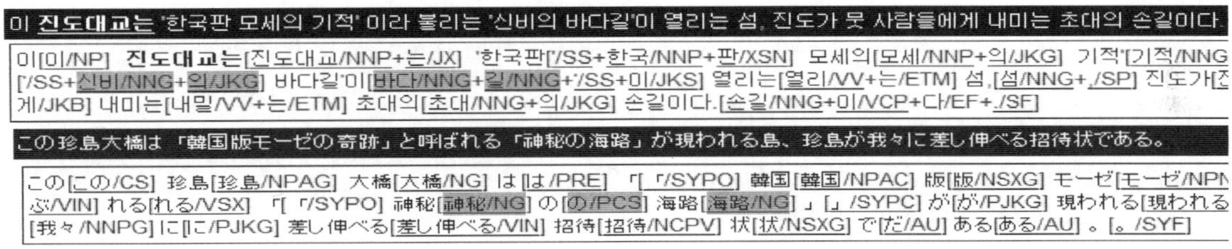

Figure 4. Phrase Alignment for 'a mysterious sea route'

Turning to the output screen, as shown in Figure 4, each underlined word has its corresponding word or phrase. When the pointer is over an underlined word, the system highlights the related words and phrases. If it is necessary to check out more information (e.g. source), one can use 'INFO' buttons. Finally, the interface offers a function to save the current result to a spreadsheet (MS-Excel).

6 Conclusion

Focusing on the *Sejong Korean Japanese Bilingual Corpus* (SKJBC), this paper covers three matters about how to use and show bilingual resources, and provides a user-friendly online interface to search the SKJBC. The NARA interface is applicable to any other bilingual resources in further researches, because it has been designed data-independently. We have already used it for aligned Korean-English text.

Acknowledgments

Part of this work was carried out while the first author was an intern at the NICT Language Infrastructure Group. The fist author was also sponsored by the BK21 Project (Global Internship). We owe special thanks to Prof. Jae-Woong Choe, Prof. Han-Seop Lee, Dr. Dong-Sung Kim, Eric Nichols, Yeolwon Seong, and Inbean Lim.

References

Anne Abeillé. 2003. *Treebanks*. Kluwer Academic Publishers, Hingham, MA, USA.

Franz J. Och and Hermann Ney. 2003. A Systematic Comparison of Various Statistical Alignment Models, *Computational Linguistics*, 29(1): 19-51.

Kishore Papineni, Salim Roukos, Todd Ward, and Wei-Jing Zhu. 2002. *BLEU: a Method for Automatic Evaluation of Machine Translation.* Annual Meeting of the ACL.

Philipp Koehn, Marcello Federico, Wade Shen, Nicola Bertoldi, Ondˇrej Bojar, Chris Callison-Burch, Brooke Cowan, Chris Dyer, Hieu Hoang, Richard Zens, Alexandra Constantin, Christine Corbett Moran, and Evan Herbst. 2007. *Moses: Open Source Toolkit for Statistical Machine Translation.* Annual Meeting of the ACL.

Yuji Matsumoto, Akira Kitauchi, Tatsuo Yamashita, and Yoshitaka Hirano. 1999. *Japanese Morphological Analysis System ChaSen version 2.0 Manual.* NAIST-ISTR99009.

Annotating Semantic Relations Combining Facts and Opinions

Koji Murakami† Shouko Masuda†‡ Suguru Matsuyoshi†
Eric Nichols† Kentaro Inui† Yuji Matsumoto†
†Nara Institute of Science and Technology
8916-5, Takayama, Ikoma, Nara 630-0192 JAPAN
‡Osaka Prefecture University
1-1, Gakuen, Naka-ku, Sakai, Osaka 599-8531 JAPAN
{kmurakami,shouko,matuyosi,eric-n,inui,matsu}@is.naist.jp

Abstract

As part of the STATEMENT MAP project, we are constructing a Japanese corpus annotated with the semantic relations bridging facts and opinions that are necessary for online information credibility evaluation. In this paper, we identify the semantic relations essential to this task and discuss how to efficiently collect valid examples from Web documents by splitting complex sentences into fundamental units of meaning called "statements" and annotating relations at the statement level. We present a statement annotation scheme and examine its reliability by annotating around 1,500 pairs of statements. We are preparing the corpus for release this winter.

1 Introduction

The goal of the STATEMENT MAP project (Murakami et al., 2009) is to assist internet users with evaluating the credibility of online information by presenting them with a comprehensive survey of opinions on a topic and showing how they relate to each other. However, because real text on the Web is often complex in nature, we target a simpler and more fundamental unit of meaning which we call the "statement." To summarize opinions for the statement map users, we first convert all sentences into statements and then, organize them into groups of agreeing and conflicting opinions that show the logical support for each group.

For example, a user who is concerned about potential connections between vaccines and autism would be presented with a visualization of the opinions for and against such a connection together with the evidence supporting each view as shown in Figure 1.

When the concerned user in our example looks at this STATEMENT MAP, he or she will see that some opinions support the query "Do vaccines cause autism?" while other opinions do not, but it will also show what support there is for each of these viewpoints. So, STATEMENT MAP can help user come to an informed conclusion.

2 Semantic Relations between Statements

2.1 Recognizing Semantic Relations

To generate STATEMENT MAPs, we need to analyze a lot of online information retrieved on a given topic, and STATEMENT MAP shows users a summary with three major semantic relations.

AGREEMENT to group similar opinions
CONFLICT to capture differences of opinions
EVIDENCE to show support for opinions

Identifying logical relations between texts is the focus of Recognizing Textual Entailment (RTE). A major task of the RTE Challenge (Dagan et al., 2005) is the identification of [ENTAILMENT] or [CONTRADICTION] between Text (T) and Hypothesis (H). For this task, several corpora have been constructed over the past few years, and annotated with thousands of (T,H) pairs.

While our research objective is to recognize semantic relations as well, our target domain is text from Web documents. The definition of contradiction in RTE is that T contradicts H if it is very unlikely that both T and H can be true at the same time. However, in real documents on the Web, there are many examples which are partially contradictory, or where one statement restricts the applicability of another like in the example below.

(1) a. Mercury-based vaccines actually cause autism in children.

Proceedings of the Third Linguistic Annotation Workshop, ACL-IJCNLP 2009, pages 150–153,
Suntec, Singapore, 6-7 August 2009.

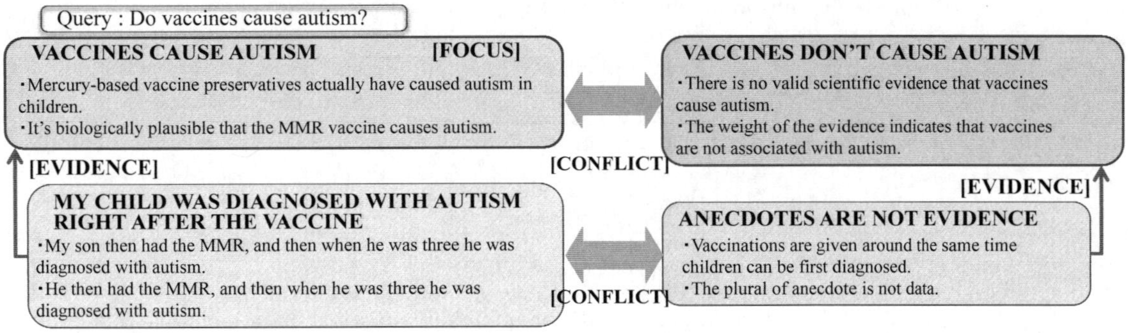

Figure 1: An example STATEMENT MAP for the query "Do vaccines cause autism?"

b. Vaccines can trigger autism in a vulnerable subset of children.

While it is difficult to assign any relation to this pair in an RTE framework, in order to construct statement maps we need to recognize a contradiction between (1a) and (1b).

There is another task of recognizing relations between sentences, CST (Cross-Document Structure Theory) which was developed by Radev (2000). CST is an expanded rhetorical structure analysis based on RST (Mann and Thompson, 1988), and attempts to describe relations between two or more sentences from both single and multiple document sets. The CSTBank corpus (Radev et al., 2003) was constructed to annotate cross-document relations. CSTBank is divided into clusters in which topically-related articles are gathered. There are 18 kinds of relations in this corpus, including [EQUIVALENCE], [ELABORATION], and [REFINEMENT].

2.2 Facts and Opinions

RTE is used to recognize logical and factual relations between sentences in a pair, and CST is used for objective expressions because newspaper articles related to the same topic are used as data. However, the task specifications of both RTE and CST do not cover semantic relations between opinions and facts as illustrated in the following example.

(2) a. There must not be a connection between vaccines and autism.
b. I do believe that there is a link between vaccinations and autism.

Subjective statements, such as opinions, are recently the focus of many NLP research topics, such as review analysis, opinion extraction, opinion QA, or sentiment analysis. In the corpus constructed by the MPQA Project (Multi-Perspective Question Answering) (Wiebe et al., 2005), individual expressions are marked that correspond to explicit mentions of private states, speech events, and expressive subjective elements.

Our goal is to annotate instances of the three major relation classes: [AGREEMENT], [CONFLICT] and [EVIDENCE], between pairs of statements in example texts. However, each relation has a wide range, and it is very difficult to define a comprehensive annotation scheme. For example, different kinds of information can act as clues to recognize the [AGREEMENT] relations. So, we have prepared a wide spectrum of semantic relations depending on different types of information regarded as clues to identify a relation class, such as [AGREEMENT] or [CONFLICT]. Table 1 shows the semantic relations needed for carrying out the anotation. Although detecting [EVIDENCE] relations is also essential to the STATEMENT MAP project, we do not include them in our current corpus construction.

3 Constructing a Japanese Corpus

3.1 Targeting Semantic Relations Between Statements

Real data on the Web generally has complex sentence structures. That makes it difficult to recognize semantic relations between full sentences. but it is possible to annotate semantic relation between parts extracted from each sentence in many cases. For example, the two sentences A and B in Figure 2 cannot be annotated with any of the semantic relations in Table 1, because each sentence include different types of information. However, if two parts extracted from these sentences C and D are compared, the parts can be identified as [EQUIVALENCE] because they are semantically close and each extracted part does not contain a different type of information. So, we attempt to break sentences from the Web down into reasonable text segments, which we call "statements." When a real sentence includes several pieces of se-

Table 1: Definition of semantic relations and example in the corpus

Relation Class	Relation Label	Example
AGREEMENT	Equivalence	A: The overwhelming evidence is that vaccines are unrelated to autism. B: There is no link between the MMR vaccine and autism.
	Equivalent Opinion	A: We think vaccines cause autism. B: I am the mother of a 6 year old that regressed into autism because of his 18 month vaccinations.
	Specific	A: Mercury-based vaccine preservatives actually have caused autism in children. B: Vaccines cause autism.
CONFLICT	Contradiction	A: Mercury-based vaccine preservatives actually have caused autism in children. B: Vaccines don't cause autism.
	Confinement	A: Vaccines can trigger autism in a vulnerable subset of children. B: Mercury-based vaccine actually have caused autism in children.
	Conflicting Opinion	A: I don't think vaccines cause autism. B: I believe vaccines are the cause of my son's autism.

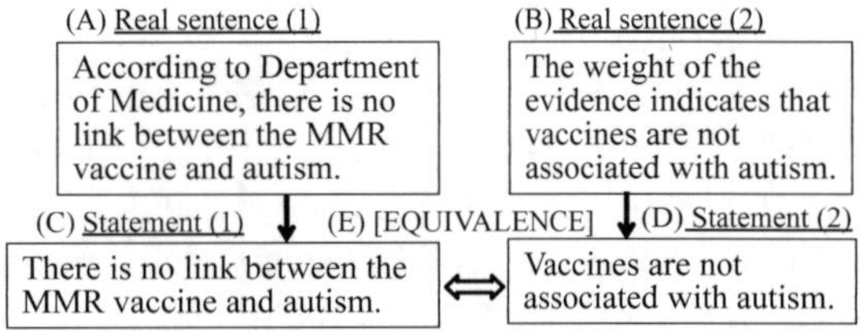

Figure 2: Extracting statements from sentences and annotating a semantic relation between them

mantic segments, more than one statement can be extracted. So, a statement can reflect the writer's affirmation in the original sentence. If the extracted statements lack semantic information, such as pronouns or other arguments, human annotators manually add the missing information. Finally we label pairs of statements with either one of the semantic relations from Table 1 or with "NO RELATION," which means that two sentences (1) are not semantically related, or (2) have a relation other than relations defined in Table 1.

3.2 Corpus Construction Procedure

We automatically gather sentences on related topics by following the procedure below:

1. Retrieve documents related to a set number of topics using a search engine
2. Extract real sentences that include major subtopic words which are detected based on TF or DF in the document set
3. Reduce noise in data by using heuristics to eliminate advertisements and comment spam
4. Reduce the search space for identifying sentence pairs and prepare pairs, which look feasible to annotate.

Dolan and Brockett (2005) proposed a method to narrow the range of sentence pair candidates and collect candidates of sentence-level paraphrases which correspond [EQUIVALENCE] in [AGREEMENT] class in our task. It worked well for collecting valid sentence pairs from a large cluster which was constituted by topic-related sentences. The method also seem to work well for [CONFLICT] relations, because lexical similarity based on bag-of-words (BOW) can narrow the range of candidates with this relation as well.

We calculate the lexical similarity between the two sentences based on BOW. We also used hyponym and synonym dictionaries (Sumida et al., 2008) and a database of relations between predicate argument structures (Matsuyoshi et al., 2008) as resources. According to our preliminary experiments, unigrams of KANJI and KATAKANA expressions, single and compound nouns, verbs and adjectives worked well as features, and we calculate the similarity using cosine distance. We did not use HIRAGANA expressions because they are also used in function words.

4 Analyzing the Corpus

Five annotators annotated semantic relations according to our specifications in 22 document sets as targets. We have annotated target statement pairs with either [AGREEMENT], [CONFLICT] or [NO RELATION]. We provided 2,303 real sentence pairs to human annotators, and they identified 1,375 pairs as being invalid and 928 pairs as being valid. The number of annotated statement pairs are 1,505 ([AGREEMENT]:862, [CONFLICT]:126, [NO RELATION]:517).

Next, to evaluate inter annotator agreement, 207 randomly selected statement pairs were annotated by two human annotators. The annotators agreed in their judgment for 81.6% of the examples, which corresponds to a kappa level of 0.49. The annotation results are evaluated by calculating recall and precision in which one annotation result is treated as a gold standard and the other's as the output of the system, as shown in Talbe 2.

Table 2: Inter-annotator agreement for 2 annotators

		Annotator A			
		AGR.	CON.	NONE	TOTAL
Annotator B	AGR.	146	7	9	162
	CON.	0	13	1	14
	NONE	17	4	10	31
	TOTAL	163	24	20	207

5 Discussion

The number of sentence pairs that annotators identified as invalid examples shows that around 60% of all pairs were invalid, showing that there is still room to improve our method of collecting sentence pairs for the annotators. Developing more effective methods of eliminating sentences pairs that are unlikely to contain statements with plausible relations is important to improve annotator efficiency. We reviewed 50 such invalid sentence pairs, and the results indicate two major considerations: (1) negation, or antonyms have not been regarded as key information, and (2) verbs in KANJI have to be handled more carefully. The polarities of sentences in all pairs were the same although there are sentences which can be paired up with opposite polarities. So, we will consider the polarity of words and sentences as well as similarity when considering candidate sentence pairs.

In Japanese, the words which consist of KATAKANA expressions are generally nouns, but those which contain KANJI can be nouns, verbs, or adjectives. Sharing KATAKANA words was the most common way of increasing the similarity between sentences. We need to assign a higher weight to verbs and adjectives that contain KANJI, to more accurately calculate the similarity between sentences.

Another approach to reducing the search space for statement pairs is taken by Nichols et al. (2009), who use category tags and in-article hyperlinks to organize scientific blog posts into discussions on the same topic, making it easier to identify relevant statements. We are investigating the applicability of these methods to the construction of our Japanese corpus but suffer from the lack of a richly-interlinked data source comparable to English scientific blogs.

6 Conclusion

In this paper, we described the ongoing construction of a Japanese corpus consisting of statement pairs annotated with semantic relations for handling web arguments. We designed an annotation scheme complete with the necessary semantic relations to support the development of statement maps that show [AGREEMENT], [CONFLICT], and [EVIDENCE] between statements for assisting users in analyzing credibility of information in Web. We discussed the revelations made from annotating our corpus, and discussed future directions for refining our specifications of the corpus. We are planning to annotate relations for more than 6,000 sentence pairs in this summer, and the finished corpus will consist of around 10,000 sentence pairs. The first release of our annotation specifications and the corpus will be made available on the Web[1] this winter.

Acknowledgments

This work is supported by the National Institute of Information and Communications Technology Japan.

References

Ido Dagan, Oren Glickman, and Bernardo Magnini. 2005. The pascal recognising textual entailment challenge. In *Proc. of the PASCAL Challenges Workshop on RTE.*

Bill Dolan and Chris Brockett. 2005. Automatical ly constructing a corpus of sentential paraphrases. In *Proc. of the IWP 2005*, pages 9–16.

William Mann and Sandra Thompson. 1988. Rhetorical structure theory: towards a functional theory of text organization. *Text*, 8(3):243–281.

Suguru Matsuyoshi, Koji Murakami, Yuji Matsumoto, , and Kentaro Inui. 2008. A database of relations between predicate argument structures for recognizing textual entailment and contradiction. In *Proc. of the ISUC 2008.*

Koji Murakami, Eric Nichols, Suguru Matsuyoshi, Asuka Sumida, Shouko Masuda, Kentaro Inui, and Yuji Matsumoto. 2009. Statement map: Assisting information credibility analysis by visualizing arguments. In *Proc. of the WICOW 2009*, pages 43–50.

Eric Nichols, Koji Murakami, Kentaro Inui, and Yuji Matsumoto. 2009. Constructing a scientific blog corpus for information credibility analysis. In *Proc. of the Annual Meeting of ANLP.*

Dragomir Radev, Jahna Otterbacher, and Zhu Zhang. 2003. CSTBank: Cross-document Structure Theory Bank. http://tangra.si.umich.edu/clair/CSTBank.

Dragomir R. Radev. 2000. Common theory of information fusion from multiple text sources step one: Cross-document structure. In *Proc. of the 1st SIGdial workshop on Discourse and dialogue*, pages 74–83.

Asuka Sumida, Naoki Yoshinaga, and Kentaro Torisawa. 2008. Boosting precision and recall of hyponymy relation acquisition from hierarchical layouts in wikipedia. In *Proc. of the LREC 2008.*

Janyce Wiebe, Theresa Wilson, and Claire Cardie. 2005. Annotating expressions of opinions and emotions in language. *Language Resources and Evaluation*, 39(2-3):165–210.

[1] http://cl.naist.jp/stmap/corpus/ja

Ingesting the Auslan Corpus into the DADA Annotation Store

Steve Cassidy
Centre for Language Technology,
Macquarie University, Sydney, Australia
Steve.Cassidy@mq.edu.au

Trevor Johnston
Department of Linguistics
Macquarie University, Sydney, Australia
Trevor.Johnston@mq.edu.au

Abstract

The DADA system is being developed to support collaborative access to and annotation of language resources over the web. DADA implements an abstract model of annotation suitable for storing many kinds of data from a wide range of language resources. This paper describes the process of ingesting data from a corpus of Australian Sign Language (Auslan) into the DADA system. We describe the format of the RDF data used by DADA and the issues raised in converting the ELAN annotations from the corpus.

1 Background

The DADA system is being developed to support collaborative access to and annotation of language resources over the web. DADA provides a web accessible annotation store that delivers both a human browsable version of a corpus and a machine accessible API for reading and writing annotations. DADA is able to ingest data from a number of different annotation formats and the data model it supports is intended to be a general model of annotation data. This paper reports on our efforts to ingest data from the Australian Sign Language (Auslan) corpus which has been annotated with the ELAN tool[1]. The primary goal of this project is to provide a read-only web-accessible version of the corpus but a longer term goal is to allow research groups to collaborate in extending the annotation.

DADA follows the principle of *linked data* (Bizer et al., 2008), every object (e.g. annotation) within the store is associated with a URL and accessing that URL generates a description of the object which includes links to the URLs of related objects. So, accessing the URL of an annotation might return a web page describing that annotation linked to its parent or the annotation set or corpus that it is part of. Linked data is an emerging design pattern in semantic web research which is being used to enable data discovery and general purpose browsing tools. For our purposes, the idea that every component of a corpus has a web-accessible URL is very powerful; it means that individual annotations could be cited in publications and opens up a whole new range of possibilities in communicating results and analysis.

There have been a number of earlier projects that aimed to develop web accessible versions of data annotated in ELAN. EOPAS (Thieberger and Schroeter, 2006) aimed to provide a means of exploring ethnographic data on the web. Various kinds of annotation data, including ELAN, could be ingested into the EOPAS XML format using stylesheets. The flexibility of an XML database was used to allow the web views of data to be generated via calls to XSLT and XQuery scripts. Because of the nature of the data being displayed, EOPAS developed views particularly suited to interlinear text although the same infrastructure could be used to generate other kind of display.

Like EOPAS, DADA makes use of an industry standard data store, however we choose RDF instead of XML because of the very close fit between the RDF data model (a directed graph) and the data model that has been shown to be needed to represent annotation data (Bird and Liberman, 2001).

The choice of RDF also allows us to leverage existing work on annotation on the web. The Annotea project at the W3C and the later Vannotea project (R.Schroeter et al., 2003) define an RDF format for storing annotations on media on the web. The models developed for DADA owe a lot to these earlier systems but build on them to provide an appropriate data model for linguistic annotation.

1.1 The Auslan Corpus

The Auslan corpus is a digital video archive of Australian Sign Language (Auslan) (Johnston and Schembri, 2006). The archive is the product of an Endangered Languages Documentation Project funded through the Hans Rausing Endangered Languages Documentation Program (ELDP) at the

[1] `http://www.lat-mpi.eu/tools/elan/`

Proceedings of the Third Linguistic Annotation Workshop, ACL-IJCNLP 2009, pages 154–157,
Suntec, Singapore, 6-7 August 2009. ©2009 ACL and AFNLP

School of Oriental and African Studies (SOAS), University of London (grant #MDP0088 awarded to Trevor Johnston). The corpus brings together into one digital archive a representative sample of Auslan in video recordings to which are added metadata files and annotation files created in ELAN. It is consists of two sub-corpora: data collected through the ELDP and data collected as part of the Sociolinguistic Variation in Auslan Project (SVIAP) conducted by Adam Schembri and Trevor Johnston (ARC #LP0346973). Both datasets are based on language recording sessions conducted with deaf native or early learner/near-native users of Auslan.

Many tiers are needed in an ELAN file to annotate a text in a signed language because sign languages can have several simultaneous levels of linguistically significant behavior. For example, each hand may utter a separate manual sign at the same time, or grammatically important body movements and facial expressions (which are not unlike prosody) may co-occur with the production of individual manual signs. All this needs to be identified and time aligned.

2 Mapping ELAN to RDF

RDF, the Resource Description Framework, is the core language of the semantic web used to make assertions about resources, describing them in terms of properties and relations to other resources. DADA stores annotations as RDF in a dedicated database called a *triple store* and uses semantic web technologies to manipulate and present data. To represent annotations, DADA defines a core ontology that maps to the data structures inherent in annotation data. The ontology is designed to be able to represent many kinds of annotation data and as such owes much to similar *lingua franca* efforts such as Annotation Graphs (Bird and Liberman, 2001) and the Linguistic Annotation Format (Ide and Suderman, 2007).

To ingest the annotations from the Auslan Corpus into DADA requires transcoding of ELAN XML annotation files into the RDF format. This section provides an overview of the DADA RDF ontology and then discusses the issues raised by mapping ELAN data.

The core object types within the DADA ontology are: the **corpus**, a collection of annotation sets; the **annotation set**, a collection of annotations on one or more media files denoting a single event or stimulus; the **annotation**, the basic unit of annotation associated with a region within the source media and the **anchor**, an abstraction of the idea of a location within a source media file. Each of these written in this paper as, for example, `dada:Annotation` but this is shorthand for a URL (`http://purl.org/dada/schema/0.1#Annotation`) which provides a unique name for the property. Each of these object types can have arbitrary properties and relations defined from the DADA or other ontologies. DADA properties define the basic structure of annotations; an example is given in Figure 1. In the figure the lines between nodes define the named relations; for example, the offset times of the anchors are defined by relations denoting the units of measurement (`time:seconds`). The data associated with the annotation is encoded by one or more relations (e.g. `auslan:RH_ID_gloss`); in this way, each annotation is associated with a *feature structure* that can encode multiple properties of the annotation.

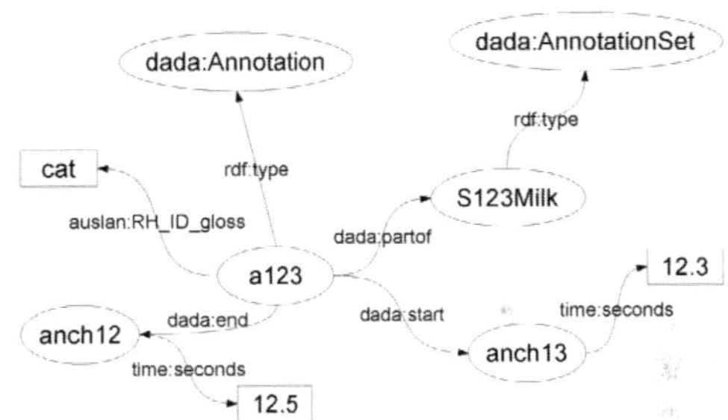

Figure 1: An example annotation structure in RDF.

The mapping between the ELAN EAF format used by the Auslan Corpus and the DADA RDF format is relatively straightforward. EAF stores annotations for a single media file (or group of related media) in an XML format which can be transformed into the RDF/XML format via an XSLT stylesheet. ELAN annotations exist on a set of *tiers* which have associated type information; for example, Auslan uses the *RH ID Gloss* tier to represent the sign being made by the right hand.

The type of annotation on a tier is defined by the associated *linguistic type* which gives a name for the type and defines it as one of five *stereo-*

types that describe how the annotation divides the timeline and relates to other annotations. There are a number of stereotypes defined by ELAN but the Auslan corpus only makes use of two: a simple time aligned type and a *symbolic association* type. The simple time aligned tiers form the base of the annotation and denote the start and end of signs and other events in the video stream. Symbolic association tiers provide additional information about these base level annotations; each annotation on one of these tiers is associated with a base level annotation which defines its start and end points. This is modeled in RDF by additional properties denoting the associated annotations. For example, Auslan defines the *RH ID Gloss* tier as a base segmentation of the video timeline and has associated tiers *RH gram cls* and *RH loc* among others. Instead of building separate annotations for each of these, they are modeled in RDF as three properties of a single annotation as illustrated in Figure 2.

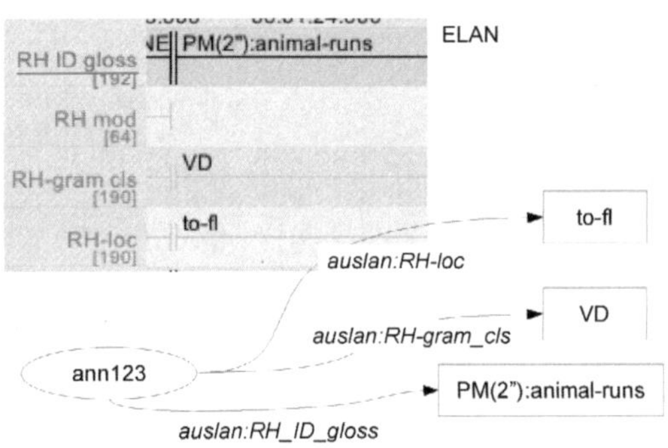

Figure 2: Conversion of associated tiers in ELAN to RDF properties

ELAN does support other types of inter-tier relationships, in particular one tier can be a *symbolic subdivision* of its parent. In this case, additional annotations must be made for each tier and the RDF model becomes a little more complex. This is not discussed further here as it is not required for modeling annotations in the Auslan corpus.

Since the RDF representation of annotations requires us to use formal relation names for properties corresponding to tiers, we are required to define these names in an ontology specific to the style of annotation being used in the corpus. While ELAN does not provide a mechanism to define a *schema* – definitions of a set of tiers – for a corpus, most corpora will use the same tiers in every file. As a side effect of importing a set of ELAN files into the DADA RDF format we generate an RDF schema that defines the linguistic types being used. These types form a point of reference for the corpus and can form a useful part of the documentation of the annotation system being used. In the longer term, the availability of such public documented linguistic types might lead to more effective sharing of annotation types between corpora. While these are stored as RDF documents, it is easy to generate template ELAN annotation files or indeed templates for other annotation tools from the same data.

While the current definitions of linguistic types are generated entirely from the ELAN source file, there is scope to link these to external ontologies being developed for linguistic analysis. Relatedly, ELAN supports linking to external controlled vocabularies (Sloetjes and Wittenburg, 2008) such as the ISO Data Category Registry (ISO 12620) which allows sharing of terms (such as Verb, Noun) that might be used as annotation labels.

3 Publishing on the Web

Once ingested into the RDF store, the ELAN annotations can be manipulated by the DADA system using standard interfaces such as the SPARQL query language. The primary interface to DADA is via the web, either through a standard web browser or via the well defined HTTP based interface for application programs. This interface presents machine-readable versions of the annotation data in well known formats; for example, returning an ELAN or Transcriber XML formatted version of a set of annotations or even a lower level XML representation. The application would not generally see the annotations in raw RDF form although such an interface can be supported if needed.

The primary view of the annotation data on the web is via HTML pages generated by the server that can contain any data derived from the annotation store. We have developed a set of generic displays for each kind of object (corpus, annotation set, etc) that are generated in response to a request for the appropriate URI from a web browser. These display all of the relevant data for the object and could be customised to provide an appropriate view of different kinds of data.

The web browser is not the only kind of client

that can retrieve data from the DADA server over the web. DADA makes use of HTTP *content negotiation* between the client and the server to enable a client to request one of a number of alternate forms of data. For example, the server can generate an ELAN format XML file which closely mirrors the original data ingested into the system. Since the output is generated via templates, other formats could also be generated to feed into alternate tools. In addition to generating existing XML formats it is also useful to generate data in a form that is easily consumed by custom applications. JSON (Javascript Object Notation[2]) is a data format that is frequently used to transport data in modern web applications and is easily parsed by libraries in many target languages. The DADA JSON interface will deliver descriptions of any kind of object in the data store in a way that makes it easy to implement clients that present interactive displays of the data.

4 A Javascript Client

As a demonstration of the web based API allowing remote clients to read annotation data from the server, we have implemented a Javascript based browser for annotation data that is able to show data aligned with the source video data. The Javascript client can be hosted on a website unrelated to the DADA server since it gains access to data purely via HTTP requests for JSON formatted data.

The client provides a web interface that is entirely dynamic, allowing the user to choose from a list of corpora hosted on the server, then choose an annotation set and finally select a type of annotation to display. The client also queries the server for details of the media files associated with the annotation set and embeds the web accessible FLV formatted video in the page. The user is able to interact with the page and navigate through the video via links from the annotation.

5 Summary

The DADA system aims to provide general purpose infrastructure for collaborative annotation of language resources. Built on core semantic web technologies it provides a server based solution that is able to ingest annotation data from a number of sources and deliver them both to human browsers and to client applications. In the first

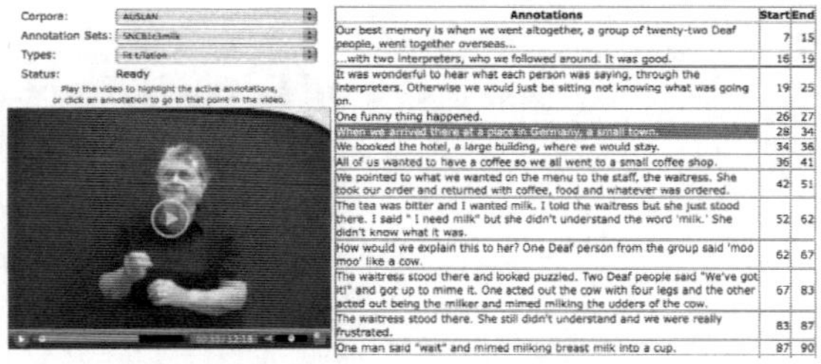

Figure 3: A screenshot from the Javascript client

phase of development the emphasis is on delivering views of existing corpora on the web.

A demonstration version of the DADA server is hosted at `http://dada.ics.mq.edu.au/` and contains a link to the Auslan data described here. More information on the Auslan corpus can be found at `http://www.auslan.org.au/`.

References

S. Bird and M. Liberman. 2001. A Formal Framework for Linguistics Annotation. *Speech Communication*.

Christian Bizer, Tom Heath, Kingsley Idehen, and Tim Berners-Lee. 2008. Linked data on the web (ldow2008). In *WWW '08: Proceeding of the 17th international conference on World Wide Web*, pages 1265–1266, New York, NY, USA. ACM.

N. Ide and K. Suderman. 2007. GrAF: A Graph-based Format for Linguistic Annotations. In *Proceedings of the Linguistic Annotation Workshop, held in conjunction with ACL 2007*, Prague. `http://www.cs.vassar.edu/~ide/papers/LAW.pdf`.

T. Johnston and A. Schembri. 2006. Issues in the creation of a digital archive of a signed language. In L. Barwick and N. Thieberger, editors, *Sustainable data from digital fieldwork: Proceedings of the conference held at the University of Sydney*, pages 7–16, Sydney, December. Sydney University Press.

R.Schroeter, J.Hunter, and D.Kosovic. 2003. Vannotea A Collaborative Video Indexing, Annotation and Discussion System for Broadband Networks. In *Proceedings of the Knowledge Markup and Semantic Annotation Workshop, K-CAP*, Sanibel, Florida, Oct.

Han Sloetjes and Peter Wittenburg. 2008. Annotation by category: Elan and iso dcr. In European Language Resources Association (ELRA), editor, *Proceedings of the Sixth International Language Resources and Evaluation (LREC'08)*, Marrakech, Morocco, may.

Nicholas Thieberger and Ronald Schroeter. 2006. EOPAS, the EthnoER online representation of interlinear text. In Linda Barwick and Nicholas Thieberger, editors, *Sustainable Data from Digital Fieldwork*, pages 99–124, University of Sydney, December.

[2] `http://www.json.org/`

The Hindi Discourse Relation Bank

Umangi Oza[*], Rashmi Prasad[†], Sudheer Kolachina[*], Dipti Misra Sharma[*] and Aravind Joshi[†]

*Language Technologies Research Centre
IIIT Hyderabad, Gachibowli, Hyderabad, Andhra Pradesh, India 500032
oza.umangi,sudheer.kpg08@gmail.com,dipti@iiit.ac.in

†Institute for Research in Cognitive Science/Computer and Information Science
3401 Walnut Street, Suite 400A
Philadelphia, PA USA 19104
rjprasad,joshi@seas.upenn.edu

Abstract

We describe the Hindi Discourse Relation Bank project, aimed at developing a large corpus annotated with discourse relations. We adopt the lexically grounded approach of the Penn Discourse Treebank, and describe our classification of Hindi discourse connectives, our modifications to the sense classification of discourse relations, and some cross-linguistic comparisons based on some initial annotations carried out so far.

1 Introduction

To enable NLP research and applications beyond the sentence-level, corpora annotated with discourse level information have been developed. The recently developed Penn Discourse Treebank (PDTB) (Prasad et al., 2008), for example, provides annotations of discourse relations (e.g., causal, contrastive, temporal, and elaboration relations) in the Penn Treebank Corpus. Recent interest in cross-linguistic studies of discourse relations has led to the initiation of similar discourse annotation projects in other languages as well, such as Chinese (Xue, 2005), Czech (Mladová et al., 2008), and Turkish (Deniz and Webber, 2008). In this paper, we describe our ongoing work on the creation of a Hindi Discourse Relation Bank (HDRB), broadly following the approach of the PDTB.[1] The size of the HDRB corpus is 200K words and it is drawn from a 400K word corpus on which Hindi syntactic dependency annotation is being independently conducted (Begum et al., 2008). Source corpus texts are taken from the Hindi newspaper *Amar Ujala,* and comprise news articles from several domains, such as politics, sports, films, etc. We present our characterization of discourse connectives and their arguments in Hindi (Section 2), our proposals for modifying the sense classification scheme (Section 3), and present some cross-linguistics comparisons based on annotations done so far (Section 4). Section 5 concludes with a summary and future work.

2 Discourse Relations and Arguments

Following the PDTB approach, we take discourse relations to be realized in one of three ways: (a) as *explicit connectives,* which are "closed class" expressions drawn from well-defined grammatical classes; (b) as *alternative lexicalizations* (AltLex), which are non-connective expressions that cannot be defined as explicit connectives; and (c) as *implicit connectives*, which are implicit discourse relations "inferred" between adjacent sentences not related by an explicit connective. When no discourse relation can be inferred between adjacent sentences, either an *entity-based coherence relation* (called EntRel) or the absence of a relation (called NoRel) is marked between the sentences. The two abstract object relata of a discourse relation are called the relation's arguments (named Arg1 and Arg2), and argument annotation follows the "minimality principle" in that only as much is selected as the argument text span as is minimally necessary to interpret the relation. Finally, each discourse relation is assigned a sense label based on a hierarchical sense classification.

2.1 Explicit Connectives

In addition to the three major grammatical classes of Explicit connectives in the PDTB – subordinating conjunctions, coordinating conjunctions, and adverbials – we recognize three other classes, described below.

[1] An earlier study of Hindi discourse connectives towards the creation of HDRB is presented in Prasad et al. (2008).

Proceedings of the Third Linguistic Annotation Workshop, ACL-IJCNLP 2009, pages 158–161,
Suntec, Singapore, 6-7 August 2009.

Sentential Relatives: These are relative pronouns that conjoin a relative clause with its matrix clause. As the name suggests, only relatives that modify verb phrases are treated as discourse connectives, and not those that modify noun phrases. Some examples are (so that), (because of which).

1) [ ] ____ { }

"[Dropping all his work, he picked up the bird and ran towards the dispensary], **so that** {it could be given proper treatment}."

Subordinators: These include postpositions (Ex. 2), verbal participles, and suffixes that introduce non-finite clauses with an abstract object interpretation.[2]

2) [ ]__ { - - }

"**Upon** [hearing *Baa*'s words], {*Gandhiji* felt very ashamed}."

Particles: Particles such as , act as discourse connectives. is an emphatic inclusive particle used to suggest the inclusion of verbs, entities, adverbs, and adjectives. Instances of such particles which indicate the inclusion of verbs are taken as discourse connectives (Ex. 3) while others are not.

3)] { } __ { }

"[People see this as a consequence of the improving relation between the two countries]. {The *Kashmiris* are} **also** {learning an political lesson from this}."

2.2 Arguments of Discourse Relations

In the PDTB, the assignment of the Arg1 and Arg2 labels to a discourse relation's arguments is syntactically driven, in that the Arg2 label is assigned to the argument with which the connective was syntactically associated, while the Arg1 label is assigned to the 'other' argument. In HDRB, however, the Arg1/Arg2 label assignment is semantically driven, in that it is based on the "sense" of the relation to which the arguments belong. Thus, each sense definition for a relation specifies the *sense-specific semantic role* of each of its arguments, and stipulates one of the two roles to be Arg1, and the other, Arg2. For example, the 'cause' sense definition, which involves a causal relation between two eventualities, specifies that one of its arguments is the cause, while the other is the effect, and further stipulates that the cause will be assigned the label Arg2, while the effect will be assigned the label Arg1. Apart from giving meaning to the argument labels, our semantics-based convention has the added advantage simplifying the sense classification scheme. This is discussed further in Section 3.

2.3 Implicit Discourse Relations

The HDRB annotation of implicit discourse relations largely follows the PDTB scheme. The only difference is that while implicit relations in PDTB are annotated only between paragraph-internal adjacent sentences, we also annotate such relations across paragraph boundaries.

3 Senses of Discourse Relations

Broadly, we follow the PDTB sense classification in that we take it to be a hierarchical classification, with the four top level sense *classes* of "Temporal", "Contingency", "Comparison", and "Expansion". Further refinements to the top class level are provided at the second *type* level and the third *subtype* level. Here, we describe our points of departure from the PDTB classification. The changes are partly motivated by general considerations for capturing additional senses, and partly by language-specific considerations. Figure 1 reflects the modifications we have made to the sense scheme. These are described below.

Eliminating argument-specific labels: In the PDTB sense hierarchy, the tags at the type level are meant to express further refinements of the relations' semantics, while the tags at the subtype level are meant to reflect different orderings of the arguments (see Section 2.2). In HDRB, we eliminate these argument-ordering labels from the subtype level, since these labels don't directly pertain to the meaning of discourse relations. All levels in the sense hierarchy thus have the purpose of specifying the semantics of the relation to different degrees of granularity. The relative ordering of the arguments is instead

[2] Subordinators that denote the manner of an action are not discourse connectives, but since such disambiguation is a difficult task, we have decided to annotate subordinators in a later phase of the project.

specified in the definition of the type-level senses, and is inherited by the more refined senses at the subtype level.

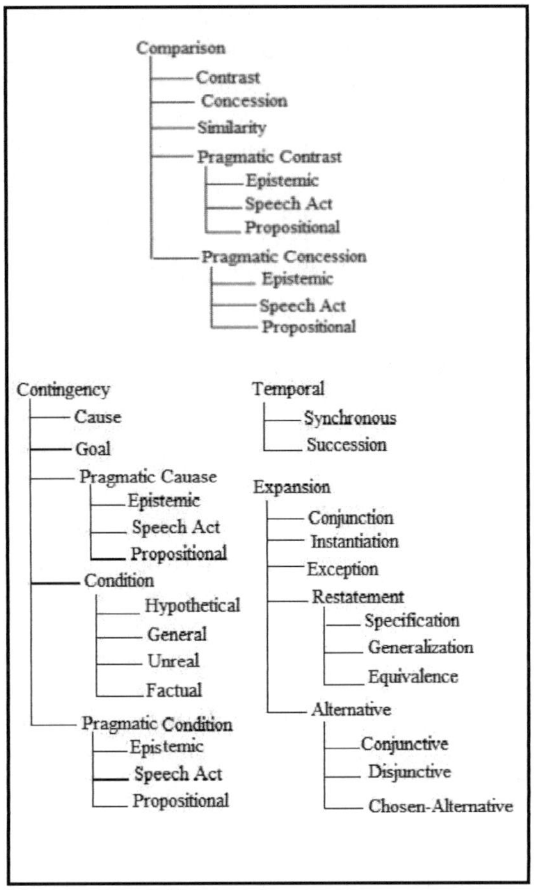

Figure 1: HDRB (Modified) Sense Classification

Uniform treatment of pragmatic relations: As in PDTB, discourse relations in HDRB are pragmatic when their relations have to be inferred from the propositional content of the arguments. However, we replace the PDTB pragmatic senses with a uniform three-way classification. Each pragmatic sense at the type level is further distinguished into three subtypes: "epistemic" (Sweetser 1990), "speech-act" (Sweetser 1990), and "propositional". The propositional subtype involves the inference of a complete proposition. The relation is then taken to hold between this inferred proposition and the propositional content of one of the arguments.

The "Goal" sense: Under the "Contingency" class, we have added a new type "Goal", which applies to relations where the situation described in one of the arguments is the goal of the situation described in the other argument (which enables the achievement of the goal).

4 Initial Annotation Experiments

Based on the guidelines as described in this paper, we annotated both explicit and implicit relations in 35 texts (averaging approx. 250 words/text) from the HDRB corpus. A total of 602 relation tokens were annotated. Here we present some useful distributions we were able to derive from our initial annotation, and discuss them in light of cross-linguistic comparisons of discourse relations.

Types and Tokens of Discourse Relations: Table 1 shows the overall distribution of the different relation types, i.e., Explicit, AltLex, Implicit, EntRel, and NoRel. The second column reports the number of unique expressions used to realize the relation – Explicit, Implicit and AltLex – while the third column reports the total number of tokens and relative frequencies.

Relations	Types	Tokens (%)
Explicit	49	189 (31.4%)
Implicit	35	185 (30.7%)
AltLex	25	37 (6.14%)
EntRel	NA	140 (23.25%)
NoRel	NA	51 (8.5%)
TOTAL	**109**	**602**

Table 1: Distribution of Discourse Relations

These distributions show some interesting similarities and differences with the PDTB distributions (cf. Prasad et al., 2008). First, given that Hindi has a much richer morphological paradigm than English; one would have expected that it would have fewer explicit connectives. That is, one might expect Hindi to realize discourse relations morphologically more often than not, just as it realizes other syntactic relations. However, even in the small data set of 602 tokens that we have annotated so far, we have found 49 unique explicit connectives, which is roughly half the number reported for the 1 million words annotated in English texts in PDTB. It is expected that we will find more unique types as we annotate additional data. The relation type distribution thus seems to suggest that the availability of richer morphology in a language doesn't affect connective usage. Second, the percentage of AltLex relations is higher in HDRB – 6.14% compared to 1.5% in PDTB, suggesting that Hindi makes greater usage of non-connective cohesive links with the prior discourse. Further studies are needed to characterize the forms and functions of AltLex expressions in both English and Hindi.

Senses of Discourse Relations: We also examined the distributions for each sense class in HDRB and computed the relative frequency of the relations realized explicitly and implicitly. Cross-linguistically, one would expect languages to be similar in whether or not a relation with a particular sense is realized explicitly or implicitly, since this choice lies in the domain of semantics and inference, rather than syntax. Thus, we were interested in comparing the sense distributions in HDRB and PDTB. Table 2 shows these distributions for the top class level senses. (Here we counted the AltLex relations together with explicit connectives.)

Sense Class	Explicit (%)	Implicit (%)
Contingency	57 (58.2%)	41 (41.8%)
Comparison	68 (76.5%)	21 (23.5%)
Temporal	43 (65.2%)	23 (34.8%)
Expansion	64(40%)	94(60%)

Table 2: Distribution of Class Level Senses

The table shows that sense distributions in HDRB are indeed similar to those reported in the PDTB (cf. Prasad et al., 2008). That is, the chances of "Expansion" and "Contingency" relations being explicit are lower compared to "Comparison" and "Temporal" relations.

5 Summary and Future Work

This paper has reported on the Hindi Discourse Relation Bank (HDRB) project, in which discourse relations, their arguments, and their senses are being annotated. A major goal of our work was to investigate how well the Penn Discourse Treebank (PDTB) and its guidelines could be adapted for discourse annotation of Hindi texts. To a large extent, we have successfully adapted the PDTB scheme. Proposed changes have to do with identification of some new syntactic categories for explicit connectives, and some general and language-driven modifications to the sense classification. From our initial annotations, we found that (a) there doesn't seem to be an inverse correlation between the usage frequency of explicit connectives and the morphological richness of a language, although there does seem to be an increased use of cohesive devices in such a language; and (b) sense distributions confirm the lack of expectation of cross-linguistic "semantic" differences. Our future goal is to complete the discourse annotation of a 200K word corpus, which will account for half of the 400K word corpus being also annotated for syntactic dependencies. We also plan to extend the annotation scheme to include attributions.

Acknowledgements

This work was partially supported by NSF grants EIA-02-24417, EIA-05-63063, and IIS-07-05671.

References

Rafiya Begum, Samar Husain, Arun Dhwaj, Dipti Misra Sharma, Lakshmi Bai, and Rajeev Sangal. 2008. Dependency annotation scheme for Indian languages. *Proc. of IJCNLP-2008.*

Lucie Mladová, Šárka Zikánová and Eva Hajičová. 2008. From Sentence to Discourse: Building an Annotation Scheme for Discourse Based on Prague Dependency Treebank. *Proc. of LREC-2008.*

Rashmi Prasad, Nikhil Dinesh, Alan Lee, Eleni Miltsakaki, Livio Robaldo, Aravind Joshi, and Bonnie Webber. 2008. The Penn Discourse TreeBank 2.0. *Proc. of LREC-2008.*

Rashmi Prasad, Samar Husain, Dipti Mishra Sharma, and Aravind Joshi. 2008. Towards an Annotated Corpus of Discourse Relations in Hindi. *Proc. of IJCNLP-2008.*

Eve Sweetser.1990. *From etymology to pragmatics: Metaphorical and cultural aspects of semantic structure* . Cambridge University Press.

Nianwen Xue. 2005. Annotating Discourse Connectives in the Chinese Treebank. *Proc. of the ACL Workshop on Frontiers in Corpus Annotation II: Pie in the Sky.*

Deniz Zeyrek and Bonnie Webber. 2008. A Discourse Resource for Turkish: Annotating Discourse Connectives in the METU Corpus. *Proc. of IJCNLP-2008.*

Simple Parser for Indian Languages in a Dependency Framework

Akshar Bharati, Mridul Gupta, Vineet Yadav, Karthik Gali and Dipti Misra Sharma
Language Technologies Research Center,
IIIT-Hyderabad, India
{mridulgupta,vineetyadav}@students.iiit.ac.in,
karthikg@research.iiit.ac.in,dipti@iiit.ac.in

Abstract

This paper is an attempt to show that an intermediary level of analysis is an effective way for carrying out various NLP tasks for linguistically similar languages. We describe a process for developing a simple parser for doing such tasks. This parser uses a grammar driven approach to annotate dependency relations (both inter and intra chunk) at an intermediary level. Ease in identifying a particular dependency relation dictates the degree of analysis reached by the parser. To establish efficiency of the simple parser we show the improvement in its results over previous grammar driven dependency parsing approaches for Indian languages like Hindi. We also propose the possibility of usefulness of the simple parser for Indian languages that are similar in nature.

1 Introduction and Related Work

Broad coverage parsing is a challenging task. For languages such as the Indian languages, it becomes all the more difficult as these languages are morphologically richer and the word order for these languages is relatively variable and less bound. Although dependency grammar driven parsing is much better suited for such type of languages (Hudson, 1984; Mel'Cuk, 1988), robust broad coverage parsing (Bharati et. al, 2008) still involves extensive analysis. Achieving good results in parsing for these languages may require large amount of linguistic resources such as annotated corpora, verb frames, lexicon etc. On the other hand, pure shallow parsing techniques (PVS and Gali, 2007) are not enough for providing sufficient information for applications such as machine translation, query answering etc.

It is here that the notion of a simple parser is born where the idea is to parse a sentence at a coarser level. One could go to a finer level of parse depending on the ease with which such a parse can be generated. The simple parser that we describe here is a grammar oriented model that makes use of linguistic features to identify relations. We have modeled the simple parser on the Paninian grammatical model (Begum et al., 2008; Bharati et al., 1995) which provides a dependency grammar framework. Paninian dependency grammar works well for analyzing Indian languages (Bharati et al., 1993). We have followed *karaka*[1] based approach for parsing.

An effort has been previously made in grammar driven parsing for Hindi by us (Gupta et al., 2008) where the focus was not to mark relations in a broad coverage sense but to mark certain easily identifiable relations using a rule base. In this paper, we show improvements in results over our previous work by including some additional linguistic features which help in identifying relations better. Our previous work focused only on inter-chunk annotation. In this paper, however, we have worked on both inter as well as intra chunk annotation. We later show their effectiveness and results at different levels of dependency annotation. We also propose how useful the simple parser is for Indian languages which are similar in nature.

2 Paninian Dependency Annotation Scheme at Various Levels

Paninian dependency scheme is based on a modifier-modified relationship (Bharati et al., 1995). The modified chunk (or group) is classified on the basis of its part of speech category. A hierarchy of dependency relations is thus established on the basis of this category. For example, all those relations whose parent (modified group) is a verb are classified under the verb modifier (vmod) category. Subsequent levels further classify these relations (or labels). Depth of a level in the hierarchy reflects the fineness of the dependency relations/labels. There are five labels at the

[1] The elements modifying the verb participate in the action specified by the verb. These participant relations with the verb are called *karakas*.

Proceedings of the Third Linguistic Annotation Workshop, ACL-IJCNLP 2009, pages 162–165,
Suntec, Singapore, 6-7 August 2009.

coarsest level namely, vmod, nmod (noun modifier), jjmod (adjective modifier), advmod (adverbial modifier) and ccof (conjunct of). Athough, ccof is not strictly a dependency relation (Begum et al., 2008). Figure 1 shows the hierarchy of relations used in the scheme.

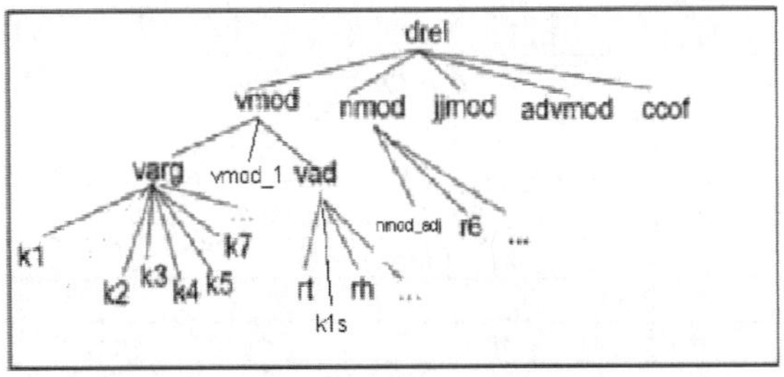

Figure 1: Hierarchy of Dependency Labels.

The next level comprises of varg (verb argument), vad (verb adjunct) and vmod_1[2] labels under vmod. Under the nmod label, nmod_adj (adjective), r6 (genitive) are classified. At the most fine grained level, varg and vad further branch out into labels like k1, k2, k3, k5, k7 and rh, rt, rd, k1s etc. The relations under varg are the six karakas that are the most essential participants in an action. All the other dependency labels[3] are non-karakas (for a more detailed explanation see Begum et al. (2008) and Bharati et al. (1995)).

Languages often have constructions that are ambiguous, owing to similar feature and context distribution. Thus, in such cases, it is appropriate to under-specify the relations (labels) or group some of them together. Also, some labels have very less frequency of occurrence in the corpus and it is thus appropriate to leave them out for marking by the simple parser. One can later, on the availability of more information, try to identify and mark such instances with appropriate labels.

The dependency tagset described in this section is used to mark inter-chunk relations. For marking relations between words within a chunk (intra-chunk), a similar tagset has been developed.

3 Procedure

Our approach is corpus based where rules have been crafted after studying the corpus. We used the Hyderabad Dependency Treebank (HyDT) for development and testing our rules. The treebank consists of about 2100 sentences in Hindi, of which 1800 were part of the development set and 300 were used as test data. Each sentence is POS tagged and chunked (Bharati et al., 2006) in SSF format (Bharati et al., 2005).

3.1 Approach

The simple parser we propose here is a language independent engine that takes a rule file specific for a particular language (Gupta et. al, 2008). Indian languages are similar in various respects (Emeneau 1956; 1980). Hence, rules made for one language can be efficiently transferred for other similar languages. However, there can be cases where rules for one language may not work for another. These cases can be handled by adding some new rules for that particular language. The relative closeness among such languages, determines the efficiency of transference of rules from one language to another. We have taken Hindi and Punjabi, as example languages to support our proposal. 1(a) below is in Hindi,

1(a). *raama ko* *mithaaii* *acchii* *nahii*
„Ram - *dat*' „sweets' 'good' „not'
lagatii.
„appear'

"Ram does not like sweets."

Its corresponding Punjabi sentence,
1(b). *raama nuu mitthaai changii* *nii*
„Ram - *dat*' „sweets' „good' „not'
lagadii.
„appear'

"Ram does not like sweets."

Now, the rules for identifying k1[4] and k2 in Hindi are similar to that of Punjabi. For instance, in both the cases, the noun chunk possessing a nominative case marker (chunks take the properties of their heads) and the TAM (tense, aspect and modality of the main verb) should agree in

[2] vmod_1: A dependency relation in the vmod category, that exists between a non-finite verb and its parent verb. It has been under-specified for simplicity.

[3] A comprehensive list of the dependency tagset can be found at http://ltrc.iiit.ac.in/MachineTrans/research/tb/dep-tagset.pdf

[4] k1 (karta) and k2 (karma) are syntactico-semantic labels which have some properties of both grammatical roles and thematic roles. k1 for example, behaves similar to subject and agent. Likewise, k2 behaves like object/theme (Begum et al., 2008)

GNP for the noun to be a k2. It is easy to see how rules made for identifying certain relations in Hindi can be transferred to identify the same relations in Punjabi and similarly for other languages. However, not all rules can be transferred from one language to another.

3.2 Intra-chunk Relations

We also mark intra-chunk dependency relations. The procedure of marking intra-chunk labels is also rule based. Rules have been crafted using a common POS[5] tagset for Indian languages (Bharati et al., 2006). Rules can be applied to other languages. However, some rules may not work. In those cases we need to add some rules specific to the language. The rule format is a five-tuple containing the following fields,

1. Modified word
2. Modified constraints
3. Modifier word
4. Modifier constraints
5. Dependency relation

Rules for marking intra-chunk relations have been marked studying the POS tagged and chunked corpus. Commonly occurring linguistic patterns between two or more nodes are drawn out in the form of statistics and their figures are collected. Such patterns are then converted into robust rules.

4 Experiments and Results

We conducted experiments using the simple parser to establish its efficacy in identifying a particular set of relations explained in section 2. Experiments were conducted on gold standard test data derived from HyDT. The experiments were carried out on Hindi.

4.1 Marking Relations at Various Levels

We marked dependency labels at various levels described above using the proposed simple parser. The results are shown below We report two measures for evaluation, labeled (L) and labeled attachment (LA). Table 1 shows results for marking relations at the top most level (cf. Figure 1).

It should be noted that we have not marked relations like jjmod and advmod because the frequency of their occurrence in the treebank is quite low. The focus is only on those relations whose frequency of occurrence is above a bare minimum (>15). The frequency of labels like jjmod and advmod is not above that threshold value (Relations like k1 and k2 occur more than 1500 times in the treebank).

Relation	Precision		Recall	
	L	LA	L	LA
vmod	**93.7%**	**83.0%**	**76.1%**	67.4%
nmod	83.6%	79.1%	77.5%	**73.3%**
ccof	92.9%	82.9%	53.5%	50.4%
Total	91.8%	82.3%	72.9%	65.4%

Table 1. Figures for relations at the highest level.

Table 2 below depicts the figures obtained for the next level.

Relation	Precision		Recall	
	L	LA	L	LA
varg	77.7%	69.3%	77.9%	69.4%
vad	75.2%	66.6%	30.3%	26.9%
vmod_1	**89.6%**	75.8%	46.0%	38.9%
r6	83.2%	78.5%	**90.2%**	**85.2%**
nmod__adj	77.8%	**77.8%**	10.9%	10.9%
Total	79.1%	71.2%	64.6%	58.2%

Table 2. Figures for level 2.

In section 1, improvement in marking certain relations over our previous attempt (Gupta et. al, 2008) was mentioned. We provide a comparison of the results for the simple parser as opposed to the previous results. Figures shown in table 3 have been reproduced for comparing them against the results of the simple parser shown in this paper.

Relation	Precision		Recall	
	L	LA	L	LA
k1	66.0%	57.7%	65.1%	57.6%
k2	31.3%	28.3%	27.8%	25.1%
k7(p/t)	80.8%	77.2%	61.0%	58.4%
r6	82.1%	78.7%	89.6%	85.8%
nmod__adj	23.2%	21.9%	27.4%	25.8%

Table 3. Figures reproduced from our previous work.

Table 4 shows results of the simple parser. Note the improvement in precision values for all the relations.

Relation	Precision		Recall	
	L	LA	L	LA
k1	72.6%	68.0%	67.9%	63.5%
k2	61.6%	54.1%	29.9%	26.2%
k7(p/t)	84.6%	77.9%	73.5%	68.7%
r6	83.2%	78.6%	90.2%	85.5%
nmod__adj	77.8%	77.8%	10.9%	10.9%
pof	89.4%	87.7%	25.7%	25.2%

Table 4. Figures for simple parser.

[5] POS: Part of Speech

4.2 Intra-chunk Experiments

We also carried out some experiments to determine the efficiency of the simple parser with respect to annotating intra-chunk relations for Hindi. Results shown below were obtained after testing the simple parser using gold standard test data of about 200 sentences. Table 5 shows figures for labeled accuracy as well as labeled attachment accuracy.

Relation	Precision		Recall	
	L	LA	L	LA
nmod	100%	89.3%	70.0%	62.5%
nmod__adj	100%	92.7%	85.2%	79.0%
nmod__dem	100%	100%	100%	100%
nmod__qf	97.0%	92.4%	80.0%	76.2%
pof	84.5%	82.1%	94.5%	92.0%
ccof	91.8%	80.0%	70.9%	62.0%
jjmod__intf	100%	100%	100%	100%
Total	96.2%	90.4%	82.6%	77.7%

Table 5. Figures for intra-chunk annotation.

5 Conclusion

We introduced the notion of a simple parser for Indian languages which follows a grammar driven methodology. We compared its performance against previous similar attempts and reported its efficiency. We showed how by using simple yet robust rules one can achieve high performance in the identification of various levels of dependency relations.

The immediate tasks for the near future would be to identify relative clauses in order to reduce labeled attachment errors and hence to come up with rules for better identification of clauses. We also intend to thoroughly test our rules for Indian languages that are similar in nature and hence evaluate the efficiency of the simple parser.

Acknowledgements

We sincerely thank Samar Husain, for his important role in providing us with valuable linguistic inputs and ideas. The treebank (Hyderabad dependency treebank, version 0.05) used, was prepared at LTRC, IIIT-Hyderabad.

References

Rafiya Begum, Samar Husain, Arun Dhwaj, Dipti Misra Sharma, Lakshmi Bai, and Rajeev Sangal. 2008. Dependency annotation scheme for Indian languages. In *Proceedings of IJCNLP-2008*.

Akshar Bharati, Vineet Chaitanya and Rajeev Sangal. 1995. *Natural Language Processing: A Paninian Perspective*, Prentice-Hall of India, New Delhi, pp. 65-106.

Akshar Bharati, Samar Husain, Dipti Misra Sharma, and Rajeev Sangal. 2008. A Two-Stage Constraint Based Dependency Parser for Free Word Order Languages. In *Proc. of the COLIPS International Conference on Asian Language Processing 2008 (IALP).* Chiang Mai, Thailand. 2008.

Akshar Bharati and Rajeev Sangal. 1993. Parsing Free Word Order Languages in the Paninian Framework, *ACL93: Proc. of Annual Meeting of Association for Computational Linguistics.*

Akshar Bharati, Rajeev Sangal and Dipti M. Sharma. 2005. ShaktiAnalyser: SSF Representation.

Akshar Bharati, Rajeev Sangal, Dipti Misra Sharma and Lakshmi Bai. 2006. AnnCorra: Annotating Corpora Guidelines for POS and Chunk Annotation for Indian Languages. *Technical Report (TR-LTRC-31), Language Technologies Research Centre IIIT, Hyderabad http://ltrc.iiit.ac.in/MachineTrans/publications/technicalReports/tr031/posguidelines.pdf*

Murray B. Emeneau. 1956. India as a linguistic area. *Linguistics,* 32:3-16.

Murray B. Emeneau. 1980. *Language and linguistic area. Essays by Murray B. Emeneau. Selected and introduced by Anwar S. Dil.* Stanford University Press.

Mridul Gupta, Vineet Yadav, Samar Husain and Dipti M. Sharma. 2008. A Rule Based Approach for Automatic Annotation of a Hindi Treebank. In *Proc. Of the 6th International Conference on Natural Language Processing (ICON-08),* CDAC Pune, India.

R. Hudson. 1984. *Word Grammar*, Basil Blackwell, Oxford, OX4 1JF, England.

I. Mel'cuk . 1988. *Dependency Syntax: Theory and Practice*, State University, Press of New York.

Avinesh PVS and Karthik Gali. 2007. Part-of-speech tagging and chunking using conditional random fields and transformation based learning. In *Proc. Of IJCAI-07 Workshop on "Shallow Parsing in South Asian Languages", 2007.*

Annotating Discourse Anaphora

Stefanie Dipper
Institute of Linguistics
Bochum University
dipper@linguistics.rub.de

Heike Zinsmeister
Institute of Linguistics
Konstanz University
Heike.Zinsmeister@uni-konstanz.de

Abstract

In this paper, we present preliminary work on corpus-based anaphora resolution of discourse deixis in German. Our annotation guidelines provide linguistic tests for locating the antecedent, and for determining the semantic types of both the antecedent and the anaphor. The corpus consists of selected speaker turns from the Europarl corpus.

1 Introduction

An important component of text understanding is *anaphora resolution*, i.e. to determine the reference of constituents whose interpretation depends on (the reference of) other textual elements. The majority of anaphora are instances of noun phrase anaphora, which relate a noun phrase anaphor to a nominal antecedent. Grammatical restrictions (gender, number agreement) and saliency (grammatical function, recency) guide the resolution process in these cases. In addition to pronouns, definite noun phrases can be viewed as anaphoric in that they may corefer to some other NP in the given context. To solve the latter type of anaphora, lexical semantic knowledge is required, as provided by an ontology or a database like WordNet.

Another type of anaphora is discourse deixis (Webber 1988; 1991), which relates a noun phrase anaphor to a verbal or (multi-)clausal antecedent. The discourse entities that are introduced by antecedents of discourse deictic pronouns are called "abstract objects" since they refer to properties and propositional entities (Asher, 1993). Grammatical restrictions cannot apply since the antecedent is non-nominal and the anaphor—commonly in the form of a personal or demonstrative pronoun—is usually in neuter singular. We assume that in addition to saliency the resolution process needs to take semantic restrictions into account (cf. Hegarty et al. (2002)).

The automatic procedure of our research effort can be envisaged as follows: Given some text we first locate discourse anaphors. Next, the semantic (= abstract) type of each anaphor is determined, based on contextual features that are derived from annotated corpus data. The anaphor's semantic type restricts the semantic type of the antecedent, and thus narrows down the search space. Finally, the antecedent is located with the help of these semantic restrictions and, again, with contextual features derived from the corpus.

2 Related Work

Corpus-based studies have shown that abstract objects are less salient than other discourse referents, which has an effect on the choice of the anaphoric element (Hegarty et al., 2002). The abstract type of the antecedent and that of the anaphor do not necessarily coincide. The data suggests that reference to other types (referred to in the literature as coërcion) is possible only in accordance to an abstractness hierarchy (Hegarty, 2003; Consten and Knees, 2005; Consten et al., 2007). The hierarchy starts with events as the most concrete type, which are anchored in spatial-temporal dimensions, and ends with propositions as the most abstract types. Anaphoric reference is possible to antecedents that are of the same type or less abstract than the anaphor (Consten and Knees, 2005).

Most works concerning the annotation of anaphora resolution do not make reference to abstract entities. OntoNotes, for example, only annotates reference to verbs (Pradhan et al., 2007). Annotation research efforts on discourse deixis include: Eckert and Strube (2000), Byron (2002), Poesio and Modjeska (2005), Poesio and Artstein (2008), and Müller (2007) for English; Navarretta (2000) for Danish; and Recasens (2008) for Spanish/Catalan. To our knowledge, there has been no attempt to systematically annotate such a corpus of German.

Proceedings of the Third Linguistic Annotation Workshop, ACL-IJCNLP 2009, pages 166–169,
Suntec, Singapore, 6-7 August 2009.

Test: Die Zusammenführung der nationalen und europäischen Ebene ist sehr wohl notwendig , obwohl natürlich die Haupttätigkeit in den Mitgliedstaaten stattfinden sollte und nur dann auf europäischer Ebene eingegriffen werden sollte , wenn **dies — *nämlich auf europäischer Ebene einzugreifen* —** unbedingt notwendig ist .

Anno: Die Zusammenführung der nationalen und europäischen Ebene ist sehr wohl notwendig , obwohl natürlich die Haupttätigkeit in den Mitgliedstaaten stattfinden sollte und nur dann [auf europäischer Ebene eingegriffen]$_{prop}$ werden sollte , wenn [**dies**]$_{prop}$ unbedingt notwendig ist .

Engl: 'It is indeed necessary to bring the national and European levels together, even though, of course, the main work should be done in the Member States, with the European level intervening only when **this** is absolutely necessary.'

Figure 1: Paraphrase test to determine the extension of the antecedent.

3 The Corpus

Our corpus consists of texts from the Europarl corpus (Koehn, 2005). As our basis, we selected all contributions whose original language is German (including Austrian German).

For the annotation task, we isolated medium-sized turns, consisting of 15–20 sentences. This was done to guarantee that the turns were not too lengthy but still provided enough information for the annotators to understand the broader context of discussion, so that they could resolve the anaphors without comprehension problems. From these turns, we selected those that contained the anaphor *dies* 'this'. This is the only anaphor in German which unambiguously refers to discourse units.

4 The Guidelines

Our guidelines are based on theoretical research on discourse semantics as well as work on annotating discourse phenomena.

Given some discourse anaphor (i.e., anaphoric *das, dies, was, es* 'that, this, which, it'), the guidelines define (i) how to locate the antecedent, (ii) how to determine the semantic type of the antecedent, and (iii) how to determine the semantic type of the anaphor. For each of these tasks, the guidelines provide linguistic tests (Dipper and Zinsmeister, 2009).

4.1 Locating the antecedent

To determine the antecedent of the anaphoric relation, a "paraphrase test" is applied: The annotator supplements the anaphor by a paraphrase in the form of *nämlich ...* 'namely ...'. The part that fills the ... corresponds to the antecedent that we are looking for, cf. Fig. 1.[1] Antecedents can consist of VPs, (fragments of) main or subordinate clauses, or multiple sentences.[2]

4.2 The semantic type of the antecedent

We distinguish 10 types of propositional entities. Many verbs prototypically denote one type of propositional entity; *gewinnen* 'win', for instance, usually expresses an event. Often, however, the type of entity that is denoted depends on the context and usage of the verb; *Hans hat Äpfel gegessen* ('Hans ate apples') denotes a process, whereas *Hans hat zwei Äpfel gegessen* ('Hans ate two apples') denotes an event because the action has an end (when both apples are eaten)—i.e., the action is telic. The semantic types are defined in terms of the following features: world-dependent, time-dependent, dynamic, telic, and modal (with subtypes deontic and epistemic, generic, subjective) (see e.g., Vendler (1967), Asher (1993)). Table 1 displays the different types of propositional entities and their defining features. It also lists the labels used for annotating these entities. The entity types are ordered according to their degree of abstractness.

The entity type "deict" (deictic) does not fit in the abstractness hierarchy of the table. It refers to extra-linguistic entities, such as the external situation, or an issue that is currently the focus of attention in parliament, etc.

[1]The *Test* line displays the sentence with the anaphor (marked in bold-face) followed by the inserted paraphrase (in bold-face and italics). The *Anno* line shows the same example with the identified antecedent underlined. Both the antecedent and the anaphor are labeled with their semantic types (see below). The *Engl* line presents an English translation that is based on the original translations from Europarl. We used the tool OPUS (`http://urd.let.rug.nl/tiedeman/OPUS`) to retrieve the English translations.

[2]E.g., the anaphor *dies alles* 'all this' often refers to an antecedent consisting of multiple sentences. The actual antecedent can diverge from the one constructed by the paraphrase test in minor aspects, such as active-passive-alternations, or bare infinitive vs. *zu*-infinitive vs. participle. In some cases, the divergences are more important and could involve, for instance, the insertion or modification of the main verb. In such cases, annotators were asked to note and record the differences.

Prop. Entity		Label	Defining Features					Replacement Test
			W	T	Dyn	Tel	Mod	
1.	Event	ev	+	+	+	+	-	*Ereignis* ('event')
2.	Process	proc	+	+	+	-	-	*Vorgang* ('process')
3.	State	state	+	+	-	(-)	-	*Zustand* ('state')
4.	Circumstance	circ	+	+	-	-	-	*Umstand* ('circumstance')
5.	Modal (deontic + epistemic)	mod	+	+	-	-	mod	*Notwendigkeit, Möglichkeit, Chance, ...* ('necessity, possibility, opportunity, ...')
6.	Opinion, claim	op	+	+	-	-	subj	*Meinung, Ansicht, Behauptung, Einschätzung, Forderung, ...* ('opinion, view, claim, assessment, request, ...')
7.	Generic	gen	+	+/-	-	-	gen	*wohlbekannte, allgemeingültige Tatsache* ('the well-known, universal fact')
8.	Fact	fact	+	+/-	+/-	+/-	-	*Tatsache* ('fact')
9.	Proposition	prop	-	-	+/-	+/-	-	*(Art von) Aktivität, Aktion, Eigenschaft, ...* '(kind of) activity, action, property, ...')

Table 1: Semantic types and their defining features: W(orld), T(ime), Dyn(amic), (Tel)ic, Mod(al)

4.3 The semantic type of the anaphor

To determine the type of anaphors, we defined a "replacement test". With this test, the demonstrative anaphor *dies, das,* etc. is replaced by a suitable NP, such as *dieses Ereignis, dieser Vorgang*. The head noun indicates the type of the propositional entity (e.g., event, process).[3] Table 1 lists the different types of propositional entities and suitable replacement nouns. The annotators are asked to choose the *most concrete*, suitable noun.

5 Results

As a first pilot study on the reliability of our annotation guidelines, two student annotators annotated 32 texts that included 48 instances of the demonstrative pronoun *dies* 'this'. The pronouns were marked in bold face, and the annotation was performed on paper. After annotating 17 texts, the annotators discussed their intermediate results.

Locating the antecedent: In one case, one of the annotators decided on a deictic reading and did not mark an antecedent at all. 40 out of 47 antecedents (85%) were marked with identical spans. In four cases they chose differing but adjacent spans and in one case one of the annotators chose a longer string than the other.

The semantic type of the antecedent: The type of the antecedents coincided in 28 out of 47 cases (60%, α=0.52).[4] Agreement improved after the discussion period: 11/17 cases matched (α=0.60).

The semantic type of the anaphor: The results with respect to the semantic type of the anaphor seemed more disappointing: the annotators agreed in only 22 out of 48 instances (46%, α=0.37). However, after the discussion period, agreement leveled that of the type of the antecedent: 12 out of 17 cases coincided (α=0.66). In addition to the semantic type, we annotated the grammatical role of the anaphor, which occurred as the subject in 79% of cases and as objects elsewhere.

Annotators agreed most often on the four most concrete types ('ev, proc, state, circ') and least often on the three most abstract types ('gen, fact, prop'). This might be due to the fact that the most abstract types are applicable in many cases, but annotators are advised to choose the most concrete type that is available. In the majority of the cases (73%), the anaphor's type was identical with or more abstract than the antecedent's type.

6 Conclusion

In this paper, we presented a corpus-driven approach to discourse deictic anaphora in German. We introduced annotation guidelines that provide linguistic tests for locating the antecedent, and for determining the semantic types of both the antecedent and the anaphor. Further work will include exploitation of contextual information in combination with the semantic types to confine the set of potential antecedents.

Our corpus consists of selected speaker turns from the Europarl corpus. In this study, 32 texts (providing 48 instances of discourse deixis) were

[3]We use the term "semantic type of the anaphor" in a somewhat sloppy way. Put more precisely, the "semantic type of the anaphor" indicates the way that the anaphor refers to (parts of) the propositional discourse referent that is denoted by the antecedent.

[4]We computed α according to `www.asc.upenn.edu/usr/krippendorff/webreliability.doc`.

annotated according to these guidelines, and first results concerning inter-annotator agreement are promising (with an agreement of 85% on the extension of the antecedent, 60% on the antecedent type, and 46% on the type of the anaphor). The pilot study indicates that the paraphrase test helps the annotators in determining on the extension of the abstract antecedent.[5] It also shows that the linguistic tests for the semantic types have to be refined.

In the next steps, we will switch from paper-and-pencil annotation to annotation based on the tool MMAX2[6]. In addition to manually determining the semantic types of anaphors, we will investigate robust, fully-automatic approaches to the derivation of contextual features for anaphora resolution. For instance, we plan to take into account anaphors of the form *dieses Ereignis, dieser Umstand,* etc. ('this event, this circumstance'), which explicitly name the semantic type of the anaphor. In a later step other, more ambiguous, types of anaphors will be included in the investigation.

Acknowledgments

We would like to thank the anonymous reviewers for their helpful comments, and our student annotators: Doris Aimer, Iris Bräuning, Christine Enzinger, Stefanie Konetzka, Barbara Mrzyglod. The work was in part supported by Europäischer Sozialfonds in Baden-Württemberg.

References

Nicholas Asher. 1993. *Reference to Abstract Objects in Discourse*. Kluwer Academic Publishers, Boston MA.

Donna K. Byron. 2002. Resolving pronominal reference to abstract entities. In *Proceedings of the ACL-02 conference*, pages 80–87.

Manfred Consten and Mareile Knees. 2005. Complex anaphors — ontology and resolution. In P. Dekker, editor, *Proceedings of the 15th Amsterdam Colloquium*, Amsterdam: University.

Manfred Consten, Mareile Knees, and Monika Schwarz-Friesel. 2007. The function of complex anaphors in texts: Evidence from corpus studies and ontological considerations. In *Anaphors in Text*, pages 81–102. John Benjamins, Amsterdam/Philadephia.

Stefanie Dipper and Heike Zinsmeister. 2009. Annotation guidelines "Discourse-Deictic Anaphora". Draft. Universities of Bochum and Konstanz.

Miriam Eckert and Michael Strube. 2000. Dialogue acts, synchronising units and anaphora resolution. *Journal of Semantics*, 17(1):51–89.

Michael Hegarty, Jeanette K. Gundel, and Kaja Borthen. 2002. Information structure and the accessibility of clausally introduced referents. *Theoretical Linguistics*, 27(2-3):163–186.

Michael Hegarty. 2003. Type shifting of Entities in Discourse. Presentation at the First International Workshop on Current Research in the Semantics-Pragmatics Interface, Michigan State University.

Philipp Koehn. 2005. Europarl: A parallel corpus for statistical machine translation. In *Proceedings of MT Summit*.

Christoph Müller. 2007. Resolving it, this, and that in unrestricted multi-party dialog. In *Proceedings of the 45th Annual Meeting of the ACL*, pages 816–823, Prague, Czech Republic, June.

Costanza Navarretta. 2000. Abstract Anaphora Resolution in Danish. In *1st SIGdial Workshop on Discourse and Dialogue*, pages 56–65, Hong Kong, China, October.

Massimo Poesio and Ron Artstein. 2008. Anaphoric annotation in the ARRAU corpus. In *Proceedings of the LREC 2008*, Marrakech, Morocco.

Massimo Poesio and Natalia N. Modjeska. 2005. Focus, activation, and *this*-noun phrases: An empirical study. In António Branco, Tony McEnery, and Ruslan Mitkov, editors, *Anaphora Processing*, volume 263 of *Current Issues in Linguistic Theory*, pages 429–442. John Benjamins.

Sameer Pradhan, Lance Ramshaw, Ralph Weischedel, Jessica MacBride, and Linnea Micciulla. 2007. Unrestricted coreference: Identifying entities and events in OntoNotes. In *Proceedings of the IEEE International Conference on Semantic Computing (ICSC)*, Irvine, CA.

Marta Recasens. 2008. Discourse deixis and coreference: Evidence from AnCora. In *Proceedings of the Second Workshop on Anaphora Resolution (WAR II)*, pages 73–82.

Zeno Vendler, 1967. *Linguistics in Philosophy*, chapter Verbs and Time, pages 97–121. Cornell University Press, Ithaca.

Bonnie L. Webber. 1988. Discourse deixis: Reference to discourse segments. In *Proceedings of the ACL-88 conference*, pages 113–122.

Bonnie L. Webber. 1991. Structure and ostention in the interpretation of discourse deixis. *Language and Cognitive Processes*, 6:107–135.

[5]The study was restricted to instances of the unambiguous anaphor *dies* 'this', which might have simplified the task of selecting an antecedent.

[6]MMAX2: `http://mmax2.sourceforge.net/`.

Annotating Wall Street Journal Texts Using a Hand-Crafted Deep Linguistic Grammar

Valia Kordoni & Yi Zhang
DFKI GmbH and Dept. of Computational Linguistics, Saarland University
66041 Saarbrücken, GERMANY
{kordoni,yzhang}@coli.uni-sb.de

Abstract

This paper presents an on-going effort which aims to annotate the Wall Street Journal sections of the Penn Treebank with the help of a hand-written large-scale and wide-coverage grammar of English. In doing so, we are not only focusing on the various stages of the semi-automated annotation process we have adopted, but we are also showing that rich linguistic annotations, which can apart from syntax also incorporate semantics, ensure that the treebank is guaranteed to be a truly sharable, re-usable and multi-functional linguistic resource[†].

1 Introduction

The linguistic annotation of a corpus is the practice of adding interpretative linguistic information in order to give "added value" to the corpus. Linguistically annotated corpora have been shown to help in many kinds of automatic language processing or analysis. For example, corpora which have been POS-tagged can automatically yield frequency lists or frequency dictionaries with grammatical classification. Another important use for linguistically annotated corpora is in the area of automatic parsing. In terms of re-usability of linguistic annotations, what is to be advocated here is that – as long as the annotation provided is a kind useful to many users - an annotated corpus gives "value added" because it can be readily shared by others, apart from those who originally added the annotation. In short, a linguistically annotated corpus is a sharable resource, an example of the electronic resources increasingly relied on for research and study in the humanities and social sciences.

In this paper, we present an on-going project whose aim is to produce rich syntactic and semantic annotations for the Wall Street Journal (henceforward WSJ) sections of the Penn Treebank (henceforward PTB; Marcus et al. (1993)). The task is being carried out with the help of the English Resource Grammar (henceforward ERG; Flickinger (2002)), which is a hand-written grammar for English in the spirit of the framework of Head-driven Phrase Structure Grammar (henceforward HPSG; Pollard and Sag (1994)).

2 Background & Motivation

The past two decades have seen the development of many syntactically annotated corpora. There is no need to defend the importance of treebanks in the study of corpus linguistics or computational linguistics here. Evidently, the successful development of many statistical parsers is attributed to the development of large treebanks. But for parsing systems based on hand-written grammars, treebanks are also important resources on the base of which statistical parse disambiguation models have been developed.

The early treebanking efforts started with manual annotations which are time-consuming and error-prone procedures. For instance, the WSJ sections of the PTB has taken many person years to get annotated. Similar efforts have been carried out in many more languages, as can be seen in the cases of the German Negra/Tiger Treebank (Brants et al., 2002), the Prague Dependency Treebank (Hajič et al., 2000), TüBa-D/Z[1], etc. Although many of these projects have stimulated research in various sub-fields of computational linguistics where corpus-based empirical methods are used, there are many known shortcomings of the manual corpus annotation approach.

Many of the limitations in the manual treebanking approach have led to the development of several alternative approaches. While annotating linguistically rich structures from scratch is clearly inpractical, it has been shown that the different

[†]We thank Dan Flickinger and Stephan Oepen for their support with the grammar and treebanking software used in this project. The second author is supported by the German Excellence Cluster: Multimodal Computing & Interaction.

[1]http://www.sfs.nphil.uni-tuebingen.de/en_tuebadz.shtml

Proceedings of the Third Linguistic Annotation Workshop, ACL-IJCNLP 2009, pages 170–173,
Suntec, Singapore, 6-7 August 2009.

structures in various linguistic frameworks can be converted from annotated treebanks to a different format. And the missing rich annotations can be filled in incrementally and semi-automatically. This process usually involves careful design of the conversion program, which is a non-trivial task. In very recent years, based on the treebank conversion approach and existing manually annotated treebanks, various "new" annotations in different grammar frameworks have been produced for the same set of texts. For example, for the WSJ sections of the PTB, annotations in the style of dependency grammar, CCG, LFG and HPSG have become available. Such double annotations have helped the cross-framework development and evaluation of parsing systems. However, it must be noted that the influence of the original PTB annotations and the assumptions implicit in the conversion programs have made the independence of such new treebanks at least questionable. To our knowledge, there is no completely independent annotation of the WSJ texts built without conversion from the original PTB trees.

Another popular alternative way to aid treebank development is to use automatic parsing outputs as guidance. Many state-of-the-art parsers are able to efficiently produce large amount of annotated syntactic structures with relatively high accuracy. This approach has changed the role of human annotation from a labour-intensive task of drawing trees from scratch to a more intelligence-demanding task of correcting parsing errors, or eliminating unwanted ambiguities (cf., the Redwoods Treebank (Oepen et al., 2002)). It is our aim in this on-going project to build a HPSG treebank for the WSJ sections of the PTB based on the hand-written ERG for English.

3 The Annotation Scheme

3.1 Grammars & Tools

The treebank under construction in this project is in line with the so-called dynamic treebanks (Oepen et al., 2002). We rely on the HPSG analyses produced by the ERG, and manually disambiguate the parsing outputs with multiple annotators. The development is heavily based on the DELPH-IN[2] software repository and makes use of the English Resource Grammar (ERG; Flickinger (2002), PET (Callmeier, 2001), an efficient unification-based parser which is used in our project for parsing the WSJ sections of the PTB, and [incr tsdb()] (Oepen, 2001), the grammar performance profiling system we are using, which comes with a complete set of GUI-based tools for treebanking. Version control system also plays an important role in this project.

3.2 Preprocessing

The sentences from the Wall Street Journal Sections of the Penn Treebank are extracted with their original tokenization, with each word paired with a part-of-speech tag. Each sentence is given a unique ID which can be used to easily look up its origin in the PTB.

3.3 Annotation Cycles

The annotation is organised into iterations of parsing, treebanking, error analysis and grammar/treebank update cycles.

Parsing Sentences from the WSJ are first parsed with the PET parser using the ERG. Up to 500 top readings are recorded for each sentence. The exact best-first parsing mode guarantees that these recorded readings are the ones that have "achieved" highest disambiguation scores according to the current parse selection model, without enumerating through all possible analyses.

Treebanking The parsing results are then manually disambiguated by the annotators. However, instead of looking at individual trees, the annotators spend most of their effort making binary decisions on either accepting or rejecting constructions. Each of these decisions, called discriminants, reduces the number of the trees satisfying the constraints (see Figure 1). Every time a decision is made, the remaining set of trees and discriminants are updated simultaneously. This continues until one of the following conditions is met: i) if there is only one remaining tree and it represents a correct analysis of the sentence, the tree is marked as gold; ii) if none of the remaining trees represents a valid analysis, the sentence will be marked as "rejected", indicating an error in the grammar[3]; iii) if the annotator is not sure about any further decision, a "low confidence"

[2]http://www.delph-in.net/

[3]In some cases, the grammar does produce a valid reading, but the disambiguation model fails to rank it among the top 500 recorded candidates. In practice, we find such errors occuring frequently during the first annotation circle, but they diminish quickly when the disambiguation model gets updated.

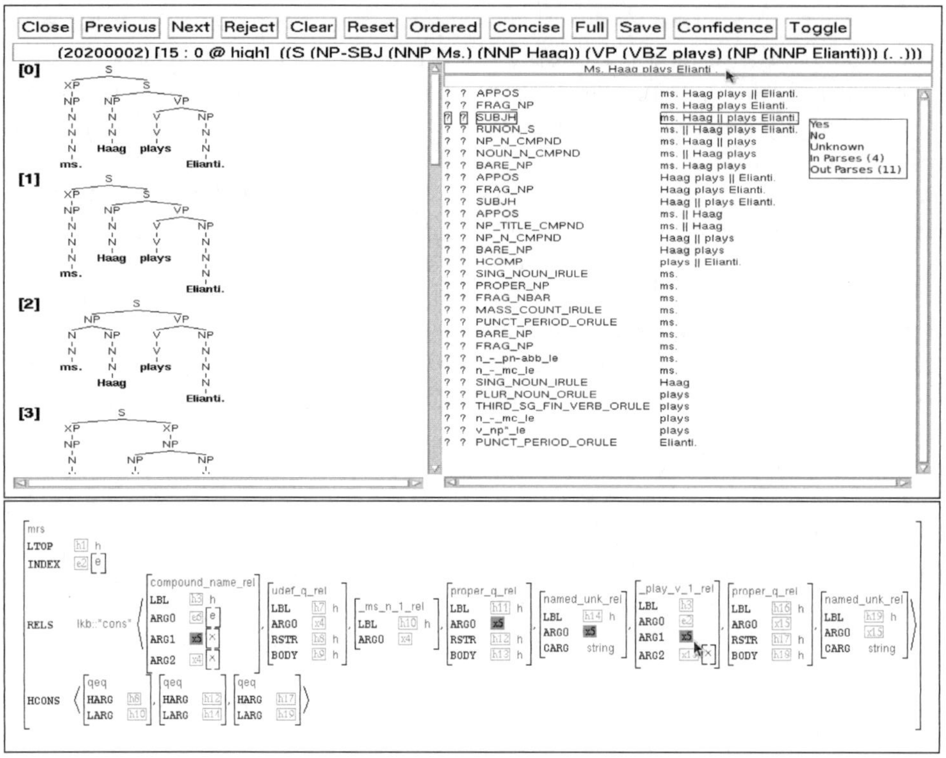

Figure 1: Treebanking Interface with an example sentence, candidate readings, discriminants and the MRS. The top row of the interface is occupied by a list of functional buttons, followed by a line indicating the sentence ID, number of remaining readings, number of eliminated readings, annotator confidence level, and the original PTB bracket annotation. The left part displays the candidate readings, and their corresponding IDs (ranked by the disambiguation model). The right part lists all the discriminants among the remaining readings. The lower part shows the MRS of one candicate reading.

state will be marked on the sentence, saved together with the partial disambiguation decisions. Generally speaking, given n candidate trees, on average $\log_2 n$ decisions are needed in order to fully disambiguate. Given that we set a limit of 500 candidate readings per sentence, the whole process should require no more than 9 decisions. If both the syntactic and the MRS analyses look valid, the tree will be recorded as the gold reading for the sentence. It should be noted here that the tree displayed in the treebanking window is an abbreviated representation of the actual HPSG analysis, which is much more informative than the phrase-structure tree shown here.

Grammar & Treebank Update While the grammar development is independent to the treebanking progress, we periodically incorporate the recent changes of the grammar into the treebank annotation cycle. When a grammar update is incorporated, the treebank will be updated accordingly by i) parsing all the sentences with the new grammar; ii) re-applying the recorded annotation decisions; iii) re-annotating those sentences which are not fully disambiguated after step ii. The extra manual annotation effort in treebank update is usually small when compared to the first round annotation.

Another type of update happens more frequently without extra annotation cost. When a new portion of the corpus is annotated, this is used to retrain the parse disambiguation model. This improves the parse selection accuracy and reduces the annotation workload.

3.4 Grammar coverage & robust parsing

Not having been specifically tuned for the newspaper texts, the ERG achieved out-of-box coverage of over 80% on the WSJ dataset. While this is a respectably high coverage for a hand-written precision grammar, the remaining 20% of the data is not covered by the first round of annotation. We plan to parse the remaining data using a less-restrictive probabilistic context-free grammar extracted from the annotated part of the treebank. The PCFG parser will produce a pseudo-derivation tree, with which robust unifications can be applied to construct the semantic structures (Zhang and Kordoni,

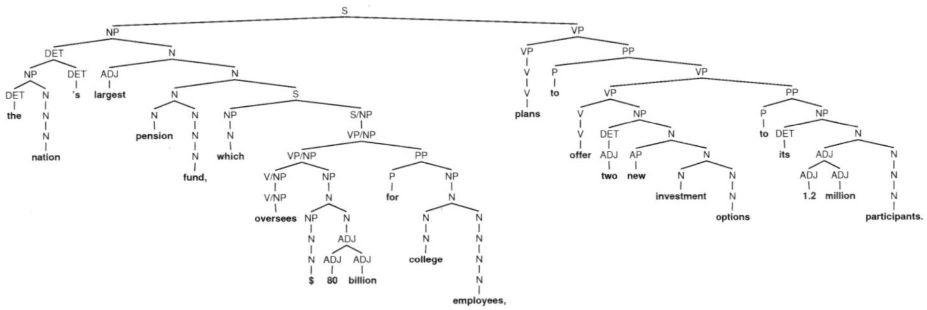

Figure 2: An example tree including a "heavy" NP-subject, a relative clause, and noun-noun compounds

2008).

3.5 Multiple annotations

To speed up the annotation, the project employs three annotators. They are assigned with slightly overlapping sections of the WSJ dataset. The overlapping part allows us to measure the inter-annotator agreement for the purpose of quality control. To estimate the agreement level, the WSJ Section 02 has been completely annotated by all three annotators. Analysis shows that the annotators reach exact match agreement for around 50% of the sentences. Many disagreements are related to subtle variations in the linguistic analyses. The agreement level shows improvement after several treebanker meetings. For future development, a more fine-grained disagreement assessment is planned.

4 Discussion

The WSJ section of the PTB is not only a challenging corpus to parse with a hand-written grammar. It also contains various interesting and challenging linguistic phenomena. Figure 2, for instance, shows the syntactic analysis that the ERG produces for a sentence which includes a "heavy" NP (noun phrase) containing a relative clause introduced by *which* in the subject position, as well as many interesting compound nouns whose interpretations are missing from the PTB annotation.

The newly annotated data will be also very important for the cross-framework parser development and evaluation. While almost all of the state-of-the-art statistical parsers for English use PTB annotations for training and testing, it would be interesting to see whether a comparable level of parsing accuracy can be reproduced on the same texts when re-annotated independently.

References

Sabine Brants, Stefanie Dipper, Silvia Hansen, Wolfgang Lezius, and George Smith. 2002. The tiger treebank. In *Proceedings of the workshop on treebanks and linguistic theories*, pages 24–41.

Ulrich Callmeier. 2001. Efficient parsing with large-scale unification grammars. Master's thesis, Universität des Saarlandes, Saarbrücken, Germany.

Dan Flickinger. 2002. On building a more efficient grammar by exploiting types. In Stephan Oepen, Dan Flickinger, Jun'ichi Tsujii, and Hans Uszkoreit, editors, *Collaborative Language Engineering*, pages 1–17. CSLI Publications.

Jan Hajič, Alena Böhmová, Eva Hajičová, and Barbora Vidová-Hladká. 2000. The Prague Dependency Treebank: A Three-Level Annotation Scenario. In A. Abeillé, editor, *Treebanks: Building and Using Parsed Corpora*, pages 103–127. Amsterdam:Kluwer.

Mitchell P. Marcus, Beatrice Santorini, and Mary Ann Marcinkiewicz. 1993. Building a large annotated corpus of english: The penn treebank. *Computational Linguistics*, 19(2):313–330.

Stephan Oepen, Kristina Toutanova, Stuart Shieber, Christopher Manning, Dan Flickinger, and Thorsten Brants. 2002. The LinGO Redwoods treebank: motivation and preliminary applications. In *Proceedings of COLING 2002: The 17th International Conference on Computational Linguistics: Project Notes*, Taipei, Taiwan.

Stephan Oepen. 2001. [incr tsdb()] — competence and performance laboratory. User manual. Technical report, Computational Linguistics, Saarland University, Saarbrücken, Germany.

Carl J. Pollard and Ivan A. Sag. 1994. *Head-Driven Phrase Structure Grammar*. University of Chicago Press, Chicago, USA.

Yi Zhang and Valia Kordoni. 2008. Robust Parsing with a Large HPSG Grammar. In *Proceedings of the Sixth International Language Resources and Evaluation (LREC'08)*, Marrakech, Morocco.

A general scheme for broad-coverage multimodal annotation

Philippe Blache
Laboratoire Parole et Langage
CNRS & Aix-Marseille Universités
blache@lpl-aix.fr

Abstract

We present in this paper a formal and computational scheme in the perspective of broad-coverage multimodal annotation. We propose in particular to introduce the notion of *annotation hypergraphs* in which primary and secondary data are represented by means of the same structure.

This paper addresses the question of resources and corpora for natural human-human interaction, in other words broad-coverage annotation of natural data. In this kind of study, most of domains have do be taken into consideration: prosody, pragmatics, syntax, gestures, etc. All these different domains interact in order to build an understandable message. We need then large multimodal annotated corpora of real data, precisely annotated for all domains. Building this kind of resource is a relatively new, but very active research domain, illustrated by the number of workshops (cf. (Martin, 2008)), international initiatives, such as MUMIN (Allwood, 2005), annotation tools such as NITE NXT (Carletta, 2003), Anvil (Kipp, 2001), etc.

1 A characterization of primary data

Different types of primary data constitute the basis of an annotation: speech signal, video input, word strings, images, etc. But other kinds of primary data also can be used, for example in the perspective of semantic annotations such as concepts, references, types, etc. Such data are considered to be atomic in the sense that they are not built on top of lower level data. When looking more closely at these kinds of data, several characteristics can be identified:

- **Location**: primary data is usually localized with respect to a timeline or a position: gestures can be localized into the video signal, phonemes into the speech one, words into the string or objects into a scene or a context. Two different kinds of localisation are used: *temporal* and *spatial*. In the first case, a data is situated by means of a time interval whereas spatial data are localised in terms of relative or absolute positions.
- **Realization**: primary data usually refer to *concrete* (or physical) objects: phonemes, gestures, referential elements into a scene, etc. However, other kinds of primary data can be *abstract* such as concepts, ideas, emotions, etc.
- **Medium**: The W3C recommendation EMMA (*Extensible Multi-Modal Annotations*) proposes to distinguish different medium: *acoustic, tactile* and *visual*. This classification is only relevant for data corresponding to concrete objects.
- **Production**: the study of information structure shows the necessity to take into account accessibility of the objects: some data are directly accessible from the signal or the discourse, they have an existence or have already been mentioned. In this case, they are said to be "*produced*". For example, gestures, sounds, physical objects fall in this category. On the other hand, other kinds of data are deduced from the context, typically the abstract ones. They are considered as "*accessible*".

In the remaining of the paper, we propose the following definition:

***Primary data**: atomic objects that cannot be decomposed. They represent possible constituent on top of which higher level objects can be built. Primary data does not require any interpretation to be identified, they are of direct access.*

This primary data typology is given in figure (1). It shows a repartition between *concrete* vs. *abstract* objects. Concrete objects are usually those taken into account in corpus annotation. As a consequence, annotation usually focuses on speech and gestures, which narrows down the set of data to those with a temporal localization. However, other kinds of data cannot be situated in the

Proceedings of the Third Linguistic Annotation Workshop, ACL-IJCNLP 2009, pages 174–177,
Suntec, Singapore, 6-7 August 2009.

	Phonemes	Words	Gestures	Discourse referents	Synsets	Physical objects
Produced	+	+	+	+/-	-	+
Accessible	-	-	-	+/-	+	-
Concrete	+	+	+	+/-	-	+
Abstract	-	-	-	+/-	-	+
Temporal	+	+	+	+/-	-	-
Spatial	-	-	+/-	+/-	-	+
Acoustic	+	+/-	-	-	-	-
Visual	-	-	+	+/-	-	+
Tactile	-	-	+/-	+/-	-	+

Figure 1: *Primary data description*

timeline (e.g. objects in the environment of the scene) nor spatially (e.g. abstract data).

We need to propose a more general approach of data indexing that has to distinguish on the one hand between temporal and spatial localization and on the other hand between data that can be located and data that cannot.

2 Graph representation: nodes and edges semantics

One of the most popular linguistic annotation representation is *annotation graphs* (Bird, 2001) in which nodes are positions whereas edges bear linguistic information. This representation is elaborated on the basis of a temporal anchoring, even though it is also possible to represent other kinds of anchoring. Several generic annotation format has been proposed on top of this representation, such as LAF and its extension GrAF (cf. (Ide, 2007)). In these approaches, edges to their turn can be interpreted as nodes in order to build higher level information. One can consider the result as an hypergraph, in which nodes can be subgraphs.

In order to explore farther this direction, we propose a more general interpretation for nodes that are not only positions in the input: nodes are complex objects that can be referred at different levels of the representation, they encode all annotations. In order to obtain an homogeneous representations, the two node types used in hypergraphs (*nodes* and *hypernodes*) share the same information structure which relies on the following points:

- **Index**: using an index renders possible to represent any kind of graphs, not only trees. They give to nodes the possibility of encoding any kind of information.

- **Domain**: prosody, semantics, syntax, gesture, pragmatics, etc. It is important to indicate as precisely as possible this information, eventually by means of sub-domains

- **Location**: annotations generally have a spatial or a temporal situation. This information is optional.

- **Features**: nodes have to bear specific linguistic indications, describing its properties.

Hypernodes bear, on top of this information, the specification of the subgraph represented by its constituents and their relations. We propose to add another kind of information in the hypernode structure:

- **Relations**: secondary data are built on top of primary one. They can be represented by means of a set of properties (constituency, linearity, coreference, etc.) implemented as edges plus the basic characteristics of a node. A secondary data is then graph with a label, these two elements composing an hypernode.

The distinction between node and hypernodes makes it possible to give a homogeneous representation of primary and secondary data.

3 An XML representation of annotation hypergraphs

We propose in this section an XML encoding of the scheme presented above.

3.1 Atomic nodes

The first example of the figure (2) illustrates the representation of a *phoneme*. The node is indexed, making its reference possible in higher level structures. Its label corresponds to the tag that would be indicated in the annotation. Other elements complete the description: the linguistic domain (specified by the attributes type and sub-type), the specification of the medium, the object localization (by means of anchors). In this example, a phoneme being part of the acoustic signal, the anchor is temporal and use an explicit timeline reference.

The same kind of representation can be given for transcription tokens (see node `n21` in figure (2)). The value of the node is the orthographic form. It is potentially aligned on the signal, and then represented with a temporal anchoring. Such

```
<node ID="n1" label="u">
   <domain type="phonetics" subtype="phoneme"
         medium="acoustic"/>
   <anchor type="temporal" start="285" end="312"/>
</node>

<node ID="n21" label="book">
   <domain type="transcription" subtype="token"/>
   <anchor type="temporal" start="242" end="422"/>
</node>

<node ID="n24" label="N">
   <domain type=" morphosyntax" subtype="word"/>
   <anchor type="temporal" start="242" end="422"/>
   <features ms="ncms---"/>
</node>

<node ID="n3" label="deictic">
   <domain type="gestures" subtype="hand"/>
   <anchor type="temporal" start="200" end="422"/>
   <features hand="right" deictic_type="space"
         object="ref_object"/>
</node>

<node ID="n4" label="discourse-referent">
   <domain type="semantics" subtype="discourse_universe"
         medium="visual"/>
   <anchoring type="spatial" x="242" y="422" z="312"/>
   <features isa="book" color="red" />
</node>
```

Figure 2: *XML encoding of atomic nodes*

anchoring makes it possible to align the orthographic transcription with the phonetic one. In the case of written texts, temporal bounds would be replaced by the positions in the texts, which could be interpreted as an implicit temporal anchoring.

The next example presented in node `n24` illustrates the representation of part-of-speech nodes. The domain in this case is *morphosyntax*, its subtype is "`word`". In this case too, the anchoring is temporal, with same bounds as the corresponding token. In this node, a feature element is added, bearing the morpho-syntactic description.

The atomic node described in node `n3` represents another physical object: a *deictic gesture*. Its domain is gesture and its subtype, as proposed for example in the MUMIN scheme (see (Allwood, 2005)) is the part of the body. The anchoring is also temporal and we can observe in this example a synchronization of the gesture with the token "`book`".

The last example (node `n4`) presents an atomic node describing a physical object present in the scene (a book on a shelf of a library). It belongs to the semantics domain as a discourse referent and is anchored spatially by its spatial coordinates. One can note that anchoring can be *absolute* (as in the examples presented here) or *relative* (situating the object with respect to other ones).

3.2 Relations

Relations are represented in the same way as nodes. They are of different types, such as constituency, linearity, syntactic dependency, semantic specification, etc. and correspond to a certain domain. The example `r1` in figure (3) illustrates a `specification` relation between a noun (node `n21`, described above) and its determiner (node `n20`). Non-oriented binary relations also occur, for example cooccurrency. Relations can be expressed in order to represent a set of objects. The next example (relation `r2`) presents the case of three constituents of an higher-level object (the complete description of which being given in the next section).

Finally, the alignment between objects is specified by two different values: *strict* when they have exactly the same temporal or spatial marks; *fuzzy* otherwize.

3.3 Hypernodes

Hypernodes encode subgraphs with the possibility of being themselves considered as nodes. Their structure completes the atomic node with a set of relations. Hypernodes encode different kinds of objects such as phrases, constructions, referential expressions, etc. The first example represents a *NP*. The node is indexed, bears a tag, a domain, an anchoring and features. The set of relations specifies two types of information. First, the *NP* node has three constituents: `n20` (for example a determiner), `n22` (for example an adjective) and `n24` (the noun described in the previous section). The alignment is said to be *strict* which means that the right border of the first element and the left border of the last one have to be the same. The resulting structure is an hypernode describing the different characteristics of the *NP* by means of features and relations.

The second example illustrates the case of a referential expression. Let's imagine the situation where a person points out at a book on a shelf, saying "*The book will fall down*". In terms of information structure, the use of a definite *NP* is possible because the referent is accessible from the physical context: the alignment of the *NP* (`n50`) and the deictic gesture (`n3`, see previous section) makes the coreference possible. This construction results in a discourse referent bringing together all the properties of the physical object (`n3`) and that of the object described in the discourse

```
<relation id="r1" label="specification">
   <domain type="syntax" subtype="oriented_rel"/>
   <edge from="n20" to="n24">
</relation>
```

```
<relation id="r2" label="constituency">
   <domain type="syntax" subtype="set_rel"/>
   <node_list>
      <node id="n20"/> <node id="n22"/> <node id="n24"/>
   </node_list>
   <alignment type="strict"/>
</relation>
```

Figure 3: *XML encoding of relations*

```
<node ID="n50" label="NP">
   <domain type="syntax" subtype="phrase"/>
   <anchor type="temporal" start="200" end="422"/>
   <features cat="NP" agr="ms" sem_type="ref"/>
   <relations>
      <relation id="r1" type="constituency">
         <domain type="syntax" subtype="set_rel"/>
         <node_list>
            <node id="n20"/> <node id="n22"/> <node id="n24"/>
         </node_list>
         <alignment type="strict"/>
      </relation>
      <relation id="r2" type="specification">
         <domain type="syntax" subtype="oriented_rel"/>
         <edge from="n20" to="n24">
      </relation>
   </relations>
</node>
```

```
<node ID="n51" label="ref_expression">
   <domain type="semantics" subtype="discourse_referent"/>
   <features referent="book'" color="red" />
   <relations>
      <relation id="r3" type="constituency">
         <domain type="semantics" type="set_rel"/>
         <node_list>
            <node id="n50"/> <node id="n3"/> <node id="n4"/>
         </node_list>
         <alignment type="fuzzy"/>
      </relation>
      <relation id="r4" type="pointing">
         <domain type="gesture" type="oriented_rel"/>
         <edge from="n3" to="n4">
         <alignment type="strict"/>
      </relation>
   </relations>
</node>
```

Figure 4: *XML encoding of hypernodes*

(n50). In this expression, the alignment between the objects is fuzzy, which is the normal situation when different modalities interact. The second relation describes the pointing action, implementing the coreference between the noun phrase and the physical object. This representation indicates the three nodes as constituents.

4 Conclusion

Understanding the mechanisms of natural interaction requires to explain how the different modalities interact. We need for this to acquire multimodal data and to annotate them as precisely as possible for all modalities. Such resources have to be large enough both for theoretical and computational reasons: we need to cover as broadly as possible the different phenomena and give the possibility to use machine learning techniques in order to produce a new generation of multimodal annotation tools. However, neither such resource, and a fortiori such tools, already exist. One reason, besides the cost of the annotation task itself which is still mainly manual for multimodal information, is the lack of a general and homogeneous annotation scheme capable of representing all kinds of information, whatever its origin.

We have presented in this paper the basis of such a scheme, proposing the notion of *annotation hypergraphs* in which primary as well as secondary data are represented by means of the same node structure. This homogeneous representation is made possible thanks to a generic description of primary data, identifying four types of basic information (index, domain, location, features). We have shown that this scheme can be directly represented in XML, resulting in a generic multimodal coding scheme.

References

Allwood J., L. Cerrato, L. Dybkjaer, & al. (2005) "The MUMIN Multimodal Coding Scheme", *NorFA yearbook*

Bird S., M. Liberman (2001) "A formal framework for linguistic annotation" *Speech Communication*, Elsevier

Carletta, J., J. Kilgour, and T. O'Donnell (2003) "The NITE Object Model Library for Handling Structured Linguistic Annotation on Multimodal Data Sets" in procs of the EACL Workshop on Language Technology and the Semantic Web

Ide N. & K. Suderman (2007) "GrAF: A Graph-based Format for Linguistic Annotations", in proceedings of the *Linguistic Annotation Workshop at the ACL'07 (LAW-07)*

Kipp M. (2001) "Anvil-a generic annotation tool for multimodal dialogue" in procs of 7th European Conference on Speech Communication and Technology

Martin, J.-C., Paggio, P., Kipp, M., Heylen, D. (2008) Proceedings *of the Workshop on Multimodal Corpora : From Models of Natural Interaction to Systems and Applications* (LREC'2008)

The SILT and FlaReNet International Collaboration for Interoperability

Nancy Ide
Department of Computer Science
Vassar College
Poughkeepsie, New York USA
ide@cs.vassar.edu

James Pustejovsky
Department of Computer Science
Brandeis University
Waltham, Massachusetts USA
jamesp@cs.brandeis.edu

Nicoletta Calzolari
CNR-ILC
Pisa, Italy
glottolo@ilc.cnr.it

Claudia Soria
CNR-ILC
Pisa, Italy
claudia.soria@ilc.cnr.it

Abstract

Two major projects in the U.S. and Europe have joined in a collaboration to work toward achieving interoperability among language resources. In the U.S., a project entitled "Sustainable Interoperability for Language Technology" (SILT) has been funded by the National Science Foundation under the INTEROP program, and in Europe, FLaReNet Fostering Language Resources Network has been funded by the European Commission under the eContentPlus framework. This international collaborative effort involves members of the language processing community and others working in related areas to build consensus regarding the sharing of data and technologies for language resources and applications, to work towards interoperability of existing data, and, where possible, to promote standards for annotation and resource building. In addition to broad-based US and European participation, we are seeking the participation of colleagues in Asia. This presentation describing the projects and their goals will, we hope, serve to involve members of the community who may not have been aware of the effort before, in particular colleagues in Asia.

1 Overview

One of today's greatest challenges is the development of language processing capabilities that will enable easy and natural access to computing facilities and information. Because natural language processing (NLP) research relies heavily on such resources to provide training data to develop language models and optimize statistical algorithms, language resources–including (usually large) collections of language data and linguistic descriptions in machine readable form, together with tools and systems (lemmatizers, parsers, summarizers, information extractors, speech recognizers, annotation development software, etc.)– are critical to this development.

Over the past two decades, the NLP community has invested substantial effort in the creation of computational lexicons and compendia of semantic information (e.g., framenets, ontologies, knowledge bases) together with language corpora annotated for all varieties of linguistic features, which comprise the central resource for current NLP research. However, the lack of a thorough, well-articulated longer-term vision for language processing research has engendered the creation of a disjointed set of language resources and tools, which exist in a wide variety of (often incompatible) formats, are often unusable with systems other than those for which they were developed, and utilize linguistic categories derived from different theoretical frameworks. Furthermore, these expensive investments are often produced only for one of several relatively isolated subfields (e.g., NLP, information retrieval, machine translation, speech processing), or even worse, for one application in one subfield. In addition, the high cost of resource development has prevented the creation of reliable, large-scale language data and annotations for many phenomena, and for languages other than English.

Interoperability of resources, tools, and frameworks has recently come to be recognized as perhaps the most pressing current need for language processing research. Interoperability is especially

Proceedings of the Third Linguistic Annotation Workshop, ACL-IJCNLP 2009, pages 178–181,
Suntec, Singapore, 6-7 August 2009.

critical at this time because of the widely recognized need to create and merge annotations and information at different linguistic levels in order to study interactions and interleave processing at these different levels. It has also become critical because new data and tools for emerging and strategic languages such as Chinese and Arabic as well as minor languages are in the early stages of development.

Two major projects in the U.S. and Europe have joined in a collaboration to work toward achieving interoperability among language resources. In the U.S., a project entitled "Sustainable Interoperability for Language Technology" (SILT) has been funded by the National Science Foundation under the INTEROP program, and in Europe, FLaReNet Fostering Language Resources Network has been funded by the European Commission under the eContentPlus framework. This international collaborative effort involves members of the language processing community and others working in related areas to build consensus regarding the sharing of data and technologies for language resources and applications, to work towards interoperability of existing data, and, where possible, to promote standards for annotation and resource building. In addition to broad-based US and European participation, we are seeking the participation of colleagues in Asia.

To ensure full community involvement and consolidation of effort, SILT and FLaReNet are establishing ties with major ongoing projects and consortia, including the International Standards Organization TC37 SC4 (Language Resource Management)[1], The World Wide Web Consortium (W3C), the Text Encoding Initiative, the ACL Special Interest Group on Annotation (SIGANN)[2], and others. The ultimate goal is to create an Open Language Infrastructure (OLI) that will provide free and open access to resources, tools, and other information that support work in the field, in order to facilitate collaboration, accessibility for all members of the community, and convergence toward interoperability.

The following sections outline the goals of SILT and FLaReNet.

[1] http://www.tc37sc4.org

[2] http://www.cs.vassar.edu/sigann

2 SILT

The creation and use of language resources spans several related but relatively isolated disciplines, including NLP, information retrieval, machine translation, speech, and the semantic web. SILT's goal is to turn existing, fragmented technology and resources developed within these groups in relative isolation into accessible, stable, and interoperable resources that can be readily reused across several fields.

The major activities of the effort are:

- carefully surveying the field to identify the resources, tools, and frameworks in order to examine what exists and what needs to be developed, and to identify those areas for which interoperability would have the broadest impact in advancing research and development and significant applications dependent on them;
- identifying the major efforts on standards development and interoperable system design together with existing and developing technologies, and examining ways to leverage their results to define an interoperablity infrastructure for both tools and data;
- analyzing innovative methods and techniques for the creation and maintenance of language resources in order to reduce the high costs, increase productivity, and enable rapid development of resources for languages that currently lack them;
- implementing proposed annotation standards and best practices in corpora currently under development (e.g., American National Corpus[3], TimeBank[4]) to evaluate their viability and feed into the process of further standards development, testing, and use of interoperability frameworks (e.g., GATE[5], UIMA[6]) and implementation of processing modules, and distributing all software, data, and annotations.
- ensuring the broadest possible community engagement in the development of consensus and agreement on strategies, priorities, and

[3] http://www.anc.org

[4] http://www.timeml.org/site/timebank/timebank.html

[5] http://gate.ac.uk

[6] http://www.oasis-open.org/committees/uima/

best approaches for achieving broad interoperability by means of sessions, open meetings, and special workshops at major conferences in the field, together with active maintenance of and involvement in open web forums and Wikis;

- providing the technical expertise necessary to turn consensus and agreement into robust interoperability frameworks along with the appropriate tools and resources for their broad use and implementation by means of tutorials and training workshops, especially for undergraduate and graduate students in the field.

3 FLaReNet

The multilingual Europe urgently needs language technologies in order to bridge its language barriers. In order to achieve better quality and fast development of language technologies that seamlessly work on all devices, for spoken and written language alike, the European scenario now needs a coherent and unified effort. The demand for cross-lingual technologies is pressing, the expectations are high, and at the same time, the field is suffering from fragmentation, lack of vision and direction. The main objective of FLaReNet is to steer the process that in the near future will define the actors, the overall direction and the practical forms of collaboration in language technologies and their "raw material", language resources. Under this respect, the goals of FLaReNet lie at a higher level than those of SILT, as they are oriented towards consolidating a community around a number of key topics that, in the end, will allow networking of language technology professionals and their clients, as well as easy sharing of data, corpora, language resources and tools.

From this perspective, FLaReNet has three main lines of action:

The creation and mobilization of a unified and committed community in the field of Language Resources and Technologies. To this end, FLaReNet is bringing together leading experts of research institutions, academies, companies, funding agencies, public and private bodies, both at European and international level, with the specific purpose of creating consensus around short, medium and long-term strategic objectives. The Network is currently composed of around 200 individuals belonging to academia, research institutes, industries and government.

The identification of a set of priority themes on which to stimulate action, under the form of a roadmap for Language Resources and Technologies. In order to avoid scattered or conflicting efforts, the major players in the field of Language Resources and Technologies need to consensually work together and indicate a clear direction of action and a shared policy for the next years. This will take the form of identification of priorities of intervention as well as short, medium, and long-term strategic objectives at all levels, from research directions to implementation choices, from distribution and access policies to the landscape of languages, domain and modalities covered by Language Resources and Technologies.

The elaboration of a blueprint of priority areas for actions in the field and a coherent set of recommendations for the policy-makers (funding agencies especially), the business community and the public at large. Whatever action cannot be implemented on a long term without the help of the necessary financial and political framework to sustain them. This is even most true for actions regarding Language Resources that typically imply a sustained effort at national level. To this end, the FLaReNet Network will propose the priority themes under the form of consensual recommendations and a plan of action for EC Member States, other European-wide decision makers, companies, as well as non-EU and International organizations.

The following Thematic Areas are currently covered by FLaReNet:

- The Chart for the area of LRs and LT in its different dimensions
- Methods and models for LR building, reuse, interlinking, and maintenance
- Harmonisation of formats and standards
- Definition of evaluation and validation protocols and procedures
- Methods for the automatic construction and processing of Language Resources

FLaReNet builds upon years of research and development in the field of standards and language resources, as well as on the achievements (both in terms of results and community awareness), of past EU projects such as EAGLES[7], ISLE[8],

[7] http://www.ilc.cnr.it/EAGLES/home.html

[8] http://www.ilc.cnr.it/EAGLES/isle/ISLE_Home_Page.htm

INTERA[9], and LIRICS[10]. Close collaboration is also established with many relevant ongoing EU projects, such as CLARIN[11].

[9]http://www.elda.org/intera
[10]http://lirics.loria.fr/
[11]http://www.clarin.eu

Building a Large Syntactically-Annotated Corpus of Vietnamese

Phuong-Thai Nguyen
College of Technology, VNU
thainp@vnu.edu.vn

Xuan-Luong Vu
Vietnam Lexicography Centre
vuluong@vietlex.vn

Thi-Minh-Huyen Nguyen
University of Natural Sciences, VNU
huyenntm@vnu.edu.vn

Van-Hiep Nguyen
University of Social Sciences and Humanities, VNU
hiepnv@vnu.edu.vn

Hong-Phuong Le
LORIA/INRIA Lorraine
lehong@loria.fr

Abstract

Treebank is an important resource for both research and application of natural language processing. For Vietnamese, we still lack such kind of corpora. This paper presents up-to-date results of a project for Vietnamese treebank construction. Since Vietnamese is an isolating language and has no word delimiter, there are many ambiguities in sentence analysis. We systematically applied a lot of linguistic techniques to handle such ambiguities. Annotators are supported by automatic-labeling tools and a tree-editor tool. Raw texts are extracted from Tuoi Tre (Youth), an online Vietnamese daily newspaper. The current annotation agreement is around 90 percent.

1 Introduction

Treebanks are used for training syntactic parsers, part-of-speech taggers, and word segmenters. These systems then can be used for applications such as information extraction, machine translation, question answering, and text summarization. Treebanks are also useful for linguistic studies, for example the extraction of syntactic patterns or the investigation of linguistic phenomena. Recently, treebanks and other large corpora have become more important since the development of powerful machine learning methods.

As mentioned above, Vietnamese is an isolating language. There is no word delimiter in Vietnamese. The smallest unit in the construction of words is syllables. Words can be single or compound. Vietnamese script is invented based on Latin alphabet in which the expansion includes accent characters and stressed accents.

Since Vietnamese word order is quite fixed, we choose to use constituency representation of syntactic structures. For languages with freer word order such as Japanese or Czech, dependency representation is more suitable. We apply annotation scheme proposed by Marcus et al. (1993). This approach has been successfully applied to a number of languages such as English, Chinese, Arabic, etc.

For Vietnamese, there are three annotation levels including word segmentation, POS tagging, and syntactic labeling. Word segmentation identifies word boundary in sentences. POS tagging assigns correct POS tags to words. Syntactic labeling recognizes both phrase-structure tags and functional tags. Our main target is to build a corpus of 10,000 syntactically-annotated sentences (trees) and an additional POS tagged data set of 10,000 sentences. Treebank construction is a very complicated task including major phases: investigation, guideline preparation, building tools, raw text collection, and annotation. This is a repeated process involving especially three phases: annotation, guideline revision, and tool upgrade. Raw texts are collected from a newspaper source, the Youth online daily newspaper, with a number of topics including social and politics. We completed about 9,500 trees and 10,000 POS tagged sentences.

In order to deal with ambiguities occurring at various levels of annotation, we systematically applied linguistic analysis techniques such as deletion, insertion, substitution, questioning, transformation, etc. Notions for analysis techniques are described in guideline. These techniques are originated in literatures or proposed

Proceedings of the Third Linguistic Annotation Workshop, ACL-IJCNLP 2009, pages 182–185,
Suntec, Singapore, 6-7 August 2009.

by our group. They are described with examples, arguments, and alternatives. For automatic labeling tools, we used advanced machine learning methods such as CRFs for POS tagging or LPCFGs for syntactic parsing. These tools helped us speed up labeling process. Besides, tree editor was also very helpful.

Our treebank project is a branch project of a national project which aims to develop basic resources and tools for Vietnamese language and speech processing. This national project is called VLSP [1]. In addition to treebank, other text-processing resources and tools include: Vietnamese machine readable dictionary, English-Vietnamese parallel corpus, word segmenter, POS tagger, chunker, and parser. Treebank and tools are closely related. Tools are trained using treebank data, and then they can be used in treebank construction.

The rest of this paper is organized as follow: First, we present issues in Vietnamese word segmentation problem. Second, POS tagging and syntactic parsing are described. Third, tools and annotation process are represented. Fourth, we present annotation agreement evaluation. And last, some conclusion is drawn.

2 Word Segmentation

There are many approaches to word definition, for example based on morphology, based on syntax, based on semantics, or linguistic comparison. We consider words as syntactic atoms (Sciullo and Williams, 1987) according to the sense that it is impossible to analyze word structure using syntactic rules, or that words are the smallest unit which is syntactically independent. We choose this criterion partly because the first application of word segmentation is for syntactic analysis (build trees).

According to application view, machine translation researchers may argue that Vietnamese words and foreign words should match each other. The problem is that there are so many possible foreign languages which are different in vocabulary. Dictionary editors may want to extract phrases from text which need to be explained in meaning. For this application, syntactic parsers can be used as tool for editors. Parsers can extract candidates for phrase/word entry.

The following word types are considered in word segmentation phase: single words, compound words, repeated words, idioms, proper names, date/time, number expressions, foreign words, abbreviations.

Word segmentation ambiguity is the major problem annotators have to deal with. Suppose that three words "nhà cửa", "sắc đẹp", and "hiệu sách" are being considered. Annotators need to identify these combinations as words in:

a. Nhà cửa bề bộn quá
b. Cô ấy giữ gìn sắc đẹp.
c. Ngoài hiệu sách có bán cuốn này

And not words in:

a. Ở nhà cửa ngõ chẳng đóng gì cả.
b. Bức này màu sắc đẹp hơn.
c. Ngoài cửa hiệu sách báo bày la liệt.

We used dictionaries as a reference. In practice, we consider dictionary words as candidate for word segmentation and make decision using context.

3 POS Tagging and Syntactic Annotation Guidelines

3.1 POS Tag Set

For European languages, word classes closely relate to morphological aspects such as gender, number, case, etc. For Vietnamese, words are often classified based on their combination ability, their syntactic functions, and their general meaning. We choose first two criteria, combination ability and syntactic function, for POS tag set design. Therefore our POS tag set will not contain morphological information (number, aspect, tense, etc.), sub-categorization information (transitive/intransitive verbs, verbs followed by clauses, etc.), and semantic information.

3.2 Syntactic Tag Set

Our tag set contains three tag types: constituency tags, functional tags, and null-element tags. We use the tag H to label phrase head. If a phrase has more than one head, connected by coordination conjunctions or commas, then all heads are labeled with H tag. Other treebanks often does not use head tag. Therefore researchers on syntactic parsing (Collins, 1999) used heuristic rules to determine CFG rules' head. Machine learning methods also can be used (Chiang and Bikel, 2002). Null elements are often used for adjective clauses, ellipsis, passive voice, and topic.

3.3 Sentence and Phrase Analysis Techniques

Annotation of real text requires various techniques to be applied. Ambiguity may occur in many steps of analysis such as determining

[1] Vietnamese Language and Speech Processing

phrase's head, discriminating between possible complements, discriminating between adjuncts and other sentence elements, etc. Sentence analysis techniques include deletion, substitution, insertion, transformation, questioning. These techniques exploit contextual information, word combination, word order, and functional words to disambiguation between possible structures.

3.4 Linguistics Issues

The problem of treebank construction can be considered as an application of linguistic theories though treebanks can also be used for linguistic studies. However, there are still disagreements among linguists as to solutions for many linguistic issues. For example, that the classifier noun is noun phrase's head or pre-modifier is controversial. Another example, Vietnamese sentence structure is subject-predicate or topic-comment is also controversial. Our treebank relies more on subject-predicate structure. Moreover, we choose linguistic solutions most appropriate to our design.

4 Tools

We designed a tool for supporting annotators in most all phases of the annotation process. Main functions of our editor are as follows:

- Edit and view trees in both text mode and graphical mode
- View log files, highlight modifications
- Search by words or syntactic patterns
- Predict errors (edit, spell, or syntax)
- Compute annotation agreement and highlight differences
- Compute several kinds of statistics

For encoding the treebank, we have developed an exchange format named vnSynAF, a syntactic annotation framework which is conformed to the standard framework SynAF of ISO. The framework SynAF is built on top of an XML-based annotation scheme which is recommended by ISO for the encoding of treebanks[2]. Our tool also supports bracketing representation (or Lisp style) of Penn English Treebank. These formats can be converted into each other.

For the task of word segmentation, we used vnTokenizer, a highly accurate segmenter which uses a hybrid approach to automatically tokenize Vietnamese text. The approach combines both finite-state automata technique, regular expression parsing, and the maximal-matching strategy which is augmented by statistical methods to resolve ambiguities of segmentation (Phuong et al., 2008).

We used JVnTagger, a POS tagger based on Conditional Random Fields (Lafferty et al., 2001) and Maximum Entropy (Berger et al., 1996). This tagger is also developed under supported of VLSP project. Training data size is 10,000 sentences. Experiments with 5-fold cross validation showed that F1 scores for CRFs and Maxent are 90.40% and 91.03% respectively.

A syntactic parser based on Lexicalized Probabilistic Context-free Grammars (LPCFGs) is another tool we used. Another group in VLSP customized Bikel's parser[3] for parsing Vietnamese text. This parser is a well designed and easy to adapt to new languages. The group implemented a Vietnamese language package which handles treebank, training, finding head of CFG rules, and word features. This parser can output text with constituent tags only or both constituent tags and functional tags.

5 Annotation Process and Agreement

There are three annotation levels: word segmentation, POS tagging, and syntactic labeling. Since the word segmentation tool had been available before the start of our project, it was used for the first annotation level (word segmentation) immediately. As to the other annotation levels (POS tagging and syntactic parsing), first several thousand sentences were labeled manually. After that a POS tagger and a parser are trained bimonthly, then the annotation task becomes semi-automatic. According to our annotation process, each sentence is annotated and revised by at least two annotators. The first annotator labels raw sentences or revises automatically-analyzed sentences. Then the second annotator revises the output of the first annotator. In addition, we also check corpus by syntactic phenomena, for example direction words, questions, etc. This process is supported by tool. So there are many sentences which are revised more than twice.

Table 2 shows a number of important corpus statistics such as sentence count, word count, and syllable count for two data sets. We completed the POS tagged data set and will complete the syntactically-labeled data set soon. The average sentence length is about 21.6 words.

[2] ISO/CD/24615, Language Resource Management-Syntactic Annotation Framework (SynAF) TC37/SC 4 N421, 22th Aug 2007, http://tc37sc4.org/documents

[3] http://www.cis.upenn.edu/~dbikel/software.html

Data set	Sentences	Words	Syllables
POS tagged	10,368	210,393	255,237
Syntactically labeled	9,633	208,406	251,696

Table 1. Corpus statistics

Annotation agreement measures how similar two texts annotated independently by different annotators are. Since this problem is similar to parsing evaluation, we use parseval measure. First, syntactic constituents in the form (i, j, label) are extracted from syntactic trees. Then tree comparison problem is transformed into constituent comparison. We can compute three kinds of measurement: constituent and function similarity, constituent similarity, and bracket similarity. By using this method, we can evaluate both overall agreement and constituency agreement.

Annotation agreement A between two annotators can be computed as follows:

$$A = \frac{2 \times C}{C_1 + C_2}$$

where C_1 is the number of constituents in the first annotator's data set, C_2 is the number of constituents in the second annotator's data set, and C is the number of identical constituents. Table 3 shows an example of constituent extraction from trees. From Table 3, we can compute: C_1=6; C_2=7; C=6; A=12/13=0.92 .

1st annotator	2nd annotator
(S (NP (Np Hằng)) (VP (V ngắm) (NP (N mưa)) (PP (E trong) (NP (N công viên)))) (. .))	(S (NP (Np Hằng)) (VP (V ngắm) (NP (NP (N mưa)) (PP (E trong) (NP (N công viên))))) (. .))
(1,6,S); (1,1,NP); (2,5,VP); (3,3,NP); (4,5, PP); (5,5,NP)	(1,6,S); (1,1,NP); (2,5,VP); (3,3,NP); *(3,5,NP)*; (4,5, PP); (5,5,NP)

Table 2. Constituent extraction from trees

We carried out an experiment involving 3 annotators. They annotated 100 sentences and the result is shown in Table 4.

Test	A1-A2	A2-A3	A3-A1
Full tags	90.32%	91.26%	90.71%
Constituent tags	92.40%	93.57%	91.92%
No tags	95.24%	96.33%	95.48%

Table 3. Annotation agreement

6 Conclusions

In this paper, we presented our most up-to-date results on Vietnamese treebank construction. This project is coming to final stage. We continue to annotate more text, revise data by syntactic phenomenon and feedback from users. We also use statistical techniques to analyze treebank data to find out errors and fix them. We intend to publish these data on LDC this year.

Acknowledgments

This paper is supported by a national project named Building Basic Resources and Tools for Vietnamese Language and Speech Processing, KC01.01/06-10.

Reference

Diệp Quang Ban. 2005. Ngữ pháp tiếng Việt (2 tập). *NXB Giáo dục.*

Cao Xuân Hạo. 2006. Tiếng Việt sơ thảo ngữ pháp chức năng. *NXB Khoa học Xã hội.*

Nguyễn Minh Thuyết và Nguyễn Văn Hiệp. 1999. Thành phần câu tiếng Việt. *NXB ĐHQG Hà Nội.*

Ủy ban Khoa học Xã hội Việt Nam. 1983. Ngữ pháp tiếng Việt. NXB Khoa học Xã hội.

Adam Berger, Stephen D. Pietra, and Vincent D. Pietra. 1996. A maximum entropy approach to natural language processing. Computational Linguistics, (22-1).

David Chiang and Daniel M. Bikel. 2002. Recovering Latent Information in Treebanks. COLING.

Michael Collins. 1999. Head-Driven Statistical Models for Natural Language Parsing. PhD thesis, University of Pennsylvania.

John Lafferty, Andrew McCallum, and Fernando Pereira. 2001. Conditional random fields: Probabilistic models for segmenting and labeling sequence data. ICML.

Mitchell P. Marcus et al. Building a Large Annotated Corpus of English: The Penn Treebank. 1993. Computational Linguistics.

L. H. Phuong, N. T. M. Huyen, R. Azim, H. T. Vinh. A hybrid approach to word segmentation of Vietnamese texts. Proceedings of the 2nd International Conference on Language and Automata Theory and Applications, Springer LNCS 5196, Tarragona, Spain, 2008.

Anna M.D. Sciullo and Edwin Williams. 1987. On the definition of word. The MIT Press.

Fei Xia et al. Developing Guidelines and Ensuring Consistency for Chinese Text Annotation. 2000. COLING.

A Multi-Representational and Multi-Layered Treebank for Hindi/Urdu

Rajesh Bhatt
U. of Massachusetts
Amherst, MA, USA
bhatt@linguist.umass.edu

Bhuvana Narasimhan
U. of Colorado
Boulder, CO, USA
narasimb@colorado.edu

Martha Palmer
U. of Colorado
Boulder, CO, USA
mpalmer@colorado.edu

Owen Rambow
Columbia University
New York, NY, USA
rambow@ccls.columbia.edu

Dipti Misra Sharma
Int'l Institute of Info. Technology
Hyderabad, India
dipti@iiit.ac.in

Fei Xia
University of Washington
Seattle, WA, USA
fxia@u.washington.edu

Abstract

This paper describes the simultaneous development of dependency structure and phrase structure treebanks for Hindi and Urdu, as well as a PropBank. The dependency structure and the PropBank are manually annotated, and then the phrase structure treebank is produced automatically. To ensure successful conversion the development of the guidelines for all three representations are carefully coordinated.

1 Introduction

Annotated corpora have played an increasingly important role in the training of supervised natural language processing components. Today, treebanks have been constructed for many languages, including Arabic, Chinese, Czech, English, French, German, Korean, Spanish, and Turkish. This paper describes the creation of a Hindi/Urdu ***multi-representational and multi-layered treebank***. *Multi-layered* means that we design the annotation process from the outset to include both a syntactic annotation and a lexical semantic annotation such as the English PropBank (Palmer et al. 2005). *Multi-representational* means that we distinguish conceptually *what* is being represented from *how* it is represented; for example, in a case of long-distance *wh*-movement in English as in *Who do you think will come,* we can choose to represent the fact that *who* is an argument of *come*, or not (*what* to represent). Having made this choice, we can determine *how* to represent it: For example, we can use a discontinuous constituent (crossing arcs), or we can use a trace and co-indexation.

Flexibility of representation is important because the proper choice of representation of the syntax of a language is itself an issue in parsing research. In the application of the Collins parser to the Prague Dependency Treebank (Collins et al. 1999) the automatic mapping from dependency to phrase-structure was a major area of research. Similarly, automatically changing the representation in a phrase structure treebank can also improve parsing results (for example Klein & Manning 2003). Finally, there is increasing interest in the use of dependency parses in NLP applications, as they are considered to be simpler structures which can be computed more rapidly and are closer to the kinds of semantic representations that applications can make immediate use of (McDonald et al. 2005, CoNLL 2006 Shared Task). We first provide a comparison of dependency structure and phrase structure in Section 2. Section 3 describes our treebank, Section 4 explores language-specific linguistic issues that require special attention to ensure consistent conversion, and Section 5 summarizes our conversion approach.

2 Two Kinds of Syntactic Structure

Two different approaches to describing syntactic structure, dependency structure (DS) (Mel'čuk 1979) and phrase structure (PS) (Chomsky, 1981), have in a sense divided the field in two, with parallel efforts on both sides. Formally, in a PS tree, all and only the leaf nodes are labeled

Proceedings of the Third Linguistic Annotation Workshop, ACL-IJCNLP 2009, pages 186–189,
Suntec, Singapore, 6-7 August 2009.

with words from the sentence (or empty categories), while the interior nodes are labeled with nonterminal labels. In a dependency tree, all nodes are labeled with words from the sentence (or empty categories). Linguistically, a PS groups consecutive words hierarchically into phrases (or constituents), and each phrase is assigned a syntactic label. In a DS, syntactic dependency (i.e., the relation between a syntactic head and its arguments and adjuncts) is the primary syntactic relation represented. The notion of constituent is only derived.

In a dependency representation, a node stands for itself, for the lexical category (or "preterminal") spanning only the word itself (e.g., N), and for its maximal projection spanning the node and all words in the subtree it anchors (e.g., NP). Thus, intermediate projections which cover only some of the dependents of a word (such as N' or VP) do not directly correspond to anything in a dependency representation. Attachments at the different levels of projection are therefore not distinguished in a dependency tree. This has certain ramifications for annotation. Conisder for example scope in conjunctions. The two readings of *young men and women* can be distinguished (are the women young as well or not?). If a dependency representation represents conjunction by treating the conjunction as a dependent to the first conjunct, then the two readings do not receive different syntactic representations, unless a scope feature is introduced for the adjective. Suppose y depends on x in a DS, we need to address the following questions in order to devise a DS-to-PS conversion algorithm that builds the corresponding phrase structure: *1) What kinds of projections do x and y have? 2) How far should y project before it attaches to x's projection? 3) What position on x's projection chain should y's projection attach to?* These questions are answered by the annotation manual of the target PS representation – there are many possible answers. If the source dependency representation contains the right kind of information (for example, the scope of adjectives in conjunctions), and if the target phrase structure representation is well documented, then we can devise a conversion algorithm.

Another important issue is that of "non-projectivity" which is used to represent discontinuous constituents. Non-projectivity is common in dependency-based syntactic theories, but rare in phrase structure-based theories. The next section highlights our most salient representation choices in Treebank design.

3 Treebank Design

Our goal is the delivery of a treebank that is *multi-representational*: it will have a syntactic dependency version and a phrase structure version. Another recent trend in treebanking is the addition of deeper, semantic levels of annotation on top of the syntactic annotations of the PTB, for example PropBank (Palmer et al. 2005). A multi-layered approach is also found in the Prague Dependency Treebank (Hajič et al. 2001), or in treebanks based on LFG (King et al. 2003) or HPSG (Oepen et al. 2002). A lesson learned here is that the addition of deeper, more semantic levels may be complicated if the syntactic annotation was not designed with the possibility of multiple layers of annotation in mind. We therefore also propose a treebank that is from the start *multi-layered*: we will include a PropBank-style predicate-argument annotation in the release. Crucially, the lexical subcategorization frames that are made explicit during the process of propbanking should always inform the syntactic structure of the treebanking effort. In addition, some of the distinctions made by PS that are not naturally present in DS, such as unaccusativity and null arguments, are more naturally made during PropBank annotation. Our current approach anticipates that the addition of the PropBank annotation to the DS will provide a rich enough structure for accurate PS conversion.

In order to ensure successful conversion from DS to PS, we are simultaneously developing three sets of guidelines for Hindi: dependency structure, phrase structure, and PropBank. While allowing DS and PS guidelines to be based on different, independently motivated principles (see Section 4), we have been going through a comprehensive list of constructions in Hindi, carefully exploring any potentially problematic issues. Specifically, we make sure that both DS and PS represent the same syntactic facts *(what is represented)*: we know that if PS makes a distinction that neither DS nor PropBank make, then we cannot possibly convert automatically. Furthermore, we coordinate the guidelines for DS and PS with respect to the examples chosen to support the conversion process. These examples form a conversion test suite.

4 Syntactic Annotation Choices

4.1 Dependency Structure Guidelines

Our dependency analysis is based on the Paninian grammatical model (Bharati et al 1999, Sharma et al. 2007). The model offers a syntactico-semantic level of linguistic knowledge with an especially transparent relationship between the syntax and the semantics. The sentence is treated as a series of modifier-modified relations which has a primary modified (generally the main verb). The appropriate syntactic cues (relation markers) help in identifying various relations. The relations are of two types – karaka and others. 'Karakas' are the roles of various participants in an action (arguments). For a noun to hold a karaka relation with a verb, it is important that they (noun and verb) have a direct syntactic relation. Relations other than 'karaka' such as purpose, reason, and possession are also captured using the relational concepts of the model (adjuncts). These argument labels are very similar in spirit to the verb specific semantic role labels used by PropBank, which have already been successfully mapped to richer semantic role labels from VerbNet and FrameNet. This suggests that much of the task of PropBanking can be done as part of the dependency annotation.

4.2 Phrase Structure Guidelines

Our PS guidelines are inspired by the Principles-and-Parameters methodology, as instantiated by the theoretical developments starting with Government and Binding Theory (Chomsky 1981). We assume binary branching. There are three theoretical commitments/design considerations that underlie the guidelines. First, any minimal clause distinguishes at most two positions structurally (the core arguments). These positions can be identified as the specifier of VP and the complement of V. With a transitive predicate, these positions are occupied by distinct NPs while with an unaccusative or passive, the same NP occupies both positions. All other NPs are represented as adjuncts. Second, we represent any displacement of core arguments from their canonical positions, irrespective of whether a clause boundary is crossed, via traces. The displacement of other arguments is only represented if a clause boundary is crossed. Third, syntactic relationships such as agreement and case always require c-command but do not necessarily require a [specifier, head] configuration. Within these constraints, we always choose the simplest structure compatible with the word order. We work with a very limited set of category labels (NP, AP, AdvP, VP, CP) assuming that finer distinctions between different kinds of verbal functional heads can be made via features.

4.3 Two Constructions in Hindi

We give examples for two constructions in Hindi and show the DS and PS for each.

Simple Transitive Clauses:

(1) raam-ne khiir khaayii
ram-erg rice-pudding ate
'Ram ate rice-pudding.'

The two main arguments of the Hindi verb in Figure 1(b) have dependency types k1 and k2. They correspond roughly to subject and object, and they are the only arguments that can agree with the verb. In the PS, Figure 1(a), the two arguments that correspond to k1 and k2 have fixed positions in the phrase structure as explained in Section 4.2.

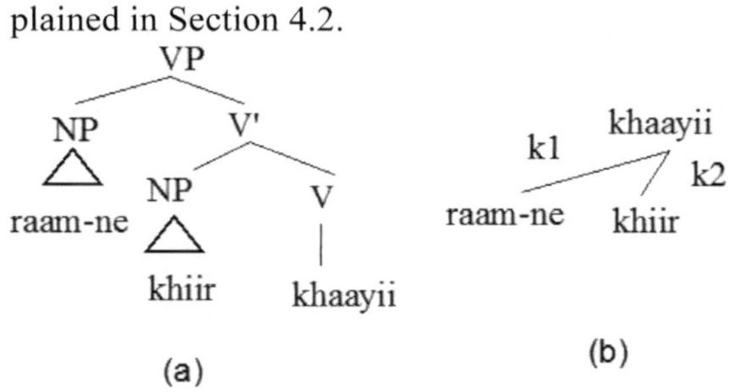

Figure 1: PS and DS for transitive clause in (1).

Unaccusative verbs:

(2) darwaazaa khul rahaa hai
door.M open Prog.MSg be.Prs.Sg
'The door is opening.'

Here, the issue is that the DS guidelines treats unaccusatives like other intransitives, with the surface argument simply annotated as k1. In contrast, PS shows a derivation in which the subject originates in object position.

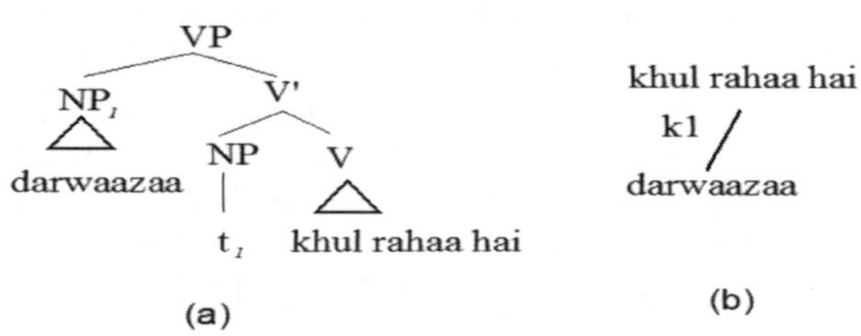

Figure 2: PS and DS for the unaccusative in (2).

5 Conversion Process

The DS-to-PS conversion process has three steps. First, for each (DS, PS) pair appearing in the conversion test suite, we run a consistency checking algorithm to determine whether the DS and the PS are consistent. The inconsistent cases are studied manually and if the inconsistency cannot be resolved by changing the analyses used in the guidelines, a new DS that is consistent with the PS is proposed. We call this new dependency structure "DS_{cons}" ("cons" for "consistency"; DS_{cons} is the same as DS for the consistent cases). Because the DS and PS guidelines are carefully coordinated, we expect the inconsistent cases to be rare and well-motivated. Second, conversion rules are extracted automatically from these (DS_{cons}, PS) pairs. Last, given a new DS, a PS is created by applying conversion rules. Note that non-projective DSs will be converted to projective DS_{cons}. (For an alternate account of handling non-projective DSs, see Kuhlman and Möhl (2007).) A preliminary study on the English Penn Treebank showed promising results and error analyses indicated that most conversion errors were caused by ambiguous DS patterns in the conversion rules. This implies that including sufficient information in the input DS could reduce ambiguity, significantly improving the performance of the conversion algorithm. The details of the conversion algorithm and the experimental results are described in (Xia et al., 2009).

6 Conclusion

We presented our approach to the joint development of DS and PS treebanks and a PropBank for Hindi/Urdu. Since from the inception of the project we have planned manual annotation of DS and automatic conversion to PS, we are developing the annotation guidelines for all structures in parallel. A series of linguistic constructions with specific examples are being carefully examined for any DS annotation decisions that might result in inconsistency between DS and PS and/or multiple conversion rules with identical DS patterns. Our preliminary studies yield promising results, indicating that coordinating the design of DS/PS and PropBank guidelines and running the conversion algorithm in the early stages is essential to the success of building a multi-representational and multi-layered treebank.

Acknowledgments

This work is supported by NSF grants CNS-0751089, CNS-0751171, CNS-0751202, and CNS-0751213.

References

A. Bharati, V. Chaitanya and R. Sangal. 1999. *Natural Language Processesing: A Paninian Perspective*, Prentice Hall of India, New Delhi.

N. Chomsky. 1981. *Lectures on Government and Binding: The Pisa Lectures*. Holland: Foris Publications.

M. Collins, Jan Hajič, L. Ramshaw and C. Tillmann. 1999. A Statistical Parser for Czech. *In the Proc of ACL-1999,* pages 505-512.

J. Hajič, E. Hajicova, M. Holub, P. Pajas, P. Sgall, B. Vidova-Hladka, and V. Reznickova. 2001. The Current Status of the Prague Dependency Treebank. *Lecture Notes in Artificial Intelligence (LNAI)* 2166, pp 11—20, NY.

T. H. King, R. Crouch, S. Riezler, M. Dalrymple and R. Kaplan. 2003. The PARC700 Dependency Bank. *In Proc. of the 4th Int' Workshop on Linguistically Interpreted Corpora (LINC-2003),* Budapest, Hungary.

D. Klein and C. D. Manning. 2003. Accurate Unlexicalized Parsing. *In the Proc of ACL-2003,*.Japan

M. Kuhlmann and M. Möhl. 2007. Mildly context-sensitive dependency language. *In the Proc of ACL 2007.* Prague, Czech Republic.

R. McDonald, F. Pereira, K. Ribarov and J. Hajič. 2005. Non-Projective Dependency Parsing using Spanning Tree Algorithms. *In Proc. of HLT-EMNLP 2005.*

I. Melčuk. 1979. *Studies in Dependency Syntax.* Karoma Publishers, Inc.

S. Oepen, K. Toutanova, S. M. Shieber, C. D. Manning, D. Flickinger, and T. Brants, 2002. The LinGO Redwoods Treebank: Motivation and Preliminary Applications. *In Proc. of COLING, 2002.* Taipei, Taiwan.

M. Palmer, D. Gildea, P. Kingsbury. 2005. The Proposition Bank: An Annotated Corpus of Semantic Roles.*Computational Linguistics, 31(1)*:71-106.

D. M. Sharma, R. Sangal, L. Bai, R. Begam, and K.V. Ramakrishnamacharyulu. 2007. *AnnCorra : TreeBanks for Indian Languages,* Annotation Guidelines (manuscript), IIIT, Hyderabad, India.

F. Xia, O. Rambow, R. Bhatt, M. Palmer and D. Sharma, 2009. Towards a Multi-Representational Treebank. *In Proc. of the 7th Int'lWorkshop on Treebanks and Linguistic Theories (TLT-7).*

Author Index

Aktas, Berfin, 44
Albert, Camille, 130

Baker, Collin F., 125
Bali, Kalika, 10
Banski, Piotr, 64
Bharati, Akshar, 162
Bhatt, R, 186
Biswas, Priyanka, 10
Bittar, André, 48
Blache, Philippe, 174
Bond, Francis, 146
Bozsahin, Cem, 44
Buscail, Laurie, 130

Cakici, Ruket, 44
Calzolari, Nicoletta, 178
Cassidy, Steve, 154
Chen, Ying, 1
Chiarcos, Christian, 35
Chodorow, Martin, 60
Choi, Jinho, 121
Choudhury, Monojit, 10

Dandapat, Sandipan, 10
Demirsahin, Isin, 44
Diab, Mona, 68
Dipper, Stefanie, 166

Ehrmann, Maud, 142

Fellbaum, Christiane, 125
Fort, Karën, 142

Gali, Karthik, 162
Garnier, Marie, 130
Guo, Weiwei, 68
Gupta, Mridul, 162

Hahn, Udo, 112
Harper, Mary, 116
Hladka, Barbora, 90
Hladká, Barbora, 52
Homola, Petr, 74
Huang, Chu-Ren, 1

Ide, Nancy, 27, 178
Inui, Kentaro, 150

Ji, Heng, 116
Johnston, Trevor, 154
Joshi, Aravind, 158

Klyueva, Natalia, 74
Kolachina, Sudheer, 158
Kordoni, Valia, 170
Kosaka, Michiko, 116

Le, Hong Phuong, 182
Lee, John, 60
Lee, Sophia Y. M., 1
Leong, Chee Wee, 56
Levin, Lori, 68
Liao, Shasha, 116
Lopatkova, Marketa, 74
Luís, Tiago, 99

Martins de Matos, David, 99
Masuda, Shouko, 150
Matsumoto, Yuji, 150
Matsuyoshi, Suguru, 150
Meyers, Adam, 116
Mihalcea, Rada, 56
Mírovský, Jií, 52, 108
Misra Sharma, Dipti, 158
Mitamura, Teruko, 68
Murakami, Koji, 150

Nagarajan, Arun, 134
Narasimhan, B, 186
Nazarenko, Adeline, 142
Nedoluzhko, Anna, 108
Nguyen, Phuong Thai, 182
Nguyen, Thi Minh Huyen, 182
Nguyen, Van Hiep, 182
Nichols, Eric, 150
Novák, Václav, 138

O'Halloran, Kay, 134
Ogel, Hale, 44
Oza, Umangi, 158

Pajas, Petr, 108
Palmer, M, 186
Palmer, Martha, 121
Podlasov, Alexey, 134
Prabhakaram, Vinodkumar, 68
Prasad, Rashmi, 158
Przepiórkowski, Adam, 64
Pustejovsky, James, 178

Rambow, O, 186
Rambow, Owen, 68
Razímová, Magda, 138
Rehbein, Ines, 19
Ritz, Julia, 35
Ruppenhofer, Josef, 19
Rykner, Arnaud, 130

Saint-Dizier, Patrick, 130
Schlesinger, Pavel, 52
Schneiker, Christian, 82
Seipel, Dietmar, 82
Sevdik-Calli, Ayisigi B., 44
Sharma, D, 186
Sharma, Dipti Misra, 162
Smith, Bradley, 134
Song, Sanghoun, 146
Soria, Claudia, 178
Sporleder, Caroline, 19
Stede, Manfred, 35
Suderman, Keith, 27
Sun, Ang, 116

Tan, Sabine, 134
Tetreault, Joel, 60
Tomanek, Katrin, 112
Turan, Umit Deniz, 44

Uresova, Zdenka, 90

Vu, Xuan Luong, 182

Wegstein, Werner, 82

Xia, F, 186
Xu, Wei, 116
Xue, Nianwen, 116, 121

Yadav, Vineet, 162
Yalcinkaya, Ihsan, 44

Zeyrek, Deniz, 44
Zhang, Yi, 170
Zinsmeister, Heike, 166

Association for Computational Linguistics
209 N. Eighth Street
Stroudsburg, Pennsylvania 18360